Heritage as Aid
and Diplomacy
in Asia

The **ISEAS – Yusof Ishak Institute** (formerly Institute of Southeast Asian Studies) is an autonomous organization established in 1968. It is a regional centre dedicated to the study of socio-political, security, and economic trends and developments in Southeast Asia and its wider geostrategic and economic environment. The Institute's research programmes are grouped under Regional Economic Studies (RES), Regional Strategic and Political Studies (RSPS), and Regional Social and Cultural Studies (RSCS). The Institute is also home to the ASEAN Studies Centre (ASC), the Singapore APEC Study Centre and the Temasek History Research Centre (THRC).

ISEAS Publishing, an established academic press, has issued more than 2,000 books and journals. It is the largest scholarly publisher of research about Southeast Asia from within the region. ISEAS Publishing works with many other academic and trade publishers and distributors to disseminate important research and analyses from and about Southeast Asia to the rest of the world.

The International Institute for Asian Studies (IIAS) is a global humanities and social sciences research institute and knowledge exchange platform. It aims to contribute to a better and more integrated understanding of present-day Asian realities as well as to rethink "Asian Studies" in a changing global context. IIAS acts as a global mediator, bringing together academic and non-academic institutes in Asia and other parts of the world, including cultural, societal and policy organizations. Originally established in 1993 by the Dutch Ministry of Education as an interuniversity institute, IIAS today is based at Leiden University, where it works as a globally oriented interfaculty institute with strong connections throughout the Netherlands, Europe, Asia and beyond.

Institute of Sociology, Academia Sinica, Taiwan, is devoted (1) to implement indigenous research and to build up the identity of Taiwanese sociology; (2) to strengthen research on neighboring societies, aiming to foster regional and cross-national comparative studies; (3) to deepen and further to systematize the findings of important fields of sociology; (4) to explore groundbreaking and distinctive research areas; (5) to promote collaboration with domestic and international sociological institutions and to enhance the academic status of Taiwanese sociology.

Heritage as Aid and Diplomacy in Asia

Edited by
Philippe Peycam
Shu-Li Wang
Hui Yew-Foong
Hsin-Huang Michael Hsiao

ISEAS YUSOF ISHAK
INSTITUTE

International
Institute for
Asian Studies

中央研究院
社会学研究所
Institute of Sociology, Academia Sinica

First published in Singapore in 2020 by
ISEAS Publishing
30 Heng Mui Keng Terrace
Singapore 119614
E-mail: publish@iseas.edu.sg
Website: http://bookshop.iseas.edu.sg

ISEAS Library Cataloguing-in-Publication Data

Names: Peycam, Philippe, editor. | Wang, Shu-Li, editor. | Hui Yew-Foong, editor. | Hsiao, Hsin-Huang Michael, editor.
Title: Heritage as aid and diplomacy in Asia / edited by Philippe Peycam, Shu-Li Wang, Hui Yew-Foong and Hsin-Huang Michael Hsiao.
Description: Singapore : ISEAS–Yusof Ishak Institute, 2020. | Includes bibliographical references.
Identifiers: ISBN 9789814881159 (paperback) | 9789814881166 (PDF) | 9789814881609 (epub)
Subjects: LCSH: Asia—Cultural policy. | Cultural property—Conservation and restoration—Government policy—Asia. | Historic preservation—Government policy—Asia. | Economic assistance—Asia—Case studies. | National interest—Asia. | Asia—Politics and government. | Cultural diplomacy—Asia.
Classification: LCC DS12 H54

Typeset by Superskill Graphics Pte Ltd

Contents

Contributors

Victor C.M. CHAN is Assistant Professor, Department of Social Science, the Hang Seng University of Hong Kong.

Brigitta HAUSER-SCHÄUBLIN is Professor Emerita of Anthropology, Göttingen University, Germany.

Hsin-Huang Michael HSIAO is Adjunct Research Fellow, Institute of Sociology, Academia Sinica, and Chair Professor of Hakka Studies, National Central University, Taiwan.

Yew-Foong HUI is Associate Professor, Department of Sociology, Hong Kong Shue Yan University; and Visiting Senior Fellow, ISEAS – Yusof Ishak Institute.

J. Eva MEHARRY is a Doctoral Candidate in the Cambridge Heritage Research Centre, Department of Archaeology, University of Cambridge, Jesus College.

Lynn MESKELL is the Shirley R. and Leonard W. Ely, Jr Professor of Humanities and Sciences in the Department of Anthropology, Stanford University and A.D. White Professor-at-large at Cornell University.

Min Yen ONG is a Teaching Associate in the Faculty of Music, University of Cambridge; Bye-Fellow at Murray Edwards College; and Research Associate at Darwin College, University of Cambridge.

Philippe PEYCAM is Director, International Institute for Asian Studies.

Jayde Lin ROBERTS is Senior Lecturer, Architecture and Urbanism in Asia, Faculty of Built Environment, UNSW Sydney.

Anran WANG is a Doctoral Candidate in History, Cornell University.

Shu-Li WANG is Assistant Research Fellow, Institute of Ethnology, Academia Sinica.

Agung WARDANA holds a teaching position at the Faculty of Law, Gadjah Mada University, Indonesia.

Lauren YAPP is a Postdoctoral Fellow in International Humanities at Brown University.

Mary ZURBUCHEN was a Ford Foundation Program Officer and Regional Representative in both South and Southeast Asia, and is now Senior Advisor to the Henry Luce Foundation in New York.

1

Heritage as Aid and Diplomacy in Asia: An Introduction

Shu-Li Wang, Philippe Peycam, Hui Yew-Foong and Hsin-Huang Michael Hsiao

In spite of a growing academic interest in the politics of heritage in Asia, few studies have directly questioned the role of international and transnational cooperation in heritage conservation. First, even though the literature has widely addressed the role of the United Nations Educational, Scientific and Cultural Organization (UNESCO) as a powerful disseminator of international standards of conservation (e.g., Askew 2010; Daly and Winter 2012; Labadi 2010, 2013a; Logan 2001), it has not yet tackled the impact of UNESCO's normative discourse on other cultural policy agents. Secondly, the social sciences have largely neglected other international structures such as the International Monetary Fund (IMF), the World Bank, the European Union, USAid, the Asian Development Bank and many others that have their own engagements in the conservation of heritage in Asia. These organizations often collaborate with UNESCO or participate in bilateral or multilateral initiatives by providing funding and "expertise" in the management of sites. The IMF, for instance, played an important role in the establishment of the International Coordinating Committee of the World Heritage Site (hereafter WHS) of Angkor under the aegis of UNESCO. Many of these initiatives are carried out by states' cultural diplomacies in often well-thought-out strategies. Pioneer countries in cultural diplomacy include France, Italy and the Netherlands, but also India and Japan. Today, most Asian states are also engaging in cultural diplomacy. In the last two decades, China, South Korea, Thailand, Vietnam and Indonesia have considerably strengthened their investments in regional "heritage cooperation". Some of them, like India or Japan, have a long history of cultural international intervention (Ray 2012). Thirdly, private "philanthropic" programmes like the Ford Foundation, the Agha Khan Foundation, the World Monuments Fund and the Getty Trust have long had a major impact on the management of heritage in Asia. They are now joined by newly established Asia-based foundations such as Korea's Samsung Foundation. Finally, new connections have recently been drawn between market-driven "development" schemes explicitly linking "culture" and "economic opportunities" as part of the global capital-driven developmentalist discourse, as when WHS become mass tourism destinations incorporated in national economic development schemes (Labadi and Logan 2016). This new model of "cultural-capitalism" is fast becoming prominent, as is the global campaign of systematic digitization of library collections by the multinational Google, "responsible capitalism", or micro-credit schemes. These essentially capitalist constructions collaborate with state-sponsored cultural heritage structures, including UNESCO, as well as with elite-originated private cultural philanthropy.

In Asia, historical colonial legacies and postcolonial negotiations of these experiences have inflected the heritage discourse in dynamic ways (cf. Logan 2001, 2016; Huang and Lee 2018). The relative shortage of historical, sociological, political and ethnographic research on these multiple incarnations of "Heritage as Aid or as Diplomacy" in Asia is all the more surprising when we consider how cultural and heritage management represents a major area of international cooperation as well as a powerful instrument of "soft power" by states, corporate forces and social elites. These national, international, transnational state and non-state agents are prolific producers of knowledge on heritage. Often following the theoretical (and sometimes ideological) avenues set by UNESCO and its different state proponents, they provide thoughtful historical and philosophical legitimating arguments in favour of the idea of heritage as aid. When confronted with local situations, however, they may offer alternative approaches to the dominant discourses. Their interactions with local educational institutions, especially universities, are another aspect of their capacity to produce normative knowledge on heritage that are worth reflecting upon.

But we need to reflect first on UNESCO and its capacity to shape a referential framework of knowledge and values around the notion of heritage, and its role and impact in Asia. Following the establishment of the World Heritage List (WHL) programme in the 1970s, UNESCO became instrumental in defining the "universal value" of cultural heritage and in guiding heritage discourses and conservation practices all over the world. The WHL ranking process has contributed to reinforce a "global hierarchy of [cultural] values" (Herzfeld 2004). As pointed out by Lowenthal (1985), what we now understand as "Heritage" is socially and politically constructed. What is considered as "heritage" often results from state-initiated actions through regulations, legal determinations and also practices of selection and classification. This is what Smith points out when she stresses how the state, through its multifaceted incarnations and roles, via the use of appointed "experts", technocratic apparatuses and bureaucracies, defines the meaning of heritage (Smith 2006; Rico 2014, 2015). For instance, states use heritage discourse and ideology to legitimate their own authority and build their soft power in the domestic and international arenas, and to expand their control over citizens. Scholars/experts are making local, national and global recommendations. In the world of heritage regime, what are the mechanisms and manipulations of ideological, political and cultural transmissions?

This book seeks especially to explore the international projection of state power through the use of heritage, heritage preservation and notions of world heritage or *Patrimoine Mondial* as defined by UNESCO (Meskell 2018). David Harvey (2014) noted how contemporary heritage-making is embedded in cultural politics operating at multiple scales, ranging from the local to the national and the international. Different players with multiple interests and roles participate in the making and unmaking of "Heritage". The complexity of a multi-scalar process in defining what we call "heritage" in the present reflects a discursive construct of heritage assemblages. The notion in fact corresponds to a messy congregation of discourses, visions and ideologies. As a subject of study, we have to recognize heritage as a discursive construct that can only be understood in its particular social, political and cultural contexts. In general the agents that define heritage involve players like nation states, but also local communities, policymakers, bureaucrats, corporations, NGOs and international organizations. In its international projection, the "heritage discursive and ideological assemblage" is influenced by shifting global political and economic power relations and the complex institutional and legal international apparatus that is supposed to mediate them. Transnational actors such as churches, social movements or transnational business ventures are also involved in the definition of canons of heritage beyond borders.

While several important works have focused on the role of the state and its related apparatus (Smith 2006), how heritage is consumed by tourists (Salazar 2010), and the social impacts on local communities (cf. Brumann and Berliner 2016), with recent attention paid to the upper echelons of UNESCO itself (Meskell 2014, 2016, 2018), there remains a broad scope for players situated in the middle in the global heritage assemblage. Through a selection of cases highlighting the complex interaction between different social and institutional actors on the international scene, we want to point to the critical role heritage discourse plays in international policy as well. We note that behind various "heritage sites" there is a complex discursive assemblage that needs to be unpacked.

Since the establishment of the World Heritage Convention, a newly formed "international heritage regime" has emerged in which different interests—mainly those of states—compete through regulated or unregulated international relations mechanisms resulting in a regime of competitive internationalism. UNESCO, the cultural and educational agency of the United Nations was set up in 1945 to ensure peace in "international society". The concept of World Heritage emerged out of the Cold War competition for political influence between the two blocs over Egypt, the construction of the Aswan High Dam and the salvation of Egyptian temples such as those at Abu Simbel, an initiative largely triggered by countries from the Western bloc as a reaction to the building of the dam in collaboration with the Soviet Union (Bett 2015; Meskell 2018). The World Heritage convention of the 1970s and contemporary heritage discourses were framed by transnational institutions such as UNESCO, the International Council on Monuments and Sites (ICOMOS), the International Centre for the Study of the Preservation and Restoration of Cultural Property (ICCROM), and the International Union for Conservation of Nature (IUCN), which led to the construction of a real UNESCO-connected and UNESCO-inspired international heritage-focused regime, with its codes, values, circles of influence, experts and internal power mechanisms, etc. We argue that a new symbolic and professional "field" of "Heritage Studies", with new forms of knowledge and new relations between people and places emerged from this apparatus. This form of "heritage internationalism" has gained traction to the point that other national and international organizations have sought to include it in their own operations. This is the case of the World Bank. Nation states, for their part, have gained in experience and sophistication to use heritage internationalism as a powerful force of legitimation for their domestic or international strategies. The normative power of UNESCO is so effective that scholars have named this official discursive apparatus the "heritage regime", a process in which one international organization (UNESCO) hegemonizes cultural heritage practices through its heritage-related bureaucratic bodies, expertise and funding schemes, as well as conventions, policies and rules (De Cesari 2013).

Since the 1990s, however, a number of voices have criticized these UNESCO-led heritage preservation practices and the Eurocentric bias of this global hierarchy of cultural values (cf. Smith 2006; Harrison 2013). Drawn from the Japanese and Korean practices of heritage conservation, the concept of "intangible heritage" was introduced to the hitherto Western-dominated official debate on heritage in places like UNESCO (Aikawa-Faure 2014). In 2003, the UNESCO Convention for the Safeguarding of Intangible Cultural Heritage was adopted. Although the concept of intangibility, itself defended by state entities, has been accepted and taken on by a number of Western countries, the new category largely expands heritage discourse on a global scale. It has introduced a plurality of definitions for what is called "cultural heritage" in different geographical and historical contexts. This led to the inclusion of non-Western and marginalized cultural practices. As a result, the definition of heritage has gained in fluidity while its scope has expanded. Scholars have come to realize that "Heritage conservation" that imbibes universal meaning should incorporate ways in which local people understand these cultural forms and how they should be preserved. They have also critically analysed some of the problematic aspects of this "heritage regime" as developed by UNESCO.

First of all, they found that states use heritage discourse for territorial boundary-making to assert their sovereignty over forms of heritage whose practice predates the modern nation-state framework (and its universalizing projection through UNESCO) at the expense of "non-national communities". The state becomes the dominant actor defining these invented "national" categories by claiming their exclusive identities. Tangible and intangible heritage are not just "nationalized". They are, thanks to UNESCO, internationally proclaimed as such. This is the case of Court "Ballet" Dance in Cambodia, registered in 2008 as an Intangible Heritage of Humanity, a "tradition" also practised in neighbouring Thailand and Laos. The UNESCO registration carried out by the Cambodian government was made at the expense of the latter countries. Nation-states can also use heritage for grand diplomatic schemes. There is a trend towards bilateral or multilateral cooperation over heritage conservation, such as the proposal to inscribe the "Silk Road" as World Heritage in 2014, which was a joint effort by China, Kazakhstan and Kyrgyzstan. At present, China is working on another transnational inscription of what is called the "Maritime Silk Road", which starts from Quanzhou in Southeast China, passes through the Indo-Chinese Peninsula and crosses the Indian Ocean and Red Sea until finally reaching East Africa and Europe. While the first Silk Road links China to Central Asia through political, economic and cultural cooperation with the surrounding countries, the Maritime Silk Road does the same with respect to Southeast Asia and beyond. Both the Silk Road and Maritime Silk Road nominations echo China's soft-power strategy of Chairman Xi Jinping's "Belt and Road Initiative" (cf. Tim Winter 2015). We see here a new form of interregional economic and political ties legitimized through international heritage-making. This mode of heritage-making can also take the form of bilateral cooperation between former colonies and their former "metropoles", often problematically referred to as "shared heritage". These new constructions have the ability to create new configurations of allegiance towards states among people on the ground.

Secondly, state and international actors are competing with each other on the ground of heritage sites. Not only does the heritage site become a locus in which strategies carried out by nation-states are put on open display, it is also fertile ground where international organizations can help legitimize a mixing of business and public ventures. One WHS therefore becomes a theatre in which teams supported by different nation-states or international organizations promote a multiplicity of visions and models of conservation practices, building infrastructure as well as developing tourism. In general, closer relationships between international institutions, governments and private interests over heritage projects are sought, usually at the expense of local communities. This has recently become the subject of critical examination on the part of a number of researchers such as Meskell (2013) and Brumann (2014), who suggest a reflexive approach to interrogate unstated motives behind institutional mechanisms and implementing procedures of UNESCO heritage listing.

The best example of this normative expansion of the concept of heritage in its utilitarian self-serving (state-serving) definition is the UNESCO Secretariat of the Angkor International Cooperation Committee (hereafter ICC). Supporting the concerns of one of its founding members, the French government, one of its "co-chairs", the ICC not only facilitates France's engagement in favour of the integrity of the World Heritage Site but it also seeks to promote the interests of the French multinational company that operates the international airport of Siem Reap–Angkor, with the tacit agreement of the other co-chairs, the representative of Japan and the representative of the Cambodian (host) government. Likewise, the Japanese government representative's official stance in favour of the heritage preservation of Angkor should be read as a way to facilitate the work of the Japanese state aid agency JICA, which itself facilitates the sealing of lucrative contracts for Japanese infrastructure-building companies to operate in the Siem Reap–Angkor zone (see chapter 4 by Peycam in this volume). Lynn Meskell's article in the present book points to the manoeuvres of US diplomacy in facilitating the resolution of tensions existing between Thailand and Cambodia over the sovereignty of the world heritage monument of Preah Vihear as a way to secure access to oil-rich zones off the coasts of both Cambodia and Thailand on behalf of the US oil giant Exon.

Here, we take a "Latourian" approach to apply the "Actor Network Theory" (1987, 2005)—where everything involved in the social and natural worlds, including objects, ideas, processes, people and other factors as well as networks interact with each other in making and remaking social situations—to examine the multifaceted mechanisms at play to define heritage in particular contexts or locations, and how state and non-state institutions negotiate and take decisions that become new international norms. At different levels, human and non-human agencies ranging from international institutions, UNESCO-driven laws and policy mechanisms, national authorities, heritage professionals and "experts", academics and "heritage bearers" or practitioners of "intangible heritage" are all involved in processes of making heritage discourses. For instance, UNESCO makes abundant use of the word "culture" to promote economically or politically driven "development" projects, a mode of operation that amounts to a new kind of cultural imperialism instrumentalized through the promotion of "universal heritage values" (Nielsen 2011; Labadi 2013b). Berliner (2012) uses the term "UNESCO-isation" to describe the impact upon local communities of such politically saturated discourse on heritage and heritage value. For example, as described by Wang (2016), while the stated aim of UNESCO is to promote sites contributing to "universal values", that carried by state-led nationalism in China is to bring "civilization" and "progress", in overt contradiction with the views of the local villagers who have been displaced or who are fighting to remain in their homes. Local communities are, as a result, often excluded from the management plans prescribed under the UNESCO banner. They find themselves forced to either relocate outside the World Heritage Site or, if they stay, their living conditions deteriorate. Unfortunately, International organizations such as UNESCO, the Asian Development Bank, the World Bank and other inter-state agencies, as well as transnational heritage organizations or funds, have adopted and co-opted the UNESCO definition of culture to define heritage practices in Asia.

We must therefore consider international heritage discourses as evolving in the nexus of competing claims between state and non-state actors, both locally and internationally. Heritage diplomacy reveals a complex process of global exchange and gift giving (Meskell 2015). World heritage status mobilizes a network of multilateral cooperation and dependency. Heritage-making therefore represents one of the dimensions in international diplomatic relations that helps forge transnational alliances and dependencies. As Meskell notes (2015, p. 13), "heritage sites have become thing-like: their mattering is not in their physicality but in their possibilities for circulation beyond culture to expanding global networks". In this sense, "sites then become gifts, objects and tokens that garner and bestow benefits, developments and ultimately, world peace" (2015, p. 13). Heritage is not used to legitimate itself, but to reflect the expansion of power. At the local level, heritage sites are nowadays given a facelift through place-making, regeneration, and development projects.

The cases presented in this book are part of a larger discussion initiated by IIAS (the Netherlands), the ISEAS – Yusof Ishak Institute (Singapore) and the Institute of Sociology, Academia Sinica (Taiwan) on cultural heritage in Asian contexts in the form of a series of topical conferences. The first event (Singapore, January 2014) focused on the role of the state in heritage-making. The second (Taipei, December 2014) investigated the role of citizens, local communities and civil society organizations in defining what heritage means to them. The last (Leiden, May 2016) examined the politics of international organizations, transnational institutions, as well as nation-states in their capacity to influence the global heritage discourses. With the aim of recovering or reclaiming the specificity of local agencies and the creativity of Asian actors in their grappling with the concept of heritage as an expression of "knowledge as power" (Foucault 1980), these conferences considered various factors and actors involved in heritage-making processes and the ways in which they are intertwined in the production and reproduction of "Heritage".

The present book is a result of the third of these three conferences. Drawing from different disciplinary approaches, it seeks to feature a diversity of situations where cultural heritage is invoked or promoted to serve interests or visions that supposedly transcend local or national paradigms. The book also represents an interdisciplinary endeavour to reflect the interwoven social, cultural, economic and political nature of heritage as aid and diplomacy. The making of heritage sites is a negotiation and contestation in the cultivation of heritage values among interest groups. Through a collection of case-specific articles, we intend to explore some of the following questions. Under the current international heritage regime, what are the mechanisms and manipulations of ideological, political and cultural transmissions? What is heritage diplomacy and how can we conceptualize it? How do the complicated history and colonial past of Asia constitute the current practices of heritage diplomacy and shape heritage discourse in Asia? How do international organizations, nation-states, NGOs, heritage brokers and experts contribute to the history of global heritage discourse? How has the flow of global knowledge been transferred and transformed? How does the global hierarchy of cultural values function? This edited book introduces examples of these interconnections and contestations as they operate in Asia at a global level. We are aware that "Asia" is a very imperfect and arbitrary notion. It is not different from other regions of the world or human groups. This set of conferences only sought to highlight a number of situational modes of power relations and human agency different than those—mostly from Western countries, regions and societies—that are usually considered in Western and/or "northern" academic institutions and circles, another reflection of the continuing imbalances within a larger "hierarchy of cultural values" that these edited volumes seek to break open.

One of the assumptions in approaching these questions is that the notion of heritage conservation in Asia is deeply influenced by the region's colonial legacies. For example, Ray (2018) investigates British agency in the archaeological survey in India. And Huang and Lee (2018) explore how China and Korea deal with their difficult Japanese imperial and military heritages, often resulting in geopolitical tensions in northeast Asia. A number of chapters in this volume comment on the complex interactions between ex-colonial countries and their former colonies in managing so-called "shared heritage" sites. In addition to formal state-sanctioned networks, professions such as academics or expert consultants live off international organizations or programmes to provide legitimating "expertise". Scholars working with organizations like UNESCO and the World Bank make recommendations and produce schemes that assign scientific and "universal" value (as well as national heritage values) to certain sites or cultural practices. Consequently, they situate the extant traditions of groups in new socio-political relationships (Meskell 2005). Other cases involve competing heritage ownership between different countries or ethnic and religious groups of people.

Asian countries are, moreover, engaged in classic international relations politics and competition, and heritage becomes a convenient instrument of diplomacy. After its reduction as an economic power with little political clout, post–World War II Japan sought to secure its influence over the Asian region through an active strategy of aid and cultural diplomacy. From the 1970s it began to massively invest in international structures like UNESCO. It began to distribute aid and technical resources for sites such as Angkor Wat, the Mogao Caves and Borobudur with the intention of projecting a positive image as an economic and cultural leader of Asia. More recently, China started its "Belt and Road Initiative" in 2013, which includes regional economic cooperation and the inscription of cross-national cultural heritage. China started the bid for UNESCO heritage on the Silk Road with some countries in Central and Southeast Asia. The Voyage of Admiral Zheng He across the Indian Ocean is also being used to project a vision of power beyond what is commonly regarded as Asia.

By now it should be apparent that the field of heritage as an arena where diplomacy and aid operate is indispensable for understanding the role of heritage in international and regional politics. The book is arranged in five parts that interrogate various aspects of this dynamics.

The first part centres on international heritage production. Physical cultural heritage sites are attached to specific places, but heritage production involves actors on several scales. In the heritage field, actors negotiate and compete. The discussion of heritage aid and diplomacy concentrates on the international production of heritage. Meskell argues that capitalist logic and neoliberalism have influenced the state's management of heritage resources. Colonizing projects have been done through heritage projects. Cambodia's Angkor dynasty is famous for its Angkor site, but there are other Angkor heritages in other countries in Indochina. For example, the conflict between Thailand and Cambodia over the Preah Vihear Temple intensified in the winter of 2008 when the latter country nominated the temple for inclusion on the World Heritage List. Hauser-Schäublin examines the genealogy of three expert reports concerning Preah Vihear and their situatedness in different political regimes of truth. She shows how each report drew on the previous one, starting with French colonial politics, via the 1962 case at the International Court of Justice up to the UNESCO heritage listing—with dramatic political consequences. These international discourses shape the way contemporary society treats Preah Vihear as a World Heritage Site. Peycam's chapter argues how a series of programmes aimed at spatial transformations of the "Angkor region" featured crucial strategies by the official teams of the French and Japanese governments in framing the committee's activities and its interactions with the Cambodian authorities. ICC and UNESCO representatives made self-legitimizing claims asserting the success of their work as a model of international cooperation for the safeguarding of World Heritage Sites. But can a proper mechanism of international cooperation for the safeguarding of a major heritage site like Angkor be realized, or sustained, without the effective participation of the communities living in and around these sites?

The second part of the book moves on to discuss heritage as aid through money, knowledge and technology. Aid to developing countries is very important, and power relations between developed and developing countries is the theme of this part. Zurbuchen's case study shows how private philanthropic foundations from developed countries are engaged in the cultural sector of developing countries in the name of heritage. She analyses how the Ford Foundation from the United States developed a specific cultural strategy for Southeast and South Asian countries in parallel with more political or economically driven ones, including during the Cold

War and the foundation's involvement in anti-communist activities. Yapp's paper examines the city of Kota Semarang in Indonesia and discusses aid from developed to developing countries. Aid is not only economic support but is also entangled in "colonial" connections. Indonesia was under Dutch colonial rule for almost 150 years and Dutch colonial heritage is apparent in many Indonesian cities. The city port of Semarang is home to many experts on Dutch heritage. Yapp analyses how experts from the "previous colonial state" interact with local heritage in Semarang. She explains how formerly colonized states face challenges emanating from projects and organizations originating from former colonizing countries. This paper also discusses how personal actors establish and affect heritage practice through private social networks.

The third part of the book focuses on how international relations affect heritage policy and how heritage reconstructs international relations. How do states with different historical perspectives interpret the same cultural heritage? Heritage is both a tool and a means. Chan demonstrates how China and Japan have used heritage in diplomatic competition and historical national narrative discourses. Their diplomatic relations caused tension after the change of Japanese leadership in 2012. Japan would bid for UNESCO World Heritage status for its industrial heritage of the Meiji period, but this was regarded as the outcome of Chinese and Korean forced labour. In another case, the Chinese government planned to apply to have the Nanjing Massacres listed on the UNESCO Memory of the World Programme. However, though Japanese textbooks recognized the killing of civilians in Nanjing by Japanese forces, Japan disagreed with China on the factual history, the numbers of victims and the forms of violence. In fact, Japan's official discourses about World War II history have evolved along with its leaders. Wang's chapter discusses the heritage of the Goguryeo period in China and North Korea. When North Korea made its bid for the Goguryeo site, China applied for the same site as a protest. Relations between North Korea and China affect the respective discourses of the Goguryeo site. Moreover, South Korea claims authority over this site, and this has complicated international relations and diplomacy.

The fourth part turns to the shifting meanings of heritage. Meharry explains how the excavation of the Bamiyan Buddhas—the classic cultural heritage of Afghanistan—has been affected by regime changes in Afghanistan, a country that has been alternately dominated by nationalist, progressive or conservative Islamist governments. Ong's chapter describes the changes in the Chinese handling of intangible heritage, in particular that of *kunqu* opera. With the Cultural Revolution, the country's economic reform and the World Heritage Regime, both *kunqu* opera and its performers changed.

The last part of the book discusses neoliberalism, a rather new topic in heritage studies. Cultural heritage becomes valuable in combination with the tourism market, and it becomes an object that can be used to support private economic interests. Wardana's chapter discusses how democratized and decentralized politics produced neoliberal spatial strategies after the overthrow of the Suharto dictatorship in Indonesia in 1998. Wardana uses the listing of rice terraces in Bali in the World Heritage List to suggest that the benefits from listing the terraces drives competition and the goals for a "neoliberalized heritage". Roberts is concerned with the collaboration between international aid and local preservation organizations. This chapter focuses on Myanmar, which partially opened to international aid in 2010. As opposed to the diplomatically isolated relations under the era of military rule, the new Myanmar, and especially its capital Yangon, have become an attractive locus for international organizations. However, the neoliberal tendencies of international organizations along with the elitism of the local heritage trust organizations that emanate from the new international connections has led to competition for heritage resources and to strategies that assign a lower priority to—and which often exclude—local communities and social groups.

Drawing from these Asian experiences, this collection of articles thus not only considers processes of "UNESCO-ization" of heritage (or their equivalents when conducted by other international or national actors) by exploring the diplomatic and developmentalist politics of heritage-making at play and its transformational impact on societies. It also describes how local and outside states often collude with international mechanisms to further their interests at the expense of local communities and of citizens' rights. As was however articulated in the volume *Citizens, Civil Society and Heritage-Making in Asia*, such transnational and international modes of power exertion through culture must grapple with an increased number of situations in which social movements can emerge that seek to preserve vernacular heritages and (re-)claim local identities, a trend that reflects the steady growth of civil society as a potent political actor in the region (cf. Hsiao et al. 2017).

References

Askew, Marc. 2010. *The Magic List of Global Status: UNESCO, World Heritage and the Agendas of States*. Abingdon: Routledge.

Berliner, David. 2012. "Multiple Nostalgias: The Fabric of Heritage in Luang Prabang (Lao PDR)". *Journal of the Royal Anthropological Institute* 18, no. 4: 769–86.

Betts, Paul. 2015. "The Warden of World Heritage: UNESCO and the Rescue of the Nubian Monuments". *Heritage in the Modern World: Historical Preservation in International Perspective, Past & Present Supplement* 226, no. 10: 100–25.

Bjarke, Nielsen. 2011. "UNESCO and the 'Right' Kind of Culture: Bureaucratic Production and Articulation". *Critique of Anthropology* 31, no. 4: 273–92.

Brumann, C. 2014. "Shifting Tides of World-Making in the UNESCO World Heritage Convention: Cosmopolitanisms Colliding". *Ethnic and Racial Studies* 37, no. 12: 2176–92.

Brumann, C., and David Berliner. 2016. *World Heritage on the Ground*. New York: Berghahn Books.

Coombes, Rosemary J. 2016. "The Knowledge Economy and Its Cultures: Neoliberal Technologies and Latin American Reterritorializations". *Hau: Journal of Ethnographic Theory* 6, no. 3: 247–75.

Daly, Patrick, and Tim Winter. 2012. "Heritage in Asia: Converging Forces, Conflicting Values". In *The Routledge Handbook of Heritage in Asia*, edited by Patrick Daly and Tim Winter, pp. 1–34. London: Routledge.

De Cesari, C. 2013. "Thinking through Heritage Regimes". In *Heritage Regimes and the State*, edited by Regina F. Bendix, Aditya Eggert, and Arnika Peselmann, pp. 399–413. Göttingen: Universitätsverlag Göttingen.

Foucault, M. 1980. *Power/Knowledge: Selected Interviews and Other Writings, 1972–1977*. Sussex: Harvester.

Gentry, K., and Laurajane Smith. 2019. "Critical Heritage Studies and the Legacies of the Late-Twentieth Century". *International Journal of Heritage Studies*. https://www.tandfonline.com/doi/full/10.1080/13527258.2019.1570964 (accessed 18 December 2018).

Giovine, Michael A. Di. 2010. "World Heritage Tourism: UNESCO's Vehicle for Peace?" *Anthropology News* 51, no. 8: 8–9.

Harrison, Rodney. 2013. *Heritage: Critical Approaches*. New York: Routledge.

Harvey, David. 2014. *Seventeen Contradictions and the End of Capitalism*. New York: Oxford University Press.

Herzfeld, M. 2002. "The Absent Presence: Discourses of Crypto-Colonialism". *South Atlantic Quarterly* 101, no. 4: 899–926.

———. 2004. *The Body Impolitic: Artisans and Artifice in the Global Hierarchy of Value*. Chicago: University of Chicago Press.

Hsiao, Hsin-Huang Michael, Hui Yew-Foong, and Philippe Peycam. 2017. *Citizens,*

Civil Society and Heritage-Making in Asia. Singapore: ISEAS – Yusof Ishak Institute.

Huang, Shu-Mei, and Lee Hyun-Kyung. 2018. "Difficult Heritage Diplomacy? Re-articulating Places of Pain and Shame as World Heritage in Northeast Asia". *International Journal of Heritage Studies* 25, no. 2: 143–59.

Labadi, Sophia. 2010. "World Heritage, Authenticity and Post-Authenticity: International and National Perspectives". In *Key Issues in Cultural Heritage*, edited by William Logan and Laurajane Smith. London: Routledge.

———. 2013a. "Culture: A Driver and Enabler of Social Cohesion". In *UNESCO International Congress "Culture: Key to Sustainable Development"*. UNESCO, 2013.

———. 2013b. *UNESCO, Cultural Heritage, and Outstanding Universal Value: Value-Based Analyses of the World Heritage and Intangible Cultural Heritage Conventions*. USA: AltaMira.

Labadi, Sophia, and William Logan, eds. 2016. *Urban Heritage, Development and Sustainability: International Frameworks, National and Local Governance*. London: Routledge.

Latour, Bruno. 1987. *Science in Action: How to Follow Scientists and Engineers through Society*. Cambridge: Harvard University Press.

———. 2005. *Reassembling the Social: An Introduction to Actor-Network-Theory*. Oxford: Oxford University Press.

Logan, W.S. 2001. "Globalising Heritage: World Heritage as a Manifestation of Modernism and Challenges from the Periphery". *Twentieth Century Heritage: Our Recent Cultural Legacy: Proceedings of the Australia ICOMOS National Conference 2001, 28 November – 1 December 2001, University of Adelaide*. Australia: University of Adelaide and Australia ICOMOS.

———. 2016. "Whose Heritage? Conflicting Narratives and Top-Down and Bottom-Up Approaches to Heritage Management in Yangon, Myanmar". In *Urban Heritage, Development and Sustainability*, edited by Sophia Labadi and William Logan, pp. 256–73. London: Routledge.

Lowenthal, David. 1985. *The Past is a Foreign Country*. New York: Cambridge University Press.

Mauss, Marcel. 1990. *The Gift: The Form and Reason for Exchange in Archaic Societies*. New York: Routledge.

Meskell, Lynn. 2005. "Sites of Violence: Terrorism, Tourism, and Heritage in the Archaeological Present". In *Embedding Ethics*, edited by Lynn Meskell and Peter Pels, pp. 123–46. Oxford: Berg.

———. 2014. "States of Conservation: Protection, Politics, and Pacting within UNESCO's World Heritage Committee". *Anthropological Quarterly* 87, no. 1: 217–43.

———. 2015. "Gridlock: UNESCO, Global Conflict and Failed Ambitions". *World Archaeology* 47, no. 2: 225–38.

———. 2016. "World Heritage and WikiLeaks: Territory, Trade, and Temples on the Thai-Cambodian Border". *Current Anthropology* 57, no. 1: 72–95.

———. 2018. *A Future in Ruins: UNESCO, World Heritage, and the Dream of Peace*. Oxford: Oxford University Press.

Noriko, Aikawa-Faure. 2009. "From the Proclamation of Masterpieces to the Convention for the Safeguarding of Intangible Cultural Heritage". *Intangible Heritage*. London: Routledge.

———. 2014. "Excellence and Authenticity: 'Living National (Human) Treasures' in Japan and Korea". *International Journal of Intangible Heritage* 9: 37–51.

Ray, Prabha Himanshu. 2012. "From Multi-Religious Sites to Mono-Religious Monuments in South Asia: The Colonial Legacy of Heritage Management". In *Routledge Handbook of Heritage in Asia*. London: Routledge.

Rico, T. 2014. "The Limits of a 'Heritage at Risk' Framework: The Construction of Post-disaster Cultural Heritage in Banda Aceh, Indonesia". *Journal of Social Archaeology* 14, no. 2: 157–76.

———. 2015. *Heritage Keywords: Rhetoric and Redescription in Cultural Heritage*. Colorado: University Press of Colorado.

Salazar, Noel B. 2010. "The Globalisation of Heritage through Tourism: Balancing Standardisation and Differentiation". In *Heritage and Globalisation*. New York: Routledge.

Smith, Laurajane. 2006. *Uses of Heritage*. London: Routledge.

Wang, Shu-Li. 2016. "Civilization and the Transformation of Xiaotun Village at China's Yinxu Archaeological Site". *World Heritage on the Ground: Ethnographic Perspectives*. New York: Berghahn Books.

Winter, Tim. 2015. "Heritage Diplomacy". *International Journal of Heritage Studies* 21, no. 10: 997–1015.

2

World Heritage and WikiLeaks: Territory, Trade and Temples on the Thai-Cambodian Border*

Lynn Meskell

It is typically said that heritage is always political. Such a statement might refer to the everyday politics of local stakeholder interests on one end of the spectrum or the volatile politics of destruction and erasure of heritage during conflict on the other. If heritage is always political, then one might expect that the workings of World Heritage might be especially fraught, given the international dimension. In particular, the intergovernmental system of the United Nations Educational, Scientific and Cultural Organization (UNESCO) World Heritage programme must navigate the inherent tension between state sovereignty and nationalist interests and the wider concerns of a universal regime (Francioni 2008; Pavone 2007).

* This chapter is republished with permission of University of Chicago Press Journals, from *Current Anthropology* 57, no. 1 (February 2016); permission conveyed through Copyright Clearance Center, Inc.

The 1972 Convention concerning the Protection of World Cultural and Natural Heritage and its list of over a thousand properties has many such contentious examples, including sites in Israel, Mali, Syria, Crimea, Congo and Cambodia. As an organization, UNESCO was born of war, with an explicit mission to end global conflict and help the world rebuild materially and morally (Guitton 2006), but it has found its own history increasingly entwined with that of international politics and violence.

If heritage is, and always has been, political, then I would argue that the scale and complexity of those politics is intensifying (Meskell 2013; Meskell et al. 2015). Globalization and world-making projects, like the UNESCO World Heritage programme, have changed the stakes for particular heritage sites through processes of greater interdependence and connectivity, transforming them into transactional commodities with exchange values that transcend their historical or material characteristics and that can be wrested from those contexts to serve other international interests. Of course, heritage is also always political, too, in domestic arrangements, particularly when governments intervene in the material lives of their citizens, local peoples and other connected communities. But how do archaeologists assess the political when so much remains largely anecdotal, imagined, protected and typically occluded from view in complex international circuits? How might we see realpolitik at work? In this article, I show how the diplomatic cables released by WikiLeaks in 2010 allow us an unprecedented vantage on to one contested archaeological site, Preah Vihear Temple in Cambodia (Figure 2.1). Launched in 2006, and with a continued Web presence today, WikiLeaks is a global nonprofit organization dedicated to transparency through the publication of classified, secret and private information (Saunders 2011). There are, of course, other high-profile sites, such as Jerusalem, that are contained in the disclosures but which lie beyond the scope of this paper.

In the case of Preah Vihear Temple, thrust into the international spotlight with its inscription on the UNESCO World Heritage List in 2008, followed by the International Court of Justice (ICJ) rulings in 2011 and 2013 (Barnett 2012; Chesterman 2015; Vrdoljak 2014),[1] we can trace the site's connectivity across national political intrigues, international border wars, bilateral negotiations surrounding gas and steel contracts, and military alignments. The very fact that so much politicking occurred around this one site, which was largely invisible in international heritage circles until its controversial UNESCO listing and the resultant border war, is telling. Each of the strands can be traced and documented separately, substantiated

FIGURE 2.1 Temple of Preah Vihear. Photograph courtesy of Dara Mang.

by a host of different scholars, disciplines and lines of evidence. What the cables essentially reveal are the linkages between seemingly unrelated spheres and events. In this instance, it may not reveal new information, but it underscores the intricate hyperconnectivity of heritage. The politics underwriting that connectivity are having new repercussions, particularly in spheres of conflict, such as the recent ISIS (Islamic State in Iraq and Syria) destruction of sites in Syria and Iraq. No longer collateral damage, heritage properties now reside at the heart of struggles for international recognition, self-determination and defiance.

Perhaps the conflation of heritage with other international interests, whether cultural or economic, may be the very connectivity that compounds violence in particular contexts. World Heritage sites that draw greater international intervention, coverage and concern might be the very ones where we will see escalating violence, as we have in Afghanistan, Mali, Syria and Iraq (Joy 2016; Meskell 2015a). Their internationalism may be at the heart of their destruction, something that UNESCO is now attempting to grapple with,[2] the demolitions by ISIS in Iraq being just the most recent example.

In the Corridors of Power

Since 2011, my research has focused on the politics of UNESCO World Heritage, specifically the workings of its twenty-one-member World Heritage Committee and the implications of site listing and conservation. Some of this work has focused on political pacting within the committee, as by the BRICS nations (Brazil, Russia, India, China and South Africa), and lobbying by States Parties to ensure successful outcomes for their properties (Meskell 2012; see also Claudi 2011). For example, members of BRICS on the committee ardently supported South Africa, enabling them to keep World Heritage status for the Mapungubwe Cultural Landscape while controversially retaining mining licences and initiating coal extraction in the buffer zone of the property (Meskell 2011). South Africa returned the favour when the same World Heritage Committee discussed illegal mining in Russia's Virgin Komi Forests. In other research, I examine high-profile World Heritage properties, like the Historic District of Panama, and show how lobbying and international support are not geared primarily to promote conservation, as the 1972 convention intended, but rather to protect government business interests, international corporations and, ultimately, Panama Canal contracts (Meskell 2014). In all of this work, heritage properties are wrested from their particular context and mobilized instead as transactional devices that both mask and enable a multifarious network of political and economic values. Transaction here not only refers to the process of "doing business" and the exchange of commodities and services in the World Heritage arena, but also encompasses the reciprocal influences and communicative activities between parties (Meskell 2015b). Indeed, I argue that World Heritage Committee debates over specific cultural and natural properties, their inscription on the World Heritage List, and their protection or even destruction are becoming largely irrelevant in substance yet remain highly valuable in state-to-state negotiations and exchanges of social capital.

My ethnographic study includes participation in the annual World Heritage Committee meetings as well as sustained interviews with members of the UNESCO secretariat, officials from the Advisory Bodies (International Council on Monuments and Sites [ICOMOS], International Union for Conservation of Nature [IUCN], and International Centre for the Study of the Preservation and Restoration of Cultural Property [ICCROM]),[3] ambassadors and members of national delegations, archaeologists and conservators involved in site nominations, as well as evaluators, consultants and academics involved in all aspects of World Heritage. This work has also taken me to Peru, India, Turkey, France, Cambodia and Myanmar to follow UNESCO's mission in-country, asking how and why specific nations seek and later utilize inscription. To avoid any conflict of interest, I have not accepted any official role in missions that evaluate World Heritage properties, nor do I have a formal affiliation with UNESCO. My research focuses on the 1972 World Heritage Convention, and although UNESCO has produced additional conventions dedicated to intangible heritage or the return of cultural property, these lie beyond the scope of the current research. Alongside in-depth interviews and long-term participation, I have analysed documents archived in Paris as well as extensive UNESCO Web-based materials. In collaborative work with cultural economists from the University of Turin, I have also incorporated statistical and network analyses to trace the international political pacting, economic interests and voting blocs that shape today's World Heritage agenda (Meskell et al. 2015). With my training as an archaeologist, I am concerned with discerning long-term patterns and evidence of change that can be observed by calibrating documentary materials, historical accounts, statistical records, interviews with a wide cross section of players, observation and participation.

Anthropologists have written extensively about the difficulty of studying the bureaucratic elite (Bendix 2013; Shore 2007), where official documentation is required for access and "deep hanging out" is typically curtailed by elaborate security measures. Ambassadors and members of national delegations, as well as officials in the UNESCO Secretariat, require letters, emails, and follow-up telephone calls before an appointment is granted. Many interviewees are happy to discuss issues, even sensitive ones like those outlined in this article, but do not want to be identified. As Shore (2007) suggests, the most valuable method is simply making the most of the desire of informants to talk and to be heard. As a result of my being sympathetic and eager to learn about the difficulties, inherent tensions and pressures of their position, officials tend to reveal much about their experiences within the World Heritage arena. As one delegate opined, he had previously been a diplomat in Geneva working on human rights issues and had found that experience far less contentious than his experience in the World Heritage Committee.

As an academic and an archaeologist researching World Heritage politics, this affords an understanding of specific heritage sites and their issues, as well as the overall system, but I am set apart from the institutional politics that individuals encountered and typically find burdensome, whether from their government or from UNESCO itself. Researchers like myself are also connected to the issues, such that navigating both closeness and distance entails a certain degree of loyalty and discretion (Müller 2013, p. 6). Yet some individuals expect a level of allegiance from me that it is not possible to maintain if multiple viewpoints are to be represented, sometimes leading to antipathy (see also Mosse 2011). My interlocutors are neither faceless nor neutral bureaucrats (see Hoggart 2011; Källén 2014); many have advanced degrees in economics, architecture or anthropology and are highly analytical about our academic issues and critiques.

UNESCO is constituted not only at its Paris headquarters but also in a vast network of regional sites that are both inherently material and increasingly virtual, as demonstrated by WikiLeaks. Following Berliner and Bortolotto (2013, p. 7), UNESCO can be viewed as a localized structure articulating a variety of concrete places where heritage, culture and conservation practices are thought about and debated by people made of "flesh and bone", working in offices surrounded by a landscape of paper. Understanding World Heritage entails acknowledging a host of institutional actors who, in a sense, "make" heritage: officials based in Paris, regional experts and consultants (architects, archaeologists and anthropologists), as well as ambassadors and diplomats who have to work within their own national bureaucracies. In seeking to protect global patrimony, there is an ever-expanding number of actors with differing expertise, perceptions, politics and agendas. Recently, this research has led me to focus on emerging Asian nations and their particular penchant for World Heritage listing. For example, in 2014, Myanmar had its first World Heritage Site, Pyu Ancient Cities, inscribed, and it did so with strong regional support from Malaysia, the Philippines, India, Japan and Vietnam. The ICOMOS expert decision to defer the site was overturned. That same year, Myanmar was appointed chair of the Association of Southeast Asian Nations (ASEAN) in a controversial decision that was widely viewed as a reward for Myanmar's national reform. Most World Heritage Committee delegates spoke about the Pyu Cities being important because it was Myanmar's first World Heritage nomination, rather than addressing the archaeological merits of the site. The decision to inscribe had little to do with the archaeological components and more to do with Myanmar's participation in world government, its nascent democracy and development, and the timing of this international recognition. Moreover, as chair of ASEAN, Myanmar would be overseeing issues that involved many Asian nations, such as maritime disputes in the South China Sea, not to mention balancing pro- and anti-China forces in the association.[4] This is a prime example of how World Heritage decision-making processes have transformed the inscription of sites into exchange values that mobilize ancillary effects in other domains, driven by economic and political imperatives.

At present, almost a third of the World Heritage Committee is composed of Asian nations, which poses a direct challenge to the established North American and European hegemony that has long dominated World Heritage (Cleere 2011; De Cesari 2014; Labadi 2005, 2007). I wanted to understand the stakes involved, specifically for Southeast Asian nations that have more recently ratified the 1972 convention, and the reasons why this was happening now. This entailed interviews with Asian ambassadors to UNESCO stationed in Paris, members of their national delegations, and officials posted in regional offices in Asia. In various meetings in Paris, Phnom Penh and Bangkok, some of my informants speculated about the political machinations leading up to the controversial inscription of Cambodia's Preah Vihear Temple. They prompted me to investigate the many seemingly unrelated international connections around the inscription and resultant conflict on the ground. One high-ranking diplomat advised me to follow the money, the oil and, indeed, the leaks. "It's all there", I was told in hushed tones against the backdrop of besuited international diplomats having their coffee and going about their business. High-ranking officials were clearly concerned about their identities being leaked, too, but I took these confidences more as conspiratorial gestures and doubted that they could be fully corroborated given the layers of secrecy and diplomacy that surround United Nations agencies.

In the case of Preah Vihear, one diplomat told me to look closely at the American role in the ultimate inscription and to then trace the chain of events online. It seemed unlikely that I would be able to do this; from my experience of nomination dossiers, such negotiations would not be made public, and so I ventured further for the source. The diplomat indicated that American support was instrumental to Cambodia's successful UNESCO listing; evidence was available on WikiLeaks, he whispered. Previously, in Bangkok, I had heard murmurs about exchanges for oil between Thailand and Cambodia due to Thailand's unsuccessful bid to claim the territory around Preah Vihear. And yet this intensely regional dispute appeared disconnected from the United States, which shared neither a border with the countries involved nor any immediate interest in the dispute, although the United States had served on the World Heritage Committee from 2005 to 2009.[5] What asset value could an eleventh-century temple dedicated to Shiva, in such a remote location, possibly have? The official World Heritage process would involve negotiations between the sovereign states of Cambodia and Thailand, brokered to some degree by UNESCO's own brand of intergovernmental diplomacy, such as an International Coordinating Committee (ICC).[6]

WikiLeaks seemed a conspiracy too far, yet I felt obliged to follow the lead, and the diplomat was indeed correct. Preah Vihear features in some 150 diplomatic cables containing almost 100,000 words from 19 May 2005 to 12 February 2010. Significantly, these dates cover the lead-up to the temple's nomination in 2007, its inscription in 2008, the fallout with Thailand, and much of the continued violence. They can be found on Cablegate,[7] the United States diplomatic cables leak released by WikiLeaks on 28 November 2010. In total, there are over 250,000 cables containing diplomatic analysis from world leaders and the diplomats' assessments of their host countries, their foreign counterparts, and the issues of the day. This article focuses on some forty cables from embassies in Bangkok, Phnom Penh, Jakarta and the US Mission to UNESCO in Paris. Some forty per cent of those cables were designated unclassified, whereas the remaining sixty per cent are confidential: significantly, none were flagged as secret or top secret. All the diplomatic cables were marked "Sipdis", denoting "secret internet protocol distribution", which means they had been distributed via the closed US SIPRNet, the US Department of Defense's classified version of the civilian Internet. More than three million US government personnel and soldiers have access to this network.[8] Documents marked top secret are not included in Sipdis.

Every cable includes the date, author, addressee, classification level and report text itself. Much of what was written and transmitted was done so in the belief that the dispatches would remain classified for the next twenty-five years. This presumably explains why American ambassadors and envoys include much gossip and hearsay in their reports back to the State Department in Washington.[9] As such, we must remain critical with respect to their veracity and intent. The US government's first official response to the leaks was to admit that they constituted a major breach of security and classified information. Yet, once the material had circulated widely and appeared in numerous international newspapers, the response switched to minimizing the disclosures as minor and unimportant (Pieterse 2012, p. 1912).

Cablegate seems largely an international embarrassment surrounding diplomatic, and sometimes undiplomatic, practices involving 274 embassies dating from 28 December 1966 to 28 February 2010. Many of the documents that I examined were unclassified, and certainly most of the events described or concerns alluded to can now be effectively traced in other literature from the fields of Asian studies, international relations, political science, defence studies, law and government (Barnett 2012; Chachavalpongpun 2012; Chesterman 2015; Croissant and Chambers 2010; Hauser-Schäublin and Missling 2014; Von Feigenblatt 2011; Yoosuk 2013). In that respect, the diplomatic cables are "open secrets". The potential danger lies in fetishizing the medium rather than focusing on the content, itself more mundane and readily available elsewhere, if only the considerable connections can be pieced together. Although such back channels have always been available, it is the embarrassment that comes with "trespassing on the fine art of double dealing" (Pieterse 2012, p. 1917). Indeed, the "only surprising thing about the WikiLeaks revelations", Žižek (2011) reminds us, "is that they contain no surprises. Didn't we learn exactly what we expected to learn? The real disturbance was at the level of appearances: we can no longer pretend we don't know what everyone knows we know." Yet, as the sociologist Jan Nederveen Pieterse has observed,

> The notion that the cables contain "no surprises" is beside the point; the point is that they confirm and document hegemonic operations, political complicity and war crimes, so their status changes from allegation and hearsay to actionable offences or, at a minimum, information that carries political consequences. It stands to reason that the political ripple effects are greater and weightier in the target zones of hegemony than on the home front where institutions act as buffers and a jaded public has been inured to impunity. (Pieterse 2012, p. 1913)

As the cables that feature Preah Vihear demonstrate, the ever-widening circuits around heritage include both national and international economic, legal, military and political negotiations. This paper is not about the specific history of the Hindu temple or the ensuing legal battles, since these topics have been thoroughly discussed elsewhere (see Hauser-Schäublin 2011; Hauser-Schäublin and Missling 2014; Pawakapan 2013). Thus, it is not about the temple per se but, rather, its global positioning as a proxy for territory, sovereignty and security as well as international corporate agreements. Those connections are laid bare in the diplomatic disclosures and remain accessible online from Cablegate.

A History of Violence

Since 2008, Preah Vihear has been the subject of a vast outpouring of scholarly literature, ranging from archaeology and heritage studies (Croissant and Chambers 2010; Hauser- Schäublin 2011) to international law (Barnett 2012; Chesterman 2015; Ciorciari 2014; Hauser-Schäublin and Missling 2014; Shulman 2011). Originally nominated on the basis of selection criteria I, III, and IV, the site was inscribed only on the basis of the first; namely, "a masterpiece of human creative genius".[10] Importantly, the inscribed property was also reduced in area and now comprises only the temple, and not the wider promontory with its cliffs and caves. The temple is composed of a series of sanctuaries linked by a system of pavements and staircases over an 800-metre-long axis and dates back to the first half of the eleventh century AD. However, its complex history extends further, to the ninth century, when the hermitage was founded. UNESCO inscription was conferred on the basis of the outstanding Khmer architecture and in terms of the temple's plan, decoration and relationship to the spectacular landscape setting (http://whc.unesco.org/en/list/1224). Indeed, so much has been published that it might be thought that the issue of the Hindu temple was rather exhausted. However, before we examine the hyperconnectivity of this one heritage site, a brief history of the international conflict over the temple is necessary.

Tensions between Cambodia and Thailand have a long history, and their respective nationalisms are today framed by accounts of the past, by colonial and foreign relations and by the recurrent nationalist narrative of "lost territories". Taking the longer view, the bloodshed over Preah Vihear is intimately tied to understandings of the past and symbolic evocations of past grandeur and territory embodied in contentious heritage sites. Some authors have argued that the whole notion of this specific border in its regional context, not to mention the temple itself, has been fundamentally misunderstood by Western commentators (Lee 2014; Von Feigenblatt 2011; Winichakul 1994). Although a full recounting lies beyond the scope of this paper, there are many excellent and recent studies that provide rich historical detail (Chachavalpongpun 2012; Croissant and Chambers 2010; Cuasay 1998; Kasetsiri, Sothirak and Chachavalpongpun 2013; Lee 2014; Sothirak 2013; Strate 2013; Yoosuk 2013).

Thai scholar Pavin Chachavalpongpun (2012) argues that the deep animosity between these nations harks back to the advent of colonialism, when King Norodom of Cambodia signed an agreement with France in 1863 to institute a protectorate over his kingdom against his rival neighbours (Siam and Vietnam). Then, in 1904, the Siamese-Cambodian border was demarcated on the basis of the watershed, as indicated in a map sketched by the supposed "joint committee" of Siamese and French surveyors (Chachavalpongpun 2012, p. 84). Not surprisingly, today only Cambodia recognizes this map as indicating a clear boundary line between the two countries, while Thailand relies on a different, unilaterally produced map that was unveiled at the World Heritage Session in Christchurch, New Zealand, in 2007. This second map shows the disputed area of land as claimed by Thailand (Sothirak 2013, p. 88).

Chachavalpongpun (2012, p. 84) sets out how Siam's loss of the Cambodian provinces to the French continues to ignite Thai nationalism by mobilizing the trope of loss of former "Thai territories" in its dealings with foreign powers and opportunistic neighbours. Preah Vihear is situated in just one such territory. This discourse of injury and loss remains resilient today and has infused Thailand's foreign policy and bilateral arrangements. Cambodia broke off its diplomatic relations with Thailand in 1958 and 1961, allegedly as a protest against the Thai claim for Preah Vihear, almost escalating to outright war (Chachavalpongpun 2012, p. 85). In 1962, Cambodia took the dispute to the ICJ (Barnett 2012; Shulman 2011). When the ICJ ruled in favour of Cambodia, the authoritarian regime of Sarit Thanarat rewrote the story for nationalist purposes, urging the Thais to remember that the temple had been stolen from them. Yet successive Thai governments never made a request for interpretation of the ICJ ruling (Chachavalpongpun 2012, p. 88), and that decision has ongoing legal repercussions (see Hauser-Schäublin and Missling 2014).

Then, in June 2007, UNESCO announced decision 31 COM 8B.24 at the World Heritage Committee meetings in New Zealand.[11] The World Heritage Committee chairperson released a statement that had been agreed to by the Delegation of Cambodia and the Delegation of Thailand:

The State Party of Cambodia and the State Party of Thailand are in full agreement that the Sacred Site of the Temple of Preah Vihear has Outstanding Universal Value and must be inscribed on the World Heritage List as soon as possible. Accordingly, Cambodia and Thailand agree that Cambodia will propose the site for formal inscription on the World Heritage List at the 32nd session of the World Heritage Committee in 2008 with the active support of Thailand.

Another key moment in the fate of Preah Vihear, covered in detail in Cablegate as well as in official documents, came in May 2008, when the Thai foreign minister, Noppadon Pattama, signed a joint communiqué with Cambodia's deputy prime minister, Sok An, in Paris. It confirmed Thai support for Cambodia's request to propose the temple to the UNESCO World Heritage List. Upon returning to Bangkok, Noppadon was faced with hostile nationalists from the People's Democratic Alliance (PAD), shouting "Noppadon is a traitor" (Chachavalpongpun 2012, p. 90). Once again, Preah Vihear was linked to waning sovereignty and the loss of national territory, especially over the 4.6 square kilometres that surround the temple. Some even argue that Preah Vihear stands in for Thailand itself, particularly its national humiliation over territorial loss, which leads back to the 1930s (Schofield and Tan-Mullins 2008). Reigniting the hostility between neighbouring nations, PAD leader Sondhi Limthongkul resolved to take the temple and its surrounding territory by force.

On 7 July 2008, the temple was formally inscribed on the World Heritage List, and border clashes between the two nations erupted almost immediately. Not restricted to just one temple, Thai soldiers occupied the Ta Moan complex in the following month, about 150 kilometres to the west. Cambodia responded by occupying the Ta Krabei Temple, some 13 kilometres east of Ta Moan, sending 70 soldiers to the previously non-militarized site. By late October 2008, the Thai military believed that Cambodia had an estimated 2,800 troops around the Preah Vihear Temple, facing its 600 troops (International Crisis Group 2011). The frontier conflict raged on, and then, in December 2008, Abhisit Vejjajiva was elected prime minister of Thailand and relations with Cambodia initially improved. However, soon after, additional clashes further escalated bilateral tensions. This was followed by joint efforts to reduce the military presence along the border. UNESCO responded to the crisis by sending a reinforced monitoring mission from 28 March to 6 April 2009: it recorded the ongoing violence and casualties, destruction of property, relocation of civilians, and evidence of damage to the temple. Given UNESCO's intergovernmental standing, the objective of the mission was to assess "the state of conservation of the World Heritage property ... without attempting to determine the dynamics of events or the responsibilities of the parties involved".[12]

By September 2009, PAD demonstrators again attempted to storm Preah Vihear but were pushed back (Croissant and Chambers 2010, p. 151). On 6 November 2009, the Thai Foreign Ministry recalled its ambassador to Phnom Penh to protest against the official appointment of deposed former Thai prime minister Thaksin as Hun Sen's economic advisor. This prompted a review of all bilateral agreements with Cambodia, and Thailand withdrew from the maritime talks over the potentially rich supplies of oil and gas in a disputed area of the eastern Gulf of Thailand. In response, Cambodia recalled its ambassador to Bangkok (Chachavalpongpun 2012, pp. 92–93).

Military standoffs continued to flare up almost to the brink of full-scale war, not only damaging bilateral talks (Sothirak 2013, p. 87) but also threatening the unity of ASEAN. In February and April 2011, tense fighting resumed, with many casualties, property damage and the displacement of thousands of civilians. Then, the United Nations Security Council (UNSC) requested that Thailand and Cambodia withdraw their troops, while the ICJ invoked its original decision for military withdrawal.[13] They advised the two nations to resolve the dispute peacefully through dialogue facilitated by the ASEAN group (Sothirak 2013, p. 90). In 2011, ASEAN was chaired by Indonesia, which took a leading role in attempting to mediate the dispute. Indonesian foreign minister Marty Natalegawa was sent to Thailand and Cambodia, but all attempts to broker peace failed. ASEAN foreign ministers then agreed to deploy military and civilian observers to the troubled border. Both nations originally agreed to admit Indonesian observers, but Thailand soon withdrew support, claiming that to do so undermined their national sovereignty.[14] Both Cambodia and Thailand had previously addressed their concerns to the UNSC in early February, recounting grievances of military aggression, damage to the temple, and the death toll and invoking the UN Charter and 1954 Hague Convention.[15] Yet such appeals to the UN held little promise of resolution.

The Thai delegation publicly stepped down from the World Heritage Convention during the World Heritage Committee meetings in Paris on 27 June 2011.[16] I witnessed the dramatic event and remember that, at those same meetings, Cambodia distributed glossy pamphlets showing military stationed around Preah Vihear and artillery damage, calling for a cessation of violence in view of Cambodian sovereignty. Many delegates dismissed the Thai position as a performative exercise in support of the ruling government that would have little political impact. Indeed, such a resignation would not take effect immediately; they would also have several years to consider their position, and Thailand was heading for national elections, the result of which would likely change everything. Leading up to the meetings, UNESCO Director-General Bokova convened a dialogue between both States Parties, hoping to "foster common understanding of the issues affecting the World Heritage site, and to reach agreement on enhancing its state of conservation following recent threats to the property".[17] An example of failed diplomacy, the latent struggle was revived through UNESCO inscription and subsequent deliberations (Hauser-Schäublin and Missling 2014, p. 89). Afterwards, UNESCO could only issue public statements of regret and urge Thailand to reconsider their withdrawal.[18] Over the ensuing months and years, UNESCO launched its own media campaign, with diplomatic attempts to garner an agreement and, ultimately, peace. Given that the UNESCO listing sparked the recent spate of violence and that other measures perhaps should have been taken beforehand (Williams 2011), the organization was in a weaker position than usual to forge a peaceful outcome.

On 18 July 2011, the ICJ called for the installation of a demilitarized zone and urged cooperation through ASEAN, reminding both nations that the UN Charter obliged them to settle disputes peacefully.[19] Hauser-Schäublin and Missling (2014, p. 80) argue that this provisional measure transformed the UNESCO World Heritage site, which had been temporarily ruled by a military border regime, into an area exclusively restricted to civilians. Cambodian troops finally withdrew from the zone surrounding the temple in July 2012. Then, in November 2013, the ICJ reiterated its decision in the 1962 ruling and stated unanimously "that Cambodia had sovereignty over the whole territory of the promontory of Preah Vihear, as defined in paragraph 98 of the present judgment, and that, in consequence, Thailand was under an obligation to withdraw from that territory the Thai military or police forces, or other guards or keepers, that were stationed there".[20] At the time of writing, diplomatic negotiations between Thailand and Cambodia continue, and the ICC is only now starting its work.[21]

In this very brief historical account, I hope to have underscored the intersections between international legal bodies, global heritage regimes, territorial conflicts, domestic politics, and understandings of history and sovereignty. In the next section, I focus on the leveraging of this specific World Heritage Site within broader politico-economic negotiations.

Heritage and Hyperconnectivity

World Heritage properties, and the very process of inscribing and subsequently managing and conserving them, produce a dynamic market place for international trade and exchange. Sites are emblems or tokens that leverage ancillary goods and exchanges in ever-widening circuits of economic and political power (Meskell 2014). Although historically the World Heritage Committee was singularly dominated by European nations, Asian States Parties currently dominate, leading to distinct styles of politics and diplomacy (see Winter 2014a, 2014b). Moreover, in terms of regional representation, no East Asian nation possessed a property inscribed on the World Heritage List before 1987. In that one year, China successfully put forward six properties, and all were inscribed. It was only in 1991 that additional sites from other East Asian nations were inscribed, and there has been a steady increase in the regional listings ever since. While the historic dominance of European nations can be explained to some degree by the convention's early development, today, Asian states such as China, with forty-eight World Heritage properties, are increasingly active (for a full discussion, see Meskell, Liuzza and Brown 2015).

During interviews with members of Asian delegations to UNESCO at their Rue Miollis, Paris, offices, I asked specifically about the changing nature of World Heritage in Asia. Over numerous cups of tea, individual diplomats described how they saw their role as supporting other Southeast Asian nations, a tendency also noted by members of the UNESCO Secretariat. Asian regionalism is often defined by a communitarian instinct to reinforce cooperation so as to overcome the fissures that might potentially divide societies (Beeson 2005). Some suggest that Asian regionalism tends to be more culturally articulated, as opposed to economic, as in North America, or political, as with Europe (Chin 2014). My informants uniformly talked about the importance of "the brand", national pride, international recognition, and development opportunities. But many were also quick to identify the pitfalls of global tourism that accompany inscription and subsequently impinge upon site conservation.

When asked about the recent interest in Asian World Heritage, one diplomat in Paris told me that it was about getting known and "being visible" on the world stage. Inscription brings international funding, support and training. "If you have that, other things follow", he explained, "sometimes it's the easy route, but not always." He had witnessed this personally in the drawn-out negotiations over Preah Vihear. Other officials described participation in the World Heritage arena, from site inscription to World Heritage Committee membership, as being tied to ASEAN principles, the role of emerging nations, Asian identity, global branding, and economics. Speaking about the importance of a major archaeological site now being prepared for nomination, one ambassador said that it did not simply belong to his country, but "to the world". If the site is inscribed, he said with thinly veiled longing, there will be development, recognition and international support, and all of this is key to his nation in transition. But, on the other hand, some ambassadors were keen to point out that they already had expertise at home and saw World Heritage Committee membership as an opportunity to share their own technical expertise. Speaking with great pride, one official, trained as an economist, spoke of his delegation's preparedness and training in natural and cultural heritage and recounted the numerous requests for regional assistance he had received. Being on the committee was a positive statement for his country, to learn further, to show their skills, to be visible and to accrue benefits all round. This is the softer side of cultural diplomacy (Luke 2013; Luke and Kersel 2013; Winter 2014b) and very different from the conflict between States Parties that erupted around Preah Vihear.

Unlike the cordial discussions above, the leaked US diplomatic cables reveal the tense briefings leading up to a May 2008 meeting in Paris just before the annual World Heritage Committee session. Thailand clearly disapproved of Cambodia's unilateral nomination of Preah Vihear. Cambodia independently solicited technical reports and management plans from French, Belgian and US specialists.[22] One American specialist from the US National Parks Service helped the Cambodians draft the 2008 progress report, and they were apparently so grateful that they considered naming part of the Preah Vihear landscape in his honour.[23] Thai experts preferred a transboundary listing, but their views were not considered. By 10 April 2008, the American ambassador suggested that the issue had become too polemical for public meetings and that "private negotiations" would be the only way to advance. The United States was to play a significant part, as we shall see, as members of national delegations and UNESCO staff had indicated during interviews.

The leaks had effectively confirmed a great deal of what was previously just speculation.

The cables make explicit the ways in which the temple dispute was intricately tied to broader issues of foreign policy and investment. Some of the cables that I examined were dispatched to the Central Intelligence Agency, National Security Council, Secretary of State, and United Nations, as well as to the Commander in Chief US Pacific Command. Rather than simply making inferred connections, it is important to demonstrate how seemingly separate issues are conjoined. Let us take one pertinent example, a cable dated 6 May 2008, entitled "Cambodia: Investment, Temple Controversy, Debt and Overlapping Claims Headline Business Delegation Meeting".[24] In that single cable, Preah Vihear figures in six of ten paragraphs. The first paragraph opens with "riding on a wave of increased US investor interest in Cambodia", then continues to "the pending inscription of the Preah Vihear Temple on the UNESCO World Heritage List and Cambodia's bilateral debt with the US Delegation members and the embassy believe that successful resolution of the Preah Vihear issue could open the door to a resolution of the overlapping claims area in the Gulf of Thailand".

The second paragraph summarizes a meeting between Cambodian prime minister Hun Sen and the US-ASEAN Business Council president Matt Daley on the expansion of US companies like Boeing and Ford. Daley reports "that the business delegation had just come from meetings in Thailand and relayed a message from Thai Foreign Minister Noppadon Pattama that Thailand does not/not oppose the inscription of the Preah Vihear Temple on the UNESCO World Heritage List, but would like a joint Thai-Cambodian management plan for a 4.7 square kilometer area adjacent to the main temple". The third paragraph focuses entirely on Preah Vihear and the issue of overlapping claims. Hun Sen states that "a joint management plan is not politically or legally feasible", since "the proposed inscription covered the main temple site (the area awarded to Cambodia by the International Court of Justice)". In the next paragraph he is quoted as urging "a swift resolution of the issue, saying that further delay endangers the site, which is the 'heritage of humankind'".

Paragraphs five and six refer to Cambodia's outstanding bilateral debt to the United States and issues of repayment. Paragraph seven deals with the Overlapping Claims Area and oil reserves in the Gulf of Thailand and in Thailand, Hun Sen preferring to consider this issue separate from that of Preah Vihear. The next paragraph covers the Cambodian economy, as does the ninth paragraph, stressing that "major US companies have already begun operations in the Cambodian market".

Finally, paragraph ten states that

> the meetings also served as a reality check that intense political debates lie behind some key economic issues. On the Preah Vihear issue, it seems likely that—despite Thai and Cambodian statements to the contrary—the inscription of the temple is linked to resolving the maritime claims dispute, at least in the minds of senior Thai and Cambodian government leaders. Both sides are looking at the issues from political, cultural, and economic perspectives. It is in the interest of both countries to find a way to settle these differences; the challenge for the USG [United States Government] is to find a way to push both countries towards an acceptable solution ... inscribing Preah Vihear on the UNESCO World Heritage List, if handled correctly, actually could open opportunities for the two countries to work more closely both on cultural issues and the more lucrative issue of the overlapping claims in the Gulf of Thailand.

During the period covered by the diplomatic leaks, and discussed within them, there was increased US investor interest in Cambodia from major corporations like Boeing, not to mention Nike, McDonalds, Pizza Hut and Marlboro.[25] The issue of Cambodia's debt to the United States was also being considered.[26] As the 6 May 2008 cable above suggests, if the Preah Vihear dispute could be resolved, it might open a door to resolving the overlapping maritime claims in the Gulf of Thailand (Schofield and Tan-Mullins 2008). This would mean access to vast natural gas reserves to be exploited by US companies like Chevron,[27] who have subsequently been granted extended concessions. Linking territorial disputes from the temple to the sea, one Cambodian representative explained that there was "no overlapping claim" with Preah Vihear as there was with the Gulf of Thailand. The two issues of commodities and flows were inextricably linked for the main players and their US brokers. An equation began to take shape: if Cambodia retained their temple, Thailand might enhance their underwater assets, and the United States might negotiate for extended contracts. Indeed, the cables underscore how governments privilege the economic interests of large corporations, not simply national interests, abroad. The political, the economic and the cultural became inseparable, and this connection was made, not only in the leaks, but also in Thai media,[28] which accused the government of exchanging Preah Vihear and its border territories for access to natural gas rights in Cambodia's Koh Kong province (Strate 2013). While the "national" is front and centre in the Preah Vihear dispute, negotiations around the site have involved a broad range of entities, including the work of national legislatures and judiciaries, intergovernmental agencies, the international operations of national firms and markets, political projects of non-state actors, and changes in the relationship between citizens and the state (Sassen 2006). For example, the United States has had a significant military stake in the region since World War II, according to the cables, with bases in Thailand, such as Utapao, with air and sea capability. Utapao had previously supported US refuelling missions en route to Afghanistan. In one cable, we read that "the relationship has evolved into a partnership that provides the United States with unique benefits. As one of five US treaty allies in Asia and straddling a major force projection air/sea corridor, Thailand remains crucial to US interests in the Asia-Pacific region and beyond."[29] Thus, supporting Thailand in an international dispute, whether over territory or temples, had implications.

The cables reveal the eagerness of the United States to strengthen its presence in Southeast Asia, especially in light of the region's increasing links with China. The State Party of China, like the United States, is a member of the ICC for Preah Vihear, so both will be instrumental in shaping its future management. In 2008, China also had substantial investment projects around Preah Vihear, including mining and industry, and has funded a bridge and a major road to the temple.[30] In that same year, the Chinese government gave US$290 million to fund a road linking Preah Vihear to the World Heritage Site of Angkor. Winter (2010, p. 121) argues that intraregional tourism provides a valuable context for mobilizing new partnerships between the two nations. The China Railway Group was also constructing a north–south railway connecting the Chinese-owned Cambodia Iron and Steel Mining Industry Group's factory in Preah Vihear province to a new port in Koh Kong province in the Gulf of Thailand.[31] According to one informant in Paris, it was the broader issue of Chinese insertion into Cambodia that was the real stimulus behind American intervention in Preah Vihear.[32]

With reference to Cambodian relations with the United States, the temple brokered a new era of fruitful cooperation. Further cementing their relationship with the United States, the Cambodian deputy prime minister Sok An is reported in one cable as saying, "gone are the days of mistrust and suspicion". And given this new relationship, he was eager for the implementation of promised US Agency for International Development (USAID) programmes for his country. In a single paragraph, the US assistance with the inscription of Preah Vihear and the possibility of excluding Thailand on the ICC is followed by discussion of Chevron concessions and potential compromises on oil revenue taxation. Sok An then repeats his gratitude for the US delegation's support of the inscription of Preah Vihear. Not forgetting this link to the workings of World Heritage, Sok An served as the chairman for the 2013 World Heritage Committee meetings held in Phnom Penh. Moreover, in 2008 and again in 2013, the US State Department pushed to renew its Memorandum of Understanding (MOU) with Cambodia concerning cultural property, thus ignoring what was unfolding on the ground (see also Luke and Kersel 2013, pp. 63–73). Specifically, in Article II of this bilateral agreement, Cambodia agrees to "strengthen regional cooperation, especially with immediately neighboring states, for the protection of the cultural patrimony of the region, recognizing that often, present-day political boundaries and cultural boundaries do not coincide".[33]

Around the site of Preah Vihear is an assemblage of distinct elements that are denationalized through political, economic and military interventions. The 1972 convention, within the framework of the United Nations, expects properties like Preah Vihear to be nominated by the sovereign state on whose territory they are located (Pressouyre 1996). World Heritage Sites should thus embody some of the most inalienable of objects. The listing of Preah Vihear constitutes what Sassen would call a "tipping point": one that moves us from an era marked by the ascendance of the nation-state and its capture of all major components of social, economic, political and subjective life to one marked by a proliferation of orders (Sassen 2006, p. 9). What WikiLeaks does is essentially highlight that proliferation. The cables might not disclose new information, but they underscore the hyperconnectivity of World Heritage today. As one US ambassador noted with regard to the temple, "the US's overarching interest in maintaining regional stability does not allow us the luxury of indefinitely standing on the sidelines of this dispute".[34] The timing of the temple dispute was also crucial for larger security concerns and jockeying for power on high-profile UN committees. Cambodia was petitioning for support in its bid to join the UN Security Council in the 2012 elections with a campaign that foregrounded their ancient heritage.[35] Thailand had considered running in 2010 but ultimately withdrew. Cambodia was also eager to secure US backing to join the Asia-Pacific Economic Cooperation (APEC) forum and overturn the embargo on new members.

The foregoing suggests that resolving the temple and its border war was bound up in and inseparable from larger international bartering that the United States saw as advantageous. However, American diplomats seem genuinely concerned with the implementation of rule of law in Cambodia, good governance and reducing corruption as much as they are with trade facilitation, economic growth and security cooperation.[36] The cables convey that the desired outcome for the United States is a peaceful resolution and one that incorporates a role for Thailand. American diplomats note that the "U.S. remains the country of first choice for arms procurement" for Thailand, with $2 billion currently in process.[37] Speaking about US involvement in the conflict, one official based in Paris told me, "they think their business is the world". His phrase is particularly apt, because so much American intervention was directly tethered to economic interests.

In Thailand the ramifications of Cablegate were keenly felt because they reveal reactions from outside observers, like US ambassadors, who themselves were not constrained by laws prohibiting Thailand's "network monarchy" from being held publicly accountable. Moreover, they cover a time of unprecedented violence and upheaval from 2009 to 2011, including the clashes between the pro-monarchy "yellow shirts" and the opposing "red shirts". Some government supporters saw the release just days before the 2011 election as a conspiracy to overthrow the monarchy and Thai establishment (Pieterse 2012, p. 1915).

The cables describe the fate of Foreign Minister Noppadon, the legal fallout when he was accused of violating constitutional procedures, and his ultimate resignation on 14 July 2008. The next day, a monk and two other Thais crossed the border in protest, sparking the further mobilization of troops.[38] Fuelled by turmoil in domestic Thai politics, popular media portrayed the loss of territory and the temple through UNESCO inscription as former prime minister Thaksin's gain, alleging that he supported the Cambodian nomination in return for personal financial rewards (Askew 2010; Croissant and Chambers 2010). Hostilities over the temple thus stirred up both domestic political intrigues and cross-border ones. Protests organized by the People's Alliance for Democracy successfully toppled an opposition-led government and politicized the temple dispute by making it a matter of national pride. At the same time, disputes were erupting over maritime territory between the two nations in the Gulf of Thailand. As stated above, the United States has commercial interests in the gulf, including the corporate giant Chevron.

Both Cambodia and Thailand were elected to the World Heritage Committee for the very same period (2009–13), undoubtedly as an internationally driven diplomatic measure to balance national interests and find a peaceful solution to the Preah Vihear conflict. There was considerable pressure on American diplomats, especially those in the US Mission to UNESCO, to support both Cambodia[39] and Thailand,[40] respectively. Each drew on their nation's vast heritage reserves and expertise in arguing for American backing. Showcasing the past and effectively managing it in modern "expert" ways has currency in international circles, as reinforced in the majority of my interviews with Asian representatives. Having that recognized through election to the World Heritage Committee, as a key "standard setting" body, is perceived as a positive step in gaining yet further prestige and power in other United Nations forums.

I have suggested that the entire World Heritage system today creates transferable values that mobilize supplemental rewards in other global domains, driven by economic, military, religious and social imperatives (Meskell 2014, 2015). This can be traced throughout the World Heritage process, but also at the level of particular properties and participants within the system. World Heritage sites, their nomination, inscription, monitoring, and conservation further leverages and consolidates international relationships, strategic partnerships and worldviews. In these politicized transactions, cultural recognition both masks and enables a multifarious network of exchange values. One notable example of fungibility in the World Heritage arena evidenced in the leaked cables is the practice of vote swapping across UN forums, also described in detail by many World Heritage insiders (see also Dreher, Sturm and Vreeland 2009; Slaughter and Hale 2010). One cable reveals that "Thailand had entered into a vote swap deal with Germany and Italy" to support their candidates for the United Nations International Civil Service Commission "in exchange for support for Thailand's candidate for the U.N. World Heritage Committee". Membership was deemed crucial given the ongoing Preah Vihear dispute, and Cambodia was also a candidate for the committee. Both nations were successful in their 2008 bid to join the World Heritage Committee in 2009. Because vote trading has become increasingly common, the Thai official ventured that it might be more difficult for his country to support the United States without Thailand.[41]

The cables tell us a great deal about World Heritage politics, and while they may reveal practices we know or assume to be operative, the fact that they come from such high-level official sources suggests we can no longer ignore them. In Žižek's terms, we cannot pretend we do not know what everyone knows we know. It is ironic, too, that the United States has been such a vociferous critic of the so-called "politicization" of UNESCO, especially during the time period covered by the leaks, citing other nations as using the World Heritage Convention to advance their agendas (see Morris 2011; Siim 2011). It has been well documented that the United States views "politicization" as the introduction of issues that it no longer has enough votes to exclude (Dorn and Ghodsee 2012; Graham 2006; Hoggart 2011; Preston, Herman and Schiller 1989, p. 131). Yet I would posit that if, for example, we had similar access to French and Chinese diplomatic correspondence in Thailand and Cambodia at the same time we might see similar speculations about trade and territorial and security matters. This is not simply an American issue: today, hyperconnectivity is as much about heritage as it is communication or globalization. Through the processes of globalization, territory, law, economy, security, authority and membership, which may have once been conceived of as national, rarely possess the degree of autonomy evinced in national law and international treaties (Sassen 2006, p. 1).

Conclusions

Ethnographic fieldwork allows for elements of surprise and serendipity to shape the research process (Shore 2007), to follow the leads that informants offer and, in the case of diplomatic elites, to dig deeper into international bureaucracies and institutional politics. Delving into the world of WikiLeaks was never intended to constitute part of my research into World Heritage, nor could it have been anticipated. Archaeologists talk a great deal about politics, but they typically have little access to politicians or those involved in the making of international agreements and policies. The diplomatic disclosures then represent a rare opportunity to untangle the complex political transactions around one World Heritage site. Moreover, archaeologists always want the past to matter in the present, yet in complex international settings we are often unaware of the ways in which and degrees to which certain sites get bound up in political, economic and religious issues that we cannot begin to access, influence or even comprehend. Increasingly, this kind of mattering can have detrimental effects on sites and, more importantly, the people around them.

This is an article about the workings of foreign interests abroad, soft and hard power, military calculation, geopolitical manoeuvring, and the future. We see that revealed in the leaked cables, where archaeological heritage is an asset to be negotiated like any other. By finding ways to trace the hyperconnectivity that we know to be operative today, we avoid constituting heritage as a "category that conceals rather than illuminates the analysis of social processes" (Franquesa 2013, p. 348). Heritage is clearly not above value in today's world, as the transactional histories of Preah Vihear neatly illustrate. Recognition of this can be traced in UNESCO's own future-driven strategy documents. World Heritage properties were positioned in 2002 as drivers for development and "dialogue among cultures and civilizations",[42] whereas by 2014 they were transformed into "assets ... used for promoting social stability peace-building, recovery from crisis situations, and development strategies". While heritage has long been framed as a resource, whether for development or intercultural understanding, this shift to "assets" signals a form of value available for capitalization, exchange, and debt repayment that is sutured, as Preah Vihear demonstrates, to both the nation state and international community. More challenging still are the political and military implications of a global heritage regime in which sites and objects now play a very visible role in the struggle or, indeed, constitute the point of conflict. On the one hand, UNESCO claims that heritage might be deployed to "prevent conflicts and facilitate peace-building", while, on the other, it recognizes that "recent years have also been marked by an increasing trend to target culture in conflict".[43] Despite UNESCO's best efforts, and laid bare in glossy brochures distributed at World Heritage meetings as well as in ISIS-released videos, material heritage is being instrumentalized to exacerbate our fundamental differences and tensions.

Some might argue that the conflicts and subsequent diplomatic efforts over Preah Vihear are examples of soft power, yet I would instead suggest that we are witnessing clear-cut international struggles for territorial, economic and military leverage. Tied to the temple dispute were issues of resource extraction, commercial contracts, infrastructural developments, regional defence, and the continued use of military installations. All of these transactions intervolved international players, including, among others, the United States and China, and in turn any decisions had ramifications for the broader future of the region. Global regimes have long been entreated to settle territorial disputes and shore up sovereign protection in relation to ancient heritage (De Cesari 2010). Indeed, Cambodia's nineteenth-century appeal to the French to normalize colonial administrative relations on the ground is echoed in later petitions to the ICJ (in 1962, 2011 and 2013) and in Preah Vihear's nomination to UNESCO's World Heritage List in 2008 as a "masterpiece of human creative genius". While some external brokers, such as UNESCO or the United States, might view cultural sites as proxies for larger issues, whether that be for the furtherance of peace (Labadi 2013; Pavone 2008) or investor advantage, for the Thais and Cambodians, the temple and its territorial context were precisely what was at issue, and they had been at issue for decades. The case of Preah Vihear also underscores the persistent Western imaginaries that linger around heritage sites in Asia (Byrne 2007, 2009, 2014) and that still fail to account for local understandings, experiences and histories. A more confronting example of cultural and religious difference towards the material past is currently playing out in Iraq and, unfortunately, after decades of crafting multilateral treaties and conventions, we appear no closer to achieving a global understanding of culture.

It is noteworthy that UNESCO, an intergovernmental organization founded after the ravages of World War II, set its sights upon the dream of peace through global treaties that bound sovereign nations together, such as the 1972 convention. Forging an international body with a mission for mutual cultural understanding through cosmopolitan diversity, on the one hand, and conservation of global patrimony through technocracy, on the other, can sometimes engender the very type of conflict that it set out to dispel. The reasons why this dual mission remains irreconcilable and increasingly falters in today's world is another, longer and more complex story.

Acknowledgments

My research on UNESCO is made all the more rewarding thanks to Claudia Liuzza, who shares so much time with me at Stanford and abroad working through these issues. I am also grateful for the inspiration and guidance given to me by colleagues from the World Heritage Center in

Paris, the Advisory Bodies, and members of national delegations who have generously shared their expertise and experience with me. I would like to thank my "dream team" of respondents, Denis Byrne, Chiara De Cesari, Martin Hall, Brigitta Hauser-Schäublin, Charlotte Joy, Christina Luke and Maurizio Pellegi, along with other expert readers, including Elizabeth Gray, Ian Hodder, Carrie Nakamura, Nicholas Stanley-Price, Ana Vrdoljak and Gamini Wijesuriya. Nicholas Brown was a wonderful research assistant during his time at Stanford, and Mark Aldenderfer and Lisa McKamy are responsible for making it all come together so pleasantly. Field research for the article was partly supported under the Australian Research Council's Discovery scheme (Crisis in International Heritage Conservation in an Age of Shifting Global Power, DP140102991). The article was written during a brief sabbatical at Oxford University, and I would like to acknowledge Keble College and, particularly, Chris Gosden and Lambros Malfouris.

Notes

1. http://www.un.org/apps/news/story.asp?NewsIDp46461#.VOYc4mTkdeM. Underlining the high profile nature of this case, Amal Clooney represented Cambodia in the interstate territorial claim (International Court of Justice, The Hague) in Cambodia v. Thailand; see "Request for Interpretation of the Judgment of June 15, 1962, in the case concerning the Temple of Preah Vihear". She also represented Julian Assange, head of Wikileaks, in extradition proceedings (City of Westminster Magistrates' Court, London) in Sweden v. Assange.

2. http://whc.unesco.org/en/news/1242/, http://whc.unesco.org/en/news /1244/, http://whc.unesco.org/en/news/1241/; see also http://portal.unesco. org/en/ev.php-URL_IDp17718&URL_DOpDO_TOPIC&URL_SECTION p201.html and the Heritage and Cultural Diversity at Risk in Iraq and Syria International Conference, UNESCO Headquarters, Paris, 3 December 2014, as well as http://unite4heritage.org/.

3. ICCROM was set up in 1959 as an intergovernmental organization dedicated to the conservation of cultural heritage and is only involved in State of Conservation reporting in a limited manner. ICOMOS was founded in 1965 and provides evaluations of cultural properties, including cultural landscapes proposed for inscription on the World Heritage List. Both ICOMOS and the IUCN are international, nongovernmental organizations. The International Union for Conservation of Nature (IUCN) was established in 1948 and provides technical evaluations of natural heritage properties and mixed properties

and, through its worldwide network of specialists, reports on the State of Conservation of listed properties.

4. http://thediplomat.com/2014/08/myanmar-asean-and-the-china -challenge/ and http://asiafoundation.org/in-asia/2014/01/08/asean-chairmanship-offers-opportunity-for-myanmar/.

5. The United States suspended financial support to UNESCO in 2011 after the recognition of Palestine and has done so twice before: once in 1977, when Israel's petition to be considered part of Europe was denied, and again in 1984, over national interest and Cold War conspiracy.

6. http://unesdoc.unesco.org/images/0022/002299/229960e.pdf. The States Parties who served on the committee include Belgium, China, the United States, France, India, Japan and the Republic of Korea.

7. https://wikileaks.org/cablegate.html.

8. http://en.wikipedia.org/wiki/United_States_diplomatic_cables_leak.

9. http://www.spiegel.de/international/world/wikileaks-faq-what-do-the-diplomatic-cables-really-tell-us-a-731441.html.

10. http://whc.unesco.org/en/criteria/.

11. http://whc.unesco.org/en/decisions/1322.

12. http://whc.unesco.org/archive/2009/whc09-33com-7B-Adde.pdf.

13. http://www.icj-cij.org/docket/files/151/16584.pdf.

14. http://csis.org/publication/thailand-cambodia-spar-un-court-over-preah-vihear-temple.

15. S/2011/56 Letter from Cambodia transmitting a letter from H.E. Mr. Hor Namhong, Deputy Prime Minister and Minister of Foreign Affairs and International Cooperation of the Kingdom of Cambodia (5 February 2011); S/2011/58 Letter from Samdech Akka Moha Sena Padei Techo Hun Sen, Prime Minister of the Kingdom of Cambodia, regarding Thailand's aggression against the sovereignty and territorial integrity of the Kingdom of Cambodia (6 February 2011); S/2011/59 Letter from Thailand transmitting a letter from Mr. Abhisit Vejjajiva, Prime Minister of the Kingdom of Thailand, reaffirming Thailand's position and providing the facts on further developments on the recent incidents between Thailand and Cambodia (7 February 2011).

16. http://asiancorrespondent.com/58411/thailand-leaves-the-unesco-world-heritage-convention.

17. http://www.unesco.org/new/en/media-services/single-view/news/unesco_director_general_irina_bokova_convenes_meeting_between_cambodia_and_thailand_to_discuss_conservation_measures_for_temple_of_preah_vihear_world_heritage_site/#.VO30vbOsV9s.

18. http://www.un.org/apps/news/story.asp?NewsIDp38853.

19. http://www.icj-cij.org/docket/files/151/16584.pdf.

20. http://www.icj-cij.org/docket/files/151/17704.pdf.

21. http://www.akp.gov.kh/?pp54894, http://www.unesco.org/new/en/ phnompenh/about-this-office/single-view/news/first_icc_preah_vihear_ launched_in_siem_reap/#.VO4Qb7OsV9s.

22. http://www.unesco.org/new/en/phnompenh/culture/tangible-heritage/ conservation-and-management-of-preah-vihear-temple/, http://whc.unesco. org/en/decisions/1548.

23. https://search.wikileaks.org/plusd/cables/09PHNOMPENH406_a.html.

24. https://search.wikileaks.org/plusd/cables/08PHNOMPENH372_a.html.

25. https://search.wikileaks.org/plusd/cables/09PHNOMPENH71_a.html.

26. http://2001-2009.state.gov/p/eap/rls/rm/2008/02/100891.htm.

27. http://investor.chevron.com/phoenix.zhtml?cp130102&ppirol-news Article_Print&IDp1068574; http://www.chevron.com/chevron/pressreleases/ article/10242011_chevronannouncesfirstgasfromplatongii projectingulf ofthailand.news.

28. http://nationmultimedia.com/2008/05/12/national/national_30072819. php; https://antithaksin.wordpress.com/2008/10/16/preah-vihear-for- koh-kong-and-natuaral-gasoil/; https://search.wikileaks.org/plusd/ cables/08BANGKOK1486_a.html.

29. https://search.wikileaks.org/plusd/cables/09BANGKOK1720_a.html.

30. https://search.wikileaks.org/plusd/cables/08PHNOMPENH1027_a.html.

31. http://www.reuters.com/article/2013/01/02/cambodia-china-investm entidUSL4N0A71JL20130102; http://www.nytimes.com/2013/01/04/ business/global/chinese-companies-to-invest-billions-on-cambodia-projects. html?_rp0.

32. In several cables, the United States's concern with China is evident, particularly regarding their bilateral investment in Cambodia; infrastructural projects, including roads and railways; and the increasing closeness of the two nations. On 25 December 2008, the US ambassador to Cambodia expressed her concern over China, fearing that the current "'Year of China' looks to become its 'Century of China'". She describes royal banquets, the first-ever visit by a Chinese warship, a growing assistance package, and further trade and investment ties. Cambodia describes this as "blank cheque" diplomacy, and in 2009 China pledged $256 million in assistance. By contrast, the United States was likely to offer Cambodia only $50 million. The Chinese loans are often used to support projects benefitting Chinese companies, whether in oil and mineral exploration or infrastructural projects. See https://search. wikileaks.org/plusd /cables/08PHNOMPENH1027_a.html.

33. http://eca.state.gov/files/bureau/cambodia_tias.pdf.

34. https://search.wikileaks.org/plusd/cables/08PHNOMPENH581_a.html.

35. http://www.cambodianembassy.org.uk/downloads/Cambodia%20UN%20 Brochure%20BLUE.pdf.

36. https://search.wikileaks.org/plusd/cables/09PHNOMPENH142_a.html.
37. https://search.wikileaks.org/plusd/cables/09BANGKOK1720_a.html.
38. https://search.wikileaks.org/plusd/cables/08BANGKOK2167_a.html.
39. https://search.wikileaks.org/plusd/cables/09PHNOMPENH505_a.html.
40. https://search.wikileaks.org/plusd/cables/09BANGKOK2599_a.html.
41. http://wikileaks.org/cable/2009/11/09BANGKOK2806.html.
42. http://unesdoc.unesco.org/images/0012/001254/125434e.pdf.
43. http://unesdoc.unesco.org/images/0022/002278/227860e.pdf.

References

Askew, M., ed. 2010. *Legitimacy Crisis in Thailand*. Chiang Mai, Thailand: Silkworm.

Barnett, M. 2012. "Cambodia v. Thailand: A Case Study on the Use of Provisional Measures to Protect Human Rights in International Border Disputes". *Brooklyn Journal of International Law* 38: 269.

Beeson, M. 2005. "Rethinking Regionalism: Europe and East Asia in Comparative Historical Perspective". *Journal of European Public Policy* 12, no. 6: 969–85.

Bendix, R. 2013. "The Power of Perseverance: Exploring the Negotiation Dynamics at the World Intellectual Property Organization". In *The Gloss of Harmony: The Politics of Policy-Making in Multilateral Organisations*, edited by B. Müller, pp. 23–45. London: Pluto.

Berliner, D., and C. Bortolotto. 2013. "Introduction". *Le monde selon l'Unesco. Gradhiva* 2: 4–21.

Burgess, J. 2015. *Temple in the Clouds: Faith and Conflict at Preah Vihear*. Bangkok: River.

Byrne, D. 2007. *Surface Collection: Archaeological Travels in Southeast Asia*. Walnut Creek, CA: AltaMira.

———. 2009. "Archaeology and the Fortress of Rationality". In *Cosmopolitan Archaeologies*, edited by L.M. Meskell. Durham, NC: Duke University Press.

———. 2012. "Anti-superstition: Campaigns against Popular Religion and its Heritage in Asia". In *Routledge Handbook of Heritage in Asia*, edited by P. Daly and T. Winter. London: Routledge.

———. 2014. *Counterheritage: Critical Perspectives on Heritage Conservation in Asia*. London: Routledge.

Chachavalpongpun, P. 2012. "Embedding Embittered History: Unending Conflicts in Thai-Cambodian Relations". *Asian Affairs* 43, no. 1: 81–102.

Chesterman, S. 2015. "The International Court of Justice in Asia: Interpreting the Temple of Preah Vihear Case". *Asian Journal of International Law* 5, no. 1: 1–6.

Chin, G. 2014. "Asian Regionalism after the Global Financial Crisis". In *The Political Economy of Asian Regionalism*, edited by G. Capannelli and M. Kawai, pp. 39–58. Tokyo: Springer Japan.

Ciorciari, J.D. 2014. "Request for Interpretation of the Judgment of 15 June 1962 in the Case Concerning the Temple of Preah Vihear (Cambodia v. Thailand)". *American Journal of International Law* 108, no. 2: 288–95.

Claudi, I.B. 2011. "The New Kids on the Block: BRICs in the World Heritage Committee". MA thesis, University of Oslo, Norway.

Cleere, H. 2011. "The 1972 UNESCO World Heritage Convention". *Heritage and Society* 4, no. 2: 173–86.

Croissant, A., and P.W. Chambers. 2010. "A Contested Site of Memory: The Preah Vihear Temple". In *Cultures and Globalization: Heritage, Memory and Identity*, edited by H.K. Anheier and Y.R. Isar, pp. 148–56. London: Sage.

Cuasay, P. 1998. "Borders on the Fantastic: Mimesis, Violence, and Landscape at the Temple of Preah Vihear". *Modern Asian Studies* 32, no. 4: 849–90.

De Cesari, C. 2010. "World Heritage and Mosaic Universalism". *Journal of Social Archaeology* 10, no. 3: 299–324.

———. 2014. "World Heritage and the Nation-State". In *Transnational Memory: Circulation, Articulation, Scales*, edited by C. De Cesari and A. Rigney, pp. 247–70. Berlin: de Gruyter.

Devji, F. 2008. *The Terrorist in Search of Humanity: Militant Islam and Global Politics*. New York: Columbia University Press.

Dorn, C., and K. Ghodsee. 2012. "The Cold War Politicization of Literacy: Communism, UNESCO, and the World Bank". *Journal of the Society for Historians of American Foreign Relations* 36, no. 2: 373–98.

Dreher, A., J-E. Sturm, and J.R. Vreeland. 2009. "Global Horse Trading: IMF Loans for Votes in the United Nations Security Council". *European Economic Review* 53, no. 7: 742–57.

Edwards, P. 2007. *Cambodge: The Cultivation of a Nation, 1860–1945*. Honolulu: University of Hawai'i Press.

Ferrucci, Stefania. 2012. *UNESCO's World Heritage Regime and its International Influence*. Hamburg: Tredition.

Francioni, F. 2008. "Preamble". In *The 1972 World Heritage Convention: A Commentary*, edited by F. Francioni and F. Lenzerini, pp. 3–7. Oxford: Oxford University Press.

Franquesa, J. 2013. "On Keeping and Selling". *Current Anthropology* 54, no. 3: 346–69.

Graham, S.E. 2006. "The (Real)politiks of Culture: U.S. Cultural Diplomacy in UNESCO, 1946–1954". *Diplomatic History* 30, no. 2: 231–51.

Guitton, J. 2006. "N'en déplaise à quelques tenants de l'esprit pur…". In *L'Unesco racontée par ses anciens*. Paris: UNESCO.

Guneratne, A. 2002. "What's in a Name? Aryans and Dravidians in the Making of Sri Lankan Identities". In *The Hybrid Island: Culture Crossings and the Invention of Identity in Sri Lanka*, edited by N. Silva, pp. 20–40. London: Zed Books.

Handler, R. 1988. *Nationalism and the Politics of Culture in Quebec*. Madison: University of Wisconsin Press.

Harrison, R. 2011. "Surface Assemblages: Towards an Archaeology in and of the Present". *Archaeological Dialogues* 18, no. 2: 141–61.

Hauser-Schäublin, B. 2011. Preah Vihear. "From Object of Colonial Desire to a Contested World Heritage Site". In *World Heritage Angkor and Beyond: Circumstances and Implications of UNESCO Listings in Cambodia*, edited by B. Hauser-Schäublin, pp. 33–56. Göttingen: Göttingen Studies in Cultural Property.

———. 2013. "Entangled in Artefacts: Governing Differing Entitlements to Cultural Objects at UNESCO". In *The Gloss of Harmony: The Politics of Policymaking in Multilateral Organizations*, edited by B. Müller, pp. 154–74. London: Pluto.

Hauser-Schäublin, B., and S. Missling. 2014. "The Enduring Agency of Borderland Regimes: The Aftermath of Serial Regulations with Different Scopes and Temporal Scales at Preah Vihear, Cambodia". *Journal of Legal Pluralism and Unofficial Law* 46, no. 1: 79–98.

Hoggart, R. 2011. *An Idea and its Servants: UNESCO from Within*. Piscataway, NJ: Transaction.

Huxley, J. 1946. *UNESCO: Its Purpose and its Philosophy*. Paris: Preparatory Commission of the United Nations Educational, Scientific and Cultural Organisation.

International Crisis Group. 2011. *Waging Peace: ASEAN and the Thai-Cambodia Border Conflict*. Asia Report no. 215–216.

Joy, C. 2012. *The Politics of Heritage Management in Mali: From UNESCO to Djenné*. Walnut Creek, CA: Left Coast.

———. 2016. "UNESCO is What?" World Heritage, Militant Islam and the Search for a Common Humanity in Mali. In *World Heritage on the Ground: Ethnographic Perspectives*, edited by C. Brumann and D. Berliner. Oxford: Berghan.

Källén, A. 2014. The Invisible Archaeologist: Letters from the UNESCO Secretariat 1946–1947. *Journal of Social Archaeology* 14, no. 3: 383–405.

Kasetsiri, C., P. Sothirak, and P. Chachavalpongpun. 2013. *Preah Vihear: A Guide to the Thai-Cambodian Conflict and its Solutions*. Bangkok: White Lotus.

Kirshenblatt-Gimblett, Barbara. 2004. "Intangible Heritage as Metacultural Production". *Museum International* 56, nos. 1–2: 52–65.

Labadi, S. 2005. "A Review of the Global Strategy for a Balanced, Representative and Credible World Heritage List 1994–2004". *Conservation and Management of Archaeological Sites* 7, no. 2: 89–102.

———. 2007. "Representations of the Nation and Cultural Diversity in Discourses on World Heritage". *Journal of Social Archaeology* 7, no. 2: 147–70.

———. 2013. *UNESCO, Cultural Heritage and Outstanding Universal Value*. Walnut Creek, CA: AltaMira.

Lee, S.K. 2014. "Siam Mismapped: Revisiting the Territorial Dispute over the Preah Vihear Temple". *South East Asia Research* 22, no. 1: 39–55.

Logan, William S. 2008. "Cultural Diversity, Heritage and Human Rights". In *The Ashgate Research Companion to Heritage and Identity*, edited by Brian Graham and Peter Howard, pp. 439–54. Aldershot: Ashgate.

Luke, C. 2013. "Cultural Sovereignty in the Balkans and Turkey: The Politics of Preservation and Rehabilitation". *Journal of Social Archaeology* 13, no. 3: 350–70.

Luke, C., and M.M. Kersel. 2013. *U.S. Cultural Diplomacy and Archaeology: Soft Power, Hard Heritage*. London: Routledge.

Mayor, F. 1990. Address by Mr Federico Mayor Director-General of the United Nations Educational, Scientific and Cultural Organization (Unesco) at the Ceremonial Session to mark the Tenth Anniversary of the International Campaign for the Safeguarding of the Cultural Triangle of Sri Lanka. Colombo, Sri Lanka: UNESCO.

Meskell, L.M. 2011. "From Paris to Pontdrift: UNESCO Meetings, Mapungubwe and Mining". *South African Archaeological Bulletin* 66, no. 194: 149–56.

———. 2012. "The Rush to Inscribe: Reflections on the 35th Session of the World Heritage Committee, UNESCO Paris, 2011". *Journal of Field Archaeology* 37, no. 2: 145–51.

———. 2013. "UNESCO's World Heritage Convention at 40: Challenging the Economic and Political Order of International Heritage Conservation". *Current Anthropology* 54, no. 4: 483–94.

———. 2014. "States of Conservation: Protection, Politics and Pacting within UNESCO's World Heritage Committee". *Anthropological Quarterly* 87, no. 1: 267–92.

———. 2015a. "Gridlock: UNESCO, Global Conflict and Failed Ambitions". *World Archaeology* 47, no. 2: 226–38.

———. 2015b. "Transacting UNESCO World Heritage: Gifts and Exchanges on a Global Stage". *Social Anthropology/Anthropologie Sociale* 23, no. 1: 3–21.

Meskell, L.M., C. Liuzza, E. Bertacchini, and D. Saccone. 2015. "Multilateralism and UNESCO World Heritage: Decision-making, States Parties and Political Processes". *International Journal of Heritage Studies* 21, no. 5: 423–40.

Meskell, L.M., C. Liuzza, and N. Brown. 2015. "World Heritage Regionalism: UNESCO from Europe to Asia". *International Journal of Cultural Property* 22: 1–34.

Morris, S.A. 2011. Letter to the World Heritage Center from the United States Department of the Interior, 2 August 2011, UNESCO, Paris.

Mosse, D. 2011. "Politics and Ethics: Ethnographies of Expert Knowledge and Professional Identities". In *Policy Worlds: Anthropology and the Analysis of Contemporary Power*, edited by C. Shore, S. Wright, and D. Però, pp. 50–67. Oxford: Berghan.

Müller, B. 2013. "Lifting the Veil of Harmony: Anthropologists Approach

International Organizations". In *The Gloss of Harmony: The Politics of Policymaking in Multilateral Organisations*, edited by B. Müller, pp. 1–20. London: Pluto.

Pavone, V. 2007. "From Intergovernmental to Global: UNESCO's Response to Globalization". *Review of International Organizations* 2, no. 1: 77–95.

———. 2008. *From the Labyrinth of the World to the Paradise of the Heart: Science and Humanism in UNESCO's Approach to Globalization*. New York: Lexington.

Pawakapan, P. 2013. *State and Uncivil Society in Thailand at the Temple of Preah Vihear*. Singapore: Institute of Southeast Asian Studies.

Peleggi, Maurizio. 2002. *The Politics of Ruins and the Business of Nostalgia*. Bangkok: White Lotus.

———. 2007. *Thailand: The Worldly Kingdom*. London: Reaktion.

Pieterse, J.N. 2012. "Leaking Superpower: WikiLeaks and the Contradictions of Democracy". *Third World Quarterly* 33, no. 10: 1909–24.

Pressouyre, L. 1996. *The World Heritage Convention, Twenty Years Later*. Paris: UNESCO.

Preston, W., E.S. Herman, and H. Schiller. 1989. *Hope and Folly: The United States and UNESCO 1945–1985*. Minneapolis: University of Minnesota Press.

Prott, Lyndel V., and Patrick J.O'Keefe. [1992] 2012. "'Cultural Heritage' or 'Cultural Property'?" In *Cultural Heritage Law*, edited by James A.R. Nafziger, pp. 3–16. Cheltenham, UK: Elgar.

Rajasingham-Senanayake, D. 2002. "Identity on the Borderline: Modernity, New Ethnicities, and the Unmaking of Multiculturalism in Sri Lanka". In *The Hybrid Island: Culture Crossings and the Invention of Identity in Sri Lanka*, edited by N. Silva, pp. 41–70. London: Zed Books.

Sassen, S. 2006. *Territory, Authority, Rights: From Medieval to Global Assemblages*. Princeton, NJ: Princeton University Press.

Saunders, R.A. 2011. "WikiLeaks are Not Terrorists—A Critical Assessment of the Hacktivist Challenge to the Diplomatic System". *Globality Studies Journal* 25: 1–7.

Schofield, C.H., and M. Tan-Mullins. 2008. "Maritime Claims, Conflicts and Cooperation in the Gulf of Thailand". *Ocean Yearbook Online* 22, no. 1: 75–116.

Seneviratne, S. 1996. "'Peripheral Regions' and 'Marginal Communities': Towards an Alternative Explanation of Early Iron Age Material and Social Formations in Sri Lanka". In *Tradition, Dissent and Ideology: Essays in Honour of Romila Thapar*, edited by R. Champakalakshmi and S. Gopal, pp. 264–312. Delhi: Oxford University Press.

———. 2007. "Situating World Heritage Sites in a Multicultural Society: The Ideology of Presentation at the Sacred City of Anuradhapura, Sri Lanka". In *Archaeology and the Postcolonial Critique*, edited by M. Liebmann and U.Z. Rizvi, pp. 177–95. New York: Altamira.

Sharma, B.K., and A. Rasheed, eds. 2015. *Indian Ocean Region: Emerging Strategic Coooperation, Competition and Conflict Scenarios.* New Delhi: Vij.

Shore, C. 2007. "European Integration in Anthropological Perspective: Studying the 'Culture' of the EU Civil Service". In *Observing Government Elites: Up Close and Personal*, edited by R.A.W. Rhodes, P.'t Hart and M. Noordegraaf, pp. 180–205. New York: Palgrave Macmillan.

Shulman, K. 2011. "Case Concerning the Temple of the Preah Vihear (Cambodia v. Thailand): The ICJ Orders Sweeping Provisional Measures to Prevent Armed Conflict at the Expense of Sovereignty". *Tulane Journal of International and Comparative Law* 20: 555.

Siim, M. 2011. Evaluation of the Global Strategy and the PACT Initiative, Letter to the Director of the World Heritage Center, 8 August 2011, Estonian Delegation.

Silva, R. 1993. "The Cultural Triangle: International Safeguarding Campaign". In *The Cultural Triangle of Sri Lanka*, pp. 176–93. Paris: UNESCO Publishing.

Slaughter, A-M., and T. Hale. 2010. "Transgovernmental Networks". In *The Handbook of Governance*, pp. 342–52. London: Sage.

Sluga, G. 2013. *Internationalism in the Age of Nationalism.* Philadelphia: University of Pennsylvania Press.

Sothirak, P. 2013. "Cambodia's Border Conflict with Thailand". In *Southeast Asian Affairs 2013*, edited by Daljit Singh, pp. 87–100. Singapore: Institute of Southeast Asian Studies.

Sri Lanka Government. 2011. *Report of the Commission of Inquiry on Lessons Learnt and Reconciliation.* Colombo: Ministry of Defence and Urban Development.

Sri Lanka Tourism Development Authority. 2013. "Welcome to Sri Lanka, Wonder of Asia". http://www.srilanka.travel (accessed 31 October 2013).

Strate, S. 2013. "A Pile of Stones? Preah Vihear as a Thai Symbol of National Humiliation". *South East Asia Research* 21, no. 1: 41–68.

Tomlinson, John. 1991. "Cultural Imperialism: An Introduction". London: Continuum.

United Nations Educational, Scientific, and Cultural Organization (UNESCO). 1972. "Convention Concerning the Protection of the World Cultural and Natural Heritage". http://whc.unesco.org/archive/convention-en.pdf (accessed 30 August 2015).

———. 2008. *The UNESCO Courier* 5.

United Nations. 2011. *Report of the Secretary-General's Panel of Experts on Accountability in Sri Lanka.* New York: United Nations.

Von Feigenblatt, O.F. 2011. "Coping with Violence in the Thai-Cambodian Border: The Silence of the Border". *Journal of Contemporary Eastern Asia* 10, no. 2: 35–40.

Vrdoljak, A.F. 2014. "Challenges for International Human Rights Law". In *Blackwell*

Companion to the New Heritage Studies, edited by W. Logan, M. Nic Craith, and U. Kockel. New York: Blackwell.

Wagner, Roy. 1981. *The Invention of Culture*. Chicago: University of Chicago Press.

Weiss, G. 2011. *The Cage*. London: Bodley Head.

Williams, T. 2011. "The Curious Tale of Preah Vihear: The Process and Value of World Heritage Nomination". *Conservation and Management of Archaeological Sites* 13, no. 1: 1–7.

Winichakul, T. 1994. *Siam Mapped: A History of the Geo-body of a Nation*. Honolulu: University of Hawai'i Press.

Winter, T. 2007. *Post-conflict Heritage, Postcolonial Tourism: Culture, Politics and Development at Angkor*. London: Routledge.

———. 2010. "Heritage Tourism: The Dawn of a New Era?" In *Heritage and Globalisation*, edited by S. Labadi and C. Long, pp. 117–29. London: Routledge.

———. 2014a. "Beyond Eurocentrism? Heritage Conservation and the Politics of Difference". *International Journal of Heritage Studies* 20, no. 2: 123–37.

———. 2014b. "Heritage Conservation Futures in an Age of Shifting Global Power". *Journal of Social Archaeology* 14, no. 3: 319–39.

Yoosuk, U. 2013. "The Preah Vihear Temple: Roots of Thailand-Cambodia Border Dispute". *International Journal of Asian Social Science* 3, no. 4: 921–29.

Žižek, S. 2011. "Good Manners in the Age of WikiLeaks". *London Review of Books* 33, no. 2: 9–10.

3

Heritage Making — Aid for Whom? The Genealogy of Expert Reports in the Hands of Politics and Their Impact in the Case of Preah Vihear

Brigitta Hauser-Schäublin

Introduction: Expert Knowledge and Political Settings

As is well known, UNESCO is an international organization with an educational and cultural governance mandate to achieve a more equal and peaceful world through altering the minds of men (Nielsen 2011, p. 275). All UNESCO conventions dealing with "heritage" aim at contributing to these overarching idealistic goals. At the core of Operational Guidelines to the 1972 World Heritage Convention are the criteria that nominations must fulfil in order to reach approval by the Intergovernmental Committee (IGC). The first and foremost criterion a monument, a group of buildings or a site must fulfil is that of "Outstanding Universal Value" from the point of view of history, art or science. A number of circles of experts at both the national and international level are involved in the nomination and listing process. At the national level, such experts are charged with the task of describing and documenting the cultural property for the nomination file in such a way that the delegates of the member states constituting the Intergovernmental Committee to the Convention become ultimately convinced of its quality. UNESCO, on the other hand, cooperates with a number of international expert bodies such as the International Council on Monuments and Sites (ICOMOS), the International Centre for the Study of the Preservation and Restoration of Cultural Property (ICCROM) and the International Union for Conservation of Nature (IUCN). Their experts, whose names are kept confidential, evaluate the nomination with regard to the fulfilment of the criteria and submit a recommendation to the IGC, where decisions are made.[1] Though expert reports claim to focus exclusively on the quality of the cultural property (mostly monuments) and to stand above politics, the expertise expressed in them is often situated in a highly political context, which, as I am going to show, can lead to unforeseen consequences. These mostly implicit and invisible conditionings of expertise often divert UNESCO's noble goals and produce other socio-political results than those intended.

The politicization of the cultural property already begins when experts are called into action and they obediently seek to fulfil their task. This applies most strikingly to the ruins of the former Hindu Temple of Preah Vihear on the Thai-Cambodian border. This politically contested monument and the hundred-year-long conflict between Cambodia and Thailand over its ownership did not prevent the UNESCO World Heritage IGC from including Preah Vihear on the Word Heritage List as Cambodia's heritage in 2008 (see Hauser-Schäublin 2011). The long history of conflict that was brought to the International Court of Justice (Judgements of 1962 and 2013; see, among others, Cuasey 1998; Silverman 2011; Mißling 2011; Hauser-Schäublin and Mißling 2014; Vrdoljak 2015) has been extensively investigated. I will therefore not reiterate the whole story. Rather, I want to focus on the cascade of expert reports, each drawing on the previous one, that have been written since Preah Vihear was "discovered" by French travellers, archaeologists and military personnel in the mid-nineteenth century when Cambodia became a French protectorate. These expert reports all came into being under particular geopolitical conditions and power relations, as well as according to the state of knowledge and methodology of the disciplines involved at that time. When Cambodia, or rather the French colonial power, initiated the 1904 and 1907 treaties with Siam (both aimed at expanding Cambodia's "Khmer" lands and drawing territorial boundaries between the two countries), Siam was apparently not aware of the French political game or of the long-lasting consequences Siam's compliance to the French request could have. Apart from the charged relationship between the two countries, the conflict also increasingly affected the local inhabitants in the former zone of transition (Hauser-Schäublin and Mißling 2011), not least due to the growing nationalism on both sides. Previously, the inhabitants had shared the same culture and language and had been living peacefully together.

As I am going to show, all the expert reports ultimately served political interests. While I will deal mainly with reports that were used by Cambodia and its French patron, we have to note that Siam/Thailand, too, was an active player in this game with regard to foreign affairs (including economic cooperation between the two countries) as well as domestic politics (see Pawakapan 2013; Kasetsiri et al. 2013). In my paper, however, I will concentrate on an analysis of the Cambodian/French politics of the day and the way in which expert reports were used.

The impact of all these expressions of expertise and the decisions that subsequently were made finally produced the escalating drama between Cambodia and Thailand that exploded into violent border conflicts when Preah Vihear was listed as a UNESCO World Heritage site of Cambodia in 2008. The listing resulted locally in the closing of the border crossing, since it had become a military conflict zone. Consequently, worshippers and tourists no longer had access to the temple from the Thai side of the frontier. The small market that had existed at the border, right at the bottom of the main access staircase to the temple, was closed as well, and ad hoc built tourist infrastructure (guest houses and snack bars) was erased.

Expert Reports as Part of Regimes of Truth

I suggest that all of these reports as manifestations and presentations of knowledge are part of a "regime of truth". According to Foucault (1980), regimes of truth are "produced by, and function within, objective social structures of power" (Reyna and Glick Schiller 2010, p. 333). Each of the historical and political situations in which expertise on Preah Vihear was established and discussed or negotiated in order to achieve decisions (of different kinds) were indeed embedded in "structures of power". It is only by analysing these structures of power rather than "truth" as an

FIGURE 3.1 The construction of a concrete runway that should provide tourists with easy access from the Cambodian plains up to the site of Preah Vihear ended at the border of the area contested by Thailand. This was one of the consequences of the nomination of Preah Vihear as a UNESCO World Heritage of Cambodia only. Photo: Brigitta Hauser-Schäblin, 2013.

absolute given that one can understand why some reports and the way decision makers have dealt with them attained the importance they reached and the consequences they produced.

Foucault explained these regimes of truth as follows:

> Each society has its regime of truth, its 'general politics' of truth: that is the types of discourse which it accepts and makes function as true; the mechanisms and instances which enable one to distinguish true and false statements, the means by which each is sanctioned; the techniques and procedures accorded value in the acquisition of truth; the status of those who are charged with saying what counts as true. (Foucault 1980, p. 131)

These regimes of truth are not only produced by systems of power but they are also in the service of these regimes and are a tactical element in the function of power relations (see also Forrester 1997). When a new regime of truth is enforced or is being accepted, a new reality or new conditions of living arise. This approach allows one to see experts' reports—which are assumed to be objective and simply following, for example, the criteria as set by UNESCO—in a wider context. However, depending on the regime of truth, the expert reports had either a particular epistemic design that fitted the regime of truth,[2] or they were examined and discredited, even ignored, if they did not comply with the system of truth they should support. I shall present analyses of three examples of expert reports on Preah Vihear and the way they were treated according to the prevailing regimes of truth dominant at that time. The first example focuses on reports in the service of colonial strategies. The second focuses on the way expert reports were used and contested during the 1962 trial of the International Court of Justice in The Hague. The last set of reports concerns the nomination and evaluation reports written for the UNESCO listing of Preah Vihear as a World Heritage site of Cambodia.

I have chosen as parameters for the analysis of the "regimes of truth" (1) the wider socio-political context in which the experts' investigations took place; (2) the explicit and implicit objectives of the investigations and the subsequent reports; (3) the mechanisms, instances and techniques applied which allowed one to distinguish true from untrue or false statements; and (4) the consequences that the fact of these reports being declared as truthful produced.

I. Expertise in the Service of Colonial Strategies

There is no need to outline here the colonial history of Cambodia, since this has been done extensively (see, for example, Reid 2015; Chandler 2008; Edwards 2007; Winter 2007), or the academic institutions working in the French colony (Singaravélou 1999; Clémentin-Ojha and Manguin 2001). Cultural politics played a predominant role in France's territorial expansion in the mid-nineteenth century. It was the cultural side of imperialism—called Orientalism by Said (2003)—that masked France's politics to build up—in competition with other European countries—a more powerful nation by acquiring extensive overseas territories. At the same time, the "discovery" and appropriation of old civilizations and their heritage that once existed in these territories increased the attractiveness of these countries. They could bear comparison with what were seen as Europe's cultural ancestors, such as Ancient Egypt, Ancient Greece and Mesopotamia, the "cradle of civilization". "Revive the glory that was" turned the appropriation of foreign lands into the noble task of a saviour (see Seneviratne 2008, p. 178). There were two parallel ways to take possession of the country; these ways were clearly interlinked. On the one hand, there were the military expeditions sent out to explore the country, especially to areas that were of economic importance, such as those that provided access to land and means of transport (such as the Mekong) and to look for possible boundary sites for the (yet to be established) border with Thailand that would be favourable to the colonial goals. At the same time, the leaders of these military expeditions were tasked with keeping an eye out for traces of the ancient Khmer civilization, which the French interpreted as bound to a single country, Cambodia (Edwards 2007; Singaravélou 1999). The early maps established by the French colonial explorers and military show, for example, that the cartographers were also charged with the task of outlining the former Empire of Khmer. Thus we find the entry "ancient Cambodge" on maps (Pavie 1903, plate 1 and IX), which was in stark contrast to the actual size of the country when the French entered it in the 1860s. This was the broader context in which the École française d'Extrême-Orient (EFEO) (Singaravélou 1999; Clémentin-Ojha and Manguin 2001) came into being. The EFEO's scholars (at the beginning mostly architects and archaeologists), who were certainly seriously dedicated to the study of ancient Khmer monuments, carried out their studies, wittingly or unwittingly, in the context of colonial cultural politics and contributed substantially to the legitimation of French hegemony in the region through their studies (Hauser-Schäublin 2011).

The studies carried out by Parmentier can be taken as an exemplar, since he interconnected geography and the chronology of the monumental Khmer ruins with his endeavour to visually reconstruct these ruins by depicting them in an idealized, spotless way. His gaze and those of other French scholars in their major works eclipsed the living world of people dwelling near the monuments where the research was conducted. For these scholars, the way of life of local people had nothing in common with the one they romanticized for the ancient Khmer. Thus, by selectively turning their attention back in time by documenting the remains of the past and revitalizing them in their imaginations, these experts refused to acknowledge, at least in their studies, that the Khmer had been defeated several times by various neighbouring polities. By their selective historical perceptions, EFEO scholars and their works at that time provided data the French colonial administration needed. They substantiated the assumption (and political hope) that Cambodia had once been a huge empire. The territorial studies became a colonial mission. Thus, military expeditions and work by scholars on the ancient Khmer complemented each other. They legitimated and propelled the colonial goal to expand the country to what was assumed to be its original size. The reports by Commandant Lunet de Lajonquière (1907) demonstrate very clearly how the military territorial exploration coincided with establishing an inventory of temples (ruins) of the ancient Khmer (Hauser-Schäublin 2011; Falser 2013).

A consequence of these reports was the imposition of the notion of a territorial state with clear-cut borders on a formerly living world that had displayed fluid, transitional regions. There, people were part of relationships that bound them simultaneously to the courts of both countries, Siam and Cambodia (Bastian 1868, p. 5). French negotiations with Siam that aimed at retrieving former "core lands" of the ancient Khmer finally led to treaties in which Siam ceded, among other provinces, Angkor to Cambodia. Consequently, the French systematically propelled the delineation of borders drawn only on paper (mapping) but which had momentous impacts on the geography of the living world (see Thongchai 1994; Lee 2014). As is well known, the French proposed that a geographical "natural" boundary should constitute the course of the border; the decision to take the watershed as the borderline was fixed in the Siam-Cambodian treaty of 1904. Therefore, with regard to the Dangrek Mountains, the line of the watershed was drawn in the area of Preah Vihear, conceived by the French as an important outpost of the ancient Khmer capital of Angkor, in such a way that the temple ruins became located in Cambodian territory. In summary, facts were created, and with it a truth implying a new reality of the everyday living world that in the following decades was often contested by Thailand, not least by temporary occupation.

II. The Regime of Truth and the 1962 Court Case at the ICJ in The Hague

Expert reports played a crucial role in the 1962 verdict concerning the Temple of Preah Vihear at the International Court of Justice (ICJ) in The

Hague. After decades of struggle between Cambodia and Thailand over ownership of the temple and over the contested delimitation between the two countries that had been established unilaterally by the French colonial power in 1907, Cambodia brought the case to the ICJ in 1959. Although the ICJ spent a lot of time determining the correct line of the border according to the watershed and the corresponding expert reports, the court did not make a decision concerning the legitimacy of the demarcation. Thus, instead of solving the boundary conflict, the court resorted to a different argument by stating that Siam/Thailand had failed to file a complaint against the disputed map—that demarcated the border—in time (Cuasay 1998). It decreed that Cambodia, therefore, holds sovereignty over the temple.[3] The judgement of 2013 reinforced the 1962 decree (see, for example, Hauser-Schäublin and Mißling 2014; Chesterman 2015; Kattan 2015, p. 16).[4]

Though officially accepting the 1962 decree, Thailand never did really give up its claims, as the numerous border incidents in subsequent years and the dreadful revenge (sending back Cambodian refugees through the heavily mined area of Preah Vihear) at the end of the Khmer Rouge era showed (Cuasey 1998, pp. 881–82).

From today's perspective, the ICJ court case and the judgement bear the fingerprints of neo-colonialism and the Cold War period. Cambodia's lawsuit rested on the outcome of the politics of its former colonial patron. The French expansionist strategy and the neglect of raising any questions about how appropriate it was to divide a socially and culturally continuous landscape according to geographic-hydrological criteria were not mentioned at all. An evaluation of the colonial historical context was absent, as were questions about French colonial interests and their abettors (military, explorers, scholars). Colonial mapping, for example, followed the principles of the Mercator map, that is, a special—European—way not only of depicting a landscape but also of creating it. This form of mapping was assumed to be globally understood and accepted as a valid instrument. Moreover, only Latin (and no Thai) characters were used and the local names were rendered only in the Cambodian form. As the works, among others, by Thongchai (1994), Anderson (1991) and Said (2003) have shown, mapping was a crucial colonizing tool. The court did not inquire whether Siam/Thailand had been fully aware of the consequences of this colonial game or its rules, namely to draw a line on a piece of paper and declare it as binding and valid forever. Furthermore, the idea that in case of a disagreement Thailand should have filed a complaint in time but had kept silent instead, again reflects the notion that "international law", a law of basically European origin, represents shared universal principles and is applicable in all situations, regardless perhaps of other understandings of rights and rules.

The only surviving contemporary witness of the 1962 ICJ court case is the engineer/geodesist Friedrich Ackermann. In 1961, Thailand had commissioned the Dutch institute for which Ackermann was working to carry out a survey on the spot in order to identify the watershed (see below). He appeared before the court as an expert and witness. He commented in retrospect that the judgement of The Hague was a misjudgement.[5]

Nevertheless, court judgements, especially those by the ICJ, have the status of infallibility and they are usually treated as if they are unconditioned by time and politics. Moreover, no further authority exists to which Thailand could have appealed.[6] The mechanism of revising a judgement of the ICJ due to changed knowledge and perspectives simply does not exist. Thus, formally, a judgement by the ICJ is sacrosanct. However, apart from this particular case, the ICJ is political anyway. As Chesterman emphasizes, the ICJ "blatantly acknowledge[s] the politicized nature of [its] work as to allow each party to appoint 'their' judge as an ad hoc member of the bench" (2015, p. 1). The composition of the judges at the 1962 court case illustrates the politicized character indeed (see footnote 3), especially against the background of the international political situation: the Cold War.

Neo-colonialism and Cold War Politics

The regime of truth of which the ICJ was part and that finally resulted in the decree in favour of Cambodia was, as several authors confirm, heavily influenced by the Cold War politics of Southeast Asia (Cuasay 1998; Burgess 2015; Kattan 2015). "Thailand was firmly in the anti-communist, pro-American camp.... Next door, Cambodia under Sihanouk was on a very different track" (Burgess 2015, pp. 98–99). The United States was getting more involved in the Vietnam War, replacing France after its defeat (Kattan 2015, p. 22); they feared that Sihanouk, who could play off the United States vis-à-vis China and the USSR, would "turn to communist benefactors" (Burgess 2015, p. 101; Kattan 2015, p. 23). The United States, therefore, continued to supply Cambodia with money, arms and (publicly hidden) support in the escalating fight over Preah Vihear out of the fear that it might become a communist country.[7] Moreover, already in 1956, Cambodian officials consulted with the US Embassy in Phnom Penh and informed them of their intent to bring the case of Preah Vihear to the ICJ. The embassy reported to Washington that "it was inclined to favour the approach" (Burgess 2015, p. 101). The US diplomats in Bangkok were not in favour of this idea and suggested that a bilateral settlement would be the better route. Nevertheless, the State Department asked for maps and it was provided with the famous map that "goes with the 1904 Treaty" between France/Cambodia and Siam and shows the temple of Preah Vihear on Cambodian territory (ibid., p. 103).

A crucial role in the whole court case and probably also with a corresponding impact on the judgement was played by one of the attorneys of the Cambodian party, the American Dean Acheson, a keen and powerfully eloquent lawyer. Acheson had been appointed US Secretary of State by President Truman in 1949 and was a key actor in developing US foreign policy in the Cold War period. At the time of the ICJ case, he was adviser to President Kennedy for NATO affairs (Cuasay 1998, p. 855). To what extent he was still part of US official networks at the time he accepted Cambodia's request becomes apparent also in the way he was treated by King Sihanouk (official invitation, exchange of personal gifts, etc.) and also when he was flown in a USAID plane to Preah Vihear to have a look at the contested site (Burgess 2015, pp. 114–17, 163).

The political setting of the regime of truth developed even further after the case had been submitted to the ICJ. Son Sann, an influential politician and president of the central bank, who led the Cambodian delegation in The Hague, acted as what Burgess calls a "vote gatherer" (2015, p. 110). In his (posthumously published) memoir, Son Sann wrote: "The communist bloc countries were in our favour and had promised that their judges at The Hague would support us. Through an American banker friend we also received a promise of support from the judge from another powerful Asian country" (cited in Burgess 2015, p. 110).

To cut a long story short, several political considerations seem to have influenced how the court case in The Hague was instigated and played out. From today's perspective, it sounds surprising that a judge from the former colonial power, which was still acting as a kind of patron to Cambodia, was on the board of judges, as were two representatives of European colonial powers (Italy and the United Kingdom). None of them seem to have hesitated in carrying out their duty in such a delicate postcolonial context or to have signalled readiness to recuse themselves in light of the colonial histories, far from being "solved" at that time, of their own countries.

No one made a secret of the fact that France had extensively provided the Cambodian party with personal and scientific expertise for the court case. France saw her former protectorate and later the newly independent state as the legitimate successor of the old Khmer "heritage" (*patrimoine*). One of the two French attorneys (both professors of the Law Faculty of Paris) who assisted the Cambodian party in the court case explained, in detail and apparently without any reservation, the close cooperation between the former colonial power and its protectorate that has been fixed in treaties. These treaties, such as the *convention culturelle franco-khmère*[8] of 1950, as Roger Pinto, one of these lawyers, explained, highlights the importance of ancient monuments, the "archaeological patrimony" and the obligation Cambodia was willing to take to continue the objective development of scientific knowledge about "la culture de l'ancien Cambodge". France had transferred the administration of Preah Vihear to the Cambodian government in 1951 by obligating Cambodia to accept the continuing technical cooperation with French archaeological institutions (ICJ 1962a, pp. 426–27). In summary, this was the socio-political setting of the regime of truth in which the court case took place.

The Techniques of Truth-Finding: Experts under Cross-examination

The pleas, cross-examinations and replies presented during the court case allow an analysis of the mechanisms, instances and techniques applied by counsels and representatives of the two parties and the judges in order to arrive at "the truth". In Foucault's terms, these were the mechanisms of how regimes of truth work.

First of all, it is important to note that the court did not appoint experts to clarify the line of the watershed on the spot with modern technology.[9] Instead, it relied primarily on the map of 1907, supplemented by the description of more or less casual observations French scholars had made during the colonial era. Thailand had mandated three experts from the International Training Centre for Aerial Survey (ITC)—Willem Schermerhorn, founder and dean of the institute, the geodesist Friedrich Ackermann and the geomorphologist Theodore Verstappen—to scientifically explore the correct line of the watershed with modern tools.[10] During the public hearings they were interrogated by the judges and cross-examined by the attorneys of the two conflicting parties (IJC 1962 Pleadings vol. II, p. 331).[11] In contrast, the French archaeological and architectural reports written during colonial times and bearing their fingerprints were presented and quoted by the counsels as pure "facts" and above suspicion.[12] Not even the judges ever asked a question in this regard.

I cannot go into detail concerning these public hearings in this paper, but I will focus on the way the three ITC experts and their reports were treated in order to find out "the truth". Thailand had mandated them to establish a photogrammetric analysis of the area of the temple of Preah Vihear (or Phra Viharn, to use the Thai name) in order to check the information that the contested map of 1904 contained in relation to the watershed.[13] The watershed, as the treaty between the Protectorate of Cambodia and Thailand of 1904 had stated, should constitute the boundary between the two countries. Only one of these three experts is described in the ICJ records as an expert *and* witness, Friedrich Ackermann (IJC 1962 Pleadings vol. II, p. 346). Since the aerial photos left some doubts about one particular spot, Ackermann was sent to Preah Vihear to make a geological survey. He spent eleven days there in July 1961. He made a detailed survey, especially of the area that could not be determined from the aerial photographs due to the coverage of vegetation. In fact, this was a crucial area, since the contour line turned out to be decisively higher than anticipated. This "saddle", as it was called during the court case, prevented the water from flowing down to the Cambodian plain; thus, it was decisive for determining the watershed line on the eastern side of the temple.

For the natural scientists from Delft, their task seemed to be clear; they and their knowledge were needed to clarify the core issue of the conflict of the court case. For them, the geological facts constituted scientific truth. The experts did not seem to be aware of the neo-colonial regime of truth in which they became entangled during the court case. During the cross-examination by Cambodia's counsels, there existed the implicit allegation that the experts presented only the data that served Thailand's interests. Cross-examination of experts is certainly an exceptional experience for scholars, and Ackermann told me that in his long career[14] he had never found himself in such a role again.[15] Looking back at the court case and the way he was examined by Dean Acheson, he said "he tried to screw me" ("Er wollte mich aufs Kreuz legen").

The cross-examination of experts and witnesses—probably as many cross-examinations are anyway—is a kind of confusion game that aims at trapping the interrogated in contradictions and, therefore, at discrediting his testimony and questioning his competence. The reports of the cross-examination reveal a whole repertoire of strategies and techniques of "truth-finding". I will sum up and briefly illustrate these techniques:

— Questioning the credibility of the interviewee, but in a courteous manner, thus putting the interviewee into a defensive, weaker position. Dean Acheson, for example, addressed the geodesist (Ackermann):

"May I ask if you are qualified in this geological extra?" (ICJ Pleadings 1962 vol. II p. 395).

— Politely expressing disrespect with the aim of discrediting the expert and his knowledge, even if the interviewee was an internationally highly respected person such as Willem Schermerhorn, Ackermann's superior.

Mr. Dean Acheson: ... Now you have not been to the Temple of Preah Vihear, have you?

Mr. Schermerhorn: No.

Mr. Dean Acheson: And therefore you rely upon what you have been told about the state of terrain?

Mr. Schermerhorn: Yes. It is true ...

Mr. Dean Acheson: I quite understand, Professor Schermerhorn. What I wanted to make clear is what is reported to have been seen by the eyes of the person on the spot. You rely on other eyes than your own ... (ICJ Pleadings 1962 vol. II, p. 367).

— Feigning modesty towards the interrogated expert in order to make him feel superior. The following dialogue dealt with the probability of there being any subterraneous water flow at the temple site, as suggested by the attorney (the French law professor Paul Reuter). Ackermann was asked whether he had observed any. Ackermann answered that the whole rock was compact without any interrupting layers that could have favoured subterraneous water flows.

M. Reuter: You haven't discovered anything that could have raised your inquietude?

Mr. Ackermann: No, I saw positively water running at the surface.

Mr. Reuter: Fine. I would like to come back to a point which you have mentioned and on which my ignorance is very big. I am not a specialist and I ask you as a specialist. (ICJ Pleadings 1962 vol. II, p. 411, my translation)[16]

— Attempting to initially create a degree of agreement with the cross-examined expert (Verstappen) and then, if the result did not turn out as expected, harshly rebuke him:

Mr. Dean Acheson: ... No, Mr. Verstappen, let us consider together whether, if this mound [the "saddle"] had been created a long time ago, it might still not look the way it looks now. Let's start a very long time ago and suppose that when the Khmers were building Preah Vihear they must have had a lot of people there to build it, and let us suppose that those people had to have water, and suppose they then built this ridge to keep the water from flowing out into the rocky passage going down into Cambodia and make a reservoir. Suppose they had done that, it would look very much today the way it does, wouldn't it?

Mr. Verstappen: I feel that it would have been rather illogical for them to construct such a dam just on the watershed, because it is evident from the figures Mr. Ackermann gave that the valley to the west of F is down-sloping towards the west, so they constructed the dam at the highest spot.

Mr. Dean Acheson: It might or it might not have been illogical for them to do it, but that wasn't the question that I asked you. What I asked was that if they *had* done it, wouldn't the land look very much the way it does today?

Mr. Verstappen: I don't think so....

Mr. Dean Acheson: I am afraid we are not understanding one another at all. I am not talking about one stone falling every year. I am talking about the Khmers bringing up the rubble from a hundred metres down the cliff and making what you would recognize at once as a rock-filled dam right across at point F. That wouldn't be much of a job for the Khmers, would it?

Mr. Verstappen: I think it is virtually impossible. It is, first of all, not only a vertical distance ... of several hundred of meters, and then to push upwards 70,000 cubic metres of material up that steep slope, I think would not be feasible... (ICJ Pleadings 1962 vol. II, pp. 429–31)

— Playing an employed scientist off against his superior:

> Mr. Dean Acheson: Mr. Ackermann, let us go back to your *expertise*
> for a moment.... But I recall that yesterday, Dr. Schermerhorn [that is,
> Ackermann's superior] felt unable to answer questions in the geological
> field and we both retreated from doing it. Would you think you are more
> qualified than he, or the same, or less, or would you like to stay out of
> the geological issue?

> Mr. Ackermann: Of course I am not a geologist. I have told you I studied
> geology for one year, so geological terms are not absolutely new to me,
> and I am not unaware of geological events or possibilities, walking in
> the terrain, but that is all. And I may add that I have never worked as
> a geologist.

Acheson finally concludes:

> I think you and I are almost exactly the same in both our education and
> our lack of geological experience. Therefore I shall not tempt you into
> this field.... (ICJ Pleadings 1962 vol. II, p. 400)

— Disqualifying data:

> Mr. Acheson: Could you indicate to us about the table, about how high
> a pile all your papers would be.

> Mr. Ackermann: That would be about 10 to 15 centimetres high. (ICJ
> Pleadings 1962 vol. II, p. 404)

— Bossing around the expert:

> Mr. Acheson: I do not wish to seem unduly persistent, but I do wish
> to draw your attention to the fact that there is no stream 2 or anything
> apart from this map, but I am asking you to look at the map and tell me
> whether you see a stream channel, which I have just described as looking
> like a question mark being formed to the west of the red line and moving
> down and ending up with an arrow below the cliff.

> Mr. Verstappen: I only see a drainage channel starting to the east, to the
> right of the red line and going in an eastward direction into Cambodia
> and ending in an arrow. But we do not see the connection at the red
> line. Otherwise we would not have drawn the watershed. (ICJ Pleadings
> 1962, p. 426)

This interrogation was later commented on and ridiculed by Acheson as follows:

> When I called Dr. Verstappen's attention to this stream shown by his own Department of the I.T.C., he, like Lord Nelson, put his blind eye to the magnifying glass and declared that he could not see the stream at all, but saw two quite different streams. I submit that any Member of the Court who wishes to look at this spot through a magnifying glass—as one Member already has done—will see this stream drawn right through the alleged watershed and flowing into Cambodia. (ICJ Pleadings 1962 vol. II, p. 466)

Cambodia's attorneys pressed the experts by suggesting the following "facts" that the experts had either not noticed or not mentioned in their report: (1) Surface changes may have taken place during the intervening fifty years between the establishment of the 1907 map and 1962 that substantially changed the contour lines. Earthquakes or landslides could have changed the surface and altered the watershed; (2) There could have been a rock breakaway or rock falls that created the ridge/saddle; (3) One of the rivers could have changed its course over the past fifty years; (4) The "saddle"—that is a surface elevation that was invisible on the aerial photographs but which was identified during Ackermann's survey—could have been man-made during the construction of the temple; (5) The elevation of the ground could be the result of human intervention over the past fifty years; (6) There was possibly a third watershed, from which the water emptied into the Cambodian plain; (7) There could be some subterraneous flows of water and, therefore, there could have been an underground watershed; (8) The flow of the O-Tasem river could have radically changed its direction (that is, formerly, it could have flowed down where today it would be necessary to climb a mountain).

In his final reply, Dean Acheson summed up his opinion of the three experts and the reports as follows:

> ... Thailand's witnesses have reversed the slope of this valley. They have achieved this miracle, although they now testify that neither God nor His instrument—geology—could have done it in over a thousand years.... How has it been done? It has been done by another miracle. Mr. Ackermann went to Preah Vihear and there discovered the invisible

mound—a mound invisible from the aerial photographs, apparently undiscoverable from I.T.C.'s geological preparatory work, and yet happily visible to Mr. Ackermann when he went to Preah Vihear and spent 11 days in surveying, measuring and tramping about the invisible mound, looking for mud on tress and rockslides where they had never taken place. Even Mr. Verstappen was able in this courtroom to perform a somewhat more minor miracle, which was to tell just what this invisible mound looked like on the photographs on which it could not be seen.

And he concluded: "I confess that I find it harder and harder to understand how the I.T.C. school at Delft operates" (ICJ Pleadings 1962 vol. II, pp. 465–66).

The consequences of the procedures of truth-finding, including the background of the political setting of the time, are mirrored in the judgement. Instead of making a decision with regard to the factual line of the watershed—thus either verifying or labelling as false the results of the scientists' search for facts, over which there had been days-long debates—the court based its judgement on a legal formality or principle (though a Europe-biased one): "Qui tacet consentire videtur si loqui debuisset ac potuisset" (He who keeps silent is held to consent if he must and can speak; Mißling 2011, p. 61).[17] Therefore, the contested map of 1907 ("Annexe I map") that was used as a document to substantiate the 1904 Franco-Siamese treaty was validated, although there was (and is) a contradiction between the map and the treaty with regard to the determination of the frontier. With this judgement, which was revalidated by the ICJ 2013 decree, Cambodia's sovereignty over the temple was reinforced and internationally legitimized. After the 1962 judgement, the Thai minister of foreign affairs wrote in a letter to the UN acting secretary general (dated 6 July 1962) that Thailand complied "under protest and with reservation of her intrinsic rights", that is, "whatever rights Thailand has, or may have in the future, to recover the Temple of Phra Viharn by having recourse to any existing or subsequently applicable legal process" (Cuasay 1998, p. 881). Thus, it was foreseeable that the listing of Preah Vihear as a UNESCO World Heritage Site of Cambodia would only open up old wounds.

In summing up, we recognize that there exists a genealogical tree of expert reports that played a decisive role in shaping the colonial and postcolonial history of Preah Vihear by attributing sovereignty over the temple to Cambodia. This genealogical tree of expert reports and the subsequent regimes of truth were the point of departure for Cambodia's nomination of Preah Vihear as a UNESCO World Heritage site.

III. The Regime of Truth and the UNESCO Listing

Apart from the century-old conflict between Thailand and Cambodia, which has flared up time and again over the decades, the rising nationalism in both countries and domestic political intrigues and turmoil (Kasetsiri et al. 2013; Pawakapan 2013; Edwards 2007; Winter 2012; Denes 2006), world powers have also been active behind the scenes of the UNESCO Listing of Preah Vihear. Their activities were revealed by the cables published by WikiLeaks and have been analysed by Meskell (2016). The geopolitics of Southeast Asia, where already China was engaged, was once again one of the main reasons for US involvement and its support of Cambodia in this contested unilateral heritage-making process. Its interests also included major economic issues such as resource extraction (gas and oil reserves in the Gulf of Thailand), concessions, investments, and Cambodia's financial debt to the United States. The Temple of Preah Vihear became a site of hyperconnectivity (Meskell 2016). While the WikiLeaks cables allow some fundamental insights into the global political setting in which the listing of the temple ruins took place, they are restricted to the actions of the United States. Thus, we do not know the manner in which other states, such as France, were involved in the case.

Most of the UNESCO diplomats in Paris, and especially the experts charged with evaluating the Temple of Preah Vihear, were full of enthusiasm (Meskell 2016). However, it seems that most of them were unaware of the delicate political history and the fragile contested situation. The expert reports commissioned by Cambodia were written by "ten distinguished experts of international acclaim" (Sahai 2009, p. 2). The UNESCO World Heritage Centre submitted these reports to ICOMOS for evaluation. All the reports were written according to the Operational Guidelines for the Implementation of the World Heritage Convention, following the qualitative, legal and organizational requirements that the guidelines stipulate.[18] The qualitative reports (those that deal with the criteria the candidate must fulfil) had been written from a perspective which looks back into time and that borrows extensively from the early French reports such as those by Lunet Lajonquière or Parmentier and the latter's reconstructive vision of an undamaged temple. These reports are also part of a regime of truth that created a kind of idealized past that seeks to revive the glory that was *Cambodge ancient*, the empire of the ancient Khmer (see above).

Consequently, they eclipse the decay of the "empire", the defeats the rulers and societies suffered, the destruction of monuments, and the iconoclasms and changes to politics that have taken place since the (assumed) golden era. The ethnographic present in which such descriptions are written intensify the picture of an imagined pristine Hindu monument.[19]

> Situated on the edge of a plateau that dominates the plain of Cambodia, the Temple of Preah Vihear is dedicated to Shiva. The Temple is composed of a series of sanctuaries linked by a system of pavements and staircases over an 800 metre long axis and dates back to the first half of the 11th century AD. Nevertheless, its complex history can be traced to the 9th century, when the hermitage was founded. This site is particularly well preserved, mainly due to its remote location. The site is exceptional for the quality of its architecture, which is adapted to the natural environment and the religious function of the temple, as well as for the exceptional quality of its carved stone ornamentation.[20]

There are a number of political slips in the nomination reports. The original ritual complex of Preah Vihear, for example, extended beyond the frontier line. However, since the application for Preah Vihear was made by a single nation, nothing further counted (or was described) than what was on the Cambodian side. Moreover, one of the most contested documents that accompanied the nomination (and which was again used in the ICOMOS 2008 evaluation) was the map ("revised graphic plan of the property") at the end of the proposal. This map should illustrate the different zones as described in the Management Plan. It shows a kind of amputated ground plan of the temple ruins, ending abruptly at the beginning of the monumental staircase (where the frontier with Thailand is); that is, the main entrance (although it is not declared as such). This main entrance definitely opened from the side of today's territory of Thailand. Instead, the steep side staircase from the Cambodian plains is depicted as if it had been the main access track to the temple. The map distorts the historical location of the temple in the landscape beyond national territorial considerations and reconfirms the former colonial regime of truth. In its (anonymous) evaluation reports in 2007 and 2008, ICOMOS relies on information provided by the World Heritage Centre. In the Management Plan of the first version ICOMOS had to evaluate, the boundary of the area destined for the World Heritage site apparently directly bordered Thai territory (2007, p. 46). In the 2008 evaluation report (following the revision of the Management Plan), ICOMOS mentions that the whole area designated for the World Heritage Site was now completely on Cambodian territory (2008, p. 7; see also Hauser-Schäublin and Mißling 2014).

There is another expert report in the nomination proposal that is quite surprising since it unknowingly deals with questions about the watershed line (see above). In the expert report on "General recommendation on water management of Preah Vihea [sic] temple", its author identifies three watersheds within the temple area: an "east temple watershed", a "pagoda watershed" and an "aerodrome watershed". At first sight, the plans provided by this expert seem to confirm Ackermann's findings: these "watersheds" show that all water flows towards the north, that is, towards Thailand. None of them flow south towards the Cambodian plains. None of the reviewers of the nomination proposal seem to have discovered this ex-post verification of Ackermann's scientific report that had been heavily contested during the ICJ case court.[21]

There are further expert reports in the Management Plan that engage with the infrastructure of the site as a tourist destination. They propose facilities that could be provided for tourists. With one exception, the reports deal—according to the goals of the nomination proposal—only marginally with local people. The priority is the monument. Similar to the colonial perspective, local people are rather a *quantité négligable,* as the advice for resettlements and the establishment of a new "old Khmer village" for tourism purposes illustrate. It is a new truth that the nomination—and finally the listing—of the World Heritage site created. The experts selected for the task (who chose them, and according to what principles?), the recommendations in their reports and the way the Cambodian government has implemented them constitute the frame of the new reality, which shares many similarities with a public open air museum conceived to exist for perpetuity.

Conclusion

The listing of the contested temple of Preah Vihear as a UNESCO World Heritage Site of Cambodia in 2008 and the subsequent outbreak of a violent border conflict was the outcome of a series of expert reports commissioned by various actors since the early twentieth century. The expert reports UNESCO had mandated in the case of Preah Vihear were only the last link in a long chain of similar expert knowledge. This tragic example illustrates the extent to which UNESCO is dependent on expert knowledge and experts' evaluations. It also demonstrates how the success or failure of UNESCO's attempts to achieve international governance by means of "culture" is conditioned by such reports and the decisions made on its behalf.

This chapter has revealed how more-or-less innocent experts and their "neutral" reports (see also Mosse 2011) became political instruments in the regimes of truth at a particular time and, consequently, in the process of heritage-making. With few exceptions, each new report was developed from the basis—the regime of truth—of previous reports, although the decision-making actors changed. As I have shown, experts in matters of "culture" and their reports have always been crucial in the establishment of and in reinforcing Cambodia's power relations with its neighbour since colonial times. The methods, techniques and procedures with which these regimes of truth have worked have differed according to the geopolitical situation, the corresponding actors and their goals. Moreover, the circle of actors involved in such decisions has widened from one stage to the next. The widest circle involved was during the nomination process of Preah Vihear as a World Heritage Site. Thanks to Meskell's (2016) analysis of WikiLeaks cables exchanged between diplomatic agencies and US government authorities over the listing of Preah Vihear, we know that even global power players and their diverse interests were pulling the strings behind the scenes in the nomination process.

As political instruments, such reports have the potential even to undermine UNESCO's noble goals; namely, to perform cultural governance in order to create a more peaceful world. As is well known, the contrary took place. The inscription of the site led to a loss of face for Thailand that resulted in armed conflict. The miniature 1:10 scale replica (600 square metres) of the temple of Preah Vihear that was built by Thai military craftsmen in spring 2016 and which overlooks the original Hindu temple on the Cambodian side demonstrates that Thailand's wounds of humiliation have not yet healed (Nanuam 2016).

Thus, the example of Preah Vihear suggests that such listings should not be evaluated only from the perspective of the criteria spelled out in the Operational Guidelines, but also from the viewpoint of the political history in which cultural property or heritage is situated.

Notes

1. Member States Delegates acting as IGC member often have their own political agenda that influences the decision-making process (Meskelll 2015). On the working of the Intergovernmental Meeting, see Brumann 2016.
2. See, for example, Hauser-Schäublin 2015.
3. The final judgement of 15 June 1962 was decreed with a majority of nine votes to three; the latter held a dissenting opinion. The judges in disagreement with the majority verdict were from Argentina, China and Australia (ICJ Judgements 1962). Under the presidency of Judge Winiarski from Poland, the vice-president from Panama and the judges from France, Italy, the United Kingdom, Japan and the USSR were members of the pro-party.
4. As Chesterman (2015, p. 1) points out, in contrast to Cambodia, Thailand (as one among many Asian countries) has not signed the Declaration Recognizing the Jurisdiction of the Court as compulsory. See also http://www.icj-cij.org/jurisdiction/index.php?p1=5&p2=1&p3=3 (1 December 2016). However, Thailand seems to have at least formally accepted the ICJ decrees.
5. I met Friedrich Ackermann for an interview at his home in Stuttgart on 9 May 2016. I am grateful to him for his preparedness to discuss the 1962 court case and his work on Preah Vihear with me.
6. The judgement is, as Article 60 of the Statute of the International Court of Justice states, final and without appeal, and Article 61, paragraph 5 notes: "No application for revision may be made after the lapse of ten years from the date of the judgement". Paragraph 1 of Article 61, however, states: "An application for revision of a judgment may be made only when it is based upon the discovery of some fact of such a nature as to be a decisive factor, which fact was, when the judgment was given, unknown to the Court and also to the party claiming revision, always provided that such ignorance was not due to negligence". The Court argued though that in the case of Preah Vihear it was a matter of negligence on the part of the Thai party.
7. Between 1953 and 1963 the United States had apparently contributed almost US$404 million to the Cambodian state to keep Cambodia from turning to communist countries (Katten 2015, p. 22n36).
8. Note that Cambodia is reduced to ethnic Khmer.
9. Judge Wellington Koo (China) stated in his dissenting opinion that the court would have been well advised to send its own experts to investigate on the spot (Peat 2014, p. 281).
10. Wilhelm (Willem) Schermerhorn, a leading international specialist of

photogrammetry at the time, was dean of the International Training Centre for Aerial Survey and director of its Consulting Department. Schermerhorn had also been the first prime minister of the Netherlands (1945–46).

11. For a critical discussion of the court case, especially the way in which cross-examination was carried out, see Burgess 2015.

12. Extracts of Henri Parmentier's book *L'art Khmer classique* were quoted by one of the Cambodian counsels in order to undermine the statements made by the ITC experts. Parmentier was presented to the court as "the distinguished French archaeologist" by the Cambodian counsel (ICJ 1962a, p. 467).

13. Based on US aerial maps of 1954 (IJC 1962a, p. 348). "When Cambodia saw the ITC mapping, they commissioned an American firm of photogeologists, Doeringsfeld, Amuedo and Ivey, to comment on it. DAI made several changes to the ITC map..." (ICJ 2012 Annexe 46, p. 6) without having ever been to Preah Vihear.

14. He founded the Institute for Photogrammetry at the University of Stuttgart in 1966 and is one of the leading experts in photogrammetry.

15. Ackermann went to the second court case concerning Preah Vihear in 2013, however, only as a private person.

16. Paul Reuter asked the questions in French; this is my translation.

17. "Given the grounds on which the Court bases its decision, it becomes unnecessary to consider whether, at Preah Vihear, the line as mapped does in fact correspond to the true watershed line in this vicinity, or did so correspond in 1904–1908, or, if not, how the watershed line in fact runs" (ICJ 1962b, p. 35).

18. http://whc.unesco.org/en/criteria/.

19. Note that the temple was dedicated to Shiva only a thousand years ago and later became a site of Buddhist worship.

20. http://whc.unesco.org/en/list/1224.

21. However, the identical term, *watershed*, blurs the fact that the author is talking about something else. A watershed is an area of land or a ridge that separates waters flowing to different rivers or lakes. The line of the watershed is the line of the border between two water systems. However, the hydrology expert did not mean watershed in this sense but rather the drainage system existing in the temple area. His task was to describe it and to make suggestions how it could be improved/used for the management of the site. I am grateful to Friedrich Ackermann for this clarification.

References

Anderson, Benedict. 1991. *Imagined Communities: Reflections on the Origin and Spread of Nationalism*. New York: Verso.

Bastian, Adolf. 1868. *Reise durch Kambodja*. Jena: Hermann Costenoble.

Brumann, Christoph. 2016. "Conclusion. Imagining the Ground from Afar: Why the Sites are so Remote in World Heritage Committee Sessions". In *World Heritage on the Ground: Ethnographic Perspectives*, edited by C. Brumann and D. Berliner, pp. 294–317. Berghahn Books.

Burgess, John. 2015. *Temple in the Clouds: Faith and Conflict at Preah Vihear*. Bangkok: River Books.

Chandler, David. 2008. *A History of Cambodia*. Westview.

Chesterman, Simon. 2015. "The International Court of Justice in Asia: Interpreting the Temple of Preah Vihear Case". *Asian Journal of International Law* 5, no. 1: 1–6.

Clémentin-Ojha, Catherine, and Pierre-Ives Manguin. 2001. *Un siècle pour l'Asie: L'École Française d'Extrême-Orient, 1898–2000*. Paris: École Française d'Extrême-Orient.

Cuasay, P. 1998. "Borders on the Fantastic: Mimesis, Violence, and Landscape at the Temple of Preah Vihear". *Modern Asian Studies* 32, no. 4: 849–90.

Denes, Alexandra. 2006. "Recovering Khmer Ethnic Identity from the Thai National Past: An Ethnography of the Localism Movement in Surin Province". PhD dissertation, Cornell University.

Edwards, Penny. 2007. Cambodia: *The Cultivation of a Nation, 1860–1945*. Honolulu: University of Hawai'i Press.

Falser, Michael, and Monica Juneija, eds. 2013. *Aracheologizing? Heritage? Transcultural Entanglements between Local Social Practices and Global Virtual Realities*. Springer.

Forrester, John. 1997. *Truth Games: Lies, Money, and Psychoanalysis*. Harvard College.

Foucault, Michel. 1980. *Power/knowledge: Selected Interviews & Other Writings, 1972–1977*, edited by Collin Gordon. New York: Pantheon Book.

Hauser-Schäublin, Brigitta. 2011. "Preah Vihear: From an Object of Colonial Desires to a Contested World Heritage Site". In *World Heritage Angkor and Beyond: Circumstances and Implications of UNESCO Listings in Cambodia*, edited by B. Hauser-Schäublin, pp. 33–56. Göttingen: Universitätsverlag.

————. 2015. "From *Homo Politicus* to Immoblized Icon: Clifford Geertz and Shifts in Anthropological Paradigms". *Bijdragen tot de Taal-, Land- en Volkenkunde* 171: 220–48. http://booksandjournals.brillonline.com/content/journals/10.1163/22134379-17102003.

Hauser-Schäublin, Brigitta, and Sven Mißling. 2014. "The Enduring Agency of Borderland Regimes: The Aftermath of Serial Regulations with Different Scopes and Temporal Scales at Preah Vihear, Cambodia". *Journal of Legal Pluralism and Unofficial Law* 46, no. 1: 79–98.

ICJ. 1962a. Pleadings, oral arguments, documents. Case Concerning the Temple of Preah Vihear. General List No. 45. Judgments of 26 May 1961 and 15 June 1962, vol. 2: Oral arguments, documents, correspondence. The Hague.

————. 1962b. Judgements. Temple of Preah Vihear (Cambodia v. Thailand). The Hague.

<http://www.icj-cij.org/docket/index.php?p1=3&p2=3&case=45&p3=4> (accessed 10 May 2016).

———. 2012: "Request for Interpretation of the Judgment of 15 June 1962 in the Case Concerning the Temple of Preah Vihear". Annexes to the further written explanations of the Kingdom of Thailand. http://www.icj-cij.org/docket/files/151/17292.pdf (accessed 12 December 2016).

———. n.d. Statute of the International Court of Justice. http://www.icj-cij.org/documents/?p1=4&p2=2 (accessed 15 May 2016).

ICOMOS. 2007. "Preah Vihear". In ICOMOS: Évaluations of Cultural Properties, pp. 2–15. UNESCO World Heritage Intergovernmental Committee, 31st ordinary session, 23 June – 2 July 2007, Christchurch, New Zealand. http://whc.unesco.org/archive/2007/whc07-31com-inf8b1e.pdf (accessed 12 May 2016).

———. 2008. "Preah Vihear". Icomos: Evaluation des bien culturels. UNESCO World Heritage Intergovernmental Committee, 32nd ordinary session, 2–10 July 2008, Québec, Canada. http://whc.unesco.org/archive/advisory_body_evaluation/1224rev.pdf (accessed 13 May 2016).

Kasetsiri, Charnvit, Sothirak, Pou, Pavin Chachavalpongpun. 2013. Preah Vihear: A Guide to the Thai-Cambodian Conflict and its Solution. Bangkok: White Lotus.

Kattan, Victor. 2015. "The Ghosts of the Temple of Preah Vihear/Phra Viharn in the 2013 Judgment". Asian Journal of International Law 5 no. 1: 16–25.

Lee, Sang Kook. 2014. "Siam Mismapped: Revisiting the Territorial Dispute over the Preah Vihear Temple". South East Asia Research 22, no. 1: 131–52.

Lunet de Lajonquière, Etienne. 1907. Inventaire descriptif des monuments du Cambodge, vol. 2. Publications de l'École Française d' Extrême-Orient 8. Paris: Leroux.

Meskell, Lynn. 2015. "Transacting UNESCO World Heritage: Gifts and Exchanges on a Global Stage". Social Anthropology 23: 3–21.

———. 2016. "World Heritage and WikiLeaks". Current Anthropology 57, no. 1: 72–95.

Mißling, Sven. 2011. "A Legal View on the Case of the Temple Preah Vihear". In World Heritage Angkor and Beyond: Circumstances and Implications of UNESCO Listings in Cambodia, edited by B. Hauser-Schäublin, pp. 57–67. Göttingen: Universitätsverlag.

Mosse, David. 2011. "Introduction: The Anthropology of Expertise and Professionals in International Development". In Adventures in Aidland: The Anthropology of Professionals in International Development, edited by D. Mosse, pp. 1–31 Oxford: Berghahn Books.

Nanuam, Wassana. "Military Builds Preah Vihear Temple Replica". Bangkok Post, 25 April 2016. http://www.bangkokpost.com/news/security/946309/military-builds-preah-vihear-temple-replica (accessed 11 December 2016).

Nielsen, Bjarke. 2011. "UNESCO and the 'Right' Kind of Culture: Bureaucratic Production and Articulation". Critique of Anthropology 31, no. 4: 273–92.

Parmentier, Henry. 1939. L'art khmer classique. Monuments du quadrant nord-est.

Planches. L'École française d'Extrême-Orient. Paris: Les éditions d'art et d'histoire.

Pavie, Auguste. 1903. *Mission Pavie Indo-Chine: Atlas, Notices et Cartes*. Paris: August Challamel.

Puangthong R. Pawakapan. 2013. *State and Uncivil Society in Thailand at the Temple of Preah Vihear*. Singapore: Institute of Southeast Asian Studies.

Peat, Daniel. 2014. "The Use of Court-Appointed Experts by the International Court of Justice". *British Yearbook of International Law* 84, no. 1: 271–303.

Reid, Anthony. 2015. *A History of Southeast Asia: Critical Crossroads*. Chichester: Wiley Blackwell.

Reyna, Stephen P., and Nina Glick Schiller. 2010. "The Pursuit of Knowledge and Regimes of Truth". In *Identities: Global Studies in Culture and Power* 4, nos. 3–4: 333–41. http://dx.doi.org/10.1080/1070289X.1998.9962594 (accessed 23 June 2014).

Sahai, Sachchidanan. 2009. *Preah Vihear: An Introduction to the World Heritage Monument*. Phnom Penh: Cambodian National Commission for UNESCO.

Said, Edward. 2003. *Orientalism*. London: Penguin.

Seneviratne, Sudharshan. 2008. "Situating World Heritage Sites in a Multicultural Society: The Ideology of Presentation at the Sacred City of Anuradhapura, Sri Lanka". In *Archaeology and the Postcolonial Critique*, edited by Matthew Liebmann and U.Z. Rizvi, pp. 177–96. Lanham, MD: Altamira.

Silverman, Helaine. 2011. "Border Wars: The Ongoing Temple Dispute between Thailand and Cambodia and UNESCO's World Heritage List". *International Journal of Heritage Studies* 17, no. 1: 1–21.

Singaravélou, Pierre. 1999. *L'École francaise d'Extrême-Orient ou l'institution des marges (1898–1956)*. Paris: L' Harmattan.

Thongchai, Winichakul. 1994. *Siam Mapped: A History of the Geo-Body of as Nation*. Honolulu: University of Hawai'i Press.

Vrdoljak, A. 2015. "Challenges for International Cultural Heritage Law". In *A Companion to Heritage Studies*, edited by W. Logan, M. Nic Craith, and U. Kockel. pp. 541–56. Chichester: Wiley.

Winter, Tim. 2007. *Post-Conflict Heritage, Postcolonial Tourism: Culture, Politics and Development at Angkor*. London: Routledge.

———. 2010. "Heritage Tourism: The Dawn of a New Era?" In *Heritage and Globalisation*, edited by S. Labadi and C. Long, pp. 117–29. London: Routledge.

4

The International Coordinating Committee for Angkor: A World Heritage Site as an Arena of Competition, Connivance and State(s) Legitimation[*]

Philippe Peycam

> Angkor, a jewel of the Cambodian heritage, has become a shared concern. The interest of the international community has been a turning point in the history of Cambodia. (UNESCO 1993, p. 34)

One year before these self-congratulatory lines were written, the United Nations Educational Scientific and Cultural Organization (UNESCO) listed the archaeological and monumental complex of Angkor in Cambodia as a World Heritage Site. The listing process had closely paralleled the negotiations that led to the Paris Agreements in 1991 and thus to the

---

[*] First published in *SOJOURN: Journal of Social Issues in Southeast Asia* 31, no. 3 (2016).

unprecedented post-conflict mission in the country led by the United Nations. The United Nation's Transitional Authority in Cambodia (UNTAC) sought to restore the political integrity of the country following decades of war and isolation. In this context, UNESCO's recognition of Angkor and its significance symbolized the return of Cambodia to the international stage, while the plan for the management of the site was part of the process of political and economic reconstruction of the country. A number of institutional "stakeholders"[1] were involved in the listing. They were for the most part members of the "international community", which in the UN diplomatico-bureaucratic jargon signifies primarily representatives of member states. Also, and in UNESCO's language, the listing of Angkor corresponded to the recognition that the site was of "outstanding" and "universal" value (UNESCO 1992, pp. 5–6).

Following the recognition of Angkor as a UNESCO World Heritage Site, an international "campaign" to conserve it was launched at a conference held in Tokyo in 1993.[2] Twenty-nine countries and eight organizations attended this event. Some of them committed to the conservation of a number of temples endangered by material degradation. At this conference, moreover, the participants agreed to establish an International Coordination Committee for the Safeguarding and Development of the Historic Site of Angkor (ICC-Angkor), whose mission was threefold. It would guarantee the "consistency of the projects" implemented in Angkor, define the "technical and financial standards" with which projects must comply, and "call the attention of interested parties" to specific aspects of the site's management (UNESCO 1993, pp. 7–8). In its first ten years of activity, about one hundred prospective projects were brought before the ICC (UNESCO and ICC-Angkor 2013, pp. 28–35). The committee's main objective has been to ensure that scientific and technical consistency prevail among different foreign-led conservation projects at Angkor.

The ICC's prime and original concern has been for the conservation and management of the archaeological ruins within the Angkor Park. The concentration of monuments delineated into a "park" during the French colonial occupation and their endangered condition as a result of war was the main reason justifying the recognition of Angkor as a World Heritage Site (UNESCO 1991, pp. 59–60). In practice, however, the World Heritage listing led to the involvement of the ICC in monitoring activities beyond the perimeter of that archaeological site, focusing primarily on activities likely to affect the protected zone: tourism, infrastructure and urban and rural development. To fulfil a condition of Angkor's World Heritage nomination, but temporarily waived because of the urgency of protection of the temples, from 1995 onward the ICC has had a domestic partner, the Authority for the Protection and Management of Angkor and the Region of Siem Reap (APSARA). APSARA was tasked with managing all aspects of the World Heritage Site across a broad territory thereafter designated as "the Angkor Region" (UNESCO 1993, p. 3). This integrated vision for Angkor and its region meant that the ICC was, with the facilitation of UNESCO, to stand as the international face of the management of the extended World Heritage Site in partnership with APSARA. The latter organization became the "national" counterpart of the efforts made by the "international community". In theory, therefore, the ICC was to consider all projects related directly or indirectly to the World Heritage Site.

If the "international community" as represented by the ICC and UNESCO claimed the existence of a formal consensus on the need to agree on methods of conservation, the second half of the 1990s and above all the period from 2000 onwards brought both an intensification of tourism and rapid urbanization. These developments put pressure on those charged with managing the ten thousand square kilometres of Siem Reap Province, within which Angkor lies. Not surprisingly, strong differences in strategies between APSARA and provincial authorities emerged. In addition, an increasing number of decisions about the World Heritage Site were made outside the purview of the ICC and APSARA. This article thus addresses the operational effectiveness of the international collaborative model embodied in the ICC. After more than twenty years of activity, has its role been limited to that of mere evaluator of projects to be implemented in Angkor? Or has it been capable of influencing—if not directly overseeing—activities occurring within the broader World Heritage Site? More generally, is it possible to achieve international heritage cooperation when nation-states—"host" states included—are the parties implementing heritage projects?

This historically contextualized study seeks to provide some preliminary responses to these questions. The article has two main sections.

The first is an examination of the general mission of the ICC, paying special attention to the politics—and geopolitics—of its establishment and operation. This examination focuses particularly on the roles of two major ICC actors—the cooperation programmes of the French and Japanese governments. As these two states have presided over the committee since its creation, their involvement was from the outset critical in the framing of the "international cooperation" discourse as it has applied to Angkor. The second section analyses a set of activities in which the two governments played an important role: planning for the spatial development of Siem Reap Province and in particular of Siem Reap town, a tourist hub located six kilometres from the temple complex.[3] The section reveals that the implementation of the international actors' plans faced fierce opposition from investors and tacit resistance within the Cambodian state itself. The influence of a structure deemed to represent the "international community" and composed of representatives of states, such as the ICC, appears to have been limited when sensitive issues such as land ownership and real estate investments were at stake. UNESCO's traditional bias in favour of monumental heritage at the expense of the welfare of local communities further contributed to a weakening of the ICC and its coordinating role, even though over time UNESCO representatives sought to modify the organization's initial approach. Some members of the ICC, particularly from within the Cambodian state, blatantly ignored the objectives of a coherent plan for the site.

In pointing to some of the ICC's structural shortcomings, shortcomings resulting from its undemocratic establishment and modus operandi, the article concludes that, as an international mechanism of cooperation for the safeguarding of a major heritage site like Angkor, the ICC is unlikely to achieve and sustain its stated objectives. Only by ensuring the effective participation of communities living in and around such sites in deliberative and decision-making processes can a platform like the ICC fulfil its promise as a mediator of international-local collaboration.

The article offers a localized—from the "field"—reflection on a number of recent critical accounts on the international institutional politics of heritage, particularly those focusing on UNESCO. Many of these accounts deal with the intergovernmental organization at either the central or macro levels. At the same time, a number of researchers have begun to study UNESCO through attention to multiple intellectual and operational facets. These researchers have pointed to a number of contradictions and internal dysfunctions plaguing the organization.[4] An inspiration for this article is the work of Lynn Meskell, who has focused on political practices within the UNESCO World Heritage Convention structure since its creation in 1972. Meskell documents a trend, largely at the initiative of member states, towards intensified politicization and nationalistic competition around heritage properties,

transforming them into transactional commodities with exchange values
that transcend their historical or material characteristics and that can be
wrested from those contexts to serve international interests. (Meskell
2016, p. 72)

These developments are in clear contradiction with stated heritage
conservation considerations, sustainable economic development objectives
and the higher philosophical principles at the origin of the World Heritage
Convention treaty. The extent to which these same forces are also at
work at the bottom end of the UNESCO pyramid, particularly at World
Heritage Sites and usually under the organization's banner of international
cooperation and cultural aid, remains to be documented.

Few accounts examine Asian, and particularly Southeast Asian, World
Heritage Sites. On sites in countries neighbouring Cambodia, I should
point to the work of David Berliner on Luang Prabang, Laos (Berliner
2012), and of Nir Avieli on Hội An, Vietnam (Avieli 2015). I should also
mention the continuing investigation of institutional practices at the World
Heritage Site of Borobodur by a number of activist-scholars from Gadjah
Mada University in nearby Yogyakarta (Kanki, Adishakti and Fatimah
2015). On Angkor–Siem Reap itself, apart from the work of Keiko Miura,
the critical literature on institutional practices of heritage management is
small, in contrast with the massive production of celebratory publications
and reports of all sorts on the World Heritage Site (Miura 2010, 2011 and
2015).

This article draws on my nine years of participation in ICC meetings
while I was the head of an educational and academic NGO in Siem Riep
between 2000 and 2009. It also draws on an extensive reading of ICC
meeting reports covering 1993–2013, on foreign consultants' reports,
conference proceedings, legislative materials and articles in the Cambodian
press.[5] The analysis of this corpus allows one to appreciate the basis
for decisions taken by the ICC and the patterns of spatial management
proposed by its members.

The Geopolitics of International Cooperation at Angkor: France, Japan and the ICC

The idea of creating an international committee for the management of
Angkor was not new to UNESCO and the States Parties that signed the

UNESCO World Heritage Convention of 1972.[6] Recommendations to establish these international entities related to a sense of urgency in the preservation of valuable heritage in areas in which states were either weak or absent. This sense of "universal responsibility" towards selected monuments emerged during the Athens Conference of 1931, which resulted in the "Athens Charter" (International Council on Monuments and Sites [ICOMOS] n.d.). In the 1960s, UNESCO was engaged in the "safeguarding" of Egyptian and Sudanese monumental heritage sites threatened by the construction of the Aswan Dam.[7] Its appeal for international cooperation led to the establishment in 1959 of an Executive Committee on which UNESCO played "the role of coordinator between the donor states and the Egyptian and Sudanese governments" (UNESCO 1999–2013, p. 1). To date, UNESCO has been the initiator of twenty-six such international structures to attend to specific sites with an overall budget of nearly one billion dollars (UNESCO 1992–2013b).

If international engagement in sites' management has always been a prerogative of the World Heritage system, the precarious situation prevailing in the early 1990s in a Cambodia that had just emerged from two decades of war exacerbated the perceived need for a collective international response. When the twenty-sixth UNESCO General Conference addressed the question of Angkor in 1991, it stressed the urgent need for the creation of an international mechanism capable of guaranteeing the conservation and the management of the temple complex (UNESCO 1991, p. 59).[8] The establishment of such a committee was indeed one of the conditions set by UNESCO for inclusion of the archaeological park of Angkor on the list of World Heritage Sites. The creation of an international coordinating committee made possible the listing of Angkor without waiting for Cambodia to fulfil two of the five basic criteria for the World Heritage Site designation; namely, the promulgation of adequate legislation in the field of heritage conservation and the approval of a management plan for the site.[9] The Inter-governmental Conference on the Safeguarding and Development of the Historical Area of Angkor, held in Tokyo on 12–13 October 1993, officially established the ICC as the sole institutional mechanism for the management of the Angkor site. With UNESCO managing the functions of the ICC's secretariat, the main task of the committee was to assist Cambodia in meeting the UNESCO conditions mentioned and at the same time to undertake urgent measures to conserve the monuments (UNESCO 1993, p. 7).

Since its inception, the ICC for Angkor has operated under the permanent co-chairmanship of the governments of France and Japan. At the Tokyo Conference, UNESCO deputy director general for culture Henri Lopes justified the prominent role of the two countries by noting that each had contributed substantially to UNESCO's funds. He added that, in the case of France, Cambodia's former colonial master had a special role to play, for it "holds parts of the country's historical memory" (UNESCO 1993, p. 57).[10] This statement reveals the ambiguous motivations that attended the establishment of the Angkor ICC.

France's and Japan's claims to special roles on the ICC were of different natures. In the case of France, the historical connection was invoked, sometimes in emotional terms (UNESCO 1993, p. 43).[11] The country was the former colonial "protector" of Cambodia, and it had been the principal actor in the restoration of the temple complex before 1973.[12] Japan's justification for a prominent role at Angkor had a clearer motive. Above all, the prominent role that Japanese political leaders and diplomats wanted their country to play in Southeast Asia made them seek the leadership of the "international effort" to preserve the historical site. There was, however, a less explicitly articulated motive associated with Japan's claim to prominence at Angkor. In selecting the formerly Buddhist temple of the Bayon as the official Japanese conservation site and labelling Angkor's Buddhist attributes "living heritage" in need of reassertion, Japan made an attempt to foster the idea of a shared Buddhist experience common to the Japanese and Cambodian peoples. The Nara UNESCO Conference of 1994 and its "Declaration on Authenticity" validated this notion (ICOMOS 1994).[13]

In an example of the kind of behind-the-scene intrigue on the part of UNESCO member states described by Meskell (2013 and 2016), the diplomats of Japan and France reached a compromise by agreeing to reserve to themselves the exclusive role of co-chairs of the ICC, somewhat at the expense of UNESCO. The latter had to content itself to serving as the ICC "secretariat". Through substantial technical and financial engagement, the two countries secured prominent influence on Angkor, making sure that the other countries that had shown an interest in being directly involved there—Australia, the United States, and later India and China—would remain, at least for some time, on the margins.

The French and the Japanese governments provided support to UNESCO-related projects through various means. They funded the involvement of scientific organizations in the management of Angkor:

the École Française d'Extrême-Orient (EFEO) and Waseda University under the aegis of the newly created Japanese Governmental Team for Safeguarding Angkor.[14] For the EFEO, this involvement represented the opportunity to regain footing on the site for which, to a large extent, the colonial Gouvernement général de l'Indochine had originally created the EFEO in 1901. The EFEO's institutional legitimacy, including vis-à-vis French state authorities, was largely owed to its stewardship of the Angkor Park starting in 1907. It had continued to serve as sole "guardian" of the park until 1973, when its last member was forced to leave the war-torn area (Peycam 2010, p. 2).[15]

The two governments also provided money to the World Heritage Fund to support the regular activities of the States Parties throughout the world, a necessary step to ensure the recognition of their prominent position on the international stage. In 1997, the French government signed the first bilateral agreement with UNESCO in the field of safeguarding heritage (UNESCO 1992–2013a, p. 1). This agreement created a trust fund of 3.7 million euros to be spent over the course of ten years. It supported nearly a hundred projects in fifty different countries. France and Japan, also together, established a trust fund at UNESCO for undertaking specific projects in Angkor. The Japanese government favoured this option, as it had as early as 1989 chosen to take the lead in the management of all World Heritage Sites in Asia. Japan thereafter provided the biggest "Funds-in-Trust" ever committed to UNESCO, of which Angkor became from 1993 onward the main recipient as measured by capital, number of projects and consultants.[16] Nearly twenty-five million US dollars were invested in Cambodia between 1989 and 2004 from a total budget of fifty million dollars (MoFA [Japan] 2011, p. 1).[17]

A fundamental divergence between the two government aid programmes became apparent when it came to providing assistance in areas beyond the preservation of the monuments. For the Japanese, the UNESCO/ICC/APSARA institutional mechanism was meant primarily to facilitate heritage conservation projects, while other types of cooperation would require different structures of collaboration and involve other Cambodian agencies. The French government, by contrast, aimed to use the mechanism to enforce a unifying and centralized strategy through the reinforcement of APSARA.

A consultant—a chief counsellor at the powerful French Cour des Comptes (Court of Auditors), Jean-Yves Rossi—designed APSARA in 1993 on the model of French public establishments (Rossi 1993). The idea was to structure an administrative agency capable of concentrating a wide array of socio-economic competencies traditionally handled by national-level ministries and the provincial government.[18] This conception explains the "region of Angkor" in APSARA's name.[19] APSARA was supposed to be financially and administratively independent, so that it could exert sole management of different kinds of projects through specialized departments (UNESCO and ICC-Angkor 1993, p. 68).[20] The Agence française de développement (AFD, formerly the Caisse française de développement) and the Special Priority Fund for Angkor provided French assistance to projects led by APSARA. Between 2000 and 2009, that latter fund accumulated six million euros received from the French Ministries of Foreign Affairs, of the Interior and of Research (Angkorvat 2015, p. 1). With hindsight, the French strategy of providing exclusive support to APSARA appears to have been an attempt to circumscribe the management of Angkor from potential interference, especially from elements in the Cambodian government that France did not trust. This strategy gave the impression that France wanted to maintain a substantial foreign influence over the site—in effect perpetuating the model that it obtained following Cambodia's formal independence in 1953, when Angkor remained under the direct management of a "foreign" entity, the EFEO.[21]

This concentration of French aid and prerogatives in one institution contrasted with the strategy pursued by Japan, which instead sought to liaise with different national institutions in the regular Cambodian government. Japan made investments simultaneously through Cambodian ministries and their provincial delegations and through Siem Reap Province. The contests for power within these institutions during the years after 1993 in which the two main parties shared political power meant that they remained weak. Although it is hard to assert that the mode of collaboration followed by Japanese cooperation programmes at Angkor amounted to a grand vision dedicated to reinforcing the Cambodian state, it was in its essence more in keeping with the nation-building process agreed upon in 1991 than the approach taken by France. The strategy of working with a diversified set of institutions also reflected the relative caution of the Japanese government, which sought to avoid appearing to invest exclusively in one Cambodian political faction over another. The existence of APSARA as a new legal entity indeed encouraged tensions among Cambodian state authorities in a country in which the whole administrative apparatus remained weak and where political allegiances

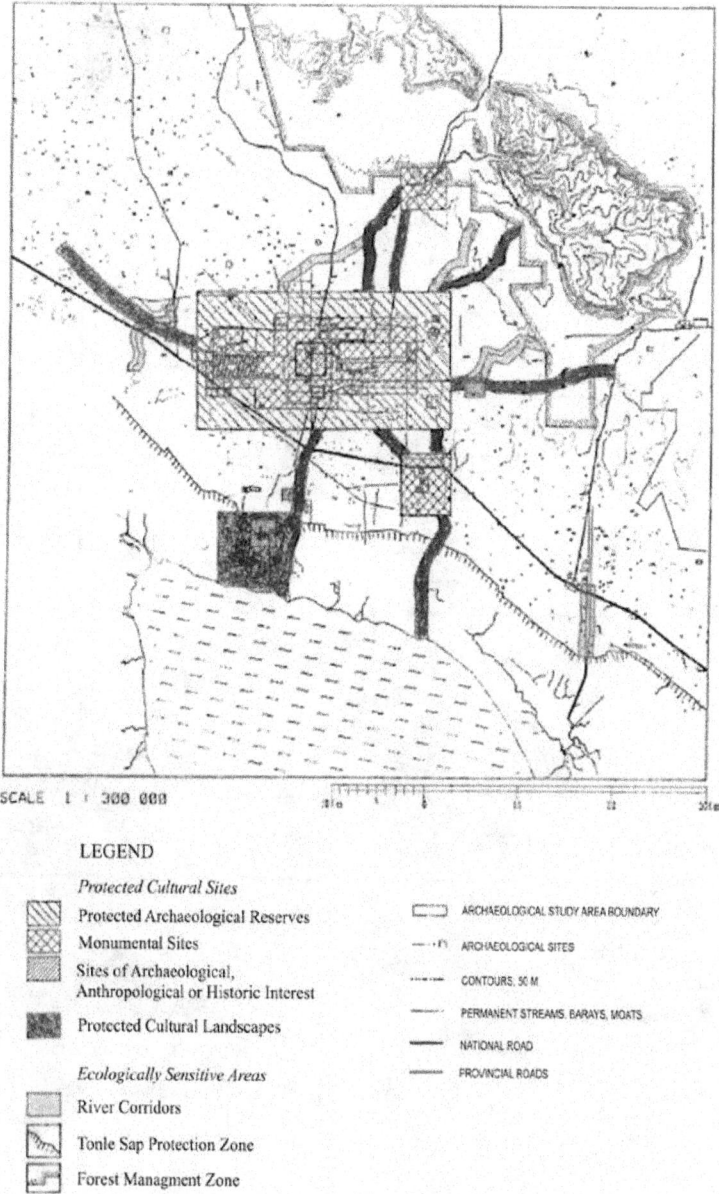

SCALE 1 : 300 000

LEGEND

Protected Cultural Sites

Protected Archaeological Reserves

Monumental Sites

Sites of Archaeological,
Anthropological or Historic Interest

Protected Cultural Landscapes

Ecologically Sensitive Areas

River Corridors

Tonle Sap Protection Zone

Forest Managment Zone

ARCHAEOLOGICAL STUDY AREA BOUNDARY

ARCHAEOLOGICAL SITES

CONTOURS, 50 M

PERMANENT STREAMS, BARAYS, MOATS

NATIONAL ROAD

PROVINCIAL ROADS

FIGURE 4.1 Proposed Zones in the Siem Reap–Angkor Region. Zoning and Environmental Management Plan for the Angkor region, 1994. ©ICOMOS Documentation Centre. Reproduced with kind permission.

SCALE 1 : 150 000

LEGEND

Protected Cultural Sites

Protected Archaeological Reserves

Monumental Sites

Sites of Archaeological,
Anthropological or Historic Interest

Urban Development Zones

Urban Conservation Zones

Urban Expansion Zones

Tourist Development Zones

- - - -   Proposed Road Corridors

FIGURE 4.2 Proposed Zones in the Siem Reap–Angkor Region. Zoning and Environmental Management Plan for the Angkor region, 1994. ©ICOMOS Documentation Centre. Reproduced with kind permission.

were divided.[22] APSARA's central position inevitably attracted the attention of Cambodia's political elite. Simultaneously, as its sphere of jurisdiction overlapped with the competencies of the Cambodian ministries and provinces, the French and the Japanese cooperation programmes found themselves at odds at the same time that their governments shared the presidency of the ICC.

French Cooperation at Angkor: The Failures of an Over-Centralized Management Plan

In this section, I will first show how the policy initiated by the French cooperation programme which exclusively supported the model whereby a super-agency like APSARA provided overall management of the site proved operationally difficult to achieve. France's state centralism certainly helped pave the way for the eventual takeover of Angkor and all the economic and political functions associated with the site by the Cambodian People's Party (CPP).

At the beginning of the 1990s, the ICC's and consultants' reports often mentioned the "region of Angkor" as the jurisdiction to be managed by the ICC. They defined this region as the Angkor Park and those parts of its surroundings likely to be affected by tourism and subsequent urban development.[23] Architect Vann Molyvann, one of the leading figures in international cooperation initiatives at the time and a minister in the newly established Cambodian government, promoted the first planning proposal for the Angkor region, which he had developed before the World Heritage listing. He defined the "Angkor region" as a broad territory that stretched from the Kulen Mountains in the north to the Tonlé Sap Lake in the south and as an area that should be managed through a comprehensive plan.

> It is necessary to delimit zones and management areas which, always responding to the needs of the monuments, also recognize existing forms of land use and land cover. (Vann Molyvann 1991, p. 74)

A team of twenty-five UNESCO-sanctioned experts endorsed this vision. Between 1993 and 1994, the team carried out a comprehensive study, finalized as the Zoning and Environmental Management Plan (ZEMP 1993),[24] in which the team members considered different aspects of the management of a "region" of ten thousand square metres. Later, another team of French experts, supported by the AFD, adopted a similar conception of a comprehensive plan at the scale of the region lying between the mountains and the lake. Their Urban Reference Plan (ARTE-BCEOM 1995) developed this approach to envision three poles of development for the region: the Angkor Park, Siem Reap town, and a "Hotel Zone" (Cité Hôtelière), in which large-scale tourist infrastructure would be built. The same year, four French teams wrote a tourism management plan (Détente, GIE, Score and Villes Nouvelles 1995) which aimed at controlling the flow of visitors in the region.

According to the Urban Reference Plan and the Tourism Management Plan, Siem Reap was to be protected from large-scale projects. Prior to the colonial era, the town, while originally a Thai administrative outpost, was just a collection of villages stretching along the river. These villages were made up of wooden houses on stilts gathered around pagodas surrounded by lush vegetation. In the 1920s and the 1930s, the French Protectorate built the commercial and administrative core of Siem Reap Province—its new provincial capital. The Grand Hôtel d'Angkor, opened in 1929, welcomed the first high-end tourists to Angkor. After Cambodia's independence in 1953, the urban development of Siem Reap slowed except for a few improvements carried out around the colonial centre. The war and raids by the Khmer Rouge—who eventually occupied and then emptied the town in 1975—both interrupted development. Following the Vietnamese occupation of Cambodia between 1979 and 1989, Siem Reap resumed its expansion towards the east with the building of shop houses leading to a new marketplace, the Phsar Leu. These developments did not compromise the village-style vernacular architecture or the integrity of neighbourhoods built during the colonial period (Hétreau-Pottier 2008, pp. 1–7).

First ZEMP and later the AFD-supported Urban Reference Plan aimed at preservation of the town's urban core and its landscape. Urban extensions were only to be permitted in the southeastern part of the town, while the western side would remain in agricultural use. New neighbourhoods would maintain low population density, with dense vegetation and open hydraulic infrastructure, and conservation measures would be adopted to preserve the historical centre and the wooden buildings scattered along the river. A large canal would delimit the Angkor Park on its southern side and a forest zone would be planted between the park and the city to mark the visible limits of urbanization. Large hotels and other tourist facilities were to be constructed in the "Hotel Zone" established on a land reserve of five hundred hectares, with the possibility of its extension by up to one thousand more hectares if the hotel developers' demands increased. Local wooden houses in their natural, village-like environment would inspire these hotels. New roads were to connect the tourist enclave directly to the Siem Reap airport, to the town of Siem Reap and of course to the World Heritage Site (ARTE-BCEOM 1995; Détente, GIE, Score and Villes Nouvelles 1995).

To ensure consistency, the plans prescribed a set of regulations for land use, infrastructure, and transport management, to be implemented through a centralized approach. Public land ownership and control over private land use were two major prerogatives of APSARA. The newly created authority's Department of Urban Development was meant to exercise exclusive prerogative over them. The French cooperation programme assisted APSARA technically and financially. With Vann Molyvann at the helm of APSARA, it benefitted from King Norodom Sihanouk's tacit support.[25] Conceived by French consultants and defended by Cambodian civil servants, this urban vision did not, however, include any provision for taking the views of the local population into account. Their voices proved missing from the whole enterprise.

Implementation of this visionary albeit technocratic French plan was impossible. Institutional and political conflicts, especially APSARA's increasing inability to exert its authority against initiatives taken by those holding power in Phnom Penh, were the reason. While APSARA was in principle charged with regulation of the management of the "Angkor region", other Cambodian governmental bodies—the Ministry of Land Management, Urban Planning, and Construction; its provincial delegations; and provincial authorities—continued to deliver construction permits and to manage transactions involving public land in Siem Reap. One particular blow was Prime Minister Hun Sen's donation in 1998 of a plot of land located on the path reserved by APSARA to connect the "Hotel Zone" to the airport (Richner 2013, p. 1). On the initiative of the minister of commerce, a concession was issued to build a third children's hospital in Siem Reap on this plot, near the temples of Angkor. The Swiss Agency for Development and Cooperation funded this project (Burnand 2013, p. 1). On numerous other occasions, the provincial authorities, under the leadership of a governor from the royalist FUNCINPEC party, issued building permits for hotels in the middle of the allegedly protected Siem Reap town. Events like these effectively decreased the attractiveness of the

"Hotel Zone" in the eyes of investors, who chose instead to build facilities in the immediate vicinity of the town centre or along the airport road.[26]

One can technically attribute these gross contraventions of plans advanced by the "international community" through the ICC to the "overlapping competencies" of Cambodian authorities and APSARA. In political terms, conflicts over land ownership and urban planning mirrored broader and deeper developments in Cambodia. The first post-UNTAC elections in 1993 inaugurated the clumsy bipartite government co-headed by the FUNCIPEC and the CPP, the former Communist Party, with Norodom Ranariddh and Hun Sen as the country's two prime ministers. This unstable situation masked the effective surrender of the "international community" to the CPP (Springer 2010, p. 73), which, despite having lost the election, maintained its effective control of all the strategic attributes of state power in the new political configuration.

In the province of Siem Reap, Cambodian authorities were split between representatives affiliated to the two parties. APSARA head Vann Molyvann, one of the protagonists in the debates held on the ICC and officially a member of the CPP, owed his true allegiances to the ailing King Sihanouk and to the representatives of the "international community". When the bipartite government fell apart in 1997, and the CPP asserted its supreme power on the national political scene, the overall system imagined by the French cooperation programme to wall Angkor off from political intrigue in Phnom Penh confronted failure. Cambodian authorities gained prominence, and the delivery of building permits increased. Appetites were sharpened when, starting in 1999, contributions to APSARA from Sokha Hotel Limited, a private company close to the CPP to which the Cambodian government entrusted the ticket concession for the Angkor Park, linked its budget directly to ticket revenues.[27] The deal required the company to pay a flat fee of one million US dollars annually to the government in exchange for the right to control the ticket concession; the government would then redistribute only 15 per cent of that sum to APSARA. Whatever money Sokha received in excess of the amount agreed upon was pure profit for the company. This arrangement, though revised in favour of APSARA in 2000, amounted to the effective privatization of the World Heritage Site.[28] Neither the ICC nor APSARA participated in any public debate or received any warning prior to this major change in what was an even more striking blow to the "international community". Two years later, a decree from the prime minister's office abruptly dismissed Vann Molyvann as head of APSARA,[29] in a move that completed the effective takeover of all important operations in Angkor by the faction in power in Phnom Penh and the overall privatization of the site.[30] We cannot blame the French cooperation programme, UNESCO or the ICC for these political convulsions or for the development of a phenomenon of "shadow state politics" at the top of Cambodia's power structure.[31] French insistence on supporting an unaccountable "state-within-a-state" organization like APSARA at the expense of a broader set of national institutions, was, however, at the core of the problem. A fundamental inability to conceive of a mechanism in which local authorities and representatives of local communities could from the outset actively participate in and share management of the region contributed greatly to the excessive bureaucratization and "elite capture" that ultimately occurred at Angkor.[32] I turn next to the approach to cooperation at Angkor pursued by Japan, the other co-president of the ICC.

Japanese Cooperation in Angkor: The Limits of Segmented Aid

While the French cooperation programme in Siem Reap invested a great deal of energy and money in assisting APSARA, which it sought to create in its own state-building image, Japan chose instead to adopt a strategy of cooperation in which it spread its investments among a range of different Cambodian institutions, including APSARA. This policy reflects in part the realities of a Japanese institutional system that involves nineteen ministries and governmental agencies in the management of international assistance (Blaise 2006, pp. 318–20). Nevertheless, in Siem Reap Province, the Japanese cooperation programme mainly operates through the Japan International Cooperation Agency (JICA) (Akagawa 2015, pp. 83–92), which has been responsible for a number of projects related to spatial planning in the province.

It is necessary to consider Japanese cooperation at Angkor, like its French counterpart, in a context broader than that of the heritage site itself. For that cooperation works hand-in-hand with Japanese economic interests, as represented by infrastructure development firms. It functions as a more utilitarian strategy in the service of Japan's economic and political interests in Southeast Asia than does French cooperation.[33] Another aim of Japanese cooperation at Angkor is the intentional display to regional and international tourists flocking to Angkor of the benevolence of Japan's role in Southeast Asia, a region that in the early 1990s still remembered Japan's military involvement half a century earlier.[34]

As of the end of 2006, Japan had invested about thirteen million US dollars in the improvement of National Highway 6, from the Siem Reap airport to the southern archaeological site of Roluos (JICA 2006). It had also provided nearly twenty-one million dollars in assistance for the expansion of the Siem Reap urban area's electricity facilities (JICA 2006). In 2004, it had improved the infrastructure supplying water to parts of Siem Reap, with two grants totalling two million dollars (JICA 2006). Between 2005 and 2006, JICA conducted a multisectoral study in order to create a master plan for the whole Siem Reap–Angkor region (JICA 2006). More recently, in 2012 JICA signed an official development assistance loan agreement with the Kingdom of Cambodia for the improvement of the water supply system for the whole city of Siem Reap (JICA 2012 and 2013b). The Japanese government also provided an additional grant of 7.161 million yen, or some 89.7 million US dollars, to build infrastructure and to assist the Siem Reap Water Supply Authority in increasing its management capacities (JICA 2012). The Cambodian counterparts for these projects included the Ministry of Public Works and Transport, the Siem Reap Water Supply Authority, and the provincial authorities.

These projects reveal two of the main priorities of Japanese cooperation: first, a concentration on investments in the water and transportation infrastructure sectors and, second, collaboration with national- and local-government authorities. These investments are generally developed in partnership with Japanese companies.[35] Involving a heritage site or not, this strategy follows the general development framework of Japanese official development assistance in Southeast Asia. It seeks to equip recipient countries with infrastructure that favours their long-term economic development. It also seeks to transfer knowledge and capacity in management to local people and governments (Blaise 2006, pp. 320–21). In general, this strategy has received a positive response from Cambodians, as the infrastructure projects have been realized.[36]

In regards to urban planning, JICA regularly appointed volunteers and consultants to Cambodian institutions. A consultant was originally attached to the provincial government to oversee the implementation of the master plan developed by the agency. The consultant's stated duties included "raising the awareness of the provincial and ministerial authorities concerning the master plan, looking for funding, and coordinating the realization of different projects scheduled by JICA's study".[37] Surprisingly, the consultant's name rarely appeared in ICC meeting minutes. Nor was he conspicuous for his visibility at public events organized by the various NGOs and other international organizations operating in Siem Riep. In 2006, JICA began to appoint "volunteer advisors" to work at APSARA's Department of Urban Development. Their official objective was to develop the skills of the local staff and ensure the implementation of specific projects developed in partnership with APSARA.[38] Eventually, it moved the work of implementing the master plan from the Siem Reap provincial administration to APSARA, as it regarded the latter as a better strategic counterpart for the project.[39]

In comparison with the French cooperation programme, JICA's strategy consisted of distributing aid to several Cambodian authorities, including APSARA and the provincial administration. Japanese cooperation initiatives sought to adapt to the confusing Cambodian politico-administrative landscape. While Japanese consultants were involved in producing overall studies of Siem Reap based on extensive data collection, JICA's representatives tried to mould their actions into the Cambodian institutional quagmire, marked by the overlap of competencies that existed among different institutions. This strategy aimed at coordinating the various planning efforts among these institutions, especially the provincial government and APSARA, as both have continued to claim responsibility for urban development under Cambodian legislation.[40]

More pragmatic in its operational capacity to deal with Cambodian political practices than its French counterpart, the Japanese strategy appeared nonetheless devoid of a clear vision for the "Angkor region". From 2000, for example, the idea of an overall management plan gave way to a fragmentation of JICA's aid, henceforth directed towards one-off projects (JICA 2013b). Yet Japan's impact on the overall development of the province, and especially the urban zone of Siem Reap, was undeniable. Moreover, given the change in the political and economic landscape of Cambodia after 1997, the Japanese approach avoided the kind of setback that the French cooperation programme, with its unconditional support for APSARA, experienced. This is not to say, however, that the Japanese programme could operate with freedom from centrifugal interests, whether in the form of investors close to the Phnom Penh government or of members of the Cambodian political elite. Japanese cooperation was no more capable of mitigating the influence of the CPP and its myriad ancillary interests than was its French counterpart. And, engulfed in the arcana of Cambodian administrative politics, it too failed to engage in any form of interaction with the members of the local community.

In fact, far from succeeding in asserting their independent influence in Cambodia, the two foreign cooperation programmes learned to negotiate new roles with national authorities while abandoning their original ambition of shaping a coherent management vision for the region. They sought never to embarrass the Cambodian authorities through their actions and their agenda. Nor did they seek to encourage transparency. Facing severe budgetary constraints, the French cooperation programme at the end of the 2000s kept its focus on projects essentially managed by the CPP-dominated APSARA while seeking to preserve some important economic interests in the area.[41] The Japanese cooperation programme for its part also suffered from reductions in funding in the wake of the global economic downturn, though its resources increased again after 2010 (Nam Pan 2014, pp. 13–14 and 17–18). It nonetheless continued to operate through its original diversified public-private partnership model, but now in closer coordination with APSARA and the prime minister's circles.

The ICC at Angkor: An Arena of States' Legitimation

The difference in their manner of operations notwithstanding, French and Japanese cooperation strategies at Angkor have had in common a fundamentally technocratic and elitist approach to development. Their projects were never viewed as accountable to a genuinely open "peer-reviewed" international forum or as involving members of the communities whose interests they claimed to serve. The two programmes were fast to overcome early and contradictory strategies in order effectively to consolidate their influence on the ICC into a tripartite arrangement made up of France, Japan and UNESCO and capable of keeping at bay potential competitors.[42] France's and Japan's early adherence to the ICC model demonstrated a common desire to maintain a visibly dominant position in the area of cultural heritage, something that they needed to cultivate by working ever more closely with Cambodia's centre of power. The ensuing configuration of power at Angkor has thus led to a "sanctuarization" of the ICC, above and beyond the reach of members of the local community. The overbearing influence of the Cambodian government and the interests of the circles that supported it was the main reason for this trend, one closely related to that government's authoritarian approach to politics. Over the years, ICC meetings became more and more hermetically sealed off from the participation of members that had not been co-opted, let alone that of members of the communities in the region. The co-chairs' offices tightly controlled the invitation process, normally handled by UNESCO in Phnom Penh.

This increased disconnection from the social reality of Siem Reap Province and, beyond that, from the whole of Cambodian society, was perhaps most clearly displayed on the occasion of a 2008 event organized by the Center for Khmer Studies, the Getty Conservation Institute, the Pacific Rim Council on Urban Development (PRCUD) and the École Nationale Supérieure d'Architecture de Paris-Belleville, in collaboration with APSARA's Urban Development Department and Siem Reap Province. The meeting on "Urban Development in the Shadows of Angkor" brought international scholars and practitioners in the field of urban studies together with representatives from different strands of Siem Reap society. The latter ranged from Buddhist monks, NGO workers and schoolchildren to members of the local business community, investors, members of women's organizations and others. UNESCO representatives and the members of the two state cooperation programmes duly ignored this event, with the exception of the JICA representative, who attended it in its entirety. The inclusive character of the meeting radically contradicted the ICC's top-down model while highlighting the committee's fundamental shortcomings with regard to democratic representation (Rabé 2008, pp. 10–11).

The fortunes and misfortunes of the Japanese and French cooperation programmes in their encounters with Cambodian political forces at play may help us to appreciate the extent to which these programmes, together with UNESCO and the Cambodian political and economic elite, shared a common interest in seeking to maintain the institutional status quo represented by the ICC-UNESCO-APSARA triangle. In fact, all these institutional partners, Cambodian and foreign, found in the ICC a useful mechanism for legitimating their roles and policies. Even after readjusting their power-sharing arrangements, the French, Japanese and Cambodian states have continued to promote the ICC, while clinging to an outdated ceremonial apparatus in which France and Japan preside over every event and the representatives of the Cambodian government are positioned—in terms of protocol and in the spatial organization of the meetings—as at the receiving end of foreign benevolence.[43]

What remains to be asked is whether an International Coordination Committee for the Safeguarding and Development of the Historic Site of Angkor retains any operational usefulness. The answer is again disappointing. Even in the case of projects presented at meetings of the ICC, decisions were typically taken behind closed doors. In most cases the committee was not concerned with projects promoted by Cambodian and foreign investors, even if they were likely dramatically to affect the Angkor region. Many examples illustrate this determination (not) to take decisions. One is the controversial Angkor National Museum, which opened in Siem Reap in 2007. The promoter of the "museum", a Thai company called Vilailuk International Holdings, secured a build-cooperate-transfer contract from APSARA and the Cambodian Ministry of Culture.[44] It rented archaeological pieces from the old Angkor Conservation Office, an institution set up during the French Protectorate, and displayed them in a massive building erected for the purpose. As it operates today, this museum offers a simplified reading of Cambodian history and presents archaeological remains in exhibition spaces located next to shopping areas. With Hun Sen's daughter as its first chairwoman, and despite its potential importance for Angkor, the project simply did not come before ICC meetings (Barton 2007). The ICC was again absent when a new harbour was built on the Tonlé Sap. In 2004, a project funded by the Asian Development Bank (ADB) was abruptly abandoned when the Council for the Development of Cambodia (CDC),[45] the country's highest decision-making agency for the promotion of private- and public-sector investments, issued a fifty-hectare land concession to a Korean company, the Sou Ching Group. The company exploited the results of the study conducted by the ADB while evicting at least three hundred fishing families, damaging the unique landscape with new concrete docks, and taking control over the tourist circuits previously managed by the villagers (Barton and Sokha Cheang 2007). A third and last example of the ICC's powerlessness is the failure of the Hotel Zone project mentioned above. While the Hotel Zone was discussed many times in the early days of the ICC and even a land reserve of 378 hectares was established and three million dollars spent to acquire land, APSARA never implemented the project. To this day, the APSARA headquarters, a Korean-funded convention centre, a museum of Asian textiles funded by the Indian cooperation programme, and a small private "museum" funded by Tokyo's Sophia University are the only facilities built on this vast otherwise empty area.

In the most important cases therefore, the ICC either endorsed decisions taken by Cambodian authorities or else chose to ignore them, especially when a risk of embarrassing the Cambodian leaders existed. It did not seek to operate as an independent public advocacy forum that could offer transparency and promote the standards that it set out to uphold. Faced with such a series of blatant failures, proponents of the ICC chose to circumvent criticism by redefining its primary objectives. As early as the committee's tenth anniversary, the 2003 Angkor conference unveiled a new ICC strategy, under the theme of "sustainable development" (UNESCO 2010a, p. 32). Discussions at the conference focused on the extent to which future projects in the region should comply with the new objective. The same gathering also rededicated the first decade of "international cooperation" a posteriori to the restoration of archaeological heritage. One may interpret the ICC's notion of "sustainability" in many ways. Its vague and non-committal nature means that almost any project might be said to satisfy this aim.

In the case of management of the Angkor region, the ICC acts primarily as a space in which foreign states and their UNESCO "facilitators" can claim a commonality of goals in order to legitimize their presence and involvement. From the Cambodian government's perspective, it serves as evidence of the capacity of national institutions to work with foreign stakeholders and to interact with them as peers rather than as the assisted party, provided that no major decisions or operations are openly debated.[46] To survive in Cambodia, the ICC has thus been condemned to serve as an official legitimator for the power in place and its shadowy state practices. The existence of the committee, as a UNESCO-derived entity, somehow reflects the degree of its "usefulness" to the "host" government. In its "international" expression, what will be interesting is whether the ICC will succeed in including more foreign states in its leadership or whether France and Japan will seek to perpetuate their exclusive stewardship.[47] More critical perhaps is the fact that the ICC has to this day remained sealed off from the views and aspirations of local communities in Siem Reap. This original weakness has arguably led to its political instrumentalization and ineffectiveness.[48]

The Angkor ICC: A Model for Replication?

That the ICC model had failed to deliver on its promises in Cambodia has not inhibited UNESCO from boasting about its "success" at Angkor, as in Director General Matsuura Koichiro's speech on the occasion of the tenth anniversary of the ICC for Angkor.

> The unanimously recognized success of the Angkor programme is due to a great extent to the wisdom and far-sighted commitment of His Majesty King Norodom Sihanouk and to the remarkable efforts of his government, resolutely supported by the international community. (Matsuura 2002, p. 8)

The anniversary fell at a time of international unease regarding the aggressive policy pursued by the United States following the 11 September 2001 attacks, a time when France opposed the American invasion of Iraq at the UN Security Council. Determination to encourage the United States to forsake its military unilateralism in favour of a more peaceful inter-state multilateralism characterized the prevailing mood. This mood coincided with the willingness of the US administration to rejoin UNESCO, a move hastened following the sacking of the National Museum in Baghdad and other embarrassing news from Iraq and Afghanistan.[49] UNESCO and its French and Japanese supporters advanced the ICC model as the one that the Americans should use in the areas controlled by their army and beyond.[50] Once again, Japan and France sought to use the Angkor ICC model to promote their international approach as an example of true intercultural dialogue. Because of its "success", the ICC model should be replicated in other endangered heritage sites, as stated in the Paris Declaration.

> We [the international community] are happy to observe that the international mechanism for cooperation which was shown to work for the knowledge, the conservation, and the development of Angkor ... is used as reference for similar actions engaged throughout the world. (UNESCO 2003b, art. 16)

UNESCO thereafter re-employed the name "International Coordination Committee" at other national cultural heritages sites—in Afghanistan (UNESCO 2003a), Iraq (UNESCO 2004) and Haiti (UNESCO 2010).[51]

It exported, that is, the Angkor model beyond Cambodia's borders. It would be interesting to assess the functioning, nature and outcome of these duplications.[52]

As this article demonstrates, in the case of Angkor the claim of ICC "success" is fundamentally flawed, undermined by the committee's original lack of accountability and its subsequent irrelevance as anything but an entity operating in the service of its main nation-state sponsors. The ICC will remain ineffective if politically and economically charged aspects of the management of a major heritage site like Angkor remain excluded from public discussions. It is moreover essential for those involved in heritage management to recognize that no long-term heritage management policy can function properly without the inclusion in processes of debate of local communities and their various components from the outset. This is especially true when the programmes discussed will affect the lives of people living in those communities. What is suggested is a more inclusive participatory model of local community involvement, based on democracy as public space, with special care devoted to the inclusion of hitherto marginalized groups. This suggestion follows Hadenius and Uggla, who write that a civil society

> (a) denotes a certain area of society which is (b) dominated by interactions of a certain kind. The area in question is the public space between the state [or state organizations] and the individual citizen. (Hadenius and Uggla 1996, p. 1621)

To realize this sort of space at Angkor, ICC meetings should be open to the public and to the national media. They should include representatives of the local community, and proceedings should at least either be conducted or made accessible in the Khmer language. In the absence of elected local institutions, as is still the case in Siem Reap–Angkor, the ICC should invite representatives of Buddhist monasteries, small and medium local business owners, neighbourhood organizations, schools, universities and local NGOs to take part in its meetings.[53] Relatively simple modes of inclusion in the deliberative process over management of the World Heritage Site, accompanied by more systematic introduction of participatory engagement at different levels of intervention, would make possible a new model of *"negotiating* conservation", as advocated by Miura. This model may ultimately justify and legitimate the continuation of an international-national, global-local hybrid mode of governance for the World Heritage Site of Angkor–Siem Reap (Miura 2010, p. 105).

The objective of this article is not to advocate the complete abandonment of the ICC experiment. In spite of its structural lack of representation, the idea of an inclusive and diverse platform in a fragmented society still coping with the aftermath of decades of civil conflict is something that is worth keeping. And it is true that, despite the unmonitored nature of the ICC, it has taken a number of positive policy measures, particularly when its members agreed to focus on emergency conservation actions. The measures have ranged from multiple technical-training schemes for Cambodian staff of APSARA to the effective end of mass looting in the temple area and the avoidance of construction within the archaeological park itself. These important achievements, dating from the early years of the ICC's operation, helped protect the temples from very real risks immediately after the end of UNTAC.

The issue with the ICC goes, however, beyond these accomplishments. For the promise of a culture of dialogue among people of different cultural and professional backgrounds should compel it to maintain a high ethical standard of governance. It is this potential to serve as an open platform for a shared coordination process that has largely been spoilt at Angkor. Genuine international and intercultural cooperation could be an effective factor in local development, if marked by inclusiveness and transparency. It could admit and accept the reality that multiple visions exist and should be in conversation, including those visions emanating from the community of local inhabitants and institutional elements that make up local "civil society". Only then could an international platform like the ICC be in a position to mediate and mitigate conflicts inherently associated with the management of heritage sites in areas where people actually live. This is the sole sure way to guarantee the long-term sustainability of these sites beyond power games and self-serving rhetoric.[54] Can states—and UNESCO—be expected to implement these changes?

Acknowledgements

I wish to thank my colleague Adèle Esposito and two anonymous reviewers for their extremely valuable contributions to my writing of this article. I also want to thank Michael Montesano for his persistent encouragement and critical comments.

Notes

1. Given the technocratic nature of the World Heritage listing process, I use the term "stakeholder", which I define as a person, a group, an organization

or a member or system that affects or can be affected by an organization's actions.

2. Words like "campaign", "mission" and "expedition"—used regularly by cultural bureaucrats and other heritage "experts" to describe conservation activities, not least under UNESCO auspices—remind me, an historian of colonialism in the region, of the terms employed and postures practised by nineteenth-century European empire builders.

3. With the expression "spatial development", I make reference to the planning, land use, infrastructure and facilities of those projects.

4. Questions about UNESCO range from those relating to governance and bureaucracy to those relating to listing practices, global strategy and representation, politics of culture and rights and cultural economics, among others. For an extensive bibliography on the subject, see Meskell 2013, p. 484.

5. Some of these reports are available on UNESCO's website, at unesdoc.unesco. org/ulis. Older reports are conserved at APSARA's documentation centre in Siem Reap.

6. France signed the convention in 1975. Japan only did so in 1992, demonstrating the late interest of this country in incorporating UNESCO into its international diplomatic strategy.

7. A striking parallel with Angkor can be found in the case of the Egyptian monuments of Abu Simbel, where UNESCO's proclaimed internationalism masked a vivid competition between member states to display—in spectacular terms—their technical superiority in preservation. This competition unfolded in the wider geopolitical context of the ideological rivalry between the two Cold War camps. See Allias 2013, pp. 6–45. I thank one of the anonymous reviewers for pointing my way to this excellent article.

8. "The General Conference requests the Director General: art. 1 (b) to set up, in collaboration with the Cambodian authorities, the international mechanism that should ensure the proper conservation and development of the site of Angkor with the assistance of specialists of this site from different countries" ("à mettre en place, en collaboration avec les autorités cambodgiennes, le mécanisme international qui convient pour assurer la conservation et la mise en valeur du site d'Angkor avec l'assistance de specialistes de ce site ressortissants de divers pays").

9. The other three conditions were the establishment of a national protection agency (APSARA, established in 1995), the definition of buffer zones based on "a Zoning and Environmental Management Plan (ZEMP) project" (effective in 1994) and the establishment of an organ for "monitoring and coordination of the international conservation effort" (the ICC itself, set up in 1993) (UNESCO 1993, p. 22).

10. "France, whose history closely connects to Cambodia, holds a memory the

Cambodians and the international community will greatly need" ("*La France, que son histoire lie au Cambodge, est détentrice d'une mémoire dont les Cambodgiens et la communauté internationale auront grandement besoin*") (UNESCO 1993, p. 57). Educated in France and the recipient of numerous honours and awards from that country, the Congolese Lopes is a senior member of the official organization La Francophonie, which brings French-speaking countries together. He can be considered a close supporter of France's cultural influence in the world.

11. In his address at the 1993 Tokyo conference on Angkor, the head of the French delegation, Ministry of Foreign Affairs representative Serge Boidevaix stressed "France's contribution [to the safeguarding of Angkor, which] must be considered in the continuity of a history in which the friendship between the Cambodian and French people never faulted" ("*La contribution de la France s'inscrit dans la continuité d'une longue historire où l'amité des peoples cambodgiens et français ne s'est jamais démentie*") (UNESCO 1993, p. 43).

12. On the complexity of France's historical relations with Cambodia and the critical role that the French Protectorate played in moulding modern Cambodian nationalism, see Edwards (2007). I thank one of the reviewers for refining my reading of the Franco-Japanese deal on Angkor.

13. By acknowledging that there are no fixed criteria to judge the value and authenticity of cultural property, that it must rather be evaluated within the cultural context to which it belongs, the Nara Document on Authenticity invited contemporary heritage actors to undertake a reappraisal of monuments in the historical and religious contexts in which they were built. The Buddhist connection of the Bayon, though not formerly expressed by the Japanese conservation team, was clearly understood in this way by a number of external observers, including the author.

14. A Sophia University "mission" was also set up, though with a much smaller share of the Japanese government funds.

15. See also UNESCO (1993, p. 40) for reference to the long and deep connection between Angkor and the EFEO at the 1996 Tokyo conference.

16. This decision corresponds to the establishment by the Japanese government of a "Funds-in-Trust" to UNESCO to cover the whole Asia-Pacific region (Akagawa 2015, p. 108).

17. For a comprehensive list and description of the numerous Japanese projects under the UNESCO/Japan trust fund projects on "tangible heritage" in Angkor and in other countries, see MoFA (2003).

18. Although representatives of various ministries—Culture, Foreign Affairs, Finance, Tourism, Public Works and Transport—and the province of Siem Reap were included on a "Cultural National Council" chaired by the king, an unintended consequence of this plan was nonetheless to sideline these

latter institutions from directly operating in the area in question (UNESCO and ICC-Angkor 1993, pp. 65–66).

19. A member of the French delegation mentioned the precedent of the French "Coastal Conservatory" (*Conservatoire du littoral*) as an "*établissement public national à caractère administrative*" (national public establishment of an administrative nature) to a colleague of the author's. The main difference from APSARA, however, is that the Conservatoire is placed under the authority of a French ministry, that of protection of the natural environment. Its governance is also more democratic than that of APSARA, as local elected leaders sit on its board of trustees and have voting rights equal to those members appointed by the central administration.

20. The funds would have been generated through taxation of tourist activities under the management of a newly created autonomous "Angkor Tourism Agency" contracted to work with APSARA under the supervision of the same Cultural National Council, with the income to be handled by the tax authorities of the Ministry of Finance. The suggested allocation of this income was 12.5 per cent for APSARA, 10 per cent for the Angkor Tourism Agency, 5 per cent for a newly created Institute of Khmer Culture under the Cultural National Council, 10 per cent for the Angkor Conservatory under the Cultural National Council, 12.5 per cent for Siem Reap Province, and 50 per cent for the national general budget (UNESCO and ICC-Angkor 1993, p. 68).

21. We do not know the extent to which the French position was influenced by King Sihanouk's own strategy aimed at "sanctuarizing" Angkor and walling it off from Phnom Penh politics.

22. This was especially true during the period of power-sharing between the Cambodian People's Party (CPP) and the royalist FUNCIPEC, which formally ended only in 2008. (FUNCIPEC is the acronym for *Front uni national pour un Cambodge indépendant, neutre, pacifique, et coopératif*, or National United Front for an Independent, Neutral, Peaceful, and Cooperative Cambodia).

23. The Zoning and Environmental Master Plan used a broad definition of this region, as corresponding to the surface area of Siem Reap Province (ten thousand square kilometres) (ZEMP Team 1993).

24. ZEMP was funded by the United Nations Development Programme and the Swedish International Development Agency. It was executed by UNESCO on behalf of the Cambodian Ministry of Culture.

25. In his long careeer, Vann Molyvann (b. 1926) was always a faithful supporter of Prince/King Sihanouk. After studying architecture in France and becoming the first trained Cambodian architect, Vann Molyvann was appointed by Prince Sihanouk as head of public works and State Architect. He was the creator of most of the important urban and architectural landmarks in pre–Khmer Rouge independent Cambodia. In 1967, he was appointed minister of education.

When the Prince was deposed in 1970, Vann went into voluntary exile, to return to Cambodia only in 1992 and to follow King Sihanouk again (Peycam 2011, pp. 20–21).

26. The unpopularity of the Hotel Zone among investors was compounded by the resistance of farmers owning land in the zone to schemes of imposed land purchase, probably at low rates, carried out by APSARA.

27. The Sokha Hotel Group is a division of the Sokimex Group, Cambodia's first and largest petroleum company. It is owned by the Vietnamese-Cambodian Sok Kong. It has close dealings with the ruling CPP. Together with Kampuchea Tela, owned by Hun Sen's family, Sokimex has monopolized Cambodian government contracts (Kay Kimsong and Ten Kate 2004; Sovan Nguon 2010). The Cambodian opposition has long complained about the CPP-Sokimex connection (Cheng 2005).

28. In August 2000, the deal was revised so that 50 per cent of the first three million dollars raised should be handed over to the government, along with 70 per cent of total tickets sales beyond three million dollars. This put APSARA in a far better financial position (*Phnom Penh Post* 2000; Sokheng Vong and Marcher 2000; see also Miura 2010, p. 115). In 2015, the Cambodian government announced that Sokimex would withdraw from the management of tickets at Angkor and return the function to the Cambodian state (Kuch Naren 2015).

29. The decree, requested by Hun Sen on 31 May 2001 and signed by King Norodom Sihanouk on 2 June, did not give a reason for the dismissal, although Vann Molyvann afterwards invoked his refusal to agree on a number of construction permits (Kay Kimsong and Reed 2001). King Sihanouk reappointed Vann Molyvann "senior advisor of the Cambodian King", an honorary appointment with no effective influence in the management of Angkor. The leadership of APSARA was later entrusted to Vice Premier Sok An, Hun Sen's close partner in the CPP and the man in charge of all economically strategic national commissions. Sok An was made president director general of APSARA, while the director general's position was given to Bun Narith, the prime minister's brother-in-law.

30. The idea of giving a concession to a private company originated in the neoliberal agenda of the International Monetary Fund, whose regional representatives sat in on ICC meetings in the early 1990s. This was later confirmed by a government spokesman when announcing the end of the concession to Sokimex (Kuch Naren 2015). On numerous occasions, however, the fund expressed "its disagreement over the way the government refused to use competitive bidding in granting or extending any concession agreement" (International Monetary Fund 2005–13).

31. "Shadow state politics" refers to the system through which leaders draw authority from their ability to informally control markets and material rewards (Springer 2010, p. 31).

32. To this day, the town of Siem Reap, inhabited by nearly 200,000 residents, does not have an elected municipal government. In the absence of a democratic representative body, efforts should be made to include commune and district delegates as well as members from Buddhist monasteries, village and neighborhood associations, professional organizations, trade unions and local NGOs.

33. Established as an Incorporated Administrative Agency under the "Act of the Incorporated Administrative Agency – Japan International Cooperation Agency" (Act No. 136, 2002), JICA is now an autonomous entity which sets out "to contribute to the promotion of international cooperation as well as the sound development of the Japanese and global economy by supporting the socioeconomic development, recovery or economic stability of developing regions" (JICA 2013a). It was originally a semi-governmental organization under the Ministry of Foreign Affairs. In Cambodia, JICA contracts its infrastructure work to Japanese companies through a competitive process (Okolotowicz 1994; Khy Sovuthy and Bartlett 2012).

34. Japan's interest in Angkor—and, before it, in Borobodur in Indonesia—must be put in the larger perspective of the Japanese government's attempt to recast the country's image in Southeast Asia. From the late 1970s onward, Japanese authorities chose to place a new emphasis on "soft diplomacy" in the cultural field, as well as in official development assistance. This trend found its full expression with the country's partial bailout of UNESCO following the withdrawal of the United States as its most important financial contributor in 1984. Quite naturally, a professional Japanese diplomat, Matsuura Koichiro, was appointed in 1999 as the organization's director general. His tenure saw Japan play the role of Asia's champion of cultural heritage preservation (Akagawa 2015, pp. 79–114).

35. Recently, JICA has been more directly involved in the facilitation of Japanese companies' penetration into Cambodia. "Up to 60 new Japanese companies are expected to apply for business licenses this year after the number tripled to about 30 in 2011, according to the Japan International Cooperation Agency's Cambodia office (JICA), which has played a major role in attracting the businesses" (Weinland 2012).

36. The Asian Development Bank, together with JICA, developed water supply and sanitation facilities in Siem Reap town beginning in 1996 (ADB 2003, p. 13). The South Korean Ministry of Public Works and Transport, together with the Korean Eximbank, also assisted Cambodian authorities to develop a sewerage system in Siem Reap town (Korean Eximbank 2011–13).

37. Adèle Esposito interview with the JICA consultant Tetsuji Goto, August 2008, Siem Reap.
38. Ibid.
39. The provincial authorities have in turn put forward another planning instrument, the Statutory Zoning Plan, designed in 2010 by the provincial Department of Land Management, Urban Planning, and Construction, apparently in cooperation with APSARA. Adding to the confusing multilayered cooperation, the Siem Reap district authority formulated in 2007 a land use plan in partnership with the German Development Service DED (JICA, PACET Corporation and Nippon Koei Ltd. 2010).
40. The conflict between the two Cambodian institutions might have less to do with competition for influence between political factions than with the contradiction in the way that competencies were distributed following the creation of APSARA.
41. The AFD, for example, planned the construction of a drainage system in the eastern part of Siem Reap, which would be connected to similar infrastructure built by the ADB in the western part of the town. Since 1995, the French construction multinational Vinci has held the lucrative concession to run the Siem Reap International Airport. Together with concessions for the Phnom Penh and Sihanoukville international airports, this presence represents the largest French economic investment in the country.
42. Such exclusionary mechanisms were particularly visible in the field of conservation of monuments. When for instance the Indian government team ventured into the ICC fray in the mid-2000s over the restoration of the Ta Phrom temple, it became the focus of suspicious scrutiny and criticism essentially orchestrated by the UNESCO secretariat of the committee. Similarly, the secretariat sought to keep at a distance a US presence temporarily interested in playing a more active role during the tenure of Ambassador Charles Ray (2003–5). With regard to the Chinese cooperation programme, the French and the Japanese tried to minimize its role while refraining from criticizing its activities. Until the beginning of the 2010s, China's representatives kept to a low-key role at Angkor.
43. An essential reason for the success of the co-chairs in sustaining their influence on the ICC is the near lifelong appointment of a handful of UNESCO-sanctioned "experts" attached to the site since its World Heritage listing. Over the years the UNESCO committee of "ad hoc experts" to Angkor has been almost invariably composed of the same structural engineer from Italy, the same *Architecte des Monuments Historiques* from France and the same architectural historian from Japan (now deceased), all under the coordination of the same archaeologist—a former minister in Tunisia and a member of the French Institute. The current French director of the UNESCO office Phnom Penh, who holds a master's

degree in law and international relations, worked under that archaeologist in UNESCO's Division of Cultural Heritage starting in 1993 (Bokova 2010, p. 1). The power and influence of this established circle within the ICC lies in its capacity to bestow UNESCO's legitimacy on the different state actors, something not lost on Cambodia's political leaders.

44. The company's chief executive, Charoenrath Vilailuck [Charoenrat Wilailak], was known for his "acquisitive interest in Cambodia's patrimony as evidenced by his own large collection" (Turnbull 2008).

45. The prime minister chairs the council, which was established in 1994. It is composed of senior ministers and representatives of relevant government agencies.

46. When they arise, sensitive issues are dealt with between plenary sessions and technical committee meetings through quadripartite gatherings among representatives of UNESCO, the Cambodian government and the two co-chairs' delegations.

47. As of December 2015, the representatives of the French and Japanese governments continued to co-chair the ICC for Angkor.

48. A number of authors have addressed this fundamental shortcoming (see Peycam and Heikkila 2009; Miura 2004).

49. The United States effectively rejoined the organization in October 2003, in a gesture warmly received by the French government (Peterson and Pollack 2003, p. 123).

50. For instance, at the Third UNESCO Experts' Meeting on the Safeguarding of the Iraqi Cultural Heritage, held in Tokyo on 1 August 2003 and in the presence of a delegation of US experts, participants recognized "the need for an international coordinating committee to be established under the auspices of the future Government of Iraq and UNESCO, based on UNESCO's experience in coordinating international efforts for the rehabilitation of cultural heritage in post conflict situations". Mounir Bouchenaki, UNESCO assistant director-general for culture specifically presented Angkor as a precedent (UNESCO 2003c, pp. 8–9).

51. Each of these new ICCs has in turn developed its own modus operandi.

52. The press release announcing the creation of the ICC for Haiti introduces it as part of a larger group of such committees that includes those for Cambodia, Afghanistan and Iraq (UNESCO Media Services 2010).

53. One simply regrets, that in the course of the negotiations on World Heritage status for Angkor, UNESCO and its international mentors did not insist that the Cambodian government include, as a precondition to listing, the establishment of an elected mechanism—perhaps a municipality—to represent the people of Siem Reap and its close vicinity. This is, after all, the third-largest urban area in the country. It is not too late for representatives of the established

"international community" to encourage their Cambodian counterparts to envisage such institutional change.

54. In her preface to the report marking the twentieth anniversary of the ICC for Angkor, UNESCO Director-General Irina Bokova again hailed the international programme for Angkor as "a spectacular example of international solidarity". She went on to celebrate the new involvement of members of the local population in what she considered as "a laboratory spurred by the relationships between culture and sustainable tourism, of handicrafts and the full mobilization of the local communities towards the harmony and construction of a whole society". This reference to "full mobilization of the local communities" has not been substantiated by any concrete change in the deliberations held at ICC meetings (UNESCO and ICC-Angkor 2013).

References

Akagawa Natsuko. 2015. *Heritage Conservation in Japan's Cultural Diplomacy*. London: Routledge.

Allias, Lucia. 2013. "Integrities: The Salvage of Abu Simbel". *Grey Room* 50 (Winter): 6–45.

Angkorvat. 2015. "Sauvegarde, Restauration et Développement d'Angkor" [Safeguarding, restoration and development of Angkor]. http://www.angkorvat.com/Sauvegarde-Angkor.htm (accessed 15 August 2016).

ARTE-BCEOM. 1995. "Plan d'urbanisme de référence et projets prioritaires. Rapport définitif" [Reference urban plan and priority projects], vol. 3. Unpublished document.

Asian Development Bank (ADB). 2003. "Water Sector Roadmap. Kingdom of Cambodia". http://www.pacificwater.org/userfiles/file/IWRM/Toolboxes/planning%20process/Roadmap-CAMBODIA.pdf (accessed 15 August 2016).

Avieli, Nir. 2015. "The Rise and Fall (?) of Hoi An, a UNESCO World Heritage Site in Vietnam". *SOJOURN: Journal of Social Issues in Southeast Asia* 30, no. 1: 35–71.

Barton, Cat. 2007. "New Angkor Museum has Eight Galleries and a Sound Dome". *Phnom Penh Post*, 20 September 2007. http://www.phnompenhpost.com/siem-reap-insider/new-angkor-museum-has-eight-galleries-and-sound-dome (accessed 15 August 2016).

Barton, Cat, and Sokha Cheang. 2007. "Plan to Build New Siem Reap Port Stalled by Protests". *Phnom Penh Post*, 14 December 2007. http://www.phnompenhpost.com/siem-reap-insider/plan-build-new-siem-reap-port-stalled-protests (accessed 15 August 2016).

Berliner, David. 2012. "Multiple Nostalgias: The Fabric of Heritage in Luang Prabang (Lao PDR)". *Journal of the Royal Anthropological Institute* 18: 769–86.

Blaise, Séverine. 2006. "De l'aide à la coopération économique: pour un réexamen de la politique japonaise" [From aid to economic cooperation: Reassessing Japanese policy]. *Revue Tiers Monde* 186, no. 2: 307–28.

Bokova, Irina. 2010. "Head of the UNESCO Office in Phnom Penh (Cambodia)". *UNESCO.* http://unesdoc.unesco.org/images/0018/001894/189415E.pdf (accessed 15 August 2016).

Burnand, Frédéric. 2013. "Beat Richner, un acteur clé de la renaissance du Cambodge" [Beat Richner, a key actor in Cambodia's renaissance]. *Coopération Suisse.* http://www.swissinfo.ch/fre/coop%C3%A9ration-r%C3%A9ussie_beat-richner--un-acteur-cl%C3%A9-de-la-renaissance-du-cambodge/34817852 (accessed 15 August 2016).

Cheng, Derek. 2005. "Sokimex Negotiating Rights for Six More Temples". *Phnom Penh Post*, 11 March 2005. http://www.phnompenhpost.com/national/sokimex-negotiating-ticket-rights-six-more-temples (accessed 16 August 2016).

Détente, GIE, Score, and Villes Nouvelles. 1995. "Mission d'étude tourisme Angkor/Siem Reap. Rapport de phase 2 — document de travail" [Tourism study mission on Angkor/Siem Reap. Phase 2 report — working document], 2 vols. Unpublished document.

Edwards, Penny. 2007. *Cambodge: The Cultivation of a Nation.* Honolulu: University of Hawai'i Press.

Esposito, Adèle, and Sylvia Nam, eds. 2008. *Siem Reap. Urban Development in the Shadow of Angkor.* Los Angeles: The Getty Conservation Institute and Pacific Rim Council on Urban Development (PRCUD); Siem Reap: APSARA Authority and Center for Khmer Studies (CKS).

Hadenius, Axel, and Uggla, Fredrik. 1996. "Making Civil Society Work, Promoting Democratic Development: What Can States and Donors Do?" *World Development* 24: 1621–39.

Hauser-Shäublin, Brigitta, ed. 2011. *World Heritage Angkor and Beyond: Circumstances and Implications of UNESCO Listings in Cambodia.* Göttingen: Universitätsverlag, pp. 9–31.

Hétreau-Pottier, Aline. 2008. "The Urban Value of Siem Reap in the Angkor Region". In *Siem Reap. Urban Development in the Shadow of Angkor*, edited by Adèle Esposito and Sylvia Nam. Los Angeles: The Getty Conservation Institute and Pacific Rim Council on Urban Development; Siem Reap: APSARA Authority and Center for Khmer Studies (CKS).

Hitchcock, Michael, Victor T. King, and Michael Parnwell, eds. 2010. *Heritage Tourism in Southeast Asia.* Copenhagen: NIAS.

International Council on Monuments and Sites (ICOMOS). 1994. "The Athens Charter for the Restoration of Historic Monuments — 1931". n.d. http://www.icomos.org/en/charters-and-texts/179-articles-en-francais/ressources/charters-and-standards/167-the-athens-charter-for-the-restoration-of-historic-monuments (accessed 16 August 2016).

———. "The Nara Document on Authenticity". http://www.icomos.org/charters/nara-e.pdf (accessed 16 August 2016).

International Monetary Fund (IMF). 2005–13. "IMF Did Not Back Sokimex Deal at Angkor". https://www.imf.org/external/np/vc/2005/082205.htm (accessed 15 August 2016).

Japanese International Cooperation Agency (JICA). 2006. "Annex: Chronological List of JICA Cambodia as of 1 December 2006". http://www.jica.go.jp/cambodia/english/activities/pdf/Annex2.pdf (accessed 16 August 2016).

———. "Signing of a Japanese ODA Loan Agreement with the Kingdom of Cambodia". 2012. http://www.jica.go.jp/english/news/press/2011/120329_02.html (accessed 16 August 2016).

———. "Organization". 2013a. http://www.jica.go.jp/english/about/organization/index.html (accessed 16 August 2016).

———. "Outline of the Project". 2013b. http://www.jica.go.jp/project/english/cambodia/013/outline/index.html (accessed 16 August 2016).

JICA, PACET Corporation, and Nippon Koei Ltd. 2010. "Follow-Up Study on an Integrated Master Plan for Sustainable Development of Siem Reap City in the Kingdom of Cambodia. Final Report". http://open_jicareport.jica.go.jp/pdf/12000220_01.pdf (accessed 16 August 2016).

Kanki Kiyoko, Lareta T. Adishakti, and Titin Fatimah, eds. 2015. *Borobodur as Cultural Landscape: Local Communities' Initiatives for the Evolutive Conservation of Pusaka Saujana Borobodur*. Melbourne:Transpacific Press; Kyoto: Kyoto University Press.

Kay Kimsong and Daniel Ten Kate. 2004. "Sokimex, Tela Win Government Oil Bid, 'Big Family' Bows Out". *Cambodia Daily*, 5 March 2004. http://www.cambodiadaily.com/archive/sokimex-tela-win-govt-oil-bid-big-family-bows-out-38792 (accessed 16 August 2016).

Kay Kimsong and Matt Reed. 2001. "Construction Permits Cited in Apsara Firing". *Cambodia Daily*, 9 June 2001. http://www.cambodiadaily.com/archive/construction-permits-cited-in-apsara-firing-23276/ (accessed 16 August 2016).

Khy Sovuthy and Kate Bartlett. 2012. "Japan to Study Angkor Wat Park Environment". *Open Development Canada*, 31 August 2012. http://www.opendevelopmentcambodia.net/japan-to-study-angkor-wat-park-environment/ (accessed 15 August 2016).

Korea Eximbank. "Press Release". 2011–13. http://211.171.208.43/edcfeng/bbs/

press/list.jsp?bbs_code_id=1404204605524&bbs_code_tp=BBS_2 (accessed 16 August 2016).

Kuch Naren. 2015. "Government to Take Control of Ticketing at Angkor Wat". *Cambodia Daily*, 7 November 2015. https://www.cambodiadaily.com/news/government-to-take-control-of-ticketing-at-angkor-wat-99671/ (accessed 16 August 2015).

Matsuura Koïchiro. 2002. "Preface". Special issue on Angkor, a Living Museum, *Museum International* 54, nos. 1–2: 7–8.

Meskell, Lynn. 2013. "UNESCO's World Heritage Convention at 40; Challenging the Economic and Political Order of International Heritage Conservation". *Current Anthropology* 54, no. 4: 484–94.

———. 2016. "World Heritage and WikiLeaks: Territory, Trade, and Temples on the Thai-Cambodian Border". *Current Anthropology* 57, no. 1: 72–95.

Ministry of Foreign Affairs, Japan (MoFA). 2003. "Preservation of Tangible Cultural Heritage through the UNESCO/Japanese Funds-in-Trust". http://www.unesco.emb-japan.go.jp/pdf/brochure-fit-tangible2003.pdf (accessed 16 July 2016).

———. 2011. "The Japanese Funds-in-trust for the Preservation of World Cultural Heritage". http://www.unesco.emb-japan.go.jp/htm/mofaworld.htm (accessed 16 August 2016).

Miura Keiko. 2004. "Contested Heritage, People of Angkor". Doctoral Dissertation, School of Oriental and African Studies, University of London.

———. 2010. "World Heritage Sites in Southeast Asia: Angkor and Beyond". In *Heritage Tourism in Southeast Asia*, edited by Michael Hitchcock, Victor T. King, and Michael Parnwell, pp. 103–29. Copenhagen: NIAS.

———. 2011. "World Heritage Making in Angkor: Global, Regional, National and Local Actors, Interplays and Implications". In *World Heritage Angkor and Beyond: Circumstances and Implications of UNESCO Listings in Cambodia*, edited by Brigitta Hauser-Schäublin, pp. 9–31. Göttingen: Universitätsverlag.

———. 2015. "Discourses and Practices between Traditions and World Heritage Making in Angkor after 1990". In *Cultural Heritage as Civilizing Mission: From Decay to Recovery*, edited by Michael Falser, pp. 251–77. Heidelberg: Springer.

Nam Pan. 2014. "Japanese ODA to Asian Countries: 'An Empirical Study of Myanmar Compared with Cambodia, Laos, and Vietnam'". Policy Research Institute, Ministry of Finance, Japan. https://www.mof.go.jp/pri/international_exchange/visiting_scholar_program/ws2014_d.pdf (accessed 16 August 2016).

Okolotowicz, Michelle-Ann. 1994. "Japan Projects get $83m Boost". *Phnom Penh Post*, 12 August 1994. http://www.phnompenhpost.com/national/japan-projects-get-83m-boost (accessed 16 August 2016).

Peterson, John, and Mark A. Pollack. 2003. *Europe, America, Bush: Transatlantic Relations in the Twenty-First Century*. London: Taylor & Francis.

Peycam, Philippe. 2010. "Sketching an Institutional History of Academic Knowledge Production in Cambodia (1863–2009) — Part 1". *SOJOURN: Journal of Social Issues in Southeast Asia* 25, no. 2: 153–77.

————. 2011. "Sketching an Institutional History of Academic Knowledge Production in Cambodia (1863–2009) — Part 2". *SOJOURN: Journal of Social Issues in Southeast Asia* 26, no. 1: 16–35.

Peycam, Philippe, and Eric J. Heikkila. 2009. "Economic Development in the Shadow of *Angkor Wat*: Meaning, Legitimation and Myth". *Journal of Planning Education and Research* 29, no. 3: 294–309.

Phnom Penh Post. 2000. "All that Glitters Seems To Be ... Sokimex". *Phnom Penh Post*, 28 April 2000. http://www.phnompenhpost.com/national/all-glitters-seems-be-sokimex (accessed 16 August 2016).

Rabé, Paul. 2008. "PRCUD Final Report". *Pacific Rim Council on Urban Development*. https://sites.google.com/site/prcudweb/roundtable-forums/siem-reap (accessed 16 August 2016).

Richner, Beat. 2013. "The Story: Beat *Beatocello* Richner". http://www.beat-richner.ch/Assets/richner_history.html (accessed 16 August 2016).

Rossi, Jean-Yves. 1993. "Un cadre juridique pour la gestion du site d'Angkor" [Legal framework for the management of the site of Angkor]. Unpublished document.

Sokheng Vong and Anette Marcher. 2000. "Sokimex and Government Revisit Angkor Deal". *Phnom Penh Post*, 18 August 2000. http://www.phnompenhpost.com/national/sokimex-and-government-revisit-angkor-deal (accessed 16 August 2016).

Sovan Nguon. 2010. "Petrolimex Targets Cambodia". *Phnom Penh Post*, 3 August 2010. http://www.phnompenhpost.com/business/petrolimex-targets-cambodia (accessed 16 August 2016).

Springer, Simon. 2010. *Cambodia's Neoliberal Order: Violence, Authoritarianism, and the Contestation of Public Space*. London: Routledge.

Turnbull, Robert. 2008. "A New Museum Puts a Thai Imprint on Angkor". *New York Times*, 2 July 2008. http://editorials.cambodia.org/2008/07/new-museum-puts-thai-imprint-on-angkor.html (accessed 16 August 2016).

United Nations Educational, Scientific and Cultural Organization (UNESCO). 1991. "26th UNESCO General Conference, Resolution 3.13". 15 October – 7 November 1991. http://unesdoc.unesco.org/images/0009/000904/090448F.pdf (accessed 16 August 2016).

————. 1992. "Operational Guidelines for the Implementation of the World Heritage Committee". 27 March 1992. http://whc.unesco.org/archive/opguide92.pdf (accessed 16 July 2016).

————. 1993."Proceedings of the Intergovernmental Conference on the Safeguarding and Development of the Historical Area of Angkor". 12–13 October 1993. http://unesdoc.unesco.org/images/0014/001493/149373mo.pdf (accessed 16 August 2016).

————. 2003a. "The International Coordination Committee for the Safeguarding of Afghanistan's Cultural Heritage (ICC)". http://whc.unesco.org/en/activities/245/ (accessed 17 August 2016).

————. 2003b. "Déclaration de Paris. Sauvegarde et Développement d'Angkor" [Paris Declaration: Safeguarding and development of Angkor]. 15 November 2003. http://portal.unesco.org/culture/fr/ev.phpURL_ID=18343& URL_DO-DO_TOPIC&URL_SECTION=201.html (accessed 16 August 2016).

————. 2003c. "Third UNESCO Experts' Meeting on the Safeguarding of Iraq Cultural Heritage, Tokyo". 1 August 2003. http://portal.unesco.org/ culture/en/files/11111/10650214625Final_Report/Final%2BReport (accessed 16 August 2016).

————. 2004. "International Coordination Committee for the Safeguarding of the Cultural Heritage of Iraq". http://whc.unesco.org/en/activities/181/ (accessed 17 August 2016).

————. 2010a. "CIC pour Angkor; 15 ans de coopération internationale pour la conservation et le développement durable" [ICC for Angkor: Fifteen years of international cooperation for conservation and sustainable development]. http://unesdoc.unesco.org/images/0018/001890/189018f.pdf (accessed 16 August 2016).

————. 2010b. "International Coordination Committee (ICC) for the protection of Haitian Cultural Heritage". http://www.unesco.org/new/en/culture/ themes/illicit-trafficking-of-cultural-property/emergency-actions/haiti/ international-coordination-committee-icc-for-the-protection-of-haitian-cultural-heritage/ (accessed 17 August 2016).

————. 1992–2013a. "Convention France–UNESCO (CFU)". http://whc.unesco. org/fr/cfu (accessed 16 August 2016).

————. 1992–2013b. "Success Stories". http://whc.unesco.org/en/107/ (accessed 16 August 2016).

————. 1999–2013. "The Executive Committee and the Trust Fund of the International Campaign". http://whc.unesco.org/en/activities/174 (accessed 16 August 2016).

UNESCO Media Services. 2010. "UNESCO Lays Foundations for International Coordinating Committee (ICC) for Haitian Culture". http://www.unesco.org/ new/en/media-services/single-view/news/unesco_lays_foundation_for_ international_coordination_committee_icc_for_haitian_culture/back/18256/#. V5RJ_GbbqT8 (accessed 16 August 2016).

UNESCO and International Coordinating Committee for The Safeguarding And Development of the Historic Site of Angkor (ICC-Angkor). 1993. "International Coordinating Committee on the Safeguarding and Development of the Historic Site of Angkor". 21–22 December 1993. http://apsaraauthority.gov.kh/imgs/documents/58/1-Session_Pl__ni__re-21-22_d__cembre_1993.pdf (accessed 16 August 2016).

———. 2013. "1993–2013: Twenty Years of International Cooperation for Conservation and Sustainable Development". http://unesdoc.unesco.org/images/0022/002272/227277e.pdf (accessed 16 August 2016).

Vann Molyvann. 1991. "Les parcs archéologiques d'Angkor" [Angkor's archaeological parks]. Unpublished document.

Weinland, Don. 2012. "Number of Japanese firms to Surge this Year". *Phnom Penh Post*, 12 July 2012. http://www.phnompenhpost.com/business/number-japanese-firms-surge-year (accessed 16 August 2016).

Zoning and Environmental Management Plan for Angkor (ZEMP). 1993. "Zoning and Environmental Management Plan for Angkor". Unpublished document.

5

Legacies of Cultural Philanthropy in Asia

Mary S. Zurbuchen

I.

There is little doubt that American philanthropy, including activities in developing countries, is experiencing fundamental shifts. Often defined as "using private wealth for public good", philanthropy has been practised in the United States for more than a century within a particular framework shaped by American laws, which made it possible for philanthropists to minimize their tax burden by giving away wealth for what are defined as "charitable purposes".

Primarily as a result of new technologies created by large and successful corporations, there is now a group of tremendously wealthy entrepreneurs and investors seeking to redefine the purposes and methods of philanthropic practice. Often called "philanthrocapitalists", these entrepreneurs assert that being successful in business gives them the know-how to solve large-scale problems of poverty and deprivation. Their philanthropic organizations promote "business-like ways of working, business-like efficiency, and market-driven solutions to social problems"

(Feinstein 2011). Instead of the "bottom line" of corporate profit, they promise a "bottom line" of social impact. Along with bottom-line thinking comes an emphasis on measuring outcomes and tangible results. The language of metrics, benchmarks, risk-reward ratios and scaling up now pervades the discourse of new philanthropies, making staff and their boards even more eager to see results quickly.

In a new book, David Callahan scrutinizes major living donors, who he argues are forming a "heterogeneous new power elite" (Callahan 2017). He describes activist megadonors who want to be celebrated for carrying out their philanthropic mission, and who maintain close personal control over their foundations, noting how in many cases donors are determined to give away all their wealth for specific purposes during their lifetimes, rather than leaving behind foundations that could evolve and chart new directions in perpetuity. The proponents of what is nowadays termed "venture philanthropy" do appear more activist than earlier generations of foundation executives. Venture philanthropists craft social media messages to explain their goals, and have created a celebrity culture of giving away wealth. Like the rock star Bono, they want to personalize their giving, and to be seen among African villagers or Indian slum dwellers directly carrying out their philanthropic mission. The people changing philanthropy paradigms today using vast personal wealth come from all political backgrounds, including progressives such as George Soros and the ultra-conservative Koch brothers. When the founder of Facebook, Mark Zuckerberg, and his wife, Priscilla Chan, recently announced the creation of a limited liability company for "advancing human potential and promoting equality" and pledged to give away 99% of their Facebook shares, public reaction to the "Chan Zuckerberg Initiative" was mixed (Soskis 2015). Would this be a breathtaking example of private largess addressing major world problems, or another instance of a mega-philanthropy promising to cure social ills while promoting its own business brand?

As philanthropy has grown, both in total assets and numbers of private foundations,[1] increased public attention is drawn to new philanthropists pledging to "change the world". The tech entrepreneurs shaping new philanthropy "believe their charitable giving is bolder, bigger and more data-driven than anywhere else" (Stanley 2015). Yet, as some critics have argued, we need to challenge venture philanthropy's assumption that business logic is the same as the logic underlying complex social processes.[2]

We might ask whether an emphasis on short-term results is leaving out more open-ended kinds of grant making that train community organizers, build institutions, or take risks through new kinds of social change experiments. We could consider whether an overarching concern with the bottom line and metrics "can drive grant making out of types of work whose results can be difficult to gauge, such as leadership development, work on race relations, [and] human rights education" (Berresford 1999). And we need to examine the notion that the most important philanthropy resonates with the urgency of today's media headlines.

Outside the United States, the manner in which concentrated wealth is employed in top-down ways in development projects—often determining local non-profit agendas and skewing public policy priorities—needs to be more carefully analysed (Massing 2016). It is not that concern for persistent poverty or disease in the world is misplaced. The problem is that promoting solutions that are designed in foundation headquarters to be implemented in distant communities, or that are expressed in terms of precise technical inputs to be measured, removes the need to "consider the cultural, humanistic, and political sides of the equation" (Anft 2015).

This essay considers whether culture itself is important, especially in non-Western contexts, as the "new philanthropy" paradigm becomes dominant. At first glance the prospects do not look promising. The philanthrocapitalist's emphasis on technical solutions and measurable results is not especially compatible with intangible subjects like the vitality of oral traditions, say, or the ways an ethnographic museum can build appreciation for a society's ethnic diversity. A tech entrepreneur may look at a multitude of world languages to be learned and taught and imagine inventing a universal translation tool, instead of less "cutting edge" approaches—such as endowing underfunded language departments of public universities. And in a world rife with injustice and inequalities, private philanthropy and governments alike tend to see cultural pursuits— including disciplines in the arts and humanities—as secondary priorities, if they count at all.

My aim here is to reflect on the record and the motivations of a leading global private foundation that for decades was active in cultural philanthropy across Asia. I will review the overall trajectory of the Ford Foundation's culture-focused philanthropy in its offices in South and Southeast Asia from the late 1970s into the twenty-first century. Tracing the various rationales underlying cultural grants leads us to a more complete view of the paradigms of engagement Ford employed in "developing" countries. It also reveals clear distinctions between field office grants and Ford's domestic arts agenda, as well as intersections between cultural programmes and other priorities of the foundation. Given both notable changes in the field of philanthropy in recent years, as well as changes in Ford's emphases and ways of working, it is important to ask whether arts and culture are still relevant to its priorities, and what turns cultural grant making in Asia has taken.

II.

First, we must evoke the background of an institution that for many years was the world's wealthiest foundation, once described as "a large body of money completely surrounded by people who want some" (Macdonald 1989, p. 3). Today, when the Bill and Melinda Gates Foundation looms over the philanthropic landscape with assets of more than $60 billion, one forgets a time when it was Ford that regularly grabbed major headlines in American discussions of private foundations. This prominence began around 1950, when the foundation was endowed with 90 per cent of the stock of the Ford Motor Company.[3] By 1960 it had a corpus of over $3 billion, along with an annual budget much larger than that of the United Nations and its specialized agencies combined.[4] Within the legal environment for American philanthropy, it is important to note that during this period the more valuable the Ford Motor Company became, the more the foundation's dividends increased, making it necessary to increase its grant making in order to preserve its tax-exempt status.[5]

Yet it was not the sheer scale of its resources that commanded attention when, in 1949, the foundation announced its intention to address issues of global importance such as peace, democracy and human welfare—it was the startling breadth and loftiness of its vision. From its beginnings in the 1930s as a small, local family foundation that had supported the communities of auto factory workers around Dearborn, Michigan, Ford set out to become a major presence on the national and international stage. The founding text for its expanded mandate was a weighty document called the Gaither Report, which came out of a process involving multiple task forces and more than a thousand people charged to consider "the ways in which the Ford Foundation can most effectively and intelligently put its resources to work for human welfare" (Gaither 1950, p. 13). The

Gaither Report provided the conceptual scaffolding for the international edifice Ford would build through its network of overseas field offices, a key part of its expansive mission to solve the world's problems. And this brings us to New Delhi, Rangoon and Jakarta, where the first field offices in Asia were launched.

Let us imagine a scene in Burma in 1953, not long after the Ford Foundation opened a field office in Rangoon as part of an expanding presence in Asia. Departing from its pattern of funding projects in public administration and agriculture, the foundation decided to support a request from the Burmese government for the creation of an International Institute of Advanced Buddhistic Studies, which would foster activities in Pali scholarship and organize the Sixth Great Buddhist Council. The council was to convene for two years between the full moons of May 1954 and 1956, gathering fifteen thousand Buddhist monks and scholars from all over Asia. According to its proponents, the institute was "expected to become the spiritual center of Southeast Asia, radiating ... irresistible and overpowering rays of Wisdom, Truth, and Righteousness".[6]

This intriguing gesture to Burma's heritage was just the first in a record of grants supporting the cultural heritage in numerous Asian countries for more than fifty years. Cultural interests first emerged for Ford in a systematic way in India, where its first overseas office had opened in New Delhi in 1952. In 1955, for example, the foundation established the Southern Languages Book Trust to publish great works of literature and philosophy in the four major languages of South India. The following year, the foundation purchased from the Museum of Modern Art in New York a thousand copies of books and multiple film prints, products of an exhibition MOMA had organized on Indian handloom textiles and crafts (Gandhi 2002, p. 4). While the ostensible aim of this grant was to reintroduce "principles of good design" to Indian cottage industry, it also clearly acknowledged the immense creative wealth of India's artisan communities.

I cite these examples of early cultural grants to note how the Ford Foundation's stance within the postcolonial Asian dynamic of continuity and change included an inclination towards the arts and humanities. The Gaither Report lauded the importance of scientific investigation and "professional experts generating objective knowledge",[7] and for some years the foundation was guided by this "heady prospectus" in setting its priorities. Arts and culture were not among those priorities initially, but thinking changed and in 1957, with its resources growing rapidly—

thus making it a necessity to disperse many more dollars each year—the foundation looked seriously at the needs of American creative artists and the potential for providing support to projects of "national significance". The Arts and Culture programme launched in the United States in 1962 aimed to raise the arts to new levels of achievement and fiscal stability through long-term support to a group of promising institutions.[8] The enormous impact of some $400 million spent into the 1980s can still be seen in the worlds of dance, regional theatre, symphony orchestras and arts management throughout the United States. The creative force behind this landmark initiative was W. McNeil Lowry, who saw the arts and humanities as an important counterbalance to the foundation's focus on social sciences and research.[9]

Cultural programming emerged very differently in the Asian settings where Ford worked. Field offices produced culture grants in a decentralized way, depending on local contexts, the inclinations of foundation staff, and direct encouragement from country directors, called representatives. The 1950s and 60s were years when issues of nation-building and economic development dominated international relations and Western states were fixed on the ideological competition with the Soviet and Chinese communist spheres.[10] In India, with its flagship field office, Ford worked with the government to find ways to improve rural life. In response to the invitation of Prime Minister Nehru, the foundation supported modernization and reorganization of village industries, which led to increased attention to traditional handloom and handicraft producers, thus raising the possibility of culture as a focus for development efforts.[11]

At the same time, efforts in language development and publishing such as the Southern Languages Book Trust, along with bilingual education and English language training, reflected the importance of India's multilingual and multicultural environment. The trust also reflected the geopolitics of the Cold War,[12] as the Soviet Union was supporting a steady stream of cheap books in Indian vernaculars at the time. In newly independent Burma, competing East/West ideologies were clearly a factor, along with the need to unite an ethnically diverse people, in the creation of the International Institute for Advanced Buddhistic Studies mentioned above. The suggestion that the Ford Foundation might support the institute—which was called "the Pali Project"—was made in writing by a US aid mission official, who cited Premier U Nu's opinion that "the popular belief that Americans work solely for the benefit of themselves or others is one of the strongest weapons in the hands of Communist propagandists in Southeast Asia" (Macdonald 1989, p. 67).

The rationale that intergroup unity and democratic values would greatly assist the nation-building process became linked to concern for culture, as reflected in foundation programme guidelines for the 1960s:

> The successful development of new nations includes, and in part depends on, cultural and intellectual factors. New nations seek to 'discover' their own cultures, and to achieve greater clarity concerning their national purposes ... it is proposed that Overseas Development support carefully selected projects designed to further these less tangible but important purposes of developing nations.

An equally significant justification for foundation involvement with India's culture was articulated in the mid-1960s by a Ford consultant, Arthur Isenberg, who argued that India's classical past and its "folk culture" were threatened by urbanization and rapid change. (By this time, the Rangoon field office had closed, as the foundation was ordered to leave Burma after the military takeover of 1962.) In 1969 a small grant for "heritage preservation" created an opening for new programming; this was reinforced by positive signals from the foundation's trustees.[13] A contraction in foundation assets through the 1970s (due to a broad US economic downturn) meant "the Foundation's enthusiastic conversion to the idea of conserving India's cultural past had to be curbed" (Gandhi 2002, p. 10). By 1978, however, a "comprehensive program centered on preservation" was approved for India. This programme would grow and evolve, sparking grants in India and other Asia offices for more than two decades.

III.

The geography and modality of the foundation's support for arts and humanities in Asia looks different from one vantage point to another. At various times the foundation made grants in the arts and humanities in Bangladesh, Bhutan, Burma, China, India, Indonesia, Japan, Malaysia, Nepal, Pakistan, The Philippines, Sri Lanka, Thailand and Vietnam. The history of this support is highly variable, with no fixed template determining which kinds of grants should be approved. There were scant policy guidelines for officers interested in working on cultural topics, and no specific annual budget allocation for such grants. On occasion, grants were conceived opportunistically, without a longer-term strategic framework. Culture programmes might be sparsely staffed, with field offices often relying on part-timers or consultants for this work. Officers whose actual assignments were in other fields such as education, social sciences, or human rights might manage culture grants. Those staff members frequently responded in a more or less ad hoc way to opportunities to support cultural activities within the constraints of time and budgets imposed by their primary programme responsibilities. In the following discussion, I will focus on the larger, sustained programmes in arts and culture in countries where officers were assigned to develop clearly articulated visions. Those offices are New Delhi (which made grants in India, Nepal and Sri Lanka) and Indonesia (which also managed activities in Thailand, the Philippines and Vietnam, at different periods).

It is vexingly hard to be precise in tracking how much the foundation spent on culture outside of the United States because the structure of Ford's programme division and its accounting codes changed over the years. For the most part, culture programmes in Asia fell under larger categories such as "Education, Media, Arts and Culture" and received small slices of annual field office budgets. Between 1984 and 1994, for example, the largest expenditures in all overseas offices went to grants under the categories of Rural Poverty and Resources, International Affairs, and Education. During this same period, Cultural Preservation and Interpretation accounted for about 13 per cent of all grant dollars in India and 18 per cent in Indonesia.[14] These amounts were probably the highest among all overseas offices, since culture grants tended to be fewer in Ford's Latin America and Africa offices. Budgets for culture never approached the scale of arts expenditures in the US programme; in the 1984–94 period, culture-related grants in Asia totalled roughly $21.5 million dollars, a mere 8 per cent of total Asia grant expenditures. In general, it seems that field office representatives could feel confident in recommending annual culture programme budgets as long as these remained subsidiary to their major "developing country" agenda. Addressing poverty, illness and injustice would claim the major portion of field office resources, even as robust cultural programmes grew.

Taking a closer look at how country programmes responded to opportunities to engage with culture, we turn to sites of the largest commitment to the arts and humanities in Asia: India, Indonesia and (on a smaller scale) Thailand, the Philippines and Vietnam. While the specifics of each field office's grants differed widely, several key themes stand out across the region and over nearly thirty years.

Heritage Conservation

The foundation initially addressed cultural issues as a matter of the material heritage—the "cultural property" that manifests history and identity in tangible form. National governments were often open to outside technical assistance for preservation of monuments, archaeological sites, and movable property such as ethnographic collections or hand-written documents. Thus, the India office worked with institutions such as the Archaeological Survey of India, Deccan College in Pune, the New Delhi School of Architecture, the cities of Jaipur and Ahmedabad, and public and private manuscript collections to support training, research and improved technologies in the fields of archaeology, urban conservation planning, and manuscript documentation. Similar grants for archaeological training and research were made in Sri Lanka, and Bhutan's National Museum received assistance in managing national art and manuscript collections. In Indonesia, conservation of monuments, advanced training for archaeologists and museologists, and manuscript preservation for endangered collections in the palaces of Central Java and the National Library were all supported. In Thailand, foundation funds helped launch an important programme to conserve the wealth of mural paintings in Buddhist temples, in partnership with the government's Fine Arts Department.

All this heritage work opened up deeper challenges and questions about the validity of culture grant making. Identifying heritage conservation as a goal is hardly helpful, one foundation staffer observed, in deciding *what* to preserve. Material remains of the past can be appropriated by power centres to legitimize dominant ideologies, as when India's Babri Masjid was claimed as a Hindu site, or when archaeological evidence of ancient Tamil settlement in Sri Lanka conflicted with the politics of national history. The conservation of the past might sharpen conflicts when, say, excavation activity threatens local settlement or livelihoods. Involvement of a foreign institution with cultural property can aggravate local or nationalistic sensitivities. And even when a project is successful—such as the microfilm documentation of thousands of pages of frail manuscripts—there remain questions of public or scholarly interest, interpretation and survival of that written heritage in its new format.

Still, the record of Ford's cultural grants produced many compelling arguments for attention to the material heritage. Learning from history and appreciating links with the past tend to be viewed as significant in most societies—a reality that needs recognition in wealthier countries where the existence of archives, libraries, museums and other cultural resources is often taken for granted. On the local level, culture grants drew attention and appreciation from government and private institutions; by means of its sustained culture programme, the foundation earned credibility among governments, artists and scholars for supporting activities other major donors would not consider. On the international level, Ford's attention to the cultural heritage reinforced the major investments it was making in the 1960s and 1970s to build international and area studies in US universities.[15] In some measure, then, the foundation's contributions to capacity-building in archaeology, museology and conservation sciences resulted in benefits for Asian institutions and communities who would, it was argued, be better able to interpret and utilize the past for the common good.

Cultural Transmission

It is not very far from conservation of the tangible heritage, of course, to the *intangible* dimensions of culture. Core issues here involve change and vitality of cultural forms over time, and processes through which meaning is conveyed to audiences and across generations within the larger social, environmental and religious settings of particular groups. The passing of skills and practice from older to younger, the dissemination of art forms to new audiences, and the formation of new relations between patrons, practitioners and consumers are all part of the "transmission" idea.

Living traditions are always in a state of change; "tradition" is neither fixed nor static. As the foundation saw it by the 1980s, many arts genres in Asia faced qualitative changes of such magnitude that their survival was threatened.[16] Minority groups under the hegemony of strong national centres and with new languages and educational systems to master found their inherited arts ignored, undervalued or otherwise marginalized. Changes in how an art form is transmitted, for instance from oral to written media, or in relations between artists and traditional sources of patronage, disrupt continuity. Formal education, the politics of language, and modern media all have profound effects on cultural transmission.

The foundation put considerable effort into assisting arts practitioners to sustain and convey older forms of expression. In India, funds helped classical musicians and dance masters document their traditions and adapt older systems of pedagogy to new social and economic conditions. Folk culture studies became a major programme for the New Delhi office, with goals of strengthening field research as well as the role of expressive arts in social development and communications. In Indonesia, meanwhile, cultural transmission required paying attention to ethnic diversity, oral traditions and performance genres across a large archipelago where heavy-handed bureaucracies were seeking to "guide" and "improve" local religious and cultural expression. Indonesian arts were also being disrupted by adaptation to modern education as masters of performance traditions were increasingly expected to become credentialed instructors in the government's conservatories and arts academies.

While in India folk culture studies provided a strong interdisciplinary focus for traditional arts, in Indonesia the field of world music or ethnomusicology became a key organizing principle, embracing both arts of the traditional aristocracy as well as diverse village-based performance genres. Foundation staff worked with arts academies and field researchers as they developed new humanities curricula and practitioner networks. Independent national organizations such as the Society for Indonesian Performing Arts and the Oral Traditions Association took shape. In the Philippines, Ford supported ethnomusicology in the academy and archiving of field recording collections developed by José Maceda, whose pioneering research illustrated commonalities among performance genres throughout Southeast Asia.

One conceptual challenge in arts grant making involves finding a balance between scholarly and activist approaches. It was important to move beyond the academic atmosphere of arts institutes to direct engagement with living traditions in the communities that keep them vital. Thus in Thailand a unique oral history project gathered stories of life and culture from displaced Khmer refugees in camps along the border. In Indonesia in the 1990s, Ford sponsored a major recording project involving the Smithsonian Institution and the Society for Indonesian Performing Arts, which over ten years documented musical styles in twenty-three provinces, resulting in a landmark twenty-CD series with the Folkways

Records label.[17] In Vietnam, support went for a competition providing small grants to community-based arts groups to record, document or research their own arts, generating materials on ritual, crafts, performing arts and languages among thirty ethnic minority communities across thirty-nine provinces.[18]

Foundation culture programmes also tried to take account of inter-linked processes of economic and social change, and of the impact of contemporary media and communications revolutions. Issues of cultural transmission involve not only changes in the arts but also the survival of entire ways of life. As struggles over control of forest land intensified across Southeast Asia, community resource use patterns, material culture and local identities all became threatened by larger political and economic forces. Culture programmes thus intersected with the foundation's concerns to reduce poverty and address issues of rights and governance.

Creative Expression

Over time, the emphasis of Ford's culture grants in Asia shifted from "cultural preservation and interpretation"—one of the frequent categories found in the documents—to include concerns for vitality and diversity. Programme officers were interested in encouraging innovative, experimental, critical work in a variety of media. They felt an emphasis on creative expression would help incorporate the experiences of underrepresented groups into national life; support the emergence of new idioms in traditional arts; develop stronger capacities, new audiences, and channels for cultural expression; and clarify the links between contemporary expression and its context, including traditional forms. What are the multiple stances towards modernity and tradition that artists attempt? What is the role of the artist in a "post-traditional", heavily state-controlled environment? Would improving the infrastructure for arts organizations result in better conditions for creative work?

Field offices supported creativity in varied ways. In India a theatre laboratory project supported contemporary theatre directors in experimental work drawing on local and folk genres, and also helped promising theatre groups to develop new methodologies and share innovations. Indonesian arts and literary groups organized national celebrations of local arts, oral tradition and regional languages. The Hanoi office provided training abroad for young Vietnamese filmmakers and helped them showcase their productions, while a new supporting organization was created in Indonesia to help arts organizations in management, strategic planning, and funding strategies. Both the India and Indonesia offices provided resources for exploring the outreach and public service potential of broadcast media, including community radio and the expanding television spectrum. The explosive growth of digital media and the Internet in the first years of the twenty-first century prompted grants for studying new media access, analysis of emerging creative and copyright issues, and innovations in documentary film.

Again, principles of selection were an issue. The foundation did not stipulate global policies to help in the choice of which artistic or expressive field to encourage. Programme staff needed to consult widely to understand the conditions that support, limit and channel creativity within a particular field. They looked to expression of local needs, selecting points of entry through cooperation with consultants and expert committees, and through stimulation of dialogues among key actors in a particular field.

Culture and Identities

In the 1950s and 60s, important changes were taking hold in postcolonial Asian states, and the consolidation of national identities was a ubiquitous project. The "unity in diversity" motto was heard in calls for integration and assimilation, both political and cultural. National unity was inscribed on the material heritage, too, as historic sites and artefacts were seen as defining a people's shared identity. If that identity was strong, it was argued, people could be resilient in the face of the manifold pressures of modernization. Even in Thailand, which had escaped direct European colonization, destabilization brought by conflicts in Indochina meant that "Thai cultural identity was ... subject to severe pressures of an accelerated westernization and modernization process."[19] A surge of thefts of valuable images from Buddhist temples, and the embarrassing disappearance of hundreds of objects from the collection of the National Museum, prompted leaders of cultural institutions to look for ways of "inculcating in the Thai public a sense of pride in their rich cultural heritage".[20] The foundation's support for research and training in both archaeology and mural painting conservation emerged in part from such locally expressed concerns, which included anxiety over the impacts of a large American military presence on Thailand's social norms.

Of course, even when nation-building ideologies were dominant, and as Cold War–related conflicts led to Vietnam's "American War" and the Indonesian annexation of East Timor, counter-narratives to the national unity theme have been regularly voiced. In the last years of the twentieth century, most areas of Ford's work, including governance, livelihoods, and human rights, became linked in one way or another to the acceptance and expression of distinct identities within the national fabric. Working with the cultural sector in Vietnam, for example, a portfolio of grants expanded effective arts management, to "create space for artists to reflect on issues of identity in the context of rapid socio-economic change" (Stern 2003, p. 42). Emphasizing diversity[21] through cultural grants both underscored and contributed to each of the other programme themes in field office settings. There is resonance between India's folk culture institutions and advocates working for rights of the *dalit* and tribal groups of the country. Local artists recording oral epics in uplands Vietnam raise the profile of minority ethnic communities whose access to forest land is being undermined by national policy. A research project on traditional arts and the Islamic heritage of Java can address a growing rhetoric of discrimination and exclusion that would seek to suppress the performing arts on grounds of religious orthodoxy.

IV.

There were, of course, other actors in the culture field in Asia during the years that I am discussing here. Most of these were bilateral or multilateral agencies representing a government, as with Germany's Goethe Institute, or groups of governments, like UNESCO, which has long promoted heritage sites of global importance and whose "Intangible Cultural Heritage" programme was defined in its 2003 convention. Embassies—including those of former colonizers—benefit from the "soft diplomacy" of sponsoring a museum exhibition or donating to a restoration project. Nonetheless, among US private charitable groups it is rare for foundations to take more than sporadic interest in international cultural matters.[22] For most of its history, for example, the Rockefeller Foundation focused on medicine and agriculture in its developing country philanthropy.[23] Organizations that focus on the tangible heritage include the J. Paul Getty Trust, which is most active in Europe and the Mediterranean. However, Getty is an operating foundation, meaning that it implements its own projects, in contrast to a grant-making foundation like Ford, which funds independent groups. Japanese foundations have been active in sponsoring cultural projects in Southeast Asian countries, but this interest has been relatively recent and primarily involves academic research and collaborations (the Japan and Nippon Foundations are good examples) or restoration of particular historic sites or shrines (as some East Asian trusts have done in Hoi An, the historic trade port of central Vietnam). The Aga Khan Trust for Culture, based in Geneva, works across the Muslim world (including Malaysia, Pakistan, India and Bangladesh) on conservation of historic cities, musical heritage, and architecture and urban design.

Still, it is clear that Ford's role in support of a wide range of cultural activities was for decades unique among donors working in Asia. By the late 1990s, professional staff with assignments in what was by then called Education, Media, Arts and Culture (EMAC) were located in Jakarta, Hanoi, New Delhi and Beijing; together with new EMAC appointments in Cairo, Lagos, Nairobi and Moscow, Ford's global "footprint" in culture reached a high point. A number of prominent initiatives in Asia from the early 1990s reflected this broadening commitment. Ford provided significant support for the Festival of Indonesia in 1990–91, an eighteen-month series of museum exhibitions, performances, film showings, conferences, folklife celebrations and other events that provided many Americans with their first glimpse of Indonesia's rich cultural heritage. At about the same time, Ford made an endowment grant to establish the India Foundation for the Arts, now one of India's leading independent foundations, with programmes encouraging new forms of creativity and arts education across the country.

What factors have been critical to the longevity and sustained focus of Ford's programmes? Doubtless Ford's commitment to having offices in the countries where it works was an essential condition enabling culture grant making. Philanthropy based in field offices made it possible for the foundation to develop long-term relationships with local individuals and institutions; to work more closely with grantees on development and implementation of projects; and to generate ground-level experience and insights important for senior management and the foundation as a whole. Even though Asian field offices have opened and closed at different moments in line with emerging opportunities or internal policy, most of Ford's culture grants were made within field offices with a well-established local presence such as in Bangkok, New Delhi, Jakarta or Dhaka.

The foundation's overseas offices have generally not functioned as branches of headquarters but have typically stressed local context and settings in shaping grant programmes. Ford's representatives in Asia tended to enjoy a high level of autonomy in exploring and setting local-office grant-making priorities, working within the broad guidelines set every few years by the foundation's trustees and the biennial grant budgets allocated by New York. Grant approvals up to a certain level are delegated to local representatives,[24] who also play a key role in selecting field office professional staff. The foundation looks for programme officers with local experience and relevant language and intercultural skills to serve terms of roughly three to six years; staff have often been recruited from university faculty, research institutes or international non-profit groups.

In building a programme of grants under a theme such as "cultural preservation, vitality and interpretation", the foundation looked for people with humanities backgrounds who could articulate a vision linking one set of grants to others in the portfolio. Deep local knowledge and professional experience were critical to working with potential grantees in responsive, creative and flexible ways. Strategic thinking in turn implied longer-term commitment to working with a group of grantee organizations, avoiding a random succession of unrelated grants. At the same time, staff were expected to look for special opportunities or new openings to work with talented people, young organizations, or to build new constituencies to address persistent issues.

This emphasis on long-term commitment, along with local autonomy and flexibility in identifying grantees, meant that foundation staff could build relationships over time through travel to different regions of a country, through broad consultations, and through bringing together different skill sets or points of view in addressing important issues. For example, when the Bangkok office decided to help the Thai government with its mural painting conservation programme, companion grants were made to the International Centre for the Study of Preservation and Restoration of Cultural Property in Rome (ICCROM), which provided important technical assistance.[25] When the Jakarta office developed a programme aimed at promoting appreciation of cultural diversity through private radio and television outlets, broadcasters and programmers from all over Indonesia were brought together to share ideas.[26] This kind of "convening power" often led to important and unexpected connections in grant making, and is the kind of role Ford could play by virtue of local offices open to different kinds of people, institutions and ideas.

Employing staff responsible for cultural grant making, the foundation built its own capacity for awareness of local priorities, values and issues beyond the mainstream technocratic focus on development followed by major donors. Within the field office, staff assigned to different programmes often worked as a team, consulting each other and sometimes jointly developing grants. One grant in Indonesia funded environmental conservation and oral traditions research in the Kayan Mentarang tropical rainforest reserve in Kalimantan, and involved programme officers working on both community resource management and cultural vitality who shared goals of strengthening the ability of forest-dwelling peoples to preserve their ways of life. The culture programme officer thus served as an example of the kind of "engaged expertise" that views heritage as something represented by whole communities and environments.[27] At the same time, Ford was cautious about claiming credit for the results of particular projects; its philosophy tended to carefully distinguish the foundation's profile as the *grantor*—sharing ideas and providing funds— from the *grantee*'s role in carrying out projects.

V.

Having worked as a foundation officer during more than two decades in Asian settings, I have wondered what place cultural interests have in American philanthropy. Is there a twenty-first century relevance in the Ford Foundation's perspectives on creativity, transmission and identities discussed above? The emergence of "new philanthropy", with its emphasis on business-like practice and measurable outcomes, has not been accompanied by a new wave of grant making in cultural fields. One reason arts and culture may be less compelling for philanthropy today is that studying foreign countries has suffered significant retrenchment in America's academic realms. Over the past two decades, the multidisciplinary "area studies" model for learning about the world, prominent since World War II, has been discounted as "orientalist" and Eurocentric. While alternative models—subaltern studies, postmodernism and cultural studies—have emerged, much social science research has turned to the study of large data sets and away from close study of cultural context. In the United States, basic government funding for area and international studies has been drastically reduced. The Ford Foundation's domestic programme in area studies was cut back in the 1980s, thus undermining the salience once fostered between domestic programmes—promoting knowledge of the world among Americans—and international cultural grant making.

The technology revolution itself may well have helped to dim the allure of international studies. With the Internet at our fingertips and social media linking anyone anywhere, much of the world now appears accessible and "knowable" through Web surfing and cyberworld networking. Further, we have seen widespread erosion of support for the humanities in US schools and universities, supplanted by a belief that only the "STEM" disciplines (science, technology, engineering, maths) can produce market-ready citizens with skills for the twenty-first century workplace.[28] Arguments that "humanities enhance our culture" or transmit "the best that has been thought and said" are no longer effective, says critic Stanley Fish, arguing that university administrators have shirked their duty to aggressively defend the humanities as an essential part of what a university should be doing (Fish 2010).

In this environment it might well seem counter-intuitive or retrograde to promote the arts and culture as important for philanthropy. Yet the new president of the Ford Foundation seems to be keeping the arts within view, at least for domestic grant-making purposes. After taking the helm in 2013, Darren Walker announced in 2015 that all foundation grant making would be organized and streamlined around the concept of "inequality". One of the seven thematic areas now featured on Ford's website is Creativity and Free Expression, which "play a central role in weaving the fabric of a just society—a society in which exclusion and inequality can never stand unchallenged". As the foundation invests in organizations "that are pivotal in fighting inequality and making meaningful progress in creativity and free expression", it will further focus grant making under two sub-themes: "Social justice storytelling" and "21st century arts infrastructure". Walker has spoken eloquently on how the arts "create economies of empathy" in building social movements. If there is crisis in the arts world, it is in part because "we have raised market-oriented thinking above all other kinds and categories of human understanding" (Walker 2015). He argues that the United States' greatness is revealed through its arts, and that America currently suffers from a poverty "of heart and mind, of spirit and soul, of civic imagination", which can be addressed through sustained funding for the arts (Walker 2017).

Some of the foundation's recent domestic grants reflect this orientation. For example, a grant of $10 million to United States Artists will build an endowment for that group to continue providing grants to individual artists in a range of fields and genres. The "storytelling" strategy in the United States embraces Ford's "JustFilms" documentary initiative, and "arts infrastructure" builds on what Ford has already been doing in the United States for some years under the rubric of "supporting diverse arts spaces". In 2015 the foundation made a total of 141 grants totalling $44.5 million under the "Freedom of Expression" theme (now superseded); over half of this support went for arts spaces, while most of the rest of the grants supported media access and the JustFilms initiative. There were also grants to a number of mainstream New York cultural institutions (Metropolitan Opera Association, New York Shakespeare Festival, New York Public Library, Vivian Beaumont Theater, etc.), suggesting that Ford intends to maintain a place among the city's prominent arts patrons.

This all sounds reassuring for culture in the United States, but the picture does not appear as bright when we look at the foundation's overseas activities. In Ford's field offices, in fact, culture programmes were curtailed under Walker's predecessor[29] and while Walker himself served as vice president for Education, Media, Arts and Culture; at the same time, a focus on public service media and Internet access was enlarged. Programme officers assigned to work on cultural vitality and interpretation disappeared around 2007, and today it is not clear whether any field office staff have specific roles under "Creativity and Free Expression".[30] The 2015 grants database includes a handful of grants under "Diverse Arts Spaces" from the Cairo and Mexico City field offices; there are none from Asia offices. In 2016, some 171 grants related to "Creativity and Free Expression" were made worldwide, for a total of $69.3 million; in Asia, there were only 7 grants (2 in China and 5 in Indonesia). So while it may still be too early to fully define new directions in cultural programming, the relative absence of culture among current Asia field office priorities is not encouraging.

There are other reasons to wonder how Ford will treat cultural issues and problems in future, and whether "new philanthropy" perspectives and models have perhaps taken root more deeply during its programme realignment. For example, the foundation for many years used a succinct media "tag" for acknowledgment on television and radio: "Ford

Foundation: A resource for innovative people and institutions worldwide."
Today, however, the Foundation sees itself as "Working with visionaries
on the frontlines of social change worldwide, to address inequality in
all its forms." The new tag posits an activist stance, putting the donor
right alongside, if not leading, grantees in the social justice struggle.
One wonders whether those who might hesitate to claim the status of
"visionaries" can still get a hearing from the foundation, and whether
support for individual artists and scholars has been eclipsed by a focus
on institution-building.

The way Ford now describes "Creativity and Free Expression" stresses
utility and purpose: art as instrument for something else. The arts do not
exist in and of themselves; they "address inequality" and "contribute to
a fairer and more just society". No doubt "storytelling" exists in myriad
contexts around the world, responding to varied social, educational or
communitarian needs; however, for the foundation it necessarily "addresses
issues of justice" and "fuels change". There is more than a hint of agenda-
setting here; how will this lexicon be translated, literally and figuratively,
outside the United States? Who decides which projects will "transform
attitudes that perpetuate injustice",[31] and how will results in terms of
"attitudes" and "more justice" be assessed? A recent profile of Darren
Walker in *The New Yorker* described ongoing debates about the implications
of addressing inequality: "Ford believed in supporting art as a means of
disrupting dominant narrative", notes the author, "but art didn't always
do what you wanted it to" (MacFarquhar 2016).

Because the foundation has long played a leading role in drawing
attention to issues of cultural vitality and interpretation in Asia, eliminating
cultural programmes is certain to have an impact on the larger field. There
is data suggesting that Ford's turn away from culture in its international
work is already having an effect. According to the Foundation Center,[32] in
2002 Ford provided by far the largest share of grants for Arts and Culture
to recipients outside the United States, making 138 grants (39 per cent of
the number of grants made in this category) with a total value of US$20.1
million (equal to 42 per cent of the amount of resources all US foundations
provided for Arts and Culture outside the US). As of 2012, Ford still made
the largest number of Arts and Culture grants (61, or 21 per cent of the total)
but provided only $12.2 million in overseas grants (just 20 per cent of the
total grant amounts). Further, while in 2002 there were 11 Asian grantee
organizations on the Foundation Center's list of the "top 50 recipients" of

Arts and Culture grants outside the US, by 2012 there were only 2 Asian grantees on that list.

Global philanthropy has been transformed by many factors, not least among them the electronic information revolution that enables instantaneous contact between staff in field offices and headquarters. This means that ways of working have changed, and that interactions among the staff of field offices and headquarters have too. Whereas field office communications with New York once took place primarily through weekly airmail pouches, today it is not uncommon for foundation staff in Asia to stay up late at night for regular teleconferences. Grants processing, meeting agendas, budgeting and accounting, personnel and other operations are increasingly uniform, digitized and centralized in the hands of managers based at headquarters.

Ford's global structure entails reaching the right balance between operational efficiency and field office creativity and autonomy. Running field offices with international staff is an expensive business that demands attention to maintaining an institutional profile in local contexts, to nurturing extensive networks, and to making sure that New York staff includes people who understand the complexity and nuance of overseas work. Some experienced hands have wondered whether Ford's "back-office" functions could more easily be centralized entirely in New York, which would mean even smaller staff levels overseas. Indeed, few philanthropies these days see utility in keeping in-country staff on the ground, preferring an approach that flies out teams of consultants and evaluators instead. This may be effective for donors who design programmes at a distance and then "contract out" to appropriate governments or non-profits for implementation; it might not be as productive an approach for Ford's traditionally more engaged philanthropy, however.

In a recent speech accepting an award from the Studio Museum in Harlem in New York City, President Walker noted that the arts are a powerful tool for challenging "persistent stereotypes and cultural narratives that undermine fairness, tolerance and inclusion". Such narratives persist outside the boundaries of the United States, and are troubling in the Asian settings of Ford's field offices. In India, for instance, exclusionary social structures persist alongside a rampant, growing religious nationalism that is leading to oppression of minority communities and growing censorship in the arts, literature and the teaching of history. Many ethnic minority peoples of China, especially in the Tibetan and Uighur regions, face relentless pressure on their languages, religions and ways of life. In Indonesia, religious intolerance is expanding into both cultural and political spheres in alarming ways. The foundation has accumulated significant experience in these countries with local activists who promote historical interpretation, appreciation of ethnic diversity, creative expression and the vitality of living traditions—experience that could be translated into changing contexts to address current challenges.

In the end, what matters for Ford's international philanthropy is not only how aspirational it might be in promoting "disruption of the drivers of inequality". What will also matter is whether it uses the unique leverage of its offices around the world to sustain grant making that is informed by local insight, in the hands of creative and engaged staff who can implement its realigned mandate in grounded, relevant ways. I have suggested that a focus on culture and humanities embeds credibility, empathy and deeper awareness within the foundation; such focus has made the foundation an exceptional donor during the rich history of its grant making in Asia. As an organization that tries to place people's real-world experience, dreams, identities and vulnerabilities foremost, the Ford Foundation has from the beginning of its work in Asia seen a role for attention to cultural vitality and creative interpretation of human experience. That is a unique and immeasurable part of Ford's own heritage—and one that its leaders should be proud to sustain.

Notes

1. According to the Foundation Center's database, in 2014 the United States had more than 86,700 grant making foundations, with total assets of over $865 billion. Some 30,000 new private foundations were created since 2000. US foundations made more than $60 billion in grants in 2014, both within the United States and abroad.
2. See Edwards (2008) on the limits of philanthrocapitalism's promise to produce far-reaching change.
3. Eventually the foundation divested from its Ford Motor Co. holdings, and the Ford family disassociated itself from the expanded global foundation.
4. At the end of 2014, the foundation had $14.4 billion in assets; it gave away some $518 million during that year.
5. The United States Congress established rules for foundations, including the requirement to use a certain percentage of their assets annually for what are defined as "charitable activities".

6. See Macdonald (1989, pp. 66–69) for more details on foundation grant 05400155. Its budget of $327,000 would be the equivalent of $2.9 million in 2015—an extraordinary amount for an initial commitment even today, and evidence of the foundation's relative wealth. At this early point, Ford's annual grant budget was about four times as large as that of the second biggest US foundation (Rockefeller).

7. Francis X. Sutton, in Macdonald (1989, p. xv). Macdonald labels the Gaither Report's language "foundationese", as in the following: "The problems of mankind must be solved, if they are to be solved at all, by a combined use of all those types of knowledge by which human affairs may be influenced" (p. 139).

8. "The arts represented a vast frontier in which no American foundation had operated a national program, nor did there exist a central agency— governmental or private—devoted to the field" (Stern 2003, p. 15).

9. It is worth pointing out that the scale and visibility of Ford's support for the arts both stimulated US private and corporate gifts to arts institutions and influenced the creation of the National Endowments for the Arts and Humanities.

10. The foundation's initial cultural efforts were focused mainly in Europe, reflecting the conviction that exchange of ideas and cultural achievements could help promote peace in the wake of World War II's "devastating effect on the European intellectual community ... American observers feared that Marxism and Communism would exert a growing appeal among these disaffected intellectuals..." (McCarthy 1987, p. 94). The foundation's first president, Paul Hoffman, had served as administrator of the Marshall Program in Europe, and firmly believed in nongovernmental cultural diplomacy.

11. The foundation helped start the National Institute of Design in 1961, urging "the cooperation of ethnologists, art historians, and village teachers with a feeling for the true cultural past" (Gandhi 2002, p. 5).

12. Much has been made of the degree to which Ford and other private foundations were linked to the Cold War policies of the US government, particularly the Central Intelligence Agency, through entities such as the Congress for Cultural Freedom. The debate over these activities is peripheral to this essay, but relevant discussion can be found in Saunders (2000), Epstein (1967), McCarthy (1987) and a variety of other sources. Coming from another direction, the foundation was also targeted as "leftist" in the press for its work on civil liberties and racial discrimination, which led to a series of congressional investigations in the 1950s and 1960s (Macdonald 1989, pp. 27–35; Rosenfield 2015, pp. 7, 23). And when Henry Ford II resigned from the Board of Trustees in 1976, severing the last Ford family ties with the foundation, he criticized the organization "for attacking the capitalist economic system that had created it" (ibid. p. 24).

13. Chairman of the board Alexander Heard wrote in 1970 that "To interpret and make visible the cultural heritage of many a developing nation ought to contribute to a sense of national pride and to the much discussed sense of identity that everyone seems to want these days..." (Zurbuchen 1994, p. 15).

14. Zurbuchen 1994, appendix tables 2 and 4.

15. As Benedict Anderson notes, post–World War II US government agencies put priority on expanding much-needed international scholarship, "[b]ut very large private institutions, especially the Rockefeller and Ford foundations, also played an important role, partly offsetting the 'policy' focus of the state. Senior officials in these foundations ... were more liberal in their outlook than state functionaries, and somewhat less obsessed with combating 'world communism'" (Anderson 2016, p. 34).

16. One document attributed the threats to a "rush toward economic growth and social modernization" and "changes in public values", suggesting "the task, then, is to help national elites be more comfortable with their own pasts" (Ford Foundation 1978, p. 20).

17. The Music of Indonesia project is described in detail in Ford Foundation (2003, p. 194).

18. The Folk Arts and Culture Fund—administered by the Center for Educational Exchange with Vietnam—has supported some 170 local projects to date (Nguyen Thi Thanh Binh, personal communication).

19. Klausner (1991). William Klausner, professor of law and specialist on Thailand since the 1950s, has written extensively on Thai culture both publicly and as a staff member of both The Asia Foundation and Ford Foundation.

20. Klausner, personal communication.

21. It is notable that the foundation took "diversity" seriously both internally and in grant making. Through the 1980s and 1990s, both Presidents Franklin Thomas and Susan Berresford stressed that racial and gender representation were important for the composition of the Board of Trustees, as well as in staffing.

22. Important exceptions here are the Henry R. Luce Foundation and a Rockefeller offshoot, the Asian Cultural Council (ACC); both are based in New York and are much smaller philanthropies than Ford. While ACC has had small offices in East Asia, its grants primarily support individual artists from the United States or Asia. The emphasis of the Luce Foundation is on strengthening knowledge of Asia among Americans, and it has no field offices.

23. From 2001 to 2007, the Rockefeller's innovative programme in the Greater Mekong Subregion recognized transnational cultural dynamics and included grants in arts and humanities; see Sciortino (2016).

24. As of 2000, for example, any field office grant with a budget up to $100,000

was approved by the representative. This kind of "delegated authority" is not typical of most international philanthropy.

25. Not incidentally, through its work with Thai conservators, ICCROM developed new techniques for the restoration of mural painting in tropical conditions—expertise that could be used in other places and contribute to building global knowledge.

26. For a more detailed account, see Ford Foundation (2003, p. 219).

27. For a fuller discussion, see Salemink (2016).

28. While there is not space here for detailed discussion, it seems clear that a decline in public support for tertiary education, and the fact that humanities subjects do not bring major research dollars to universities, has contributed to shifting priorities. In the words of one candidate in the 2016 US presidential race, "We need less [sic] philosophers, and more engineers."

29. Luis Ubiñas was president of the Ford Foundation from 2007 to 2013.

30. Staffing and assignments are still shifting in the wake of President Walker's realignment around "inequality". My comments reflect current information available at www.fordfoundation.org, as well as discussions with several field office observers.

31. From a description on Ford's website of a recent foundation grant in partnership with the Skoll and BRITDOC Foundations that "will provide second-stage funding for joint projects by social entrepreneurs and filmmakers". https://britdoc.org/flex/ (accessed May 2016).

32. See www.data.foundationcenter.org for relevant lists and tables.

References

Anft, Michael. 2015. "Of Billionaires and Hunger". *Chronicle of Philanthropy* 4 (November).

Berresford, Susan. 1999. "American Philanthropic Values and the Future of Philanthropy". Remarks at the New York Regional Association of Grantmakers Annual Meeting, 11 May 1999.

Callahan, David. 2017. *The Givers: Wealth, Power and Philanthropy in a New Gilded Age*. New York: Knopf.

Edwards, Michael. 2008. *Just Another Emperor? The Myths and Realities of Philanthrocapitalism*. New York: Demos & The Young Foundation.

Feinstein, Alan. 2012. "International Philanthropy in Southeast Asia: Case Studies from Indonesia and the Philippines". In *Understanding Confluences and Contestations, Continuities and Changes: Towards Transforming Society and Empowering People*. Bangkok: API.

Fish, Stanley. 2010. "The Crisis of the Humanities Officially Arrives". *New York Times*, 11 October 2010.

Ford Foundation. 1978. "The Foundation and Asia". Unpublished paper.
———. 2003. *Celebrating Indonesia: Fifty Years with the Ford Foundation 1953–2003.* Jakarta: Equinox.
Gaither, H. Rowan. 1950. *Report of the Study for the Ford Foundation on Policy and Program.* Detroit: The Ford Foundation.
Gandhi, Leela. 2002. *Arts and Culture: From Heritage to Folklore.* New Delhi: Ford Foundation (50th Anniversary report series).
Klausner, William. 1991. "Cultural Programming". Ford Foundation Inter-Office Memorandum, 4 December 1991.
Macdonald, Dwight. [1955] 1989. *The Ford Foundation: The Men and the Millions.* New Jersey: Transaction.
MacFarquhar, Larissa. 2016. "What Money Can Buy". *The New Yorker*, 4 January 2016.
Massing, Michael. 2016. "How to Cover the One Percent". *The New York Review of Books*, 14 January 2016.
Reich, Rob. 2013. "What Are Foundations For?" *Boston Review.* Bostonreview.net, 1 March 2013.
Salemink, Oscar. 2016. "Scholarship, Expertise, and the Regional Politics of Heritage". In *Scholarship and Engagement in Mainland Southeast Asia*, edited by Oscar Salemink. Bangkok: Silkworm Books.
Sciortino, Rosalia. 2016. "'Learning across Boundaries': Grantmaking Activism in the Greater Mekong Subregion". In *Scholarship and Engagement in Mainland Southeast Asia*, edited by Oscar Salemink. Bangkok: Silkworm Books.
Soskis, Benjamin. 2015. "Time for the Public to Weigh Good and Bad of the Zuckerberg-Chan Gift". *Chronicle of Philanthropy*, 11 December 2015.
Stanley, Alessandra. 2015. "Silicon Valley's New Philanthropy". *New York Times*, 31 October 2015.
Walker, Darren. 2015. "Open and Free: On Arts, Democracy, and Inequality". Address to the Annual Meeting of the Association of Art Museum Directors, Mexico City, 26 January 2015.
———. 2017. "The Art of Democracy: Creative Expression and American Greatness". The Nancy Hanks Lecture on Arts and Public Policy, John F. Kennedy Center for the Performing Arts, Washington DC, 20 March 2017.
Zurbuchen, Mary, with Alan Feinstein and Ruth Mayleas. 1994. "A Review of the Ford Foundation's Cultural Grantmaking in Asia". Unpublished report.

6

To Help or Make Chaos?
An Ethnography of Dutch
Expertise in Postcolonial Indonesia

Lauren Yapp

Draped over the curve of coastal hills as they give way to a sweltering plain that borders the Java Sea is the Indonesian city of Semarang. Now a moderately-sized provincial capital of 1.5 million people, Semarang was once a rival to its better-known neighbour, Batavia (now Jakarta), and for centuries boasted substantial wealth and political influence on par with some of Southeast Asia's most prominent port cities. Javanese, Chinese, Malay, South Asian and Arab communities first made their homes here, drawn to the vast network of lucrative trade routes that threaded through the city and its bustling harbour (Muhammad 2011). Then, from the late seventeenth to the mid twentieth century, waves of Dutch colonizers arrived on these shores, transforming Semarang into a foothold of their empire in the archipelago and a "gateway to modernity"[1] for the whole of central Java (Coté 2006; Cobban 1988). In the decades leading up to World War II, Semarang gained further fame as a hotbed of radical politics and local resistance to foreign rule, earning it the moniker *Kota*

Merah, or "The Red City", in reference to its association with early leftist leaders in the anti-colonial struggle (Poeze 2014). Now, over seventy years since Indonesia declared its independence, this deep history of colonialism, cosmopolitanism and conflict is etched upon the contemporary cityscape, which still bears tangible traces of this tumultuous past in the form of mosques and temples, marketplaces and railways, dwellings and warehouses, barracks and offices, lighthouses and canals.

Semarangers today regard many of these crumbling structures as sites of memory and meaning, whether for themselves, their families or their own ethnic and religious communities. However, one site in particular has drawn significant attention from government authorities, civil society groups and community organizations in recent years: Kota Lama, or "The Old Town". Strategically nestled between the city's historic port and the densely packed districts of Pecinan (Chinatown), Kauman (the Arab and Javanese quarter), Kampung Melayu (the Malay quarter) and Pekojan (the South Asian quarter), Kota Lama consists of a cluster of streets and buildings that once lay within the walls of a fortress built in the mid 1700s by the Dutch East India Company (VOC) as a base from which to extend control over the city. Today, the fortress is long gone and most of the surviving structures that make up Kota Lama date instead to the district's heyday in the late nineteenth and early twentieth centuries (Leushuis 2014). During this time, the area gained prominence as the stomping grounds of colonial elites (mainly Dutch and other Europeans, but also some wealthy members of the city's Chinese-descendent community) and their commercial enterprises, then housed in imposing office buildings and cavernous warehouses.

In the decades following Indonesia's independence in 1945, Kota Lama gradually slipped into a state of abandonment and decay as Semarang's economic centre of gravity shifted to the new developments to the south, and many of the modest number of Indonesian residents (who had moved into the district during the chaos of the 1940s) left their homes in search of cooler climes in the hilly suburbs. By the 1990s what was once a centre of business and administration in the colonial-era city had gained a local reputation as a *kawasan gelap*—a "dark district" or "no-go zone"—associated more with crime and prostitution than with history and heritage. But in recent years all this has begun to change rapidly and dramatically. What started in 2012 with efforts by local students, academics and artists to draw attention to the plight of Kota Lama through exhibitions and festivals eventually snowballed by 2016 into a vigorous (and, at the time of writing, ongoing) campaign by the governor of Central Java to have the district declared a UNESCO World Heritage Site. Indeed, Kota Lama today is a full-blown hotbed of heritage advocacy. In the space of only a few years, dozens of initiatives involving people from all corners of Semarang society have mushroomed with the aim of researching, preserving and promoting the city's ageing colonial core as newly minted "heritage".

Colonial Heritage, Postcolonial Expertise

The weathered barracks, warehouses, shops, churches, banks, hotels and offices that today constitute the heritage site of Kota Lama represent only a tiny fraction of the "imperial debris" (Stoler 2013) scattered across Indonesia today, left behind in the wake of over three centuries of Dutch conquest and colonization. However, Kota Lama's recent trajectory—decades of neglect, interrupted by a frenzy of heritage initiatives—is in fact representative of the fate of many historic districts in cities across the archipelago. Indeed, like numerous cities elsewhere in Southeast Asia (e.g., Melaka and George Town [Jenkins 2008], Bangkok [Herzfeld 2003], Luang Prabang [Berliner 2012], Manila [Byrne 2007], Singapore [Kong 2011] and Hanoi [Logan 1996]), Indonesia's urban centres are now experiencing what might best be described as a "heritage rush", with an array of government, private and community actors suddenly, in the space of only the last five to ten years, scrambling to preserve and promote aging buildings and neighbourhoods as heritage sites. In Indonesia, some of this interest has been directed towards celebrating the deep roots of minority communities across the archipelago. For instance, in Semarang there has been a modest but growing effort to see historic temples, traditional festivals and old shophouses in Pecinan (Chinatown) recognized and protected as cultural heritage (a movement that has only become possible since the fall of Suharto's military dictatorship in 1998 and the loosening of that era's strict prohibitions on public expressions of Chinese-Indonesian identity). However, here again the case of Kota Lama is indicative of wider trends throughout the country. The activism, funding and projects that now aim to preserve Indonesia's historic urban fabric have focused overwhelmingly on the built environment of the colonial period, and particularly on those sites (like Kota Lama) that are seen by city-dwellers to be clearly "Dutch" in their architectural style and urban design.

This recent transformation of "imperial debris" into "colonial heritage" across Indonesia is part of a well-documented phenomenon throughout Asia, Africa and the Middle East, where sites like Kota Lama are frequently targeted for extensive restoration and are seen by authorities as a lucrative draw for both overseas and domestic tourists (Bissell 1999, 2005; Jacobs 2010; Peleggi 2005). As is often the case in these postcolonial contexts, while Indonesia's current heritage boom has been driven primarily by the efforts of Indonesians themselves (it is *not* an imported trend), foreign "experts"[2] have also played a significant role. Many such experts—professionals in the fields of architecture, urban planning, engineering, marketing, tourism, heritage management, etc.—hail from Western nations that once colonized the countries wherein they now proffer their services. In Indonesia, for instance, a sizeable number of the visiting experts now advising or conducting heritage projects (as well as a broad range of other development and infrastructural work across the country) are Dutch.[3]

Experts and expertise have recently emerged as critical topics within the burgeoning field of heritage studies. Some scholars, including several in this volume, have explored how the activities and discourses of international organizations like UNESCO, along with a booming cottage industry of heritage-related institutes and NGOs, have produced a class of transnational heritage professionals who advise, evaluate and conduct preservation projects around the globe (James 2016; De Cesari 2010).[4] Others have considered the failures of heritage experts who, despite noble goals and sophisticated methods, struggle to make a positive impact upon (or, at least, avoid causing damage to) communities whose cultural, historical and political context is largely unfamiliar to them (Adams 2015; Rico 2016). As some authors have pointed out, Western notions of what is heritage and how best to preserve it are promoted not only by visiting professionals from the Global North but also by elites in the Global South keen to hold sites in their own countries to "international" standards of conservation practice (Byrne 1995; Roberts 2017). Recently, attention has also been paid to heritage diplomacy, wherein heritage experts are deployed as tools of soft power to bolster economic and political relationships between countries, their interventions often swathed in the language of humanitarian aid and development goals (Yapp 2016; Akagawa 2016; Luke and Kersel 2013).

The present chapter is intended as a contribution to this body of work, but it takes a rather different tack. Drawing upon extensive ethnographic research in Semarang since 2012, it presents an intimate narrative of what unfolded when two Dutch teams of self-styled "experts" arrived in the city with the intention to develop and promote Kota Lama as a heritage site. This fine-grained analysis of how these projects came about and the ways in which the involvement of the Dutch visitors was received (and managed) by the city's own lively community of heritage professionals and activists raises three key points: (1) individual cultural brokers are critically important in facilitating and actualizing the work of foreign experts, particularly so in the early stages of transnational heritage initiatives; (2) as such projects drag on, conventional understandings of relationships of aid between presumably "developed" and "developing" countries are reversed; and (3) the status of visiting experts, as opposed to the substance of their expertise, is ultimately their most useful (and sought after) asset in the eyes of their local hosts.

Each of these dynamics could be understood as symptomatic of the broader neoliberalization of heritage work around the globe (Herzfeld 2010), as evident in the shrinking of public funds available for arts and culture, and in the expansion of private initiatives that rely heavily on heritage expertise (or, at least, the appearance of it) to secure contracts and stake claims (Breglia 2006). Indeed, the very presence of Dutch teams in Semarang was premised on the increasingly popular view that heritage aid should be dispersed primarily in the form of experts, not funds. However, looking to neoliberalism as the primary framework through which to understand the work of foreign heritage professionals risks too presentist an evaluation of their significance. In other words, what appears to be a *new* development in the way that heritage is identified, managed and promoted is in fact, seen in its historical context, anything but. Rather, what is most intriguing in the case of Dutch experts conducting projects in Indonesia (or indeed citizens of any former colonial power working in regions their countrymen once colonized) is a pervasive sense of *déjà vu*—one only heightened by the fact that the two teams of heritage professionals considered here travelled from their homes in the Netherlands to Semarang with the intent to preserve the very ruins that testified to their own ancestors' conquest and control of the city.

In the account that follows of the interactions between these Dutch experts and their Indonesian hosts, the dynamics of this colonial past repeatedly re-emerge, albeit at times in unexpected ways. Echoes of history were present not only in the perpetuation of power imbalances and reinforcement of knowledge hierarchies that privileged Dutch voices over

Indonesian ones, but also, more subtly, in the configuration of interpersonal networks that tied some prominent figures in Semarang society to their foreign guests, and in the strategies used by the city's heritage activists to manage the extractive presence of these visiting experts over the short-term in an effort to secure long-term support from local authorities for their own work in Kota Lama. Finally, I conclude by considering the curious *lack* of controversy prompted by the involvement of Dutch professionals in Indonesia's heritage sector, which is paradoxically made possible by the colonial past itself and the initial (yet often misplaced) expectation harboured by citizens of both nations that historical intimacies produce contemporary expertise.

Attention from Abroad

One of Kota Lama's local nicknames is "Little Netherlands",[5] and so perhaps it is no surprise that all of the foreign-led initiatives in the district that I was aware of during my time in Semarang were the work of Dutch companies, organizations and individuals. From 2014 to 2016, in particular, there were at least half a dozen initiatives that brought citizens of the Netherlands to Kota Lama for weeks at a time, ranging from documentary films, to academic research, to photographic exhibitions, to direct consultancy work on how to best develop the historic district as an attractive site for investment and tourism. It is this latter category of Dutch involvement that this chapter is concerned with, focusing on two such projects that I was able to observe closely: one led by a Dutch non-profit organization and the other overseen by a Dutch consultancy company.

Both of these initiatives brought small groups of professionals from the Netherlands—presented as experts in the fields of urban planning, heritage management and marketing—to Semarang for several visits of two to three weeks at a time. During their initial stay in the city, each team of visitors held a series of workshops with groups of Semarangers they had identified as relevant stakeholders to discuss Kota Lama and to draw up plans for its development as a heritage attraction. The non-profit organization (which typically specializes in advising small- and medium-sized businesses across Asia and Africa) focused on drafting proposals for substantial physical changes to infrastructure and building use in the district. The consultancy company was concerned mainly with formulating a coherent narrative of Kota Lama's historical and cultural significance that could be used as the basis for a branding strategy to promote the site. Following these workshops, both Dutch teams returned to Semarang periodically to present their recommendations to the city and provincial governments, expecting (so far, with mixed success) that their work would guide the preservation and marketing of Kota Lama going into the future. More recently, the members of these two groups have aimed their sights even higher, making overtures to the municipality in the hopes of securing agreements that would authorize them to advise on matters beyond heritage—such as infrastructure, urban development, and tourism—not only for Kota Lama, but for the entire city.[6]

Crucial Cultural Brokers

The opening lines of the consultancy company's post-field report characterize their Kota Lama project as being prompted initially by a direct invitation from the Dutch embassy in Jakarta to "develop a strategy for the (re)development of the built heritage of Kota Lama in Semarang together with local stakeholders". In reality the origins of the team's involvement in heritage work in Indonesia are far less grand. About a year prior to their visit, a Dutch academic who had often conducted research in Indonesia over the past two decades happened to hear of the company's role in facilitating several participatory heritage management initiatives in the Netherlands. Thinking that their approach might be an interesting one to try in Semarang, the researcher contacted the team and, finding them eager to attempt what would be their company's first project overseas, offered to assist them. In fact it was not until much further down the pipeline of logistical preparations for their visit to Indonesia that funding from the Dutch embassy in Jakarta was sought and secured, along with the blessing of the embassy's Deputy Head of Public Diplomacy and Cultural Affairs.[7] This financial and symbolic support of the Dutch government for the consultancy company did lend their work in Kota Lama a certain gloss of authority—even more so than was warranted, with some Semarangers interpreting the team's frequent use of their embassy's logo in presentations to mean that these visitors from the Netherlands represented (and sought to promote) their nation's interests in Indonesia.

Contrary to these misperceptions of cosiness between the Dutch embassy and its citizens abroad, however, the actualization of the consultancy company's Kota Lama dreams from paper proposal to on-the-ground project depended not on the heft of ambassadorial support but on a far more local and seemingly modest source: a petite Indonesian businesswoman named Ibu Lydia.[8] Ibu Lydia is best known amongst Semarangers as the owner of an ageing but well-loved restaurant that has been in her family since the colonial period. Decorated with antiques and serving Dutch dishes alongside Indonesian favourites, the restaurant is a historic landmark in its own right. On any given day one can find pairs of weary Dutch tourists taking a respite from the city's heat to snap pictures of the interior's faded glamour, alongside well-to-do Indonesian families indulging their nostalgia for the Indo-European flavours their parents treated them to as children.

However, Ibu Lydia's passion is not only the kitchen but also Kota Lama. Several years ago she formed a foundation with the mission of attracting public attention to the historic district through arranging and financing festivals, conferences and exhibitions. A large part of Ibu Lydia's longstanding interest in her city's colonial-era buildings, and the Dutch-led initiatives to save them, are her strong personal ties to the Netherlands. Like many older generations of Chinese-descendent Indonesians from well-off families, she grew up speaking Dutch in the home and is fluent to this day. She divides her time between Semarang and the Hague (where she once ran a branch of her restaurant) and is on familiar terms with virtually every Dutch official or researcher working in the field of Indonesian heritage, including the academic who suggested the consultancy company to set its sights on Kota Lama. Due to their friendship, Ibu Lydia's foundation was soon brought on as the primary Indonesian partner for the consultancy company's project, which in reality meant that it was up to her to arrange and fund a significant portion of their visit to Semarang. Oftentimes dipping into her own accounts, Ibu Lydia set up accommodation for the team, granted them use of her restaurant for their sessions, and tapped her extensive connections to convince local officials and wealthy property owners (two notoriously tricky groups of people to track down) to attend their workshops. As a testament to her substantial clout in Semarang and her critical role in the consultancy company's project, when the team asked the Dutch embassy in Jakarta to assist them with arranging a one-on-one meeting with the city mayor to pitch their vision for Kota Lama, they were told by embassy officials that they did not have those kinds of connections—instead, they were advised to ask none other than Ibu Lydia.

The crucial involvement of Ibu Lydia in the Dutch experts' visit was not a one-off; indeed, every single Kota Lama project with Dutch involvement has depended heavily on her. She has also worked closely with the aforementioned non-profit organization since their very first trip to Semarang nearly five years ago, and she has single-handedly initiated heritage-themed exchanges between universities in the Netherlands and Semarang. I even witnessed her running into a group of bewildered students from Rotterdam who were wandering around Kota Lama in search of inspiration for their master's thesis project. Within hours of this random encounter she had set them up with research questions, a local professor to supervise them, and a plan for two months of fieldwork. Once, sitting together in the back room of her restaurant after a particularly long day of shuttling yet another set of visitors from the Netherlands around town, an exhausted Ibu Lydia joked with me that she feared the Dutch embassy and other funding institutions in the Netherlands would eventually stop supporting their countrymen's projects in Kota Lama because they would get sick of seeing her name listed as the local sponsor on every single grant application. Asking her if she had ever considered seeking support from other sources abroad, Ibu Lydia replied, to my surprise, that over the years she had in fact turned down several overtures from British and Japanese heritage professionals seeking to work in her city in favour of the Dutch institutions and individuals with whom she was already on familiar terms.

The figure of Ibu Lydia can tell us a great deal about how heritage projects led by overseas parties actually work on the ground, beyond how they are portrayed in glossy booklets after the fact. Embassies are in reality quite limited in their clout and connections, especially outside a capital city, while the private organizations attempting to carry out these initiatives are themselves rather lost in their new surroundings (sometimes literally, as was the case with the students from Rotterdam). The ability of these heritage projects to gain any traction thus depends almost entirely on individual cultural brokers, like Ibu Lydia, who may not hold a formal title but who do hold an enormous amount of cross-cultural capital that allows them to translate foreign expectations into a local context. At the same time, this translation is necessarily a partial one—while Ibu Lydia was critical to helping groups like the consultancy company to gain a foothold in Semarang, her heavy involvement in these projects meant that the Dutch team only heard one side of the story of Kota Lama. Simultaneously enabled and limited by their reliance on her, most of them were unaware that her foundation has many critics in Semarang, or that her family has property holdings in and around Kota Lama and thus an interest in managing the district in such a way that grows these investments.

Moreover, the existence and prominence of cultural brokers like Ibu Lydia today is directly related to the colonial past. The elite status of families like her's—well-off, educated Indonesians of Chinese descent with political clout, Dutch language skills and personal and business ties to the Netherlands—was in part a product of the colonial system. Connections (cultural, financial and emotional) to the former colonizer were something to be quietly preserved, not cut off, after the Dutch East Indies became the Republic of Indonesia. This historical context also helps to explain Ibu Lydia's personal views on the Dutch groups seeking to do projects in Kota Lama today. Chatting with her in the kitchen over slices of *appeltaart*, she told me again and again that Kota Lama was in crisis, the local government had no idea what they were doing when it came to heritage, and the Dutch were "top experts" whose visits were "rare opportunities" that should be seized by Semarangers if they truly wanted Kota Lama to succeed. Moreover, she was convinced that bringing groups like the consultancy company and the non-profit organization to Semarang was the *only* thing that would compel the municipality to take care of the city's heritage sites—these local officials' fear of being made "embarrassed" (*malu*) in front of their foreign visitors overcoming any bureaucratic red tape. Her strategy for attracting and facilitating Dutch-led heritage projects was thus one perhaps best described as "the more the merrier"— she would welcome with open arms any Dutch professional with an idea for Kota Lama and would swiftly put them to work.

Role Reversals

Not everyone agreed with this approach. Indeed, even some Dutch researchers familiar with the situation in Kota Lama felt that Ibu Lydia's foundation had made missteps in the past by bringing in other presumed "experts" from the Netherlands without properly vetting them or consulting with local heritage professionals to see if the proposed project was in fact redundant. One even suggested to me that their countrymen who could not find success at home actively sought out projects in developing countries, where presumably their white skin and Western credentials would be locally interpreted to mean that they knew what they were doing.

Many of the Indonesian heritage professionals and activists that I encountered in Semarang held broadly similar views to this one. They harboured great respect for Ibu Lydia and her foundation, but as more and more visitors from the Netherlands arrived in their city over the course of the year, intending to research and advise on all matters related to Kota Lama, they began to fear that they had not been nearly selective enough in choosing which projects from abroad to support. Our chats concerning these doubts about the qualifications of the Dutch teams in town often blossomed into wider discussions that revealed how they viewed the contemporary dynamics between their nation and its former colonizer.

One such conversation unfolded as Pak Indra and I took a break from the sweltering heat of Kota Lama to sip iced coffee in a cafe that had recently opened in a restored nineteenth-century shop. Pak Indra, then the director of a local organization dedicated to preserving traditional Javanese arts, is himself another key cultural broker in Semarang. Having studied in the Netherlands in his youth, he speaks Dutch fluently. He has worked closely with Ibu Lydia's foundation in the past and he counts many Dutch academics as old friends. And yet he was not so enamoured with the prospect of these two Dutch teams consulting on the future of his city's historic sites. Revealingly, his concerns stemmed not so much from whether their "experts" were technically qualified (though he had been generally unimpressed by the plans for Kota Lama drawn up by visiting architects over the years) but rather from what led them to seek out projects in Indonesia in the first place. We Indonesians know that the Dutch economy is struggling, he explained, citing the eurozone crisis and the recent deep cuts in budgets for arts and culture in the Netherlands. These Dutch people who are busy designing heritage projects to carry out in Semarang are "looking for a job", knowing that there are currently more "opportunities" available to them in Indonesia than back home. Pak Indra illustrated this with an anecdote about a Dutch colleague who he knew had been struggling for some time to set up their own heritage consultancy in Amsterdam, and so had shifted focus to developing projects in Indonesia, where there was less competition for these services. "That's fine", he continued, "we all have to earn a living, after all." But he remained deeply sceptical of how useful these "Dutch experts", like the ones that kept showing up on his doorstep, could be in improving the state of Indonesia's heritage sites, given that these visitors often lacked knowledge of the linguistic, cultural, legal and political context of their overseas work. As a result, their interventions in Kota Lama, he contended, were "chaotic" (*kacau*).

Pak Indra's reading of Dutch-led projects in his city represents a complete inversion of the typical relationship of aid that is imagined to exist between a "developed" country like the Netherlands and a "developing" counterpart like Indonesia. While Ibu Lydia and the members of the non-profit organization and the consultancy company saw their work as the generous extension of an "opportunity" to Semarangers and their imperilled heritage sites, the "opportunity" in question was alternatively understood by other Indonesians like Pak Indra to be something offered by *their* nation to the Dutch. In this latter interpretation, and with a strong flavour of colonial times, Indonesia possesses the raw resources for endless heritage-themed initiatives from abroad—abandoned historic buildings, unmanaged archaeological sites, underused archives, and a widespread assumption amongst local authorities that foreign nationality is an indication of expertise. This, coupled with the reality that in terms of macroeconomic power Indonesia is increasingly the dominant party in its relationship with the Netherlands,[9] left Pak Indra with the sense that it was not Indonesia that needed the Dutch but rather the Dutch who needed Indonesia.

I do not believe that the members of the Dutch teams realized how much they stood to gain from their projects compared to how much their local interlocutors had to give to make them possible. The Semarangers I knew were generous and genuine hosts who would rarely speak anything other than kind words about their visitors. However, one friend—a passionate heritage activist named Mas Arif who was tasked with arranging the details of their travel and workshops—admitted to me that accepting this steady stream of Dutch experts placed a strain on himself personally and on the local community of heritage activists as a whole. Preparing, in his words, an "appropriate situation"[10] for these visitors during their stay in Semarang was not easy. Arriving in Semarang with only a general understanding of the context into which they were stepping, both teams had to be filled in on local politics and bureaucracy by their Indonesian hosts, who took valuable time off from their own work in Kota Lama to bring the Dutch up to speed and to fulfil the teams' frequent requests for assistance in sorting out accommodation, paperwork and meetings with city authorities. In short, he said with a laugh, their visits "*tambah PR*"—added to his homework. But, like many Semarangers who had been involved in the local heritage sector for some time, Mas Arif was most concerned with the potential of outsiders to disrupt and confuse the work already under way to preserve his city's historic sites. When I asked him if the presence of the non-profit organization and consultancy company helped or complicated ongoing local efforts to revitalize Kota Lama, he replied in even stronger terms, echoing Pak Indra's earlier sentiments and answering with his characteristic wry smile: "They don't 'complicate' the situation; that isn't the correct term. The correct term is 'make chaos'."[11]

Not fully aware of the complexity of heritage work and city politics in Semarang, the Dutch teams certainly made many unconventional moves. In my own estimation, their lack of knowledge about the local context had some unexpected benefits; namely, their willingness to speak with everyone provided a channel for certain groups who had hitherto been left out of decisions regarding Kota Lama to become more involved in those discussions. But for many of the Semarangers who had been working steadily and quietly behind the scenes for years to convince, placate, negotiate and pressure various constituencies into supporting the cause of heritage preservation in their city, the unpredictability of their Dutch guests made these Indonesian hosts feel it necessary to adopt a mindset of constant damage control to protect the work they had thus far accomplished. This (coupled with Pak Indra's observation that it is Indonesia that has the most to offer the Netherlands on matters of heritage, not the other way around) begs the question: what exactly *was* the ultimate impact of these Dutch initiatives in Kota Lama that would make many of Semarang's heritage professionals, while sceptical, still willing to participate in them?

Status over Substance

A simple answer to the question of impact might be: There wasn't any. Or at least not in the way originally intended by the Dutch experts. Judging the success of these two initiatives by their own standards, neither of them has as yet been particularly effective in substantively moulding public perception or future development of Kota Lama as a heritage site. To my knowledge, none of the detailed plans or glossy reports that resulted from their visits to Semarang have been formally adopted by municipal authorities, let alone executed.

The Indonesian heritage professionals I came to know during my fieldwork understood full well that the projects they were assisting their

Dutch visitors in carrying out were unlikely to have significant concrete effects on Kota Lama. In spite of this, however, many felt that the experience of hosting and participating in these initiatives from abroad could potentially be worthwhile to them, even if the actual plans that were produced would eventually fall by the wayside. Specifically, while the aforementioned "chaos" was perceived as a definite risk, the possible reward of having foreigners conduct heritage projects was the chance to use perceptions of these visitors' expertise to strategically bolster local claims to knowledge and experience. Indeed, one of the strongest laments I heard from Indonesians working in the heritage field, not only those in Semarang but also in several other cities, was their frustration at being ignored by bureaucrats and policymakers. Even the most senior advocates for Kota Lama—people who had worked to bring public attention to the site for decades, developed strong relationships with residents there, or amassed libraries of information on its history—felt that they were still not seen as "experts" by the local authorities, bureaucrats who rarely listened to their recommendations or protestations as they ploughed ahead with their own plans for the historic district. To be understood by one's fellow Indonesians (especially those who worked in city hall or the governor's office) as a heritage "expert", Mas Arif explained to me, one needed advanced degrees or professional experience, preferably from an institution in a "developed country" (*negara maju*);[12] better still would be a visiting "expert" to call one's own.

Given these assumptions (however unfounded or unfair) about the relationship between foreignness and expertise, members of the non-profit organization and the consultancy company were powerful cards Semarang's heritage advocates could play in city politics. Ibu Lydia believed this when she asserted that it would be the presence of her Dutch guests, if nothing else, that would finally compel the municipal planning office to support her foundation's work in Kota Lama. Indeed, I too was understood by some of my interlocutors in Semarang as fulfilling this role,[13] having been frankly advised by my Indonesian friends that I would have easier access than them to high-ranking officials, key documents and even historic buildings because of, first, my white skin, and second, my credentials from a well-known American university—all of which turned out to be more or less true.

The two Dutch teams probably would have felt somewhat un-comfortable to know that their foreignness alone was being put to such strategic use; after all, they had come to Semarang with a certain idealism that they could help "save" the city's heritage by sharing their knowledge and experience. Nevertheless, as I followed them being shuttled around town, introduced to directors of government departments and prominent members of Semarang society, it became even clearer that it was not the substance of their expertise that was their most valuable asset to their Indonesian hosts but rather their status as experts. That is, it was not the specific *content* discussed in the workshops that ultimately mattered, but rather it was the very *presence* of these foreigners in Semarang that could have a substantial impact on the perception and management of Kota Lama as a heritage site.

Ibu Lydia, Pak Indra, Mas Arif and the many other Semarangers with a passion for Kota Lama did not need to be informed as to why their heritage was significant or what challenges it faced—they had all spent years and careers pondering these matters. But what they *could* put to practical use were flesh-and-blood "foreign experts" as means to circumvent some of the existing power dynamics within their own city that thus far had prevented their voices from being heard. At times, this strategy appeared to work. For instance, the consultancy company's local guide during their visits, a young man with an encyclopedic knowledge of Semarang's history but no formal credentials, was able to leverage his involvement with the team into a much-deserved position as the only paid, full-time member of the municipal board in charge of managing Kota Lama. In other cases, it backfired spectacularly. After the consultancy company delivered their Kota Lama proposal to the city mayor, his office announced its intention to hire an architect from overseas to design a new building in the district, inspired by one of the team's recommendations.[14] On social media, some of Semarang's heritage professionals were livid that their government would choose foreign expertise over the skill and experience of its own citizens—even though, ironically, it was they who brought the Dutch visitors to city hall in the first place.

Intimacy and Normalcy

The proverbial elephant in the room throughout all of these interactions was, of course, the history of colonialism that binds the Netherlands and Indonesia inexorably together. Counter-intuitively, however, this past (nearly 350 years of violence, extraction and oppression) actually rendered the presence of the Dutch teams in Semarang *less* controversial than might reasonably be expected, not only from the perspective of these visitors from the Netherlands but also, surprisingly, in the eyes of many of their Indonesian hosts. Yes, local heritage professionals did share misgivings, annoyances and frustrations related to the burdens unwittingly imposed by their guests. At times some even wryly expressed a desire (which I have heard echoed across Indonesia's heritage sector) to work with other countries, such as Singapore or South Korea, that they hoped would be more generous with funding than the stereotypically frugal Dutch. Yet one line of criticism was glaringly absent from the views voiced by my Indonesian interlocutors: that Dutch experts might be unqualified or unwelcome to conduct heritage projects in Semarang *because* of their country's role in the archipelago's painful past. In fact, the general consensus amongst all parties, Dutch and Indonesian, appeared to be precisely the opposite.

To better understand this paradox, it must be considered within the wider context of how citizens of the Netherlands and Indonesia today view the period of Dutch colonial rule in these islands. Even by the rather low standards set by Britain and France, the Netherlands lags behind fellow imperial powers of yore in reckoning with its colonial past (Smits 2011; van Leeuwen 2011; Bosma 2012). As Andrew Goss (2000, pp. 11–12) explains, the nation has not yet embarked upon any "serious soul-searching" in regards to this chapter in its history, in part because the period of Dutch empire has remained firmly "bracketed" in public discourse (and also in the country's academic sphere, where even some prominent researchers studying the Dutch East Indies go to great lengths to avoid engaging with postcolonial theory [Boehmer and de Mul 2012]). This "bracketing" means that when Dutch colonial history is discussed in the Netherlands today (already a rare occurrence) it is usually presented as disconnected from the wider narrative of the country's past and unrelated to national identity in the present. Often, Dutch imperial ambitions are even cast in a favourable light: as an endeavour to be celebrated (the term *VOC mentaliteit*, or "VOC mentality", is a byword for Dutch entrepreneurial spirit that regularly pops up in everyday conversation); a warm memory of *tempo doeloe* ("the good ol' days" [Goss 2000; Gouda 2007]) prompted by a sepia-toned photograph in the family album; or, at the very least, a benign mercantile pursuit of peaceful trade, not violent conquest. As one representative of the non-profit organization once explained to me, his ancestors had a "special gene for trade" but were careful not to change the "structure" of the indigenous societies they encountered. Dutch citizens today thus had no reason to feel guilty about their past empire, he reasoned cheerfully.

As would be expected, Indonesians generally do not harbour such rosy views of their own colonization. However, scholars have noted a curious lack of public interest in confronting the period of Dutch rule as *the* moment of national trauma, producing what Kusno (2000) calls a state of "postcolonial amnesia", in contrast with other former colonies in which this history is usually cast as a source of continuing "anxiety", a "painful memory" to be suppressed, or a "burden to disown" (pp. 210–11). Ironically, this is especially evident in Indonesia's booming heritage sector—the one arena in which a sober reckoning with the violence of this past would seem to be unavoidable. Just as the period of empire has been "bracketed" in the Netherlands, the history of colonial oppression, as the lived experience of one's own ancestors, appears to have been *decoupled* from the visual markers and material trappings from that time (i.e., "imperial debris") still present in the archipelago, which, relabelled as "heritage", have been rendered safe for consumption by Indonesians today. It is not that colonialism is forgiven and forgotten (as indeed some Dutch tourists interpret their encounters with smiling local tour guides), but that instead, through an exercise of selective memory, present-day Indonesians are not required to actively reckon with this past in the course of preserving, promoting or enjoying its physical traces as "heritage". As one of Semarang's young Kota Lama enthusiasts replied when I asked them how this district known for its "Dutch" architecture, so clearly constructed under the colonial yoke, could attract such admiration from their countrymen today: "For us, there isn't a relationship between 'Dutch'/the Netherlands (*belanda*) and colonialism."[15]

This notion that a postcolonial society can celebrate structures built by its own colonizers without feeling compelled to critique the colonial project itself is startling, but not unprecedented (Bissell 2005). Indeed, this is precisely what Amae (2017) describes in contemporary Taiwan, where the reappropriation of infrastructures built by Japanese engineers in the early twentieth century as popular heritage sites is indicative of a postcolonial discourse in which one can be "pro-Japanese" without necessarily being "pro-colonial" (p. 255). In much the same fashion, Kota Lama can be valued by Indonesian heritage professionals, activists, tourists and government officials as the city's "Dutch" district—its "Little Netherlands"—without prompting a public discussion of the history of conquest and extraction to which its very existence testifies.

Participating in these patterns of bracketing and decoupling, the pain
of the colonial past was completely ignored by both the Dutch visitors and
their Indonesian hosts in Semarang and replaced instead with a feeling
of personal (and apolitical) intimacy. Expressing such intimacies—that
is, the belief that both parties intuitively "get" each other because of the
Netherlands' and Indonesia's historical ties—played a key role in their
daily interactions and, especially, in propping up the Dutch teams' claims
to expertise, which were often being undermined by their own bumbling
and the resultant "chaos". While both the non-profit organization and
the consultancy company certainly wanted to be perceived as somewhat
neutral parties in Semarang (when asked by workshop participants,
"Who do you work for?", the Dutch visitors would reply emphatically,
"We work for Kota Lama!"[16]), team members would also regularly reference
their own familial connections with Indonesia in an attempt to develop
rapport with their hosts. For instance, in presentations to Indonesian
audiences, one member of the consultancy company would begin with a
slide showing a map of the archipelago, point to the easternmost province
of present-day Papua, and proudly explain that he was born there, before
returning to the Netherlands with his family while still a toddler. To anyone
with knowledge of modern Indonesian history, this statement could easily
come across as tone-deaf—Papua, also known up until the early 1960s as
Netherlands New Guinea, was the last holdout of Dutch colonial rule in
the region and continues to be a source of contention to the present day.
However, he seemed to believe, and perhaps rightly so, that revealing
this personal history would not only foster a closer relationship between
his team and their local interlocutors but would also legitimize his work
in Semarang on the grounds that Indonesia, as he would then explain to
the audience, was "a place very close to [his] heart".

Ibu Lydia, Pak Indra and other Indonesians who had personal
experience working and studying in the Netherlands often reciprocated
these expressions of intimacy with their visitors, chatting with them in
Dutch and comparing notes on the far-off cities where they had once
lived. But even amongst local heritage professionals and activists who
did *not* have any direct personal ties to the Netherlands, many similarly
harboured an initial expectation that *Dutch* expertise, as opposed to any
other generic "foreign" kind, would perhaps be better equipped to offer
insights and assistance regarding the "Dutch" district of Kota Lama. Mas
Arif and others knew that their visitors from the Netherlands would arrive

in Semarang fairly clueless about local politics, language and culture (a fact which proved to be both a burden and an opportunity), but they did, at first, hold out hope that the shared history of their two countries would mean that the Dutch teams would possess a better-than-average understanding of the city's past (or at least privileged access to Dutch archives), and thus offer advice tailored to Kota Lama. Within the first few days of their visits, however, it became clear that this was not the case; despite their claims to personal familiarities with Indonesia and its past, almost everything the Dutch "experts" came to know about Kota Lama, they learned from their Indonesian hosts and the single Dutch researcher who had invited them to Semarang in the first place. Going forward, the already sceptical Pak Indra took his disappointing experiences with the two Dutch teams into account when considering potential future collaborations with their countrymen. For instance, a few months after the departure of the consultancy company, one of their affiliates in Amsterdam sought to curate an exhibition in Semarang on an early twentieth-century Dutch architect who had designed many of the city's iconic buildings. Instead, Pak Indra handed the responsibility over to a team of local curators and heritage activists, telling me with uncharacteristic bluntness, "Well, actually, we realized we probably know as much about [this architect] as the Dutch do!"

It is not difficult to understand why heritage activists anywhere would become disillusioned with foreign experts when promised results are left undelivered. But in the case of the Dutch teams in Semarang, the disillusionment of their hosts was deepened when the initial expectation of a uniquely *Dutch* expertise, assumed to be born of shared history and personal intimacies, was unmet. This expectation was itself founded on an even more fundamental premise: that presence of experts from the Netherlands in the city of Semarang was the normal, even natural, state of affairs. The Dutch teams did not feel they needed to go to great lengths to justify their work in Kota Lama, either to each other or to the Indonesians they encountered, because it was simply taken for granted that *of course* they would be involved; for their part, local heritage professionals and enthusiasts, even those who viewed their Dutch visitors as bringing more "chaos" than "help", did not dispute this basic presumption. By way of contrast, as an American, my own interest in Semarang's heritage sites was often met with surprise from both my Dutch and Indonesian interlocutors, who were initially very curious as to why I, an individual with no apparent personal ties to the archipelago, would ever want to study its history. Once, a member of a Dutch cultural agency (one that regularly funds Dutch-led heritage projects abroad) even approached me at a conference in the Netherlands to ask, good-naturedly, what on earth drew me to "their" colony.

If nothing else, this—the normalization of Dutch expertise in Indonesia—is a testament to the enduring dynamics of the colonial past in the postcolonial present, and thus just as much a kind of "colonial heritage" as Kota Lama itself.

Notes

1. "Gateway to modernity" was the title of a prominent panel featured in a 2013 exhibition on the history of Semarang organized by local heritage activists.
2. I recognize that terms such as "foreign", "local" and "expert" are potentially problematic, being constructed categories that can obscure more than they reveal. I use these words here with this in mind (though for stylistic reasons I do not always place the words in quotation marks), in part because these are the terms used by my Dutch and Indonesian informants themselves, and in part because one of the aims of this chapter is to illustrate how these taken-for-granted descriptors are in fact strategically managed and deployed.
3. Another former occupier, Japan, is also a prominent supplier of experts and funds to Indonesia today. In this chapter, I focus on a particular category of "foreigners", but in doing so I do not mean to suggest that there are not other kinds of "foreignness" that play a role in Indonesia's heritage sector, and which are neither Western nor white. In fact, Japanese professionals have long been involved in heritage preservation work in the country (e.g., their role in the restoration of Borobudur in the 1970s [Nagaoka 2016]). However, because there were no such Japanese-led projects when I did my fieldwork in Semarang, I do not directly address them here.
4. Though Meskell (2012) observes that the recommendations of experts from ICOMOS and IUCN are increasingly ignored in World Heritage Committee proceedings when seen to impede that body's "rush to inscribe" sites.
5. This name was coined a decade or so prior by an Indonesian academic who, on a visit to Singapore, had been impressed by the city-state's marketing of ethnically defined neighbourhoods like "Little India" and "the Malay Quarter" as heritage sites. Despite the rather odd linguistic position of "Little Netherlands"—an English term coined by an Indonesian to describe a "Dutch" district—it remains a popular moniker amongst Semarangers.
6. Thus far, however, such attempts have run into bureaucratic dead ends. As

explained to me by a senior figure in Semarang's city government, despite all the talk of PPPs (public-private partnerships) being on the rise in Indonesia since the post-1998 decentralization of the country's administration, there is still no suitable template (in their office's view) for collaborations between government bodies and non-government actors, especially ones from overseas.

7. Though, crucially, this endorsement was nothing so serious as an act of granting permission for the project to go ahead; independent organizations from the Netherlands do not require the formal approval of the Dutch embassy to carry out their initiatives in Indonesia, though it is often sought as a matter of convention in the case of cultural heritage projects. This is indicative of a wider global trend, wherein heritage work is being increasingly carried out by private actors that are nonetheless somewhat connected to and, most crucial, *locally understood as* representatives of foreign governments.

8. All names of individuals mentioned in this paper are pseudonyms.

9. The fact of Indonesia's growing economy has not been lost on the Dutch politicians and diplomats engaged in formulating their country's international heritage policies. According to those involved in Erasmushuis, the Dutch cultural centre affiliated with the embassy in Jakarta, Indonesia's status as "no longer a poor country" is raised in the Dutch parliament as a reason why direct funding to heritage initiatives (and other projects) in the former colony is no longer strategic and should be replaced by Dutch experts sent to advise the Indonesian public and private sectors. This recognition of the improved financial footing of Indonesia therefore does not seem to correlate to a recognition of the country's ability to make independent decisions on how to best preserve its cultural heritage; rather, it serves as justification for even heavier involvement of foreign expertise.

10. Like many of my informants, Mas Arif frequently peppered his Indonesian speech with English terms and phrases. His use of "appropriate situation" in English was indicative of this habit.

11. In the original Indonesian: "Mereka tidak 'memperumit' situasinya, itu bukan istilahnya yang benar. Istilah yang benar adalah 'mengacaukan.'"

12. Indeed, even though several heritage advocates in Semarang had obtained masters or doctoral degrees from European, American or Australian universities, their possession of these credentials could actually be looked upon with some suspicion by local authorities as "arrogant" (*sombong*) (a judgement likely also coloured by the fact that most of these educated individuals were young and middle-aged women, while most of the Dutch "experts" were older men).

13. However, I did my best to stress to my interlocutors throughout my time in Indonesia that I was *not* a trained professional in the field of cultural heritage

management and had no desire to interject how I thought Kota Lama "should" be developed into local heritage advocates' ongoing conversations.

14. At the time of writing, this proposed plan has not been carried through (and, to my knowledge, has not even been mentioned again since the initial negative reception it received).

15. In the original Indonesian: "Bagi kami, tidak ada hubungan antara belanda dan penjajahan." In the text above, I have translated this phrase as directly as possible, but an alternative, more liberal translation of the same sentence could be: "From our perspective, 'Dutch'/the Netherlands is not synonymous with colonialism."

16. This answer was entirely unsatisfactory to the Indonesian attendees, who would often come up to me after the session was finished to ask me in lowered voices if I knew who these Dutch people *really* worked for. In saying that they "worked for Kota Lama", the team was trying to indicate that their company was beholden to no one, something they likely felt would put their Indonesian hosts at ease; in reality, it just made many of them more perplexed and apprehensive.

References

Adams, J. 2015. "Equity Polestar or Pretense? International Archaeological Tourism Development in 'Less Developed Countries'". In *Heritage Keywords: Rhetoric and Redescription in Cultural Heritage*, edited by K.L. Samuels and T. Rico. Boulder: University Press of Colorado.

Akagawa, N. 2016. "Japan and the Rise of Heritage in Cultural Diplomacy". *Future Anterior: Journal of Historic Preservation History, Theory, and Criticism* 13, no. 1: 125–39.

Amae, Y. 2017. "Becoming Taiwanese: Appropriation of Japanese Colonial Sites and Structures in Cultural Heritage-Making—A Case Study on the Wushantou Reservoir and Hatta Yoichi". In *Citizens, Civil Society and Heritage-Making in Asia*, edited by H.M. Hsiao, H. Yew-Foong, and P. Peycam. Singapore: ISEAS – Yusof Ishak Institute.

Berliner, D. 2012. "Multiple Nostalgias: The Fabric of Heritage in Luang Prabang". *Journal of the Royal Anthropological Institute* 18, no. 4: 769–86.

Bissell, W. 1999. "City of Stone, Space of Contestation: Urban Conservation and the Colonial Past in Zanzibar". PhD Dissertation, University of Chicago.

———. 2005. "Engaging Colonial Nostalgia". *Cultural Anthropology* 20, no. 2: 215–48.

Bosma, U. 2012. "Why Is There No Post-colonial Debate in the Netherlands?" In *Post-colonial Immigrants and Identity Formations in the Netherlands*, edited by U. Bosma. Amsterdam: Amsterdam University Press.

Breglia, L. 2006. *Monumental Ambivalence: The Politics of Heritage*. Austin: University of Texas Press.

Byrne, D. 1995. "Buddhist Stupa and Thai Social Practice". *World Archaeology* 27, no. 2: 266–81.

———. 2007. *Surface Collection: Archaeological Travels in Southeast Asia*. Lanham, MD: AltaMira Press.

de Cesari, C. 2010. "World Heritage and Mosaic Universalism: A View from Palestine". *Journal of Social Archaeology* 10, no. 3: 299–324.

Cobban, J. 1988. "Kampungs and Conflict in Colonial Semarang". *Journal of Southeast Asian Studies* 19, no. 2: 266–91.

Coté, J. 2006. "Staging Modernity: The Semarang International Colonial Exhibition, 1914". *RIMA: Review of Indonesian and Malaysian Affairs* 40, no. 1: 1–44.

Goss, A. 2000. "From Tong-Tong to Tempo Doeloe: Eurasian Memory Work and the Bracketing of Dutch Colonial History, 1957–1961". *Indonesia* 70: 9–36.

Gouda, F. 2007. "The Unbearable Lightness of Memory: Formations of Cultural Memory and Recycling the Dutch Colonial Past". *Historical Journal Groniek* 174: 9–27.

Herzfeld, M. 2003. "Pom Mahakan: Humanities and Order in the Historic Center of Bangkok". *Thailand Human Rights Journal* 1: 101–19.

———. 2010. "Engagement, Gentrification and the Neoliberal Hijacking of History". *Current Anthropology* 51, no. 2: 259–67.

Jacobs, J. 2010. "Re-branding the Levant: Contested Heritage and Colonial Modernities in Amman and Damascus". *Journal of Tourism and Cultural Change* 8, no. 4: 316–26.

James, L. 2016. "The Symbolic Value of Expertise in International Heritage Diplomacy". *Future Anterior: Journal of Historic Preservation History, Theory, and Criticism* 13, no. 1: 83–98.

Jenkins, G. 2008. *Contested Space: Cultural Heritage and Identity Reconstructions: Conservation Strategies within a Developing Asian City*. Münster: LIT Verlag Münster.

Kong, L. 2011. *Conserving the Past, Creating the Future: Urban Heritage in Singapore*. Singapore: Urban Redevelopment Authority.

Kusno, A. 2000. *Behind the Postcolonial: Architecture, Urban Space and Political Cultures in Indonesia*. New York: Routledge.

van Leeuwen, L. 2011. "Postcolonial Neglect in Holland". *Inside Indonesia* 103 (January–March). http://www.insideindonesia.org/weekly-articles/postcolonial-neglect-in-holland.

Leushuis, E. 2017. *Panduan Jelajah Kota-kota Pusaka di Indonesia* [Guide to exploring heritage cities in Indonesia]. Yogyakarta: Penerbit Ombak.

Logan, W. 1996. "Protecting Historic Hanoi in the Context of Heritage Contestation". *International Journal of Heritage Studies* 2, no. 2: 76–92.

Luke, C., and M. Kersel. 2013. *United States Cultural Diplomacy and Archaeology: Soft Power, Hard Heritage*. New York: Routledge.

Meskell, L. 2012. "The Rush to Inscribe: Reflections on the 35th Session of the World Heritage Committee UNESCO Paris, 2011". *Journal of Field Archaeology* 37, no. 2: 145–51.

Muhammad, D. 2011. *Semarang Sepanjang Jalan Kenangan* [Semarang down memory lane]. Semarang: Pustaka Semarang.

Nagaoka, M. 2016. *Cultural Landscape Management at Borobudur, Indonesia*. New York: Springer.

Peleggi, M. 2005. "Consuming Colonial Nostalgia: The Monumentalisation of Historic Hotels in Urban South-East Asia". *Asia Pacific Viewpoint* 46, no. 3: 255–65.

Poeze, H. 2014. *Tan Malaka, Gerakan Kiri, dan Revolusi Indonesia* [Tan Malaka, the Leftist Movement, and the Indonesian Revolution]. Jakarta: KITLV-Jakarta.

Rico, T. 2016. *Constructing Destruction: Heritage Narratives in the Tsunami City*. New York: Routledge.

Roberts, J.L. 2017. "Heritage-Making and Post-coloniality in Yangon, Myanmar". In *Citizens, Civil Society and Heritage-Making in Asia*, edited by H.M. Hsiao, H. Yew-Foong, and P. Peycam. Singapore: ISEAS – Yusof Ishak Institute.

Smits, A. 2011 "The Netherlands in Post-colonial Perspective: Compared with Other European Art Institutes, Those in the Netherlands Lag behind in Processing Their Nation's Colonial Past". *Metropolis M* 5 (October/November 2011). http://metropolism.com/magazine/2011-no5/niet-willen-weten/english.

Stoler, A. 2013. "'The Rot Remains': From Ruins to Ruination". In *Imperial Debris: On Ruins and Ruination*, edited by A. Stoler. Durham, NC: Duke University Press.

Yapp, L. 2016. "Define Mutual: Heritage Diplomacy in the Post-colonial Netherlands". *Future Anterior: Journal of Historic Preservation History, Theory, and Criticism* 13, no. 1: 67–82.

7

Heritage Conservation as a Tool for Cultural Diplomacy: Implications for the Sino-Japanese Relationship

Victor Chi-Ming Chan

The Sino-Japanese relationship has experienced ups and downs since its diplomatic normalization in the 1970s. The increasing economic interdependence has broadened and deepened mutual understanding and interests among business sectors and the general public in both countries, while historical problems, security and territorial disputes, and economic competition remain the main obstacles for building trust and confidence between the two governments. The bilateral relationship since the changes in leadership in the two countries in 2012 has substantially deteriorated. Chinese President Xi Jinping and Japanese Prime Minister Abe Shinzō were finally able to schedule their first bilateral summit in 2014, at the Beijing APEC Leaders' Summit, after they had both been in office for two years. It is expected that the Sino-Japanese relationship will continue to face many challenges, particularly in relation to security issues.

With such a pessimistic background to Sino-Japanese relations over the past few years, this chapter aims to examine how heritage conservation could operate as a tool of cultural diplomacy in the context of Sino-Japanese confrontation. Heritage not only contains cultural or historical value but also enhances and channels a national image to a country's people, and to the rest of the world. So, in order to realize the nationalist agenda, it is essential for both governments to "push" heritage conservation at the international institutional level—in this case, through the framework of the United Nations Educational, Scientific and Cultural Organization (UNESCO). The core concern of this chapter is to explore how China and Japan interact with different stakeholders through the negotiation and lobbying processes to realize their cultural and diplomatic, or nationalistic objectives.

The chapter consists of five sections. After this introduction, the second section reviews the process of heritage conservation at the domestic and international levels. I apply a constructivist approach to conceptualize heritage as a tool of cultural diplomacy. The third and fourth sections delineate two case studies related to heritage conservation and the Sino-Japanese relationship: (1) the inclusion of sites of Japan's Meiji Industrial Revolution: Iron and Steel, Shipbuilding and Coal Mining in the World Heritage List (WHL); and (2) the inclusion of Documents of the Nanjing Massacre in the Memory of the World Register (MWR) in July and October 2015, respectively. The former case reveals how the Japanese government has sought to build a national identity as a model of modernization in Asia since the late nineteenth century—in this case, positioning Japan as the first Asian nation that was able to modernize and compete with the West. The latter case shows the efforts of the Chinese government to "protect" the documenting of the Nanjing Massacre and to stereotype Japan as a "former aggressor with potential military ambitions". The final section concludes that heritage conservation may be a novel but fierce "battlefield" in future Sino-Japanese relations, that both governments may need to "rethink" their strategies of reforming the international heritage conservation process, and that the two countries should both nurture better relations with each other and also with South Korea.

Heritage Conservation as Cultural Diplomacy

According to the website of UNESCO (2016), heritage is "the legacy from the past, what the populations live with today, and what they pass on to future generations". Cultural or natural heritage is therefore an irreplaceable source of life and inspiration. In recent years, heritage conservation in various aspects at the national level has been of increasing importance. In terms of its economic contribution, tourism focussed on cultural heritage is a major and stable source of foreign income in a globalized and interconnected world (Streeten 2006). With the rapid growth of transportation and information technology, it is easier for budget-conscious tourists to visit widely recognized World Heritage Sites at an affordable cost. In order to attract potential tourists, collaborative efforts among different stakeholders, particularly government agencies and the private business sector, are essential (Tunney 2005). But a more fundamental concern is how the cultural practices or heritage sites that represent a nation's "past" are recognized internationally. UNESCO's frameworks are designed to impose "political neutral" and "professional" directions for making decisions on conservation. However, it is not too much of a stretch to observe the process as a result of cultural diplomacy.

Heritage Conservation as a Politically Neutral and Professional Evaluation Process

UNESCO has been putting enormous efforts into assisting the realization of national conservation policy initiatives. Heritage conservation involves collaboration and advanced technological knowledge and equipment. After World War II, UNESCO was able to coordinate international projects to save "the Abu Simbel temples in the Nile Valley" in 1959 and "Venice after disastrous floods threatening the survival of the City" in 1966 (Frey and Steiner 2011, p. 555). The 1972 UNESCO Convention concerning the protection of the world's cultural and natural heritage "seeks to encourage the identification, protection and preservation of cultural and natural heritage around the world considered to be of outstanding value to humanity" (UNESCO 1972). Regarding documentary heritage as another focus of this chapter, the UNESCO Memory of the World Programme established in 1992 aims to adopt appropriate techniques to preserve and disseminate the valuable archive holdings of libraries and museums worldwide (Abid 1998, pp. 51–66; UNESCO 2011). More importantly, national heritage is considered as internationally significant and influential when it is listed in the WHL and in the MWR.

The decision-making processes for the WHL are relatively more state-centric, as a nomination can only be made by state members. The nomination is then sent to two advisory (expert) bodies—the International Council on Museums and Sites (ICOMOS) and the International Union for Conservation of Nature (IUCN)—for them to "evaluate and propose the sites for inscription" (Frey and Steiner 2011, p. 558) based on ten criteria listed in article 77 of *the Operational Guidelines for the Implementation of the World Heritage Convention* (UNESCO 2015). The World Heritage Committee (WHC), which is composed of twenty-one members elected for a six-year term (but usually four years) by the General Assembly, "is responsible for the implementation of the World Heritage Convention [WHC] ... and decides on the inscription or deletion of properties on the List of World Heritage in Danger" (ibid.).

Operation of the MWR, on the other hand, is relatively less concentrated at the international level, but is deeply involved at the national and regional levels. The MWR encourages member states to implement their own national register and to coordinate with other countries to establish a regional register for promoting the significance of documentary heritage. In order to successfully register as part of the Memory of the World it is not necessary to be nominated by member states. According to article 4.3.3 of UNESCO's (2002) *Memory of the World–General Guidelines to Safeguard Documentary Heritage*, "nominations for the [World] Register may be submitted by any person or organization, including governments and NGOs". It goes on to specify that priority would be given to nominations made by the relevant regional or national Memory of the World committees, or those documentary heritages under threat and commissioned by UNESCO. The nomination should be submitted to the UNESCO Secretariat and then to the International Advisory Committee (IAC). The IAC is responsible for the policies and overall strategy of the whole Memory of the World Programme. It therefore monitors the global progress of the programme, considers reports from its sub-committees, regional committees and the Secretariat, and in turn advises these bodies on their functions and responsibilities. As necessary, it revises and updates the *General Guidelines* and any additions to or deletions from the MWR based on such criteria as authenticity, uniqueness, irreplaceability and significance (UNESCO 2002).

The WHL and the MWR, then, are subject to the approval of expert-led advisory committees/organizations, but the decisions in fact cannot entirely avoid all political interference. The WHL is expected to be relatively political, as the WHC, which is the final approving body, is a state-centric organization. According to Meskell (2013, p. 486), the WHC, "with the growing dominance of strategic political alliances", may overturn and even publicly deride "the recommendation of the Advisory Bodies and finally affect the credibility of the inscription process". In addition, in the current MWR system, even if materials recommended for registration concern multiple countries, UNESCO does not ask for the opinions of those countries. The fourteen-member IAC, based on their own personal capacity, screens applications, and the director-general makes a final decision based primarily on the committee's recommendations (*Mainichi*, 7 November 2015). Even though the director-general, Irina Bokova (2012), has said "we can decide to act and think as visionaries, to rejuvenate the WHC and confront the challenges of (heritage conservation) in the 21st century", the question can again be asked whether the process is really a fair and transparent one? In general, how far is the so-called "expert-led process" still effective and efficient? Is it sufficient to explain the current Sino-Japanese contest in heritage conservation within UNESCO frameworks?

Heritage Conservation as a Process of Cultural Diplomacy

The argument of this chapter is not intended to simply downplay the influence of heritage experts in deciding on what should be included in the WHL or the MWR. Nevertheless, in spite of rigorous institutions and rules, politics and power relationships should be considered properly in heritage conservation. As already mentioned, domestic politics matters in formulating heritage conservation policies and practices. Such influences inevitably are seen in the international institutional procedures, which may affect the final result. Nation-states nowadays do not solely focus on the traditional security concerns of military capability and economic development, but they also look to newly established arenas such as heritage conservation, which can generate revenues through cultural tourism and which, more importantly, can strengthen their own national identities or reveal the stereotypes found in other competing nations.

Cultural diplomacy, whilst it is becoming increasingly popular in international cultural relations, contains diverse meanings and practices. Gienow-Hecht (2010) examines the purposes and actors of cultural diplomacy. The Department of State in the United States (1959) characterized cultural diplomacy as "the direct and enduring contact between people of different nations ... to generate a better climate of international trust and understanding in which official relations can operate". However, in the Cold War era, cultural diplomacy was almost equivalent to cultural propaganda—an area in which the United States and the Soviet Union competed against one another (Fayet 2010; Magnusdottir 2010). The end of the Cold War, together with rapid globalization since 1990, has been broadening and deepening the cultural exchange among people from different nations and cultures. Cultural diplomacy again stresses more on "the exchange of ideas, information, art and other aspects of culture among nations and their people in order to foster mutual understanding" (Cummings 2003, p. 1) and follows the trend of the retreat of the state. Nevertheless, the process of diplomatic interaction requires substantial state involvement, particularly in the foreign policy domain (Iriye 1997; Mulcahy 1999). So the purpose of cultural diplomacy is highly political (Mitchell 1986).

Another stimulus comes from Joseph Nye's soft power analysis. It goes beyond the traditional conception of power by distinguishing between hard and soft power (Nye 1990, 2002). More importantly, Nye (2011, p. 8) emphasizes that nation-states should seek to acquire "smart power"—a "combination of the hard power of coercion (military capability) and payment (economic strength) with the soft power of persuasion and attraction". Nye's analysis opens the opportunity for different states, regardless of whether they possess military or economic power, to seek a cultural dimension for the acquisition of power. Cultural attractiveness may simply come from tangible and intangible heritage. Throughout the selection process for world heritage, however, it is important for nation-states to try to persuade members of the approving authority to endorse and approve nominations. As a result, cultural diplomacy therefore serves as a renewed platform for nation-states to work with and/or compete against each other and UNESCO.

Heritage Conservation as a National Identity/Stereotype Nexus

This chapter sheds light on how heritage conservation affects political relationships among nation-states. As mentioned earlier, the interplay between state parties occurs and develops within UNESCO frameworks. But what is it that makes such relationships become tense, deteriorate or even lead to confrontation? One suggestion is to view the heritage conservation and national identity/stereotype nexus as a social process under a constructivist approach.

National identity, in terms of representing a symbol of unity, does not develop simply as a natural process. What comes to define a nation as a nation depends on the commonalities found among the groups of people within it. As Anderson (2006) found in his analysis of nationalism and nation building, a nation-state is in fact an imagined political community in which members possess a shared cultural identity. Certain kinds of connection are found among members. In other words, according to Akagawa (2015, pp. 19–20), "it is the process of identifying 'us' and 'others' to establish the distinctiveness for collective identity as the nation" and, therefore, "construct people's attachment to the nation". More importantly, the process of finding shared characteristics makes heritage and its conservation politically important to the rulers. Graham, Ashworth and Tunbridge (2000, p. 183) mention that "the nation-state required national heritage to consolidate national identification, absorb or neutralize potentially competing heritage of socio-cultural groups or regions, combat the claims of other nations upon its territory or people while furthering claims upon nationals in territories elsewhere". Lowenthal (1998, p. 2) points out that heritage serves as "the chief focus of patriotism" and strengthens the existence of "cultural nationalism" (Yoshino 1992). So it is an intended and highly selective process "to feed the [national] brand and to create a desired image" (Minnaert 2014). The first case study of this paper traces how the nomination of industrial sites of Meiji modernization as a world cultural heritage by the Abe administration in 2014 sought to highlight pride in Japanese achievements.

On the other hand, national stereotyping presents an obstacle to the construction of a national identity and brand. According to Berting (1994, p. 11), "stereotypes do not [necessarily] result from the direct experience of the actors [usually outsiders], but from traditions, transmission, mediation and reinterpretation". They may not be positive, but are instead controversial, and are formed outside the nation. So the nation itself is considered a "victim" (Minnaert 2014, p. 107). In other words, the national stereotyping of State A is a by-product of the national branding of State B. The second case study of this paper shows how the nomination of documents from the Nanjing Massacre as an article of world memory by the Central Archives of China and a group of local archives in China in 2014 strengthened the historical significance of China's anti-Japanese aggression during World War II on the one hand and simultaneously reinforced the aggressive past of Japan on the other. Such a historical recollection was an attempt to stereotype Japan as a potential "aggressor" in Asia.

Research Design, Methodology and Framework

It is worthwhile here to outline the research design, methodology and analytical framework of the study. The research adopts a case study approach. I have selected two cases—(1) Sites of Meiji Industrialization: Iron and Steel, Shipbuilding and Coal Mining as world heritage, and (2) Documents of the Nanjing Massacre as world memory—in order to analyse heritage conservation as a political and diplomatic process among multilateral actors, such as national heritage bureaucracy, representatives of state member teams, and experts in UNESCO. The two cases took place under the framework of UNESCO, which included the participation of heritage experts, and the two were required to go through a similar approval process. It is essential to examine how national actors "responded" to the decisions made under the international framework. Of significance is that the two cases involve Japan's controversial World War II legacy. The cases reveal how Japan and China deal with the imperial/colonial past by means of heritage conservation. Japan attempts to "repack" its imperial past as momentum for future economic miracles, while China emphasizes its victimhood to justify the prolonged Japanese aggression.

The methodology is based on documentary and archival analysis (Burnham, Gilland, Grant and Layton-Henry 2004). The materials used in this study can be classified as primary source materials, including UNESCO documents (Convention, Operational Guidelines and other publications related to World Heritage and World Memory); secondary sources such as newspapers and official documents published by the governments of China and Japan; and tertiary sources such as books and academic journal articles.

Instead of focusing merely on the assumptions on rational analysis, the analytical framework depicts and explains the interactions among major stakeholders, particularly governments, national or non-governmental heritage organizations and international institutional actors, particularly those expert-led advisory bodies. The study divides heritage conservation as the construction of national identity into four stages. Stage one looks into the nomination for listing of a site as UNESCO heritage. The question to be asked is: How are the lists of heritage for UNESCO's consideration determined? Stages two and three deal with the selection process led by expert advisory bodies, and the responses by the governments to this. Here the concerns include whether the nomination is good enough for the criteria, particularly in terms of "Universal Value"; what were the comments received from the advisory bodies; and how did the respective state members respond to those comments? Stage four encompasses the announcement of the final result: What is the result? Have there been any protests by state parties against results that could affect their national identity? How does the result affect relationships among state parties? And how does the result affect the pattern of state participation in UNESCO?

Case Study 1 – Sites of Meiji Industrialization: Iron and Steel, Shipbuilding and Coal Mining

On 5 July 2015, the WHC decided to accept Japan's nomination of the sites of Meiji industrialization to include in the WHL. According to UNESCO (2016a):

> The site [of Japan's Meiji Industrialization: Iron and Steel, Shipbuilding and Coal Mining] encompasses a series of 23 component parts, mainly located in the southwest of Japan. It bears testimony to the rapid industrialization of the country from the middle of the 19th century to the early 20th century, through the development of the iron and steel industry, shipbuilding and coal mining. The site illustrates the process by which feudal Japan sought technology transfer from Europe and America from the middle of the 19th century and how this technology was adapted to the country's needs and social traditions. The site testifies to what is considered to be the first successful transfer of Western industrialization to a non-Western nation.

Even though ICOMOS evaluated that the nomination encompassed all the necessary attributes of outstanding Universal Value, a great many criticisms were levelled against the nomination, particularly from those state parties that had been under Japanese colonial rule and subject to aggression, like South Korea and China (*South China Morning Post*, 6 July 2015). This led to a delay in voting and in the announcement of the results (Kirk 2015). With further interactions and negotiation between South Korea, China and Japan, the Japanese were able to gain approval for the nomination.

Stage 1 – Nomination: Constructing National Pride as the First Modernized Asian Country

Returning to power in December 2012 in the wake of a decade of economic depression and political instability, Abe put forward his political agenda of revitalizing Japan as a first-class nation with a strong economy, as geostrategically powerful and possessing cultural importance. On the economics side, Abenomics was positioned as being able to stimulate the economy and halt deflation. On the political side, Abe set out to amend the interpretation of Article 9 of Japan's constitution in order to relax the suspension of the right of collective defence. Culturally, Abe and his government (in particular the Cultural Affairs Agency) have actively been looking for heritage sites able to reflect the historical achievement of national development. The nomination of the sites of Meiji industrialization proposed by several local governments in the southwest region fitted his political agenda. The Abe cabinet officially approved the nomination proposal and submitted it to UNESCO for consideration in 2014. In his welcome message in the nomination proposal (UNESCO 2016b), Prime Minister Abe Shinzō states,

> Central to their [Meiji and the subsequent governments] policies of modernization was the determination to establish heavy industry—most importantly shipbuilding, iron and steel, and coal—as the key to build a world industrial nation. This was based initially on a forthright embrace of Western industrial technologies which, although not always successful in the first instance, were to provide the foundation for Japan's transition within fifty years into a modern industrial state.

From a defeated, weak and divided nation to the first non-Western power to industrialize before World War II, the economic development of Japan since the Meiji period was highlighted. Tracing the historical and cultural significance of the sites in relation to the conditions of pre-war Japan, it was an important step for the Abe government to change the negative images of the imperial past and to even instil feelings of pride and superiority in the Japanese populace through the nomination.

Stage 2 – Selection Process 1: Comments from ICOMOS experts

ICOMOS recommends nomination on the basis of two criteria: (ii) and (iv) in the *Operation Guideline* (UNESCO 2016c). Criteria (ii) looks into whether the nomination "exhibit(s) an important interchange of human values, over a span of time or within a cultural area of the world, on developments in architecture or technology, monumental arts, town-planning, or landscape design". From the evaluation report (2016, p. 102) we are told that,

> [T]he sites collectively represent an exceptional interchange of industrial ideas, know-how and equipment, that resulted, within a short space of time, in an unprecedented emergence of autonomous industrial development in the field of heavy industry which had profound impact on East Asia

In addition, criteria (iv) refers to an instance of heritage as "an outstanding example of a type of building, architectural or technological ensemble, or landscape which illustrates (a) significant stage(s) in human history". The evaluation report (2016, p. 102) states that,

> [T]he technological ensemble of key industrial sites of iron and steel, shipbuilding and coal mining is testimony to Japan's unique achievement in world history as the first non-Western country to successfully industrialize. Viewed as an Asian cultural response to Western industrial values, the ensemble is an outstanding technological ensemble of industrial sites that reflected the rapid and distinctive industrialization of Japan based on local innovation and adaptation of Western technology.

The nomination was endorsed in May 2015 (*Japan Times*, 5 May 2015) but was strongly criticized by Japan's neighbours, South Korea and China.

Stage 3 – Selection Process 2: Interactions among State Members

The recommendation of the experts did not prevent the controversy that arose over the legacy of forced labour in World War II. This should have been foreseen, as China and South Korea had already lodged protests when Japan made its earlier nomination. The Chinese government strongly opposed the inception of the sites without acknowledging the Japanese practice of forced labour during the war. In a news conference on 14 May 2015, Chinese Foreign Ministry spokeswoman Hua Chunying stated that

> Many of the 23 Japanese industrial sites witnessed the use of forced labour from China, the Korean Peninsula and other Asian countries during World War II.... China shares South Korea's concerns when it comes to

Japan's move to register the relevant industrial sites as world heritage, and expresses opposition to this decision. (*Asahi Shinbun*, 15 May 2015)

According to Underwood (2015, p. 1), the South Korean government argued that the twenty-three Japanese sites failed to demonstrate the "universal values" required for World Heritage listing, pointing especially to the seven sites where some 60,000 Koreans were forced to work for Japanese companies in support of the imperial war effort. So the final decision is one that constructs Japan's pride in its modernization on the back of a grim history of overseas slave labour or forced labour, particularly from Korea. South Korea's Foreign Ministry expressed this view in a statement:

> [D]espite our efforts to carry our position, ICOMOS appears to have made the recommendation only from the technical aspect in line with its customs … without acknowledging that forced labour took place there. (Shin 2015)

Both China and South Korea took a very strong position in opposing the endorsement by ICOMOS, as both governments argued that the experts had not considered the importance of the negative colonial legacy.

Stage 4 – Result Announcement: Addressing Forced Labour in the Description of the Sites

As China was not a member of that session of the WHC, it was difficult for the country to impose further action, except through official propaganda, whilst South Korea could push for the Japanese nomination to be rejected. There was a short delay before the vote for nomination because Japan and South Korea needed more time for final negotiations. Eventually, South Korea agreed to approve the nomination under the condition that the existence of forced labour during the period of Japanese occupation and of Japan's aggression be acknowledged. The Japanese delegation at the UNESCO meeting then proposed to incorporate information centres at many of the sites, with a statement that a large number of Koreans and others (including Chinese) were "brought against their will and forced to work under harsh conditions in the 1940s at some of the sites" (Deutsche Welle, 6 July 2015). The South Korean Foreign Ministry took those comments as a breakthrough, remarking that Japan "has come to mention for the first time ever the hard historical fact that Koreans were mobilized against their will and forced to work under harsh conditions in the 1940s" (June 2015).

As a result, Japan's nomination of the sites of Meiji Industrialization: Iron and Steel, Shipbuilding and Coal Mining as a tool to promote Abe's nationalist political agenda was not very successful after Japan acknowledged the existence of forced labour and bowed to pressure from South Korea. The country's national identity and pride as the first non-Western modernized country were damaged. Japanese officials, in their corresponding remarks and statements, avoided using the phrase *kyosei rodo* (forced labour), and instead used *hatarakasareta* (were forced to work), which is a more colloquial expression used to dilute the negative impression of Japan's wartime image (*Japan Times*, 6 July 2015).

Case Study 2 – Documents of the Nanjing Massacre

On 8 October 2015, the Documents of the Nanjing Massacre from China were inscribed on the MWR by the IAC of UNESCO's Memory of the World Programme (*China Daily Asia*, 10 October 2015). The decision came after a two-year process during a meeting of the IAC tasked with studying nominations from forty countries, and was finally accepted by the director-general of UNESCO. According to the Memory of the World Programme (2016),

> Documentary heritage submitted by China and recommended for inclusion in the Memory of the World Register in 2015. The documents consist of three parts: the first part concerns the period of the massacre (1937–1938), the second part is related to the post-war investigation and trials of war criminals documented by the Chinese National Government's Military Tribunal (1945–1947), and the third part deals with files documented by the judiciary authorities of the People's Republic of China (1952–1956).

The result, however, aroused severe criticism from the Japanese government. Japan, as the largest donor of UNESCO, then called for a reform of the organization structure, and even threatened to cut off funding to UNESCO because of what it perceived as an unfair and biased process (*South China Morning Post*, 10 October 2015).

Nomination – Stereotyping Japan as an Aggressor

After China's leadership changeover in 2012, Xi Jinping became the central figure of the fifth generation of leaders. In addition to preserving economic development, Xi has put enormous efforts into combating corruption at various levels, including among retired members of the Politburo Standing Committee. In order to consolidate his power, Xi has positioned himself as a strong leader able to face external threats, such as the rise in Japan of right-wing attitudes towards World War II. The Chinese government under Xi has been looking to alternatives to traditional security responses to counter Japan's revival as a military threat, by documenting Japan's aggressive behaviour as historical fact and subsequently nominating them to a widely accepted international platform—the MWR—and at the same time also accusing Japan of a "deliberate cover-up of the truth" (Han 2015).

China submitted the nomination of documents of the Nanjing Massacre to UNESCO from the six local archives of China in 2014, with the enormous support of the State Archives Administration. The cache included documents related to atrocities committed by Japanese soldiers in Nanjing, where Japan's imperial forces went on a six-week spree of rape and destruction from December 1937, slaughtering as many as 300,000 people (*South China Morning Post*, 13 February 2014). On page 8 of the nomination form, the authenticity of the documents is highlighted as follows:

> All the Nanjing Massacre Documents collected by the above-mentioned archival institutions are original ones. Some of them were acquired during the massacre; some are from the archives of the post-war investigation of the Japanese army's crimes, or from the Tokyo International Military Tribunal and Nanjing War Criminals Tribunal. Other categories of documents include trials of Japanese war criminals by the judiciary of the People's Republic of China, and historical materials and relics donated to the archival institutions by individuals at home and abroad. All the documents and archival items have been collected, sorted and identified by experts. Hence, their identity and provenance have been reliably established.

Despite the non-standard nature of the nomination submission (it not being submitted by a state member), the Chinese government nevertheless fully supported the nomination. Chinese Foreign Ministry Spokeswoman Hua

Chunying explained the submission in a news conference, saying that China wanted to "prevent the miserable and dark days from coming back again" (An 2015). In fact, China aimed to utilize historical documents to reveal what it portrays as the criminal wartime behaviour of the Japanese.

Japan, for its part, has repeatedly accused China's nomination as being a political move taken during a period of sensitive relations between the two countries. On 18 June 2014, Japanese Chief Cabinet Secretary Suga Yoshihide stated that,

> [I]t is extremely regrettable that China has used UNESCO politically to unnecessarily play up the negative legacy of a certain period of the history of both countries when we need efforts for the improvement of the bilateral relationship .... we cannot deny that there were murders and looting [carried out] against non-combatants after the Japanese imperial army entered Nanjing. However, there are several estimates about the scale and it is difficult for the government to determine [these] clearly. (Li 2014)

From the Japanese point of view, China is still trying to use Japan's wartime misdeeds for political purposes (Yoshida 2015). The potential inscription of the Documents of the Nanjing Massacre would definitely endanger Japan's positive national identity with regard to its achievements in economic and industrial development.

Selection Process – Expert-led Recommendations

As mentioned earlier, the selection process is based on the recommendation of the IAC. The fourteen members meet every two years to examine the nominations, and they then make their recommendations to the director-general of UNESCO. According to Lothar Jordan, vice chairman of the IAC, due to the controversial nature of this nomination, prior to the final decision being made the IAC evaluated not only the documents submitted by China but also the arguments compiled by the Japanese Foreign Ministry and papers from a private scholar on the incidents of the Nanjing Massacre. However, the arguments of the Japanese officials failed to persuade the IAC members to change their minds. In fact, it is difficult for state members to intervene too much in current selection practices. Apart from submitting new evidence, nothing can be done to influence the decision of the IAC. Japan has already called for reform to improve the transparency of the selection process.

From the Chinese side, it is also important to note that its nomination of "comfort women" was not accepted because the IAC would like China, together with other "affected" countries like South Korea, to jointly submit a new nomination. If such a recommendation were to be followed, it would assist in providing a cross-check and a cooperative approach, thereby protecting various sources of documentary heritage that involve different countries (Yi 2015). The Chinese government therefore may see whether the South Korean government would be interested in making a joint nomination in the future about the "comfort women" issue.

Announcement of the Result and National Responses to it

The IAC recommendation on the Documents of the Nanjing Massacre along with the final approval by the director-general of UNESCO intensified the confrontation between China and Japan in three areas: (1) how to define "truth" with regard to the Nanjing Massacre, as well as the issue of national stereotyping of Japan; (2) matters of UNESCO funding; and (3) reforming the UNESCO framework.

Truth or National Stereotyping?

China welcomed the inscription of documents by the UNESCO decision, with Foreign Ministry Spokeswomen Hua Chunying stating that,

> China will ensure these valuable documents are protected and circulated, and make them play a positive role in remembering history, cherishing peace, looking into the future and safeguarding human dignity.... Nanjing Massacre is a severe crime committed by Japanese militarism during World War II and is a historical fact recognized by the international community.... (*China Daily*, 10 October 2015)

According to the *Manichi Shimbun* (12 October 2015), Zhu Chenshan, director of the Nanjing Massacre Memorial Hall, stated that UNESCO's approval to add the documents to the Memory of the World register meant "that people in the world share a common view on the history of the Nanjing Massacre". In other words, China is to a relatively large extent able to publicize Japan's wartime past, particularly the death toll and its wartime criminal acts. This would help China to counter-balance and compete with Japan in other arenas in the future.

Conversely, the Japanese government was angered by UNESCO's decision because the IAC ignored Japan's arguments and directly recognized Japan as an aggressor during World War II. As a result, the Abe government, which was seeking to develop a nationalist agenda, suffered a great deal. Japan subsequently lodged a protest with the Chinese government that it had used UNESCO for political purposes against the Japanese international image. Japan specifically disagreed with the figure of 300,000 cited by China for the death toll (ibid.).

Funding Issue

Japan is the largest contributor to UNESCO. Japan's Chief Cabinet Secretary Suga Yoshihide has stated that without there being, in Japan's view, a fair and transparent decision-making process, "as for Japan's [financial] contribution [to UNESCO], we plan to look into all possibilities and revisions, including halting payments" (Aljazeera, 13 October 2015). In response, China condemned Japan's threats. Hua Chunying, spokeswomen for China's Foreign Ministry, said that "Japan can threaten to remove funding to the relevant UN body but it cannot rub away its stains from history. The more it rubs, the blacker it becomes." The Japanese reaction materialized when the Abe government decided to withhold its 4.4 billion yen contribution to UNESCO for the fiscal year as leverage in its call for improving operations of the organization (*Japan Times*, 26 October 2016).

Reforming UNESCO's World Memory Programme

In the previous sections we have seen how Japan has repeatedly called for a complete reform of the entire selection procedure for the World Memory Programme. In a statement, the Japanese Foreign Ministry said:

> It is extremely regrettable that a global organization that should be neutral and fair entered the documents in the Memory of the World register, despite the repeated pleas made by the Japanese government.... As a responsible member of UNESCO, the Japanese government will seek a reform of this important project, so that it will not be used politically. (*South China Morning Post*, 10 October 2015)

In addition, Hiroshi Hase, Japan's then minister for education, culture, sports, science and technology, urged UNESCO at the 2015 General

Conference in Paris to improve the governance and transparency of the programme at an early date. Japan's view is that the main focus of reform should be to ensure fairness and transparency and to avoid politicizing documentary heritage conservation.

China's response to the discussion about reform of the Memory of the World Register was not very strong, but it emphasized that it should not be politicized. According to Hong Lei, a spokesman for the Chinese Foreign Ministry,

> The UNESCO and its subsidiary bodies have been discussing the reform of the Memory of the World Register to make better use of its positive role in protecting the world's cultural heritage and the common memory of mankind.... If some nations try to politicize the reform of the application rules of the Memory of the World Register to seek their private benefits and further to realize their goal of denying or even beautifying the history of aggression, the reform will be opposed firmly by the international community. (CCTV News Content, 22 December 2015)

On the one hand, China has been relatively cautious so as to avoid further politicizing UNESCO's decisions and the call for reform. On the other hand, China has insisted on deliberative consultation among members of the international community to allow for fair discussion and for proper decisions on any reform to be made.

The reform process began in 2015. It included a comprehensive review conducted by the IAC. In 2017 the Executive Board of UNESCO approved the IAC's Final Review Report in which highlights "questioned nominations (like comfort women) will be given more time for dialogue amongst the concerned parties, even before submission to Register Assessment Sub-committee (RASC)" (UNESCO MOW IAC 2017). In other words, such an amendment seems to "favour" the Japanese side, particularly in terms of "suspending" the comfort women inscription (Nakano 2018; Suh 2020). However, the debates of the inscription of historical controversies as MOW are still going on before the resumption of the next cycle of the inscription process.

Conclusion: Implications for Sino-Japanese Relations in Heritage Diplomacy

The conflict in heritage diplomacy between China and Japan intensified after UNESCO accepted Japan's sites of Meiji industrialization in the

WHL and China's documents of the Nanjing Massacre as part of the International MWR. Aside from territorial disputes and economic competition, heritage conservation—particularly any related to the legacy of World War II—is a highly sensitive issue for both countries. In spite of its heavy dependence on the recommendations of experts, in the two cases studied above, UNESCO became increasingly politicized. Along with building their own identities through heritage conservation, China and Japan may also seek ways to "influence" UNESCO to generate "stereotypes" and to bring disgrace to each other. Japan, as the main financial contributor, may have some advantage in pushing for the reforms. China, on the other hand, may be able to involve more parties in heritage conservation in order to rebalance the efforts of Japan. So, in order to enhance their own soft power, both countries may actively participate in these processes in the foreseeable reform, especially in redefining the composition of the IAC and in the decision-making process for the Memory of the World Programme. More importantly, leaders in both countries have their own nationalistic political agendas, and heritage—as a tool of foreign policy—is being substantially utilized in the process of realizing these interests.

In the context of the controversy over heritage related to World War II, South Korea becomes an essential card played in Sino-Japanese relations. In retrospect, it could be seen that opposition to the nomination of the sites of Meiji restoration did not come mainly from China, but rather from South Korea. It is necessary to examine the role of South Korea in balancing Sino-Japanese relations and in the processes of national identity construction by the two countries. In the discussion of colonial and World War II legacies, it is still possible to link China and South Korea, which may inhibit further development of the relationship between Japan and South Korea. Ideally, therefore, China and South Korea should keep their eyes on the potential revival of Japanese neo-conservatism. However, Japan and South Korea are major US allies in East Asia. Any further improvement in their bilateral relationship would be mutually beneficial and would accord with the interests of the United States.

A current and important observation should be highlighted with respect to the "comfort women" issue. South Korea had made a "final and irrevocable" deal with Japan on the "comfort women" issue in December 2015. Compensation has been made and the Japanese government has issued an apology; the South Korean government for its part will try actively to persuade local civil society organizations to remove the controversial comfort woman statute near the Japanese Embassy in Seoul. However, with the downfall of ex-president Park Geun-hye in March 2017, the deal was dismissed by President Moon Jae-in in December of the same year. Although the Abe government warned that there was no alternative other than the deal to settle the "comfort women" issue, Moon and his appointed comfort women task force concluded the deal could not resolve the dispute entirely and therefore new negotiations were necessary.

In conclusion, heritage diplomacy between China and Japan has been becoming increasingly important for their respective foreign policy agendas. If the spillover effect of heritage conservation (either positive or negative) is strong enough, China and Japan will need to consider various strategies such as actively participating in international frameworks and looking for proper political alliances to preserve their own constructed identities and interests.

References

Abid, A. 1998. "Memory of the World—Preserving Our Documentary Heritage". *International Journal of Special Libraries* 32, no. 1: 51–66.

Akagawa, N. 2015. *Heritage Conservation and Japan's Cultural Diplomacy: Heritage, National Identity and National Interest*. Abingdon, Oxon: Routledge.

An, B. 2015. "Japan Seeks to 'Block' Application for Nanjing". *China Daily*, 5 October 2015. http://www.chinadaily.com.cn/world/2015-10/05/content_22091194. htm (accessed 10 April 2016).

Anderson, B. 2006. *Imagined Communities*, 2nd ed. New York: Verso.

Berting, J., ed. 1994. *The Roles of Stereotypes in International Relations*. Rotterdam: Ribso.

Bokova, I. 2012. Address by Ms Irina Bokova, UNESCO director-general, on the occasion of the opening of the 36th session of the World Heritage Committee, Saint Petersburg, Russian Federation. http://unesdoc.unesco. org/images/0021/002167/216700e.pdf (accessed 10 April 2016).

Burnham, P., K. Gilland, W. Grant, and Z. Layton-Henry. 2004. *Research Methods in Politics*. London: Palgrave.

Cumming, M.C. 2003. *Cultural Diplomacy and the United States Government: A Survey*. Washington, DC: Centre for Arts and Culture.

Department of State, International Educational Exchange Service, Bureau of International Cultural Relations, United States. 1959. "Cultural Diplomacy". Washington, DC: US Department of State.

Fayet, J. Voks. 2010. "The Third Dimension of Soviet Foreign Policy". In *Searching for a Cultural Diplomacy*, edited by J.C.E. Gienow-Hecht and M.C. Donfried. New York: Berghahn Books.

Frey, B.S., and L. Steiner. 2011. "World Heritage List: Does It Make Sense?" *International Journal of Cultural Policy* 17, no. 5: 555–75.

Gienow-Hecht, J.C.E. 2010. "What Are We Searching For? Cultural, Diplomacy, Agents, and the State". In *Searching for a Cultural Diplomacy*, edited by J.C.E. Gienow-Hecht and M.C. Donfried. New York: Berghahn Books.

Graham, B., G.J. Ashworth, and J.E. Tunbridge. 2000. *A Geography of Heritage: Power, Culture and Economy*. London: Arnold.

Han, B. 2015. "UNESCO Accepts China's Nanjing Massacre". *The Diplomat*, 17 October 2015. http://thediplomat.com/2015/10/unesco-accepts-chinas-nanjing-massacre-documents/ (12 April 2016).

Iriye, A. 1997. *Cultural Internationalism and World Order*. Baltimore, MD: Johns Hopkins University Press.

Jun, H. 2015. "UNESCO Listing Renews Spat between Japan, South Korea". *Wall Street Journal*, 7 July 2015. http://blogs.wsj.com/japanrealtime/2015/07/07/unesco-listing-renews-spat-between-japan-south-korea (accessed 6 April 2016).

Kirk, D. 2015. "Japan, Korea Breakthrough: Japanese Repenting 'Forced' Korean Labor on UNESCO Heritage Sites". *Forbes*, 6 July 2015. http://www.forbes.com/sites/donaldkirk/2015/07/06/japan-agrees-with-korea-on-world-heritage-sites-admitting-forced-labor-an-omen-for-future/#6b589b1a18a4 (accessed 15 April 2016).

Li, Zoe. 2014. "UNESCO Lists Nanjing Massacre and 'Comfort Women,' China Says". CNN, 18 June 2014. http://edition.cnn.com/2014/06/13/world/asia/china-japan-nanjing-massacre-unesco (accessed 12 April 2016).

Lowenthal, D. 1998. *Possessed by the Past: The Heritage Crusade and the Spoils of History*. Cambridge: Cambridge University Press.

Magnusdottir, R. 2010. "Mission Impossible? Selling Soviet Socialism to Americans". In *Searching for a Cultural Diplomacy*, edited by Gienow-Hecht J.C.E. and M.C. Donfried. New York: Berghahn Books.

Meskell, L. 2013. "UNESCO's World Heritage Convention at 40". *Current Anthropology* 54, no. 4: 483–94.

Minnaert, T. 2014. "Footprint or Fingerprint: International Cultural Policy as Identity Policy". *International Journal of Cultural Policy* 20, no. 2: 99–113.

Mitchell, J.M. 1986. *International Cultural Relations*. London: Allen and Unwin.

Mulcahy, K.V. 1999. "Cultural Diplomacy and the Exchange Program, 1938–1978". *Journal of Arts Management, Law and Society* 29, no. 1: 7–28.

Nakano, R. 2018. "The Unintended Consequences of UNESCO's Documentary Heritage Program: Shaming without Naming". *ASR: CMU Journal of Social Sciences and Humanities Special on Heterodoxy in Global Studies* 5, no. 2: 99–113.

Nye. J.S. Jr. 1990. *Born to Lead: The Changing Nature of American Power*. New York: Basic Books.

———. 2002. *The Paradox of American Power: Why the World's Only Super-power Can't Go It Alone*. New York: Oxford University Press.

———. 2011. *The Future of Power*. New York: Public Affairs.

South China Morning Post (SCMP). 2017. "Japan Says 'No Alternative' to 'Comfort Women' Deal after South Korean President Dismisses It", 28 December 2018, https://www.scmp.com/new/asia/east-asia/article/2125943/south-korean-president-moon-jae-dismisses-2015-deal-japan (accessed 20 January 2020).

Streeten, P. 2006. "Culture and Economic Development". In *Handbook of the Economics of Art and Culture*, edited by V.A. Ginsburgh and D. Throsby. Amsterdam: Elsevier.

Suh, K. 2020. "History Wars in the Memory of the World: The Documents of the Nanjing Massacre and the 'Comfort Women'". In *The UNESCO Memory of the World Programme: Key Aspects and Recent Development*, edited by R. Edmondson et al. Cham, Switzerland: Springer.

Tunbridge, J.E., and G.J. Ashworth. 1996. *Dissonant Heritage: The Management of the Past as a Resource in Conflict*. New York: Wiley.

Tunney, J. 2005. "World Trade Law, Culture, Heritage and Tourism: Towards a Holistic Conceptual Approach". In *The Politics of Heritage: Negotiating Tourism and Conversation*, edited by D. Harrison and M. Hitchcock. Clevedon, Buffalo: Channel View.

Underwood, W. 2015. "History in a Box: UNESCO and the Framing of Japan's Meiji Era". *Asia Pacific Journal* 13, no. 26: 1–13. http://apjjf.org/2015/13/26/William-Underwood/4332.html (accessed 10 April 2016).

UNESCO. 2002. *Memory of the World: General Guidelines to Safeguard Documentary Heritage*. http://unesdoc.unesco.org/images/0012/001256/125637e.pdf (accessed 10 April 2016).

———. 2015. *The Operational Guidelines for the Implementation of the World Heritage Convention*. http://whc.unesco.org/en/guidelines (accessed 10 April 2016).

———. 2016a. "Sites of Japan's Meiji Industrial Revolution: Iron and Steel, Shipbuilding and Coal Mining". http://whc.unesco.org/en/list/1484 (accessed 10 April 2016).

———. 2016b. "Sites of Japan's Meiji Industrial Revolution: Iron and Steel, Shipbuilding and Coal Mining. Nomination proposal". http://whc.unesco.org/en/list/1484/documents (accessed 10 April 2016).

———. 2016c. "Sites of Japan's Meiji Industrial Revolution: Iron and Steel, Shipbuilding and Coal Mining—Advisory body evaluation". http://whc.unesco.org/archive/advisory_body_evaluation/1484.pdf (accessed 10 April 2016).

UNESCO Memory of the World Programme. 2014. "Nomination Form—International Memory of the World Register". http://www.unesco.org/

new/fileadmin/MULTIMEDIA/HQ/CI/CI/pdf/mow/nomination_forms/ china_nanjing_en.pdf (accessed 10 April 2016).

———. 2016. "Documents of the Nanjing Massacre". http://www.unesco.org/ new/en/communication-and-information/memory-of-the-world/register/ full-list-of-registered-heritage/registered-heritage-page-2/documents-of-nanjing-massacre (accessed 10 April 2016).

UNESCO Memory of the World Programme, International Advisory Committee. 2017. "Final Report on Memory of the World Programme Review". https:// unesdoc.unesco.org/ark:/48223/pf0000257032 (accessed 20 January 2020).

Yi, W. 2015. "China's 'Comfort Women' Offer Gets Cold Shoulder". *Korean Times*, 14 October 2015. http://www.koreatimes.co.kr/www/news/ nation/2015/11/120_188678.html (accessed 1 April 2016).

Yoshida, R. 2015. "UNESCO Strikes Political Nerve with Nanking Massacre Documents". *Japan Times*, 19 October 2015. http://www.japantimes.co.jp/ news/2015/10/19/reference/unesco-strikes-political-nerve-with-nanking-massacre-documents/#.VxNDI01Xpto (accessed 15 April 2016).

Yoshino, K. 1992. *Cultural Nationalism in Contemporary Japan: A Sociological Enquiry*. London: Routledge.

8

From Ideological Alliance to Identity Clash: The Historical Origin of the Sino-Korean Goguryeo Controversies

Anran Wang

Goguryeo (Koguryo in old romanization) is the name of an ancient kingdom that existed from 37 BCE to 668 CE in present-day North Korea and Northeast China (also known as Manchuria), as well as small portions of South Korea and the Russian Far East. In succession, its capitals were in the present-day Chinese county of Huanren (34 BCE – 3 CE), the Chinese city of Ji'an (3–427 CE) and North Korea's capital city of Pyongyang (427–668 CE). Historical relics, particularly tombs and city walls, abound in these places and their environs. During the seventh century, Goguryeo resisted numerous invasions from successive dynasties in the Chinese hinterland, particularly the Sui Dynasty (581–618 CE) and the Tang Dynasty (618–907 CE), and experienced continuous warfare with other regimes on the Korean Peninsula, such as Silla (57 BCE – 935 CE) and Baekje (18 BCE – 660 CE). The period during which Goguryeo existed is termed the era of the Three Kingdoms of Korea (57 BCE – 668 CE) because Goguryeo, Silla and Baekje were the three major powers on the Korean Peninsula. Goguryeo was eventually destroyed by a joint force of Silla and the Tang in 668, which led to the Unified Silla Era (668–935 CE) and to the Tang's rule in northern Korea.

Surprisingly, Goguryeo became an issue of severe contention among Northeast Asian countries in the early twenty-first century, more than thirteen centuries after the kingdom's collapse. A controversy among China and the two Koreas involving governments and academia over whether Goguryeo was a Korean dynasty or a local minority regime of ancient China broke out when North Korea and China nominated their respective Goguryeo relics for UNESCO World Heritage status. While nominations from both countries were eventually successful, the controversy persisted and had a significant impact on international relations in Northeast Asia.

This chapter probes the historical origin of this early twenty-first century controversy by placing it within the modern history of the three countries involved. Over the decades, Goguryeo-related narratives by the governments and academia of the three countries have changed significantly, but not as the result of archaeological discoveries. The Sino–North Korean ideological alliance in the 1960s enabled North Korea to enjoy China's full endorsement of its official historical interpretation. Nearing the end of the Cold War, however, governments and academia in Northeast Asian countries experienced various drastic changes that eventually led in the early 2000s to an identity clash surrounding Goguryeo between China and the two Koreas.

Goguryeo in the Shadow of the Sino–North Korean Ideological Alliance

North Korean Narratives, 1940s to 1970s

North Korea's exploitation of Goguryeo history for contemporary propaganda purposes began in the early 1960s, until which time North Korean historians had largely focused on fitting the history of Goguryeo into the Marxist-Leninist theoretical framework (Quan 2004). The situation changed in 1962 when the publishing house of the ruling party, the Workers' Party of Korea (WPK), published a propaganda brochure in which the author cited Goguryeo as successfully resisting invasions from the Sui Dynasty of China in order to inspire patriotic sentiment among North Korean citizens (Ri 1962). It is likely that the escalating Sino-Soviet split which created more latitude for Pyongyang to sway between the two powers contributed to North Korea's exploitation of ancient history for nationalist purposes. A similar event to also take place in 1962 was Mongolia's commemoration of the eight hundredth anniversary of Chinggis Khan's birth. While the Soviet Union soon stopped the outburst of nationalist sentiment in Mongolia, Moscow did not enjoy that level of influence in North Korea, where most pro-Soviet officials had been purged by 1961. In 1963 North Korea openly criticized a historical work by the USSR Academy of Science, accusing the latter of distorting history and of denying the independence of ancient Korea (Kim et al. 1963).

Meanwhile, North Korea began to interact with China over historical matters. In February 1963 the president of North Korea's Academy of Science met with the Chinese ambassador in Pyongyang and requested China's consent to initiate a joint excavation project of Goguryeo and other ancient relics in Northeast China that were supposed to be related to ancient Korea (China 1963a). Shortly before the start of the project in August that year, the vice chair of the WPK Central Committee presented Chinese Premier Zhou Enlai a gift of two volumes of *The Synoptic History of Korea* (*Joseon Tongsa*), which represented Pyongyang's official interpretation of Korean history (China 1963b).

The Sino–North Korean joint excavation project, which lasted from 1963 until 1965, was the first ever international archaeological cooperation undertaken with communist China. Although China did not object to North Korea's stance of considering Goguryeo part of Korean history— which was the very reason China had agreed to launch the joint project with North Korea in China's own territory and to give away most of the artefacts unearthed—the two countries had several disagreements over the interpretation of the archaeological findings. For example, North Korean archaeologists tried to find evidence for their arguments that the Balhae Kingdom (698–926 CE) was a continuation of Goguryeo, while their Chinese colleagues would not agree to this attempt (Sun Binggen 2011).

Facilitated by the abundant materials and data obtained through the research project in Northeast China, studies on Goguryeo abounded in North Korea in the 1960s and the 1970s. In 1971, North Korean leader Kim Il-Sung (2003) stressed that "It was during the Goguryeo era that our nation was the strongest." As a summary of the outcomes of historical research throughout the two decades, a multi-volume academic work titled *Complete History of Korea* was published in 1979. The volume on Goguryeo specially praised the ancient kingdom for its people's patriotic spirit and cultural achievements (KASS 1979, pp. 7–8).

Chinese Narratives, 1950s to 1970s

Traditionally, Chinese historians have considered Goguryeo as a Korean kingdom. Although a few works in the 1930s and the 1940s—such as those by Fu Sinian (1932) and Jin Yufu (1943)—argued for an essential link between historical regimes in Manchuria, including Goguryeo, and those in China proper, their arguments were more likely a response to the Japanese occupation of Manchuria and the Japanese academia's efforts to deny Chinese sovereignty over Manchuria from a historical perspective, rather than a reflection of the prevalent view among Chinese intellectuals. While narrating Goguryeo as an ancient people of Northeast China, the work by Jin (1943, pp. 21–22) also articulated that the people of Goguryeo had mostly moved south into the Korean Peninsula and constituted the Korean nation. An article in *People's Daily* by Soong Ching-ling[1] (1951) simply used the word "Koreans" (*Chaoxian ren*) to refer to the people of Goguryeo, saying that Koreans had performed iron smelting in Northeast China since 1,300 years ago. A book published in 1951 titled *The Sino-Korean Friendship since Five Millenniums Ago* (Zhang et al. 1951), which Jin Yufu participated in editing, also referred to Goguryeo as a Korean kingdom.

This narrative soon came to be at odds with China's broader historical discourse. In 1951, famous Chinese historian Bai Shouyi (1951) proposed to use the boundaries of contemporary China as a criterion to determine whether a historical regime should be considered Chinese or foreign. He also criticized the tendency to only consider the empires based in China proper as "China". According to this discourse, China should at least have a "share" of Goguryeo, since Goguryeo's territory overlaps with the northeastern borderland of modern China. Moreover, for more than four centuries the capital of Goguryeo was located in present-day China. However, the Chinese academia applied a double standard: most scholars supported the proposal by Bai that considered all historical regimes within the contemporary border as "Chinese", but they never applied this criterion to Goguryeo. An article published in 1959 (He 1959) criticized the phenomenon that history textbooks frequently listed the Xiongnu, Jurchen and Mongol people as foreigners, arguing that since the territory of those historical regimes mostly lie within the contemporary Chinese border they should all be considered ethnic minorities of ancient China. The article made no mention of Goguryeo.

After the 1959 Tibetan uprising, ancient history concerning non-Han people became a more sensitive issue in China. When Zhou Enlai commented on an opera depicting the marriage of the Tang Princess Wencheng with King Songtsan Gampo of Tibet (641 CE), he articulated that while historical operas must not alter the true history, they can nevertheless avoid mentioning unfavourable historical facts and instead stress the central point of interethnic unity (Wu 1992). In 1961, Jian Bozan (1961), a state-sponsored historian, praised a Han Empire concubine who was sent to marry the leader of Xiongnu in order to establish friendly relations. Another famous historian named Fan Wenlan (1980) described wars between empires in China proper and neighbouring states as "quarrels between brothers" in an article written in 1962 (but which was only published in 1980) because those neighbouring non-Chinese nations were also retrospectively considered "Chinese" in a civic sense. Again, this rhetoric did not apply to Goguryeo. Fan's work titled *General History of China* (Fan 1978, p. 349)—composed from the 1950s through the early 1960s, but not published until 1978—condemned the Tang Dynasty's military expedition to Goguryeo as an "invasion".

Recent Chinese scholars have provided several reasons to explain why Chinese academia in the Maoist era considered Goguryeo as Korean. These reasons include a political atmosphere in favour of Sino–North Korean friendship, the inadequateness of historical studies (Ma et al. 2001, p. viii), and the arbitrary dismissal of the outcomes of studies during the Republican era (Ma et al. 2001, p. 301). Among these reasons, the inadequateness of research does not have to necessarily result in a double standard. It could actually be the result of, rather than the reason for, designating Goguryeo as part of foreign history. Research undertaken on Goguryeo was extremely limited during the Republican era, so the effect of dismissing these studies should also have been very limited.

The first reason provided—namely, the political pressure academia faced—was the most essential one. Evidence indicates the existence and effect of political pressure over studies on Goguryeo. In 1962, Premier Zhou Enlai stopped the discussion in newspapers of a Qing era fiddle ballad because the ballad mentioned the Yuan Empire's invasion of Korea (Mu 2006). The next year, Kang Sheng[2] prohibited the publication of an academic work by the famous historian Chen Yinke that discussed the aforementioned ballad for the reason it may affect Sino–North Korean relations. Kang Sheng also criticized the history department of Peking University for disagreeing with the opinions of North Korean historians (Lu 1995, p. 370).

Siding with the North Korean historical interpretation was a technique leaders of communist China frequently employed to rally support from their North Korean counterparts. In the wake of the exodus of North Korea's pro-China officials in 1958, Mao Zedong (1958) mentioned to Kim Il-Sung that the Sino-Korean border was originally at Liao River,[3] and that the Chinese pushed the Koreans to Yalu River, which is the current border. Mao commented that "Our ancestors owe to your ancestors." By denouncing what ancient China had done to Korea, Mao was likely trying to assure Kim that communist China would recognize his leadership and would not try to subvert his regime.

The escalating Sino-Soviet Split in the early 1960s resulted in "a tug-of-war between China and the Soviet Union for North Korean allegiance" (Chung 1978, p. 54). China recognized most of the territorial claims from North Korea during the border negotiation in 1962, while North Korea in return openly voiced its objection to Moscow's attempt to isolate China (*Rodong Sinmun* 1964). It was also around this time that Chinese leaders frequently talked about the ancient history of Sino-Korean relations. In 1963, Zhou Enlai (1963) commented to a delegation from the North Korean Academy of Science that archaeological exploration had shown that the Korean nation had long resided in contemporary Northeast China. "We need to apologize to you on behalf of our ancestors, who eroded your territory until so small." Apart from rallying support from North Korea during the Sino-Soviet split, those comments may also be a self-comforting narrative to justify concessions to North Korea during the border negotiation and China's huge assistance to North Korea despite domestic economic hardships (Shen and Dong 2011). In the same year, China's official newspaper, *People's Daily*, published a Chinese translation of the aforementioned North Korean historians' criticism levelled at the Soviet Academy of Science, even though it contained several points of view that the Chinese academia had never agreed with, such as the denial of the existence of Gija Joseon.

Meanwhile, the narrative condemning ancient China's oppression of ancient Korea fitted well with Beijing's general diplomatic discourse upholding national independence and resisting hegemonies. With this narrative, Beijing condemned Washington's foreign policies and later also Moscow's, and appealed for cooperation from Third World countries. The work by Fan Wenlan (1978, p. 349), for example, written in the 1960s, commented:

> The Tang Emperor was self-assured for governing a large country and a strong force, and thought he would surely succeed in his attempt to inflict the small and weak neighbor. History turned out to not conform to his wishes. What he encountered was a defeat that was too late to regret for.

This anti-hegemonic narrative was also reflected in China's relationship with Vietnam. During his visit to Hanoi in 1960, Zhou Enlai specifically chose to pay homage to the Trung Sisters, the Vietnamese national heroines who rebelled against Chinese domination in 40 CE (Cheng 2009, p. 308).

While domestic ethnic politics was becoming an important concern in China's official historical narrative, as shown in the example of the emphasis on Sino-Tibetan friendship, it appeared less important than foreign relations. In the early 1960s, a high-ranking party official directed the editor of the state-owned Zhonghua Book Company to remind Chen Yinke, who wrote for the company, to deal cautiously with history that involved neighbouring communist countries and Southeast Asian countries because referring to the ancient regimes of these countries as vassal states of ancient China might cause "unnecessary troubles". Meanwhile, the same official also promised Chen that the party would not interfere in his history writing on other issues, and mentioned that issues concerning ethnic minorities "seems to not matter very much, because domestic issues are always easy to clarify" (Xu 2008).

This was especially true with respect to Goguryeo because Beijing at that time did not care much whether its ethnic Korean citizens identified with China or North Korea. Zhou asked Kim Il-Sung if he would like to receive some more "return migrants" from China (China 1961), and Mao (1963) told Kim that "There are more than one million Koreans in the Northeast [China]. They are yours, and also ours." In the early 1960s, most ethnic Koreans in China were either immigrants or children born to immigrants from the Korean Peninsula. While not necessarily loyal to Beijing (Jin 1957), the Korean community in China showed little secessionist tendencies because mostly they considered themselves as expatriates and acknowledged that the territory where they lived belonged to China.

South Korean Narratives, 1950s to 1970s

South Korea was largely irrelevant to the politics of Goguryeo history in this period. With most important Goguryeo relics located in communist countries, it was hard for South Korean historians to study Goguryeo. Although South Korean President Park Chung-Hee (1962, pp. 55, 95) in his book praised Goguryeo's resistance to Chinese and Japanese invasions, this did not immediately result in an increase of attention on Goguryeo in South Korea, nor any reaction from North Korea or China.

Transformation of Academia around the End of the Cold War

North Korean Narratives since the 1980s

During the two decades that sandwiched the end of the Cold War, North Korea faced economic hardship caused by a rigid command system, excessive spending on military expansion and ideological monuments, natural disasters and the discontinuation of aid from other communist states. South Korea's rise in economic strength and international status further challenged the legitimacy of the North Korean regime. Likely fuelled by the sense of crisis vis-à-vis South Korea, North Korean academia began to place Goguryeo, whose capital had been in Pyongyang, over Silla, the kingdom based in southern Korea that eventually unified Korea. An academic work published in 1990 (Son 1990, p. 10) cited the comment by Kim Jong-Il that "The history of the Three Kingdoms era did not develop centring on Silla, but rather developed centring on Goguryeo", and it commented that further studies of Goguryeo history were essential to combat the erroneous arguments made by the "imperialist historians" of Japan and Western countries and by "reactionary historians" of South Korea.

Kim Jong-Il further claimed that it was Goguryeo that aspired to the unification of Korea, that it continuously struggled for that purpose (KASS 1991, p. 100) and that it was almost about to fulfil this goal (Ch'oe 2005, p. 151). Closely following the leader's words, a new 1991 edition of the 1979

Complete History of Korea was published, which sang the praise of Goguryeo's glorious history in pursuing unification of the Korean nation, in leading the development of national culture and in fighting for independence (KASS 1991, p. 9). In a change from the 1979 edition, which discussed Goguryeo's wars with Silla and Baekje in different centuries under separate chapters with section headings such as "Territorial Expansions toward the South" (KASS 1979, pp. 135, 189), the 1991 edition reorganized these successive events into a single chapter titled "Goguryeo People's Struggle for the Unification of Nation and Territory" (KASS 1991, p. 100). More strikingly, the new edition brought forward the dating for Goguryeo's establishment by two centuries (KASS 1979, p. 7; KASS 1991, p. 30).

Kim Jong-Il also condemned Silla, which allied with the Tang to exterminate Goguryeo and achieve unification (Ch'oe 2005, p. 217). The 1991 edition (KASS 1991, p. 9) attributed Goguryeo's fall partly to Silla's collaboration with the Tang, which it described as a nation-betraying scheme (*baejokjeok chaekdong*). This narrative contrasts dramatically with the 1943 speech of Kim Il-Sung (1995), which juxtaposed Goguryeo with Silla and Baekje, praising the efforts of all three nations in resisting foreign invasions and arguing that Korea could have thrived had the three kingdoms achieved solidarity. Finally, Kim Jong-Il praised Goguryeo for making great contributions to the entire Korean nation by resisting foreign invasions, which arguably also benefited Baekje and Silla (Son 2008b, p. 6). Reflecting this emphasis on Goguryeo's defence of the Korean nation, four out of five chapters of *History of Goguryeo II* published in 1997 (Son 1997) centred on resisting foreign invasions.

South Korean Narratives since the 1980s

The softening of Cold War tensions since the 1970s enabled South Korean historians to access works by North Korean and Chinese historians, which led to a significant increase in studies on Goguryeo in South Korea. Since the 1980s, many South Korean scholars have been able to visit Goguryeo historical relics in China. This further contributed to interest in Goguryeo among South Korean scholars, many of whom enthusiastically acclaimed the greatness of Goguryeo to an extent comparable to their North Korean colleagues. A book titled *History of the Goguryeo Empire* published in 1997 (Seo, p. 7), for example, claimed that Goguryeo was a great empire that should be placed on par with the successive Chinese empires and the

Roman Empire. A group of scholars established the "Koguryo Research Center" in 1994, sponsored field research, organized international conferences and published journals thereafter. In 1997, South Korean President Kim Dae-Jung claimed during the presidential election that he would start a "New Gwanggaeto Era", referring to King Gwanggaeto of Goguryeo who defeated several neighbouring states and expanded Goguryeo's territory.

Irredentist sentiments toward Manchuria among South Korean scholars and activists began to stem from this Goguryeo fever and appeared in a plethora of publications. *History of the Korean Nation's Continental Connections* (Paeksan Jaryowon 1987, foreword), for example, claimed that the Korean nation had ruled Manchuria for 3,157 years, in contrast to the Chinese who ruled Manchuria for less than five hundred years. *On Northern Territory* (Yu 1991) claimed that the Korean nation should follow the example of the Jewish nation to retrieve the ancestral territory that had been lost to them for thousands of years. A pictorial album on Goguryeo relics published in 1994 was titled *Oh, Goguryeo! Local Stories in Our Former Territories* (*Chosun Ilbo* 1994), referring to the part of Manchuria once ruled by Goguryeo as Korea's "former territory" (*yet ttang*).

Chinese Narratives since the 1980s

Since the start of reform in 1978, the Chinese government had greatly loosened its control over academia. Instead of prescribing the way to interpret specific historical events, the government in most cases only required academia to obey the general principle of upholding national unity, and it allowed scholars to express their academic views relatively freely under this principle. Meanwhile, the importance of Sino–North Korean relations dropped significantly as China started the process of de-ideologization. Chinese academia no longer had to worry about Sino–North Korean relations when studying ancient history.

To avoid a double standard, historians in China tried to make a universal criterion to determine the national belonging of ancient regimes. In 1981, Bai Shouyi (1981) again voiced his suggestion of using the contemporary Chinese border as the criterion. The famous historical geographer Tan Qixiang (1988), on the other hand, proposed in a speech in the same year to use the border of the Qing Empire at its greatest extent as the criterion. While this makes no difference to the Sino-Korean border, which has remained basically the same since the Qing era, the significance of Tan's speech lies in that it openly claimed that Goguryeo, during its earlier centuries before moving its capital to Pyongyang, should be considered a local regime of China.

Soon after Tan's speech, many Chinese scholars took a step further to claim the entire Goguryeo as a minority regime of China. Because the present-day Sino-Korean border did not exist during Goguryeo's time, they saw it as problematic to designate part of Goguryeo history as Chinese history and the other part as Korean history based merely on a change of the location of Goguryeo's capital within its own territory. For example, one book (Xue and Li 1991, pp. 20–21) explicitly opposed using contemporary national borderlines as a criterion and argued that a regime's relationship with regimes in the Central Plain would be a better criterion. Many Chinese historical works in the 1980s and 1990s classified Goguryeo as part of Chinese history, such as *Outline History of Northeastern Nations* (Fu and Yang 1983), *History of China's Northeast* (Tong 1987), *History of Sino-Korean Border* (Yang and Sun 1993), *A Study on the History of Sino-Korean Relations* (Liu 1994), among others. A work by two Chinese scholars expressing this viewpoint was translated into Korean and published in Seoul (Li and Sun 1990).

But not all scholars in China followed this trend. In this same period, a handful of historical works in China still considered Goguryeo as part of ancient Korea. These include *Outline of World History* (Sun and Zhao et al. 1985), *General History of Korea* (Jiang 1992), *Brief History of Sino-Korean Relations* (Yang and Han 1992), *History of Sino-Korean Relations: Ancient Volume* (Jiang et al. 1998), among others. One especially noteworthy example is a Korean-language book written by an ethnic Korean scholar in China (Fang 1998) titled *Koreans Who Left Their Names in Ancient Chinese History*, the first chapter of which was dedicated to Goguryeo. Obviously, most works that treated Goguryeo as a local minority regime of China focused on Chinese history, as scholars working on Chinese history were eager to find a way to avoid the double standard that was prevalent during the Maoist era. On the other hand, Chinese scholars working on Korean history and world history showed little interest in shifting their view on Goguryeo. The potential conflict with historical interpretation of other parts of China was not a problem for them.

Among Chinese scholars who focused their studies on Goguryeo, a consensus gradually formed that Goguryeo should be considered part of

Chinese history. During the first Nationwide Academic Symposium on Goguryeo held in Tonghua[4] in 1998, almost all the scholars that addressed this issue considered Goguryeo as a minority regime of China (JASS and TNU 1999). The only remaining dispute was whether Goguryeo also belongs to Korean history. Some scholars (e.g., Zhang 2000) believed that Goguryeo belongs solely to China, based on the pre-Goguryeo Chinese rule over northern Korea, as well as the alleged integration of the Goguryeo people into China after Goguryeo's collapse.

In contrast to the strict control during the Maoist era, the coexistence of different academic understandings on Goguryeo since the 1980s suggests that Beijing did not interfere in this scholarly issue. In 1997, a college history textbook (Cui 1997) in China described Goguryeo for the first time as a local, ethnic minority regime of China. However, this does not indicate a shift in the government's stance because the narratives in the history textbooks for *secondary* schools, which reach a far wider population, remained unchanged.

The Northeast Project

Having reached a consensus on Goguryeo's Chinese status, in-system scholars in China soon started to push the government to adjust the official stance. Ma Dazheng[5] (2011b, p. 5), for example, criticized textbooks that were still presenting an outdated view on Goguryeo and cautioned that "certain neighbouring countries" were wantonly distorting history, which the Chinese government and academia should take measures to refute.

Sun Jinji, another in-system scholar, wrote numerous internal reports that were circulated among high-level officials in China. One such report written in 1998, which was leaked and re-published in Los Angeles, was likely the most influential one as it was commented on by Hu Jintao,[6] among other high-level officials (Ma Dazheng 2011a, p. 2). In this report, Sun pointed out the strange phenomenon that while researchers studying Goguryeo history still faced many restrictions, teaching and propaganda in this field lacked direction and discipline. Sun Jinji (2011, p. 162) suggested that greater latitude for the free expression of scholarly opinions should be allowed because "some scholarly opinions may not fit the current political needs, but in the future the political situation may change, and they may fit future political needs." As an in-system scholar whose academic work was supposed to serve the government, Sun justified the tolerance of diverse opinions based on the possibility that the government may need to change its rhetoric in the future and find current heterodox opinions useful. Meanwhile, to end the situation of indiscipline in propaganda, Sun proposed that the central government should, upon consultation with scholars, establish a unified official narrative on Goguryeo.

According to Sun Jinji (2011b, p. 162), the government of Liaoning province tried to organize scholars to formulate a unified line on Goguryeo, but this issue was too significant for the local government and scholars to decide. Likely following Sun's suggestion, in November 1998 the External Propaganda Leading Group of the Communist Party of China (CPC) Publicity Department formally requested the Chinese Academy of Social Sciences (CASS) to help formulate the propaganda narrative on Goguryeo. The latter completed a report in December, the details of which were not known to the public (Ma Dazheng 2011a, pp. 1–2).

In 2000, in the wake of the first Inter-Korean summit, a Xinhua News Agency journalist (Ma Yang 2011) wrote an internal report to remind the government that an improvement in inter-Korean relations would significantly promote cooperation on historical studies in the two Koreas. The strength of academia in the two Koreas combined would overpower Chinese scholars working on Northeastern history. The journalist argued that this would lead to a serious challenge to China's sovereignty because some South Korean scholars claimed that once the two Koreas unify, the Korean academia would immediately negate the Sino–North Korean border treaty. Hu Jintao again commented on this report (Ma Dazheng 2011a, p. 2). While the content of Hu's comments is unknown, the plan proposed by the CASS in 2001 to implement Hu's instructions led to the well-known Northeast Project (CASS 2011).

With approval from the central government, the CASS formally launched the Northeast Project in February 2002, which aimed at systematically studying the history of China's Northeastern borderlands, and providing support "for maintaining social stability and developing the economy of the Northeastern borderland". A large part of the Northeast Project's expenses came from central and local governments (Li 2005, p. 1). The Publicity Departments of the CPC Provincial Committees in all three Northeastern provinces also participated. This clearly shows that Beijing's interest in the ancient history of Northeast China had greatly increased. However, contrary to the widespread understanding in South Korea, there was little evidence that Beijing had a particular interest in "robbing" Goguryeo from Korea. Studies on Goguryeo constituted only a small portion of the Northeast Project, which itself was only one of the many academic projects on ancient history that Beijing approved around that time, including projects on early Chinese civilization and the history and geography of Tibet and Xinjiang. Despite its clear official background, the Northeast Project was still scholarly in nature. Beijing did not revise the existing secondary school textbooks, and did not formally step into this scholarly issue until Pyongyang's nomination of Goguryeo relics for UNESCO World Heritage status forced it to do so.

Identity Clash at UNESCO

Pyongyang's Endeavour

Recovering from the flood and famine of the early 1990s, North Korea joined the World Heritage Convention in 1998, and soon started to prepare to nominate its Goguryeo relics for World Heritage status. Considering the extent to which North Korean leaders and academia had been praising Goguryeo, it was not surprising that Pyongyang selected its Goguryeo relics as its first prospective World Heritage Site. Facilitated by US$30,000 in aid from UNESCO in 1999 (UNESCO 1999), North Korea completed its preliminary preparation for nomination in 2000 and added "Koguryo Mural Tombs" to its tentative list[7] for World Heritage status (UNESCO 2001). Experts from UNESCO helped North Korea revise its nomination to include tombs without murals, and in January 2002 North Korea formally submitted the nomination under the revised title "The Complex of Koguryo Tombs". The International Council on Monuments and Sites (ICOMOS)[8] then sent an expert named Lü Zhou, a Chinese professor from Tsinghua University, to evaluate the eligibility of Goguryeo relics in North Korea in July 2002. As later elaborated in UNESCO guidelines (UNESCO 2005, p. 112), ICOMOS prefers to appoint an expert from the same geographic region as the prospective site, so it was not a surprise that a Chinese professor was selected to lead the onsite evaluation.

Beijing's Response

China's in-system scholars were surprised by the nomination from North Korea. While they had heard about North Korea's preparation for nomination in previous years, many believed North Korea's dire economic condition would prevent it from completing the process.[9] In July 2002, the Shenyang Military Region internally circulated a specially composed education pamphlet titled *The Historical Evolution of Sino-Korean Border* (Sun et al. 2002), which claimed that historically the dominion of Korea had never passed the present-day border rivers, and that Goguryeo was an ethnic minority local regime of ancient China. China's decision to educate its military personnel stationed near the border with North Korea about ancient history was likely a silent response to North Korea's nomination.

Beijing's open reaction suddenly appeared when it nominated its own Goguryeo relics for World Heritage status on 22 January 2003, slightly over a week before the deadline of 1 February for consideration for the following year. The addition of Goguryeo relics to China's tentative list took place even later, on 28 January 2003 (Shin 2011). It is possible that China decided hastily to submit its own nomination in reaction to North Korea's and could not complete the complicated paperwork earlier. It is also possible that China wanted to avoid attracting outside attention too early and thus decided to wait until close to the deadline before submitting its nomination. The UNESCO regulation at that time did not prohibit this practice (UNESCO 2002), while a revision in 2005 (UNESCO 2005, p. 17) stated that no nomination could be considered if the site was not already on the country's tentative list, and recommended that a country add any prospective World Heritage Site to its tentative list at least a year before formal nomination. This recommendation further evolved into a mandatory requirement in 2011 (UNESCO 2011, p. 18), making it impossible for such a hasty nomination to happen again. In September 2003, eight months after its submission, China modified the English name of the proposed World Heritage Site from "Capital Cities, Imperial Tombs and Nobles' Tombs of Koguryo" to "Capital Cities and Tombs of the Ancient Koguryo Kingdom". In its explanation to UNESCO (China 2003), the Chinese government justified this change in that the linguistic difficulties of non-native English speakers had led to an imperfect title. Judging from the nature of the change of title, however, Beijing likely found the term "imperial" inappropriate to describe what it considered a local regime under Chinese empires, but failed to avoid using this inappropriate term during its initial, hasty nomination.

Evidence suggests that Beijing directly decided to nominate China's Goguryeo relics with no participation from local governments in the decision-making process. The government of Tonghua city did not mention any plan of World Heritage nomination in its December 2002 Work Report (Zhang Yong 2004), although by that time China's nomination file was almost ready, as indicated by the Chinese official's signature in the file (China 2002, p. 121). A high-level official of Ji'an mentioned (CPPCC-JMC 2004, p. 2) that the work on World Heritage nomination did not start until the spring of 2003. When Goguryeo was added to China's tentative list, there were already around sixty other sites on that list waiting to be nominated for World Heritage status (UNESCO 2003a), of which, according to UNESCO regulations at that time, only one site could be nominated each year. However, China put Goguryeo in front of all sites already on the list and nominated Goguryeo right away, indicating that Beijing had made the nomination of Goguryeo relics its top priority in UNESCO.

While hastily nominating its own Goguryeo relics, Beijing also possibly played a role in delaying the process of North Korea's nomination. The deadline for World Heritage nomination is 1 February each year for consideration for the following year. Therefore, North Korea's nomination submitted in January 2002 was to be considered in 2003, while China's nomination, submitted in January 2003, could only be considered in 2004. In March 2003, ICOMOS, which had sent a Chinese expert to evaluate North Korean sites the previous year, recommended that the World Heritage Committee (WHC) of UNESCO defer North Korea's nomination. The ICOMOS report (UNESCO 2003b, pp. 36–38) cited North Korea's lack of comparative studies with Goguryeo relics in China, among other technical reasons, to explain its decision, and recommended that North Korea consider submitting a joint nomination with China. This raised suspicion about underhanded manipulation by the Chinese government, who understandably did not want North Korea's Goguryeo relics to be inscribed as a World Heritage Site ahead of its own.

Following the suggestion from ICOMOS, the WHC formally deferred North Korea's nomination during its July 2003 session in Paris. This forced North Korea to repeat some of the procedures, including the ICOMOS evaluation, and to be considered together with the Chinese nomination in the following year. While China supported the suggestion by ICOMOS for a joint Sino–North Korean nomination, North Korea reportedly declined (UNESCO 2003c). In February 2004, ICOMOS completed its second evaluation report on North Korea's Goguryeo site. Most of the technical problems raised the previous year, such as a lack of accessibility to the tombs and poor management, still existed, but this time ICOMOS did not consider those problems to be significant concerns and recommended that the North Korean site be inscribed into the World Heritage List (UNESCO 2004a, pp. 60–62; Shin 2011). This further deepened international suspicion about possible Chinese manipulation in the 2003 evaluation.

Eventually, the 2004 session of the WHC held in Suzhou, China approved nominations from both countries on the afternoon of 1 July. The approval of China's nomination took place first (UNESCO 2004b, pp. 28–29, 35–36). Despite starting preparations three years earlier than China and submitting its nomination one year earlier, North Korea ended up being a few hours later than China in getting its Goguryeo relics inscribed as a World Heritage Site.

Reasons behind Beijing's Response

One likely reason behind Beijing's efforts to have its own Goguryeo relics inscribed on the World Heritage List ahead of those of North Korea was its concern over the stability of its Northeastern borderland, the former territory of Goguryeo where most of China's two million ethnic Korean population live today. Although ethnic Koreans have long been considered loyal to China—as one study showed that 86 per cent of ethnic Koreans would support China rather than South Korea in a football match between the two countries (Im 2004, p. 348)—Beijing nevertheless worried about their lack of the "correct sense of motherland and citizenship" (*zuguo guannian he gongmin yishi*) (Sun and Sha 1994, p. 250). This worry can also be seen in Goguryeo-related publications in China. As a state-directed academic work in 2001 (Ma et al. 2001 xiii–xiv) argued:

> We have noticed that in recent times, especially since the 1990s, some people ... have attempted to push descendants of Goguryeo to identify with the Korean ethnicity or to organize ethnic Koreans living in the Northeast to pay homage to their "ancestors" at the relics of Goguryeo. These attempts have ulterior motives, which we must under no circumstance take lightly. Such action is ethnographically groundless, inappropriate under ethnic policies, and politically toxic.

As opposed to the Maoist era, when Beijing appeared to be indifferent to the identity of its ethnic Korean population, in the early 2000s ethnic Koreans no longer had a strong sense of being expatriates, while they still retained a strong Korean identity. If it becomes their common belief that the people of Goguryeo are their ancestors and that Northeast China is their own ancestral land, Beijing would have reason to worry that their Korean identity may potentially lead to secessionism.

Adding to China's worry were voices from South Korean academia and civil society organizations that kept denying China's sovereignty over Manchuria. Since the 1980s there have been a number of South Korean lawmakers and scholars who have urged the government to negate the validity of the 1962 Sino–North Korean Border Treaty (*JoongAng Ilbo* 1983 and 1993) and the 1909 border treaty between Qing China and Japanese-controlled Korea (Paeksan Society 1998). This territorial ambition was largely underpinned by the narrative that Northeast China had historically been the territory of successive Korean kingdoms such as Goguryeo and that it was currently inhabited by significant numbers of ethnic Koreans. Beijing was deeply worried about the South Korean government granting certain privileges to ethnic Koreans from China (Piao and Piao 2006, p. 56) and about the two Korea's propaganda activities towards China's ethnic Korean community, which claimed that Northeast China was the ancient land of the Korean nation (Liu 2011a, pp. 145–47). By claiming Goguryeo as Chinese rather than Korean, China could sever the historical link between the Korean nation and the territory of Northeast China, and could argue that the Korean presence in Northeast China dates back to only the nineteenth century.

Inter-Korean coordination on this issue was another reason behind Beijing's concern. South Korean civil societies had plans to assist North Korea's World Heritage nomination by organizing academic seminars and influencing international public opinion (Kim 2004). China had been vigilant towards the development of inter-Korean cooperation on the issue of Goguryeo, as an internal report (Liu 2011b, p. 153) says:

> The "Goguryeo fever" in the two Koreas, once confluent, will definitely contribute to the further rise and expansion of the "great Korean nationalism" or "pan-Korean nationalism" on the peninsula.... Under such scenario, relevant political powers will inevitably step in, and may publicly demand territory ... from us.

Beyond concerns over the Sino-Korean borderland, Goguryeo also had broader significance in China's overall ethnopolitics. While party officials considered domestic ethnic issues as "always easy to clarify" in the

Maoist era, in the early twenty-first century, after communism had largely lost its appeal, Beijing found it necessary to intensify its manipulation of historical interpretation in order to consolidate its narrative of national unity. Beijing changed its narrative on Tibet, for example, from the claim that Tibet became part of Chinese territory since the Yuan Dynasty (Ngapoi 1989) to that Tibet had been part of China "since the appearance of human activity in the Tibetan plateau" (Zhang et al. 2009). Since Beijing claimed that its borderland territories had been integral parts of China since ancient times, and that China's conquests of those territories throughout history were wars of unification rather than invasions, it would not want to let the interpretation of Goguryeo damage the integrity of this discourse. Under these new circumstances, the Maoist-era practice of employing a double standard and designating Goguryeo part of foreign history was unacceptable, not only academically but also politically. Complying with this line, a handbook on Goguryeo for cadres (Sun and Sun 2003, p. 149) used the term "righteous wars of unification" (*zhengyide tongyi zhanzheng*) to describe the military expeditions of the Sui and Tang Empires to Goguryeo.

Meanwhile, claiming to be rising peacefully, Beijing seeks to portray itself as peace loving. While in the Maoist era Beijing based its foreign policy discourse on the denunciation of imperial Chinese dynasties, the government now wanted to give the outside world an impression that throughout history China had often been strong but had never bullied other countries (*People's Daily* 2006). Once Goguryeo is classified as a local regime of China, Sui-era and Tang-era China can no longer be considered to have invaded Korea (Sun and Sun 2008, p. 66), and Beijing no longer needs to recognize, as it did during the Maoist era, that China invaded neighbouring countries in the past.

Identity Clash beyond UNESCO

Chinese Offensive

Soon after starting its World Heritage nomination process, Beijing began to openly propagandize the idea that Goguryeo belonged to China. In April 2003, Jilin People's Press published a brochure titled "Questions and Answers of Historical Knowledges on Goguryeo", explaining to people outside academia why Goguryeo should be considered a local minority regime of China. It has one section specially designated to explain why

Goguryeo has no relation to contemporary ethnic Koreans in China (Yang and Qin 2003, pp. 65–70). A handbook on Goguryeo for cadres published in October 2003 also claimed that ethnic Koreans are one of the youngest ethnic groups in China and that they have no relation with Goguryeo. It stressed that the history of Goguryeo is "an academic issue with political sensitivity" and that academic research on this issue "should be based on the ultimate interest of the state and the nation" (Sun and Sun 2003, vol. 2, p. 188).

In June 2003, *Guangming Daily*, a newspaper directed by the CPC, published an article arguing that Goguryeo was a local minority regime of ancient China (Bian 2003). The argument itself was not new among Chinese academia, but this was the first time official media had explicitly endorsed it, thereby causing a major controversy in South Korea. Also in June, China's State Post Bureau issued a postal stationary envelop featuring a Goguryeo mural painting (Hu 2011, p. 116), and later organized a field trip to Ji'an in preparation for the planned issuance of Goguryeo-themed postage stamps (Chen 2004, p. 115). In April of the next year, China's Ministry of Foreign Affairs deleted the reference to Goguryeo on the information page about South Korea in its website. After strong protests from South Korea in July, the ministry in August deleted altogether all the information on Korean history prior to 1945 (Zhang Weiwei 2004). From July to October 2004, the Ji'an municipal government organized the first Ji'an Goguryeo Cultural Tourism Festival, featuring shows, performances and exhibitions of paintings, photography and calligraphy.

North Korean Reaction

While Pyongyang never openly commented on Beijing's actions during the World Heritage nomination process, its official media and state-controlled academia voiced their opposition to Beijing's historical narratives. In November 2003, an article (Kang 2003) titled "Goguryeo is a Dignified Millennium Strong Country of the Korean Nation" appeared in North Korea's official newspaper, which strongly refuted the interpretation that Goguryeo was subordinate to Chinese empires. A book for popular consumption named *Goguryeo Stories* released in 2007 (Cho 2007, p. 215) stressed that Goguryeo was not China's vassal state. Likely due to considerations of Sino–North Korean relations, North Korea always refrained from identifying the target of its criticism. In an academic conference held in Vladivostok in October 2007, North Korean scholars joined with their South Korean colleagues to refute China's historical narrative, but they never mentioned the name "China" or "Northeast Project" (Kim 2008).

An academic publication in 2008 included an article (Son 2008a, pp. 186–95) that stressed that Goguryeo had always been an independent kingdom that only traded with and never belonged to the Chinese empires, and that the so-called tributary relationship with the Chinese empires was merely nominal. It criticized the opinion by "certain people" that considered Goguryeo a vassal state of China based on the contemporary Sino-Korean borderline, pointing out that Russia never considered the history of Siberia before the Russian conquest as the history of the Russian Federation, and Arabs never considered ancient peoples living in North Africa as ethnic minorities of those modern Arabic states. Without naming the target of its criticism, it argued that "distorting and ignoring the history of other nations is a very wrongful deed that damages the other nation's independent identity (*jajuseong*)".

South Korean Reaction

Beijing's explicit declaration of Chinese "ownership" over Goguryeo resulted in a strong reaction from Seoul. Seoul initially tried to downplay the situation by making statements that the deferral of the North Korean nomination in 2003 was due to technical reasons rather than Chinese manipulation, and that the Northeast Project did not represent the stance of the Chinese government (*Hankyoreh Shinmun* 2004). By the summer of 2004, however, when the Chinese foreign ministry deleted mention of Goguryeo from the information page about South Korea of its website, Seoul could no longer remain mild mannered. The South Korean government understood the Goguryeo controversy as an issue more serious in nature than the Japanese history textbook controversies, since in this case the Chinese government was directly involved in the distortion of history (Park 2004). The South Korean foreign ministry summoned the Chinese ambassador multiple times to protest Beijing's action, sent diplomats to Beijing to negotiate the issue and even considered recalling its ambassador to China (Jo 2004).

The South Korean public was also outraged. Denunciation of China's action and calls for revenge abounded in South Korean newspapers and on websites (Gries 2005). A more direct reflection of their anger could be seen in the protest held outside the Chinese Embassy in Seoul, where demonstrators were dressed in Goguryeo costumes. In the South Korean National Assembly, lawmakers from both ruling and opposition parties jointly pushed through a resolution denouncing China's action and demanding the government take appropriate measures (National Assembly of the Republic of Korea 2004). Polls showed that prior to the dispute 63 per cent of South Korean lawmakers from the ruling party chose China as South Korea's most important diplomatic partner, but after the dispute had broke out less than 6 per cent of South Korean lawmakers still did so (Snyder 2004).

Resolution of the Sino–South Korean Dispute

After repeated solemn representations from Seoul, the Chinese vice foreign minister visited Seoul in August 2004 and reached a consensus with his South Korean colleagues in refraining from politicizing scholarly issues. China promised not to revise its secondary school history textbooks, which were still teaching students the old narrative that Goguryeo was a Korean kingdom (Piao and Piao 2006, p. 58), in this way bringing a conclusion to the dispute at the official level.

China kept its promise, preventing further dispute over the issue. The textbooks published immediately thereafter for high schools in China glossed over the war between the Sui Dynasty and Goguryeo without clarifying whether the Sui was unifying China or was invading a foreign country, while the textbook for middle schools did not mention Goguryeo at all. On the historical maps included in the textbooks, where the authors had no choice but to clarify whether Goguryeo belonged to historical China, the earlier narrative remained. Both middle school and high school textbooks marked Goguryeo as outside the border of ancient China, while the Eastern and Western Turkic Khanates, the Kingdom of Zhangzhung in Tibet, tribes of Mohe in present day Northeast China and the Russian Far East, together with the Sui Empire in China proper, all lay within the border (NRDT 2005, p. 3; PEPHED 2005, pp. 68–69).

Beyond textbooks, Beijing tried to prevent further controversy by keeping a low profile in regard to its stance. China's State Post Bureau eventually did not issue the planned postage stamps on Goguryeo mural paintings, while in contrast the two Koreas issued several sets of Goguryeo-related stamps in the 2000s, many featuring Goguryeo relics in China. After the first Ji'an Goguryeo Culture and Tourism Festival in 2004, the municipal government held the second and third festivals in 2005 and 2006 on a much smaller scale, and thereafter the practice was discontinued. In 2014 the publishing house affiliated to the CASS published a new edition of *History of Sino-Korean Relations* that had first been published in 1998. Despite multiple revisions and expansions, the designation of Goguryeo as part of Korean history remained unchanged (Wang et al. 2014).

Causal Factors for the Sino–South Korean Dispute

It is easy to understand why South Koreans reacted strongly to China's actions. After decades of "Goguryeo fever", by the early 2000s Goguryeo had already been "mythologized" by South Korean nationalist historians into a symbol of Korean independence from foreign powers (Mohan 2006), and therefore had "direct implications for Korean confidence and self-esteem" (Gries 2005). Any denial of Korean ownership of Goguryeo was therefore equivalent to "a denial of Korean nationhood" that "threatens the very existence of Korea" (Lee 2004).

What is harder to understand are the reasons for Beijing igniting this dispute and allowing its relations with South Korea to deteriorate, which had been highly beneficial for the economic and security prospects of both countries. Since Beijing was willing to make a significant compromise with South Korea and to show considerable restraint after 2004 to prevent any further deterioration of bilateral relations, it can be inferred that the strong reaction from South Korea must not have been anticipated by Beijing. Otherwise, there was no reason for Beijing to adopt the hard line and cause this dispute in the first place. The unexpected nomination by North Korea that pushed Beijing to react hastily is a simple but plausible explanation. Beijing might simply have not had enough time to carefully evaluate the potential effect that its new position on Goguryeo would cause.

Another possible reason is that Beijing failed to realize that the nature of an academic debate would change once a government becomes involved. During Goguryeo-related negotiations with Seoul, Beijing raised the issue of South Korean scholars and activists voicing territorial claims over China's Northeast, and Seoul responded that it played no role in those activities, but rather it was Beijing that had directly involved itself in the contention over Goguryeo since 2003 (Piao and Piao 2006, p. 58).

Beijing likely overlooked the distinction between scholarly opinions and a government stance, which is understandable since the Chinese academia is closely associated with the Chinese government and abides by the latter's stance on important political issues. This oversight might have prevented Beijing from foreseeing the seriousness of South Korean reactions. After all, opinions that Goguryeo belonged to China had already become the mainstream among Chinese academia since the 1990s, and South Koreans were not unfamiliar with this opinion. For example, scholars from the two countries fiercely debated over Goguryeo during a seminar in Ji'an in 1993 (Sun Qilin 2011, p. 129), but this did not damage the close bilateral relations between the two countries in the 1990s. Beijing might have considered its action in 2003 as merely an overdue correction of the outdated, Maoist-era ideology-based stance, and an appropriate measure to defend China's sovereignty against territorial claims by South Korean activists. Beijing, therefore, had not expected the ensuing diplomatic dispute.

Conclusion

Throughout the modern history of China and the two Koreas, the issue of Goguryeo has seldom been free from political manipulation. From the 1950s to the 1970s, China supported the North Korean narrative on Goguryeo under the Sino–North Korean ideological alliance, even though this narrative was incompatible with China's own on national unity. Since the 1980s, the partially enfranchised Chinese academia sought to revise its historical narrative to better reconstruct China's multi-ethnic national identity, while the historical narrative of the North Korean academia was gradually radicalized due to the country's domestic political situation. In parallel, a "Goguryeo fever" appeared in South Korea, leading to increasing interest both in Goguryeo itself and in inter-Korean cooperation on historical issues. Eventually, academia in China and in the two Koreas, out of their own national identities, developed an unbridgeable gap between their respective understandings of Goguryeo. An identity clash was ready to break out once an appropriately conducive international event took place, such as the UNESCO World Heritage nomination.

The Sino-Korean identity clash that arose since 2003 at and beyond UNESCO demonstrated a mixture of contingency and necessity. A clash in some form was inevitable because it was difficult for China, a multi-ethnic country facing significant secessionist threats, to share a similar understanding on the inheritance of historical regimes with the two Koreas, which are mono-ethnic countries that trace their distinct and exclusive national history to ancient times. Once China's post-Maoist reforms ended the Sino–North Korean ideological alliance, a uniform line between Chinese and North Korean academia was no longer possible. Furthermore, there was a significant overlap between the territory held by Goguryeo, the ethnic Korean areas of contemporary China, and China's borderland territory over which South Korean nationalists kept challenging Chinese sovereignty. The history of Goguryeo therefore had strong contemporary geopolitical and ethnopolitical significance to all parties concerned, which meant that politicization of this issue, which should have remained scholarly in nature, was hard to avoid.

On the other hand, none of the governments involved wanted to see a deterioration of intergovernmental relations in the wake of the controversy, and all three governments displayed significant restraint in preventing any further deterioration of relations once the clash took place. The unforeseen clash lay in the fact that North Korea's unexpected action of nominating its Goguryeo sites for World Heritage status pushed Beijing to respond hastily, and that Beijing's tendency to overlook the distinction between scholarly opinions and a government stance prevented it from foreseeing the negative effect its response would cause. Beijing's unnecessarily tough stance ignited strong resentment from the South Korean government and society, resulting in a drastic identity clash over this long-vanished ancient kingdom.

Notes

1. Soong Ching-ling (1893–1981), wife of Sun Yat-sen, was then one of the vice chairs of the Central People's Government of the newly founded communist China.
2. Kang Sheng (1898–1975) was the chief ideologist of the CPC, later becoming vice chair.
3. Liao River was the border river between Goguryeo and several dynasties of China. It now lies entirely within China.
4. Tonghua is a prefecture-level city in Jilin, China that administers the county-level city of Ji'an, where Goguryeo's capital was located between 3 CE and 427 CE.
5. Ma Dazheng (1938–) is deputy director of the Research Center for Chinese

Borderland History and Geography at the Chinese Academy of Social Sciences (CASS).

6. Hu Jintao (1942–) was China's vice president, later becoming president as well as secretary general of the CPC.

7. Each State Party of the World Heritage Convention maintains a tentative list, which is an inventory of prospective World Heritage Sites in that country that the State Party intends to consider for nomination.

8. ICOMOS is responsible for providing advice to UNESCO's World Heritage Committee on prospective World Heritage Sites.

9. Personal communication with an anonymous in-system scholar in Beijing, June 2017.

References

Bai, Shouyi. 1951. "Lun lishishang zuguo guotu wenti de chuli" [On the solution to territory issues of historical China]. *Guangming Daily*, 5 May 1951.

———. 1981. "Guanyu zhongguo minzu guanxishi shang de jige wenti: Zai zhongguo minzu guanxi shi zuotanhui shang de jianghua" [On several issues of history of ethnic relations of China: Speech on the colloquium on history of ethnic relations of China]. *Beijing Shifan Daxue Xuebao* [Beijing Normal University journal] 6.

Bian, Zhong. 2003. *Gaogouli lishi yanjiu de jige wenti* [On several issues of historical studies on Goguryeo]. *Guangming Daily*, 24 June 2003.

CASS (Chinese Academy of Social Sciences) Research Center on China's Borderland History and Geography. 2011. "Dongbei bianjiang lishi yu xianzhuang yanjiu gongzuo zuotanhui jiyao" [Outline of forum on the research of the history and current situation of the northeastern borderland]. In *Dongbei bianjiang lishi yu xianzhuang de huigu yu sikao* [Review and thoughts on the history and current situation of the Northeast borderland], edited by Ma Dazheng, internal material produced by CASS. Republished as *Zhonggong zhongyao lishi wenxian ziliao huibian* [Collections of important documents and materials in CCP history], collection 31, vol. 16, edited by the Service Center for Chinese Publications, Los Angeles.

Chen, Lianxing, ed. 2004. *Tonghua nianjian* [Tonghua yearbook]. Changchun: Jilin People's Press.

Cheng, Yuangong. 2009. *Zhou Enlai zongli weishizhang huiyilu* [Memoir of Premier Zhou's chief bodyguard]. Beijing: CCCPC Party Literature Publishing House.

China. 1961. "Zhou Enlai tongzhi huifang Jin Richeng tongzhi tanhua jilu" [Record of conversation during Comrade Zhou Enlai's return visit to Comrade

Kim Il-Sung]. Ministry of Foreign Affairs Archive, Beijing, 204-01454-01, pp. 1–12.

———. 1963a. "1963 nian zhu Chao shiguan tong Chaoxian waiwusheng jiaoshe qingkuang jianbao" [Bulletin on negotiations between embassy in DPRK and the foreign ministry of DPRK in 1963]. Ministry of Foreign Affairs Archive, Beijing, 106-00715-03, pp. 16–38.

———. 1963b. "1963 nian Zhong-Chao guanxi dashiji" [Chronicles of events in Sino-DPRK relations in 1963]. Ministry of Foreign Affairs Archive, Beijing, 106-00715-03, pp. 39-61.

———. 2002. *Capital Cities, Imperial Tombs and Nobles' Tombs of Koguryo*. Nomination of cultural property for inscription on the World Heritage List. The State Administration of Cultural Heritage of the People's Republic of China.

———. 2003. Letter from Tian Xiaogang, Secretary-General of National Commission of the People's Republic of China for UNESCO, to Francesco Bandarin, Director of UNESCO World Heritage Center, 5 September 2003 (appended to China 2002).

Cho, Hŭi-Sŭng. 2007. *Goguryeo iyagi* [Goguryeo stories]. Pyongyang: Social Sciences Publishing House.

Ch'oe Ju-Kyŏng. 2005. "5 segi maryeop 7 segi jungyeop samguktongil'eul wihan Goguryeo-ui nambangjinchul yeongu" [A study on Goguryeo's southern expedition for the sake of unification of the Three Kingdoms from the late fifth century to the mid-seventh century]. In *Goguryeosa yeongu ronmunjip (2)* [Collection of theses on Goguryeo history (2)]. Pyongyang: Social Sciences Publishing House.

Chosun Ilbo 1994. *A! Goguryeo, uri-ui yetttang geu hyeonjang iyagi* [Oh, Goguryeo! Local stories in our former territory]. *Chosun Ilbo* Culture Section I.

Chung, Chin O. 1978. *Pyongyang between Peking and Moscow: North Korea's Involvement in the Sino-Soviet Dispute, 1958–1975*. Birmingham: University of Alabama Press.

CPPCC-JMC (Chinese People's Political Consultative Conference Ji'an Municipal Committee), ed. 2004. *Jinian Gaogouli yiji lieru shijie yichan minglu – Mingcheng shengdi (Ji'an wenshi ziliao di 12 ji)* [In commemoration of the inscription of Goguryeo relics in World Heritage List: Historic city and scenic spot]. Ji'an: CPPCC-JMC Subcommittee of Cultural and Historical Data.

Cui, Lianzhong et al., eds. 1997. *Shijie tongshi (6 juan ben)* [General history of the world, in 6 volumes]. Beijing: People's Publishing House.

Fan, Wenlan, ed. 1978. *Zhongguo tongshi* [General history of China], vol. 3. Beijing: People's Press.

———. 1980. "Zhongguo lishi shang de minzu douzheng yu ronghe" [Ethnic struggles and amalgamation in Chinese history]. *Lishi Yanjiu* [Historical research] 1.

Fang, Xuefeng. 1998. *Jungguk godaesa-e ireum-eul namgin joseonsaramdeul* [Koreans who left their names in ancient Chinese history]. Yanji: Yanbian People's Press.

Fu, Langyun, and Yang Yang. 1983. *Dongbei minzu shilue* [Outline history of northeastern nations]. Changchun: Jilin People's Press.

Fu, Sinian, ed. 1932. *Dongbei shigang: di yi juan: gudai zhi dongbei* [Outline of history of the northeast, vol. 1, The northeast in ancient times]. Peiping [Beijing] and Shanghai: Institute of History and Philology, Academia Sinica.

Gries, Peter Hayes. 2005. "The Koguryo Controversy, National Identity, and Sino-Korean Relations Today". *East Asia* 22, no. 4: 3–17.

Hankyoreh Shinmun. 2004. "Junggug-e 'goguryeosa pyeonip uryeo' jeondal" [Concerns over the incorporation of Goguryeo history conveyed to China], 9 January 2004. Cited in Kim In-Seong 2004, p. 165.

He, Ziquan. 1959. "Zhongguo gudaishi jiaoxue zhong cunzai de yige wenti" [A problem that exists in the teaching of ancient Chinese history]. *Guangming Daily*, 5 July 1959.

Hu, Zhili. 2011. *Zhongguo youzheng zhuanyong youzitu putong youzifengpian mulu* [Catalogue of China Post ordinary postal stationery envelopes with dedicated indicias]. Beijing: Posts & Telecom Press.

Im, Gye-Sun. 2004. *Uri-ege dagaon joseonjog-eun nugu inga?* [Who are the Koreans in China coming up to us?]. Seoul: Hyeonamsas.

JASS and TNU (Jilin Academy of Social Sciences Goguryeo Research Center and Tonghua Normal University Institute of Goguryeo Studies), eds. 1999. *Quanguo shoujie Gaogouli xueshu taolunhui lunwenji* [Proceedings of the first national academic conference on Goguryeo studies].

Jian, Bozan. 1961. "Cong xihan de heqin zhengce shuodao zhaojun chusai" [From the political intermarriage policy of Western Han to Zhaojun's marriage into Xiongnu]. *Guangming Daily*, 5 February 1961.

Jiang, Feifei, et al. 1998. *Zhong-Han guanxi shi: Gudai juan* [History of Sino-Korean relations: Ancient volume]. Beijing: Social Sciences Academics Press.

Jiang, Mengshan, ed. 1992. *Chaoxian tongshi* [General history of Korea]. Yanji: Yanbian University Press.

Jin, Changfan. 1957. "Yanbian Chaoxianzu zizhizhou bufen ganbu, xuesheng zai zhengfeng yundong zhong baolu chulai de yixie defang minzuzhuyi sixiang" [Local nationalist thoughts among some cadres and students in Yanbian Korean autonomous prefecture exposed during the rectification movement]. Xinhua News Agency: Internal reference document no. 2393, 31 December 1957.

Jin, Yufu. [1941] 1943. *Dongbei tongshi: shangbian* [General history of the northeast, vol. 2]. Chongqing: Wushiniandai chubanshe.

Jo, Jung-Sik. 2004. "Jung, goguryeosa sijeong geobu: 'jibangjeongbu, daehakgyojae

tongje motanda.' Jeongbu, jujungdaesa sohwan geomto" [China refuses to
rectify Goguryeo history: 'Unable to regulate local governments and college
textbooks'. Government considered recalling ambassador from China]. *Chosun
Ilbo*, 7 August 2004.

JoongAng Ilbo. 1983. "Baekdusan cheonjineun hangugui yeongtoda" [The Heaven
Lake of Mount Paektu is Korean territory]. *JoongAng Ilbo*, 17 September
1983.

———. 1993. "Baekdusaneun urittang: Yeoyauiwon 64 myeong gyeoruian jechul
seomyeong" [Mount Paektu is our territory: 64 lawmakers from ruling and
opposition parties signed and submitted the draft resolution]. *JoongAng Ilbo*,
24 July 1993.

Kang, Se-Kwŏn. 2003. "Goguryeoneun joseonminjogui dangdanghan cheonnyeon
gangguk" [Goguryeo is a dignified millennium strong country of the Korean
nation]. *Rodong Sinmun*, 27 November 2003.

KASS ([North] Korean Academy of Social Science Institute of History), ed.
1979. *Joseon Jeonsa* [Complete history of Korea], vol. 3. Pyongyang: Science
Encyclopedia Publishing House.

——— ed. 1991. *Joseon Jeonsa* [Complete history of Korea], vol. 3. Pyongyang:
Science Encyclopedia Publishing House.

Kim, Hyeon-Suk. 2008. "Hanjung yeoksa munje-e daehan bukhan-ui baneunghwa
ipjang - Goguryeosa munje-e daehan choegeun yeongu seonggwareul jungsim-
euro" [North Korea's reaction and position on the South Korean-Chinese
historical dispute: Focussing on the recent studies on the issue of Goguryeo
history]. Seoul: Northeast Asia History Foundation.

Kim, Il-Sung. 1995. "Joseonhyeongmyeonggadeul-eun joseon-eul jal araya
handa" [Korean revolutionaries must know about Korea well], speech before
Korean People's Revolutionary Army political cadres and political instructor,
15 September 1943. In *Kim Il-Sung jeonjip* [The complete works of Kim Il-Sung],
vol. 1, pp. 546–71. Pyongyang: Workers' Party of Korea Press.

———. 2003. "Joseon 2.8 yesulyeonghwachwaryeongso-ui myeotgaji gwaeob-e
daehayeo" [On several tasks of Korea February 8 arts, movies and photography
group], 22 October 1971. In *Kim Il-Sung jeonjip* [The complete works of Kim
Il-Sung], vol. 47, pp. 400–14. Pyongyang: Workers' Party of Korea Press.

Kim In-Seong. 2004. "Yeoksajeok jinsil waegog-e daehan bipangwa banseong"
[Criticism and reflection on the distortion of historical truth]. *Minjok Yeongu*
[Ethnic studies] 13 (September).

Kim, Jin-Sun. 2004. "Junggug-ui goguryeosa pyeonib-e balkkeunhan bukhan"
[North Korea outraged over China's incorporation of Goguryeo History].
Sisapyeongnon [Current affairs review] 3, no. 1 (January).

Kim, Sŏk-Hyŏng et al. 1963. *Jeon segye sa (Ssoryeon gwahagweon pyeon) Joseon
gwangye seosul-ui eomjunghan chagodeul-e daehayeo* [On the serious errors in

the narratives relating to Korea in *world history* (edited by USSR Academy of Science)]. *Rodong Shinmun*, 20 September 1963.

Lee, Chi-Dong. "Korean, Chinese Academics Debate Claims to Koguryo Kingdom". *Yonhap*, 16 September 2004. Cited in Gries 2005.

Li, Dianfu, and Yuliang Sun. 1990. *Goguryeo Gansa* [A brief history of Goguryeo], translated by Ingu Gang and Young-soo Kim. Seoul: Samseon.

Li, Sheng. 2005. "Guanyu 'Dongbei Gongcheng' yu 'Gaogouli lishi yanjiu' de jidian jianjie: zai 'Gaogouli lishi wenti xueshu yantaohui' shang de jianghua" [Some thoughts on the 'northeast project' and 'research on goguryeo history': Speech on the 'symposium on goguryeo historical studies']. In *Gaogouli lishi wenti yanjiu lunwen ji* [Collection of essays in Goguryeo historical research], edited by Li, Sheng and Wenyi Piao. Yanji: Yanbian University Press.

Liu, Housheng. 2011a. "Woguo dongbei diqu wending yu fazhan yanjiu" [A Study on the strategies of stability and development in our country's northeast region]. In *Dongbei bianjiang lishi yu xianzhuang de huigu yu sikao* [Review and thoughts on the history and current situation of the northeast borderland], edited by Ma Dazheng, internal material produced by Chinese Academy of Social Sciences. Republished as *Zhonggong zhongyao lishi wenxian ziliao huibian* [Collections of important documents and materials in CCP history], collection 31, vol. 16, edited by Service Center for Chinese Publications, Los Angeles.

———. 2011b "Weihu Jilin sheng wending de sheqing yanjiu" [A social situation study on maintaining stability in Jilin Province]. In *Dongbei bianjiang lishi yu xianzhuang de huigu yu sikao* [Review and thoughts on the history and current situation of the northeast borderland], edited by Ma Dazheng, internal material produced by Chinese Academy of Social Sciences. Republished as *Zhonggong zhongyao lishi wenxian ziliao huibian* [Collections of important documents and materials in CCP history], collection 31, vol. 16, edited by Service Center for Chinese Publications, Los Angeles.

Liu, Yongzhi. 1994. *Zhong-Chao guanxishi yanjiu* [A study on the History of Sino-Korean relations]. Zhengzhou: Zhongzhou guji chubanshe.

Lu, Jiandong. 1995. *Chen Yinke de zuihou ershinian* [Chen Yinke's last twenty years]. Beijing: SDX Joint Publishing Company.

Ma, Dazheng. 2011a. "Qianyan" [Foreword]. In *Dongbei bianjiang lishi yu xianzhuang de huigu yu sikao* [Review and thoughts on the history and current situation of the northeast borderland], edited by Ma Dazheng, internal material produced by Chinese Academy of Social Sciences. Republished as *Zhonggong zhongyao lishi wenxian ziliao huibian* [Collections of important documents and materials in CCP history], collection 31, vol. 16, edited by Service Center for Chinese Publications, Los Angeles.

———. 2011b. "Dongbei bianjiang lishi yu xianzhuang de huigu yu sikao" [Review and thoughts on the history and current situation of the northeast borderland].

In *Dongbei bianjiang lishi yu xianzhuang de huigu yu sikao* [Review and thoughts on the history and current situation of the northeast borderland], edited by Ma Dazheng, internal material produced by Chinese Academy of Social Sciences. Republished as *Zhonggong zhongyao lishi wenxian ziliao huibian* [Collections of important documents and materials in CCP history], collection 31, vol. 16, edited by Service Center for Chinese Publications, Los Angeles.

Ma, Dazheng et al. 2001. *Gudai Zhongguo Gaogouli lishi conglun* [Theses on ancient Chinese Goguryeo history]. Harbin: Heilongjiang Education Press.

Ma, Yang. 2011. "Zhuanjia jianyi jinzao zuzhi Dongbei bianjiang yangeshi diaocha" [Experts suggest that investigations on northeastern borderland history be organized as soon as possible]. In *Dongbei bianjiang lishi yu xianzhuang de huigu yu sikao* [Review and thoughts on the history and current situation of the northeast borderland], edited by Ma Dazheng, internal material produced by Chinese Academy of Social Sciences. Republished as *Zhonggong zhongyao lishi wenxian ziliao huibian* [Collections of important documents and materials in CCP history], collection 31, vol. 16, edited by Service Center for Chinese Publications, Los Angeles.

Mao, Zedong. 1958. "Mao Zedong huijian Chaoxian zhengfu daibiaotuan tanhua jilu" [Record of conversation during Mao Zedong's meeting with DPRK government delegation]. 25 November 1958. Cited in Shen and Dong 2011.

———. 1963. "Mao Zedong jiejian chaoxian laodong xinwen daibiaotuan tanhua jilu" [Record of conversation during mao zedong's reception of the delegation of *Rodong Sinmun* of DPRK]. 26 April 1963. Cited in Shen and Dong 2011.

Mohan, Pankaj. 2006. "China's Nationalist Historiography of the 'Northeast Project' and the Australian Response to Its Challenge". *Journal of Inner and East Asian Studies* 3, no. 1: 29–46.

Mu, Xin. 2006. "Guo Moruo kaozheng 'Zaishengyuan'" [Guo Moruo's study on *Zaishengyuan*]. *Shiji* 5.

National Assembly of the Republic of Korea. 2004. *Junggug-ui Goguryeosa waegog mit jungguk yeoksa pyeonipsido jungdan chokgu gyeoruian* [Resolution urging for the suspension of China's distortion of Goguryeo history and attempt to incorporate it into Chinese history]. 6 August 2004.

Ngapoi, Ngawang Jigme. 1989. "Shenqie huainian Banchan E'erdeni Quejijianzan dashi" [Deep cherish for Choekyi Gyaltsen, 10th Panchen Lama]. *People's Daily*, 14 February 1989.

NRDT (National Research and Development Team for History Curriculum Standards at the Compulsory Education Stage), ed. 2005. *Lishi qinianji xiace* [History, grade 7 (2)]. Beijing: Beijing Normal University Press.

Paeksan Jaryowon, ed. 1987. *Hanminjok-ui daeryuk gwangye sa* [Continental history of the Korean nation]. Seoul: Paeksan Jaryowon.

————, ed. 1998. *Hangug-ui bukbang yeongto* [Northern territory of Korea]. Seoul: Paeksan Jaryowon.

Park, Chung-hee. 1962. *Uri minjog-ui nagal gil: Sahoejaegyeon-ui inyeom* [Our nation's path: Ideology of social reconstruction]. Seoul: Dong'a.

Park, Jung-Hyeon. 2004. "Jung, nambuktongil daebi goguryeosa waegok" [China distorts Goguryeo history in preparation for Inter-Korean reunification]. *Chosun Ilbo*, 10 August 2004.

People's Daily. 2006. "'Zhongguo weixie' haishi 'Zhongguo jiyu': Ruhe lijie zou heping fazhan daolu" ['Chinese threat' or 'Chinese opportunities': How to understand taking a peaceful development route]. *People's Daily*, 29 September 2006.

PEPHED (People's Education Press History Editorial Department), ed. 2005. *Zhongguo gudaishi quan yi ce* [Ancient history of China, single volume]. Beijing: People's Education Press.

Piao, Jianyi, and Guangji Piao, eds. 2006. *Zhong-Han guanxi yu dongbeiya jingji gongtongti* [Sino-South Korean relations and the northeast Asian economic community]. Beijing: China Social Sciences Press.

Quan, Hexiu. 2004 "Junggung hakgyega boneun hanbando nambukakgyeui goguryeoyeongu (2): 1945–1999" [Studies of Goguryeo in the south and north of the Korean peninsula as seen by Chinese academia (2): 1945–1999]. *Paeksan Hakbo*, 69: 361–77.

Ri, Sŏng-Sun. 1962. *Su nara chimnyag-eul bandaehan Goguryeo inmin-ui tujaeng* [The Goguryeo people's struggle against Sui invasion]. Pyongyang: Workers' Party of Korea Press.

Rodong Sinmun, 1964. "Sahoejuui jinyeong-ui tongil-eul suhohayeo gukje gongsanjuuiundong-ui dangyeol-eul ganghwahaja" [Maintain the unity of the socialist camp and strengthen the solidarity of international communist movement]. *Rodong Sinmun*, 30 January 1963. Cited in *Korean Central Yearbook (1964)*, edited by Korean Central Yearbook Editorial Committee, Pyongyang: Korean Central News Agency, 1964, pp. 80–84.

Seo, Byeong-Guk. 1997. *Goguryeo jeguk sa* [History of Goguryeo empire]. Seoul: Hyean.

Shen, Zhihua, and Jie Dong. 2011. "Zhong-Chao bianjie zhengyi de jiejue (1950–1964 nian)" [The solution of Sino-DPRK border disputes, 1950–1964]. *Twenty-First Century* (April): 34–51.

Shin Mi-A. 2011. "Bukhangwa Junggungnae Goguryeo yujeok segyeyusan deungjae gwallyeon juyo jaengjeom yeongu" [Review concerning the inscription of Koguryo relics in North Korea and China on the World Heritage List]. *Goguryeo Balhae Yeongu* [Studies on Goguryeo and Balhae], no. 40: 83–107.

Snyder, Scott. 2004. "A Turning Point for China-Korea Relations?" *Comparative Connections* (Fall).

Son, Yŏng-Jong. 1990. *Goguryeo sa (1)* [History of Goguryeo 1]. Pyongyang: Science Encyclopedia Publishing House.

———. 1997. *Goguryeo sa (2)* [History of Goguryeo, vol. 2]. Pyongyang: Science Encyclopedia Publishing House.

———. 2008a. *Joseon dandaesa (Goguryeo sa 3)* [Dynastic history of Korea (history of Goguryeo, vol. 3)]. Pyongyang: Science Encyclopedia Publishing House.

———. 2008b. *Joseon dandaesa (Goguryeo sa 4)* [Dynastic history of Korea (history of Goguryeo, vol. 4)]. Pyongyang: Science Encyclopedia Publishing House.

Soong, Ching-ling. 1951. "Xinzhongguo xiangqian maijin: Dongbei lüxing yinxiang ji" [New China marching forward: Impressions during trip to Northeast]. *People's Daily*, 1 May 1951.

Sun, Bingying, Liantai Zhao, et al. eds. 1985. *Shijie tongshi gangyao (gudai bufen)* [Outline of world history (ancient part)]. Changchun: Jilin Literature and History Press.

Sun, Binggen. 2011. "Guanyu Zhong-Chao lianhe kaogu fajuedui de yixie qingkuang huiyi" [Recollection of some issues of the Sino-North Korean joint archaeological excavation team]. In *Dongbei bianjiang lishi yu xianzhuang de huigu yu sikao* [Review and thoughts on the history and current situation of the northeast borderland], edited by Ma Dazheng, internal material produced by Chinese Academy of Social Sciences. Republished as *Zhonggong zhongyao lishi wenxian ziliao huibian* [Collections of important documents and materials in CCP history], collection 31, vol. 16, edited by Service Center for Chinese Publications, Los Angeles.

Sun, Jinji. 2011. "Yanjiu you jinqu, xuanchuan wu jilü: Gaogouli wenti yanjiu, xuanchaun xianzhuang" [Restrictions for research; indiscipline for propaganda: The current situation of research and propaganda on Goguryeo issue]. In *Dongbei bianjiang lishi yu xianzhuang de huigu yu sikao* [Review and thoughts on the history and current situation of the northeast borderland], edited by Ma Dazheng, internal material produced by Chinese Academy of Social Sciences. Republished as *Zhonggong zhongyao lishi wenxian ziliao huibian* [Collections of important documents and materials in CCP history], collection 31, vol. 16, edited by Service Center for Chinese Publications, Los Angeles.

Sun, Ku et al. 2002. *Zhong-Chao bianjie de lishi bianqian* [Historical evololution of the Sino-Korean border]. People's Liberation Army internal reading material. Shenyang. Republished as *Zhonggong zhongyao lishi wenxian ziliao huibian* [Collections of important documents and materials in CCP history], special vol. 43, edited by Service Center for Chinese Publications, Los Angeles.

Sun, Qilin. 2011. "Guanyu Chaoxian, Hanguo xuezhe ji zhengyao dui woguo Dongbei jiangyu yu minzu wenti yanlun de diaoyan" [A survey of speeches by North and South Korean scholars and politicians on territory and ethnic issues in our country's Northeast]. In *Dongbei bianjiang lishi yu xianzhuang de huigu yu sikao* [Review and thoughts on the history and current situation of the northeast borderland], edited by Ma Dazheng, internal material produced by Chinese Academy of Social Sciences. Republished as *Zhonggong zhongyao lishi wenxian ziliao huibian* [Collections of important documents and materials in CCP history], collection 31, vol. 16, edited by Service Center for Chinese Publications, Los Angeles.

Sun, Wenfan, and Yuliang Sun eds. 2003. *Gaogouli lishi zhishi ganbu duben* [Goguryeo historical knowledge handbook for cadres]. Changchun: Jilin Literature and History Press.

Sun, Yuliang, and Wenfan Sun. 2008. *Jianming Gaogouli shi* [A concise history of Goguryeo]. Changchun: Jilin People's Press.

Sun, Yunlai, and Yunzhong Sha, eds. 1994. *Jilin sheng bianjiang minzu diqu wending he fazhan de zhuyao wenti yu duice* [Major issues and solutions concerning the stability and development of borderland ethnic minority areas in Jilin Province]. Beijing: Central University for Nationalities Press.

Tan, Qixiang. 1988. "Lishishang de zhongguo he zhongguo lidai jiangyu" [Historical China and China's historical dominion]. *Zhongguo Bianjiang Shidi Yanjiu* [China's borderland history and geography studies] 3: pp. 1–9.

Tong, Dong, ed. 1987. *Zhongguo dongbei shi* [History of China's Northeast]. Changchun: Jilin Literature and History Press.

UNESCO. 1999. Bureau of the World Heritage Committee Twenty-Third Extra-ordinary Session. "Item 5 of the Provisional Agenda: Requests for International Assistance". WHC-99/CONF.208/6. Paris, 15 November 1999.

———. 2001. World Heritage Committee Twenty-Fifth Session, "Item 10 of the Provisional Agenda: Information on Tentative Lists and Examination of Nominations of Cultural and Natural Properties to the List of World Heritage in Danger and the World Heritage List". WHC-01/CONF.208/12, annex 1. Helsinki, 10 December 2001.

———. 2002. "Operational Guidelines for the Implementation of the World Heritage Convention". WHC 02/2. July 2002.

———. 2003a. World Heritage Committee Twenty-Seventh Session. "Item 8 of the Provisional Agenda: Tentative Lists of States Parties". WHC-03/27.COM/8A. Paris, 10 June 2003.

———. 2003b. World Heritage Committee Twenty-Seventh Session. "ICOMOS Evaluations of Nominations of Cultural and Mixed Properties to the World Heritage List". WHC-03/27.COM/INF.8. Paris.

———. 2003c. World Heritage Committee Twenty-Seventh Session. "Summary Record". WHC-03/27.COM/INF.24. Paris. Cited in Shin 2011.

———. 2004a. World Heritage Committee Twenty-Eighth Session. "ICOMOS Evaluations of Nominations of Cultural and Mixed Properties to the World Heritage List". WHC-04/28COM/INF.14A. Suzhou.

————. 2004b. World Heritage Committee Twenty-Eighth Session. "Decisions of the 28th session of the World Heritage Committee (Suzhou 2004)". WHC-04/28. COM/26. Paris, 29 October 2004.

————. 2005. "Operational Guidelines for the Implementation of the World Heritage Convention". WHC. 05/2. 2 February 2005.

————. 2011. "Operational Guidelines for the Implementation of the World Heritage Convention". WHC. 11/01. November 2011.

Wang, Xiaopu et al. 2014. *Zhong-Han guanxi shi: Gudai juan (di er ban)* [History of Sino-Korean relations: Ancient volume (2nd ed.)]. Beijing: Social Sciences Academics Press.

Wu, Xue. 1992. "'Qing Yi', zai zongli guanhuai xia chengzhang" [Youth art theatre of China grows under the care of the premier]. In *Zhou Enlai yu yishujiamen* [Zhou Enlai and artists], edited by Chen Huangmei. Beijing: CCCPC Party Literature Publishing House.

Xu, Qingquan. 2008. "Chen Yinke Lun 'Zaishengyuan' chuban fengbo" [Issues concerning the publication of Chen Yinke's *On 'Zaishengyuan'*]. *Southern Weekly*, 28 August 2008.

Xue, Hong, and Shutian Li. 1991. *Zhongguo Dongbei tongshi* [General history of Northeast China]. Changchun: Jilin Literature and History Press.

Yang, Chunji, and Shengyang Qin. 2003. *Gaogouli lishi zhishi wenda* [Questions and answers of historical knowledge on Goguryeo]. Changchun: Jilin People's Press.

Yang, Zhaoquan, and Junguang Han. 1992. *Zhong-Chao guanxi jianshi.* [Brief history of Sino-Korean relations]. Shenyang: Liaoning Nationalities Publication House.

Yang, Zhaoquan, and Yumei Sun. 1993. *Zhong-Chao bianjie shi* [History of Sino-Korean border]. Changchun: Jilin Literature and History Press.

Yu, Jeong-Gap. 1991. *Bukbang yeongtoron: Saeroun sidaejeongsin, Damuljeongsin* [On northern territories: The new zeitgeist, *Damuljeongsin*]. Seoul: Beopgyung Chulpansa, 1991.

Zhang, Bibo. 2000. "Guanyu Lishishang Minzu Guishu yu Jiangyu Wenti Zaisikao-Jianping 'Yishiliangyong' Shiguan" [Reflection on the national belongings and territorial issues in history: Comment on the historical view of 'one history for dual use']. *Zhongguo bianjiang shidi yanjiu* [China's borderland history and geography studies] 2: 1–9.

Zhang, Fan et al. 2009. "Xizang ziguyilai jiushi zhongguo de yibufen – Fang xizang shekeyuan fuyuanzhang Sun Yong" [Tibet has been a part of China since ancient times – An interview with Sun Yong, vice dean of Tibet Academy of Social Science]. *People's Daily*, 26 February 2009.

Zhang, Weiwei. 2004. "Hanguo dui 'Gaogouli shi' wenti pinglun zongshu" ["Literature review on the South Korean comments to issues of Goguryeo history"]. *Guoji Ziliao Xinxi* [International data and information] 9: 27–31.

Zhang, Yong. 2002. "Zhengfu gongzuo baogao: Zai Tonghua shi di si jie renmindaibiaodahui di si ci huiyi shang" [Government work report: At the fourth session of the fourth people's congress of Tonghua City], 16 December 2002. In *Tonghua nianjian* [Tonghua yearbook], edited by Lianxing Chen.

Zhang, Zhengliang et al. 1951. *Wuqiannianlai de Zhong-Chao youhao guanxi* [The Sino-Korean friendship since five millenniums ago]. Beijing: Kaiming shudian.

Zhou, Enlai. 1963. "Zhou Enlai jiejian Chaoxian kexueyuan daibiaotuan de tanhua" [Zhou Enlai's talk during his reception of DPRK Academy of Science delegation]. *Waishi Gongzuo Tongbao* [Foreign affairs bulletin] 10. Cited in Shen and Dong 2011.

9

Nationalism, Politics and the Practice of Archaeology in Afghanistan: A Case Study of Bamiyan

J. Eva Meharry

In 2001 the Taliban destroyed the Buddhas of Bamiyan, two of the world's tallest Buddha statues, which had stood at the crossroads of Asia for more than 1,400 years. The event was a poignant example of the dynamic relationship between archaeological heritage and politics. In the aftermath, the international community largely attributed the event to a growing trend of heritage destruction (i.e., Bahadur 2002; Bryant 2002) perpetrated by religious fundamentalists across South Asia (i.e., Chakrabarti 2003; Coningham and Lewer 1999; Ratnagar 2004). Others placed the event within a continuance of Islamic iconoclasm, extending back to the medieval period, across the broader Muslim world.[1] From 2014, the Bamiyan Buddhas' destruction was reinterpreted as a harbinger for Da'esh's iconoclastic destruction of archaeological sites across the Middle East (Williams 2015).

While the destruction of the Buddha statues linked the threats posed by religious fundamentalism to eastern and western neighbours, within Afghanistan it also underscored the relationship between the country's archaeology, nationalism and politics. Since Afghanistan's "independence" in the early twentieth century, successive political leaders have attempted to build a nation from a deeply divided society, and one of the most valuable resources available has been the ancient archaeological heritage. While numerous studies have revealed the politicization of archaeological heritage in the twentieth and twenty-first centuries across the Middle East and South Asia (i.e., Goode 2007; Meskell 1997; Silberman 1989), none have fully delved into the twentieth-century historical backdrop that shaped the events of 2001 in Afghanistan. Moving beyond the typically generalized treatment of the Taliban and their destruction of the Buddhas (for a discussion, see Bernbeck 2010, p. 30), this paper aims to place the events of 2001 in the context of the formation and development of nationalism and the archaeological discipline in Afghanistan since the country's "independence" in 1919. Using the iconic case of Bamiyan, this paper will reveal how key actors, including foreign archaeologists, conservative religious groups and Afghan political administrations, shaped the politicization of archaeology in the modern Afghan nation-state.[2] As a "negative heritage" site that stores negative memories in the collective imagination (Meskell 2002, p. 558), exploring what circumstances led to the destruction of the Bamiyan Buddhas through a longer historical lens than previous studies may also help to decipher what role the site will play in the future of Afghanistan, whether for remembering or forgetting past memories in the formation of the modern national identity.

Afghanistan's Archaeology, Nationalism and Politics: The Early Years (1919–79)

"Independence" (*esteqlal*) was reportedly the "most hard-worked word" in Afghanistan when Emir Amanullah Khan assumed the throne in early 1919 (Adamec 1974, p. 77; Maconachie 1928, p. 2), propagated by the nationalist fervour spreading across the post–World War I Middle East. To win his country's freedom from British intervention in its foreign affairs, the newly anointed leader launched the short-lived Third Anglo-Afghan War of 1919 (Adamec 1967, pp. 133–34; Adamec 1974, p. 77). Amanullah vigorously asserted this independence at home and abroad in a progressive nation-building agenda, even before the Treaty of Rawalpindi formally secured Afghanistan's autonomy in 1921 (Gregorian 1969, pp. 239–61; Sykes 2002, pp. 284–85). Within the year, the king's trusted foreign minister and influential nationalist ideologue, Mahmud Tarzi (Nawid 1999, p. 189; Schinasi 1979), travelled to Paris as the new foreign minister to cultivate bilateral cultural relations with France (Dupree 1973, p. 446).

The foreign minister's overtures to France proved fruitful. In September 1922, an Afghan-Franco cultural agreement was reached, guaranteeing exclusive excavation rights for the French archaeologists and an equal distribution of discoveries between the two countries for the next thirty years (Dupree 1974, p. 205; Grissmann 2006, pp. 62–63). As American and European archaeologists ceded excavation rights to nationalist governments across the Middle East in the inter-war years—principally the coveted partition of archaeological discoveries—the agreement generously favoured the French archaeologists (Goode 2007, p. 5). Unsurprisingly then, the first French representatives to arrive in Afghanistan were the archaeologists, Alfred Foucher and André Godard, who established the Délégation Archéologique Française en Afghanistan (DAFA) a year before the French Legation in Kabul (Fenet 2010, p. 35; Sykes 2002, p. 297).

The "Concessional" stage (1922–52) of the archaeological discipline in Afghanistan began in 1922 with DAFA's countrywide survey.[3] The archaeologists concentrated on many of the sites mentioned in the written accounts of the Chinese pilgrims Fa Hsien and Xuanzang, who traversed the ancient trade routes now known romantically as the "Silk Road" (Beal 1885, pp. 50–51; Giles 1923, p. 19; Tarzi 2006, p. 154). Located along one of the main ancient thoroughfares in the mountainous region of Central Afghanistan, and home to the politically marginalized Shi'a Hazara minority group (Barfield 2010, pp. 37–40; Mousavi 1998, p. xiii), Bamiyan was amongst the first archaeological sites surveyed by DAFA. The Bamiyan Buddhas loomed large in European consciousness and imagination after nineteenth-century explorers penned vivid accounts of their travels to Bamiyan (i.e., Eyre 1843; Masson 2011; Sale 1843), likening the monumental statues, 38 metres (c. 550 CE) and 55 metres (c. 615 CE) high, to the great "wonders of the world" (Simpson 1886a, pp. 490–91; Simpson 1886b, pp. 525–26). As the French minister plenipotentiary in Afghanistan, Maurice Fouchet, frankly stated in a 1923 correspondence to King Amanullah, who had altered his title to king, "*padshah*", that year: "The Buddhas of

FIGURE 9.1   Panoramic view of the Bamiyan Cliffs with the two colossal Buddha niches. Photography courtesy of Jake Simkin.

Bamiyan are the only visible richness of Afghanistan" (Centlivres 2008, p. 9; Fouchet 1931, p. 131). The selection also reflected the personal and professional interests of the DAFA director, Alfred Foucher, who devoted a large portion of his career to Buddhist archaeology (Foucher 1917).

Foucher and Joseph Hackin, the then-director of the Musée Guimet, completed three field seasons in Bamiyan Valley between 1923 and 1926, revealing a rich cultural landscape. The two colossal statues formed the most visible component of a Buddhist monastic complex in the Bamiyan Cliffs, encircled by close to 750 manmade caves ornately decorated with frescoes and sculptures (Ball 2008, p. 164). Caves in the lateral Kakrak and Foladi Valleys housed similarly decorative features (Klimburg-Salter 1989, p. 73; Scerrato 1959, pp. 23–56; Tarzi 1977, p. 107). South of the Bamiyan Cliffs the archaeologists also found two Islamic period sites: the fortified complex, *Shahr-i Zuhak*, "the Red City"; and the mud-brick citadel, *Shahr-i Ghulghulah*, the "City of Noise" (Ball 2008, pp. 164–67). Focusing on the pre-Islamic remains in the Bamiyan Cliffs (Hackin and Carl 1933; Tarzi 2003, p. 1), the archaeologists documented the condition of the monuments and implemented preliminary conservation measures on a portion of the frescoes (Toubekis and Jansen 2013, p. 157). Many of the frescoes from the cliffs and Kakrak Valley were subsequently removed and divided between museums in Kabul and Paris (Feroozi 2004, p. 12; Rowland 1966, pp. 92–106).

From the outset, archaeology was prioritized in Amanullah's incipient nationalist agenda, strategically implemented to help legitimate the government's territorial sovereignty and bolster national prestige on the international stage (Qureshi 2014, pp. 221–24; Tarzi 1998, p. i). Contemporary intellectual leaders in the progressive vanguard supported this sentiment, such as King Amanullah's friend Badshah Khan, known as the "Frontier Gandhi" for his activism alongside Mahatma Gandhi, who reflected in his autobiography:

> When Buddhism was spreading, our country made great progress, evidence of which can be found in the relics of that age. Even today two magnificent statues of Guatama the Buddha can be seen in Bamian. They are probably the largest statues in the world. Standing at the foot of the mountain, carved out of the rock, they present an unparalleled example of the perfection in the art of sculpture... (Khan 1969, p. 15)

The intellectual Mahmud Tarzi further argued that understanding the country's ancient past would help secure its future; a conviction that undoubtedly spurred his previous efforts in Paris (Gregorian 1969, pp. 174–75). A state-issued visitors' guide to Afghanistan captured this line of thinking in 1958: "With the passing of the era of Colonialism, a revival of the ancient tradition of cultural and artistic advance took place.... The heritage ... served to inspire the people to return to independence" (Zhobal 1958, p. 82).

In pursuit of national prestige, King Amanullah installed the Bamiyan collection in the Presidential Palace in the heart of the capital, along with the remaining "Cabinet of Curiosities" acquired by the royal family during the "Exploratory" stage (pre-1922), a period when antiquarians, drawn to the region by the "Great Game", conducted informal surveys and excavations of archaeological sites (Dupree 1958, p. 161; Grissmann 2006, p. 62). In 1924 the collection was inaugurated as the National Museum of Afghanistan (Grissmann 2009). Alfred Foucher also recalled the king's eagerness to "inaugurate a new era, that of archaeological tourism in the history of the valley of Bamiyan" (Foucher 1923, p. 368). To help realize this vision, Joseph Hackin and his wife, Ria, published the first visitor's guidebook to Bamiyan (Hackin and Hackin 1934).

The year 1924 marked a wave of broad social and cultural reforms (Gregorian 1967, p. 367). In opposition to the king's progressive scheme, the ulama, a body of conservative Muslim religious leaders, formed a rebellion in the eastern province of Khost (Dupree 1973, p. 449; McChesney 1999, pp. 13–15; Nawid 1999, pp. 100–1). During the nine-month uprising, a local mullah led a village mob to the French excavation at Hadda, a Greco-Buddhist site near the southeastern border shared with the then British India, smashing the recently excavated Buddhist artefacts—indexing the first politically motivated attack on Afghanistan's heritage in modern history (Godard n.d.; Goode 2007, p. 16).

The rebellions also highlighted Afghanistan's deeply divided society, fragmented along ethnic, linguistic and religious lines. King Amanullah's jihad against Britain during the Third Anglo-Afghan War temporarily united the societal factions around pan-Islamic and anti-colonial sentiments. At the time, the conservative ulama feared British control would corrupt the Islamic social and cultural fabric of Afghanistan, whilst the Young Afghan (*Jawanan-i Afghan*) nationalist movement viewed imperialism as a threat to nationalism and progress. This tenuous convergence of nationalist, religious and tribal agendas diverged, however, once the imperial threat had been lifted at the end of the war (Barfield 2010, pp. 176, 181).

Ignoring the internal unrest, the royal couple toured Europe, the Middle East and India from December 1927 to July 1928. En route, the king secured diplomatic relations with many of their host states, but he was particularly inspired by European and Turkish modernity (Dupree 1973, p. 451; *The Living Age* 1928, pp. 507–14). When he returned home, the king accelerated the implementation of his progressive programme, and famously unveiled Queen Soraya at a state function in Kabul, purportedly shocking their more conservative compatriots' religious views (Dupree 1973, p. 450). The combination of these events spurred the ulama into mounting a coup, forcing the king to abdicate (Nawid 1999, p. 191). As the royal family fled the country, a mob swarmed the capital, looting the collections at the Arg, including a number of Buddhist antiquities excavated at Hadda by the French archaeologists (Dupree et al. 1974, p. 24).

After King Amanullah's abdication, his successor, former minister of war, King Nadir Shah (r. 1929–33) of the Musahiban family, laid the foundation of the state's infrastructure, expanding the national road system and postal system—both of which improved the accessibility and visibility of Bamiyan (Sykes 2002, p. 331). Heeding his predecessor's fate, the king granted concessions to the tribal network, such as greater autonomy and fewer taxes (Barfield 2010, p. 200; Pattanaik 2002, pp. 125–26). Following Nadir Shah's assassination in 1933 as a result of a political family feud (Adamec 1974, p. 198), his son King Zahir Shah (r. 1933–73) oversaw a period of relative social and political stability, even steering a narrow course of neutrality through World War II.

Despite the political turmoil, archaeological activities continued at Bamiyan. The French conducted two excavations at the Bamiyan Cliffs in 1930 and 1933 (Hackin and Carl 1933). Activity then waned during the years surrounding World War II, with the French away—and in some cases killed—for the war effort (Cambon 2008, p. 147). The only exception was the "micro-excavations" made by a British team at Shahr-i Zohak in Bamiyan Valley in 1951 (Allchin and Allchin 2012, pp. 137–43; Baker and Allchin 1991, p. vii).

During the abeyance of archaeological exploration, Bamiyan imagery proliferated in state-sponsored material. In 1932 the state issued a 3-Afghanis postal stamp simply titled "Bamian", as one of twelve in the First Definitive Monuments Series (Patterson 1964, pp. 41–42). The red and white postal stamp depicted the view of the Bamiyan Cliffs, with the niche of the 55-metre Buddha statue in the central frame, though set at a slight angle so that the statue was partially obscured in the shadow of the niche. The 3-Afghanis stamp illustrated the only pre-Islamic monument in the series, alongside six stamps with ancient and modern Islamic monuments, and five with modern state monuments constructed between 1880 and 1930.

Use of the Bamiyan motif was particularly noteworthy, since postal stamps were a highly politicized form of state-sponsored material (Cohen 2012). From the 1940s the state employed postal stamps to promote Pashtunistan Day, which contested the border dividing Pashtun tribal territory along the North-West Frontier of then India; and, post-Partition, it issued annual stamps to recognize the UN and UNESCO, organizations attempting to ameliorate tensions with Pakistan (Azari 1988, p. 38; ibid., pp. 840–43). In response to the printing of the "Bamian" 3-Afghanis postal stamp, rebellions by the conservative ulama erupted again, and the stamp was swiftly withdrawn from circulation (Patterson 1964, p. 42).

In 1939 a banknote series also included Bamiyan. The 2-Afghanis banknote depicted a landscape view of Bamiyan Valley, with the large Buddha niche in the background and a profile of King Zahir Shah on the obverse. Of the remaining seven banknotes, three depicted modern monuments, two Islamic monuments, and two scenic waterways. The banknotes thus displayed a similar balance of motifs to the Definitive series of postal stamps, emphasizing the modern and Islamic monuments in favour of the pre-Islamic ones. In this case, the response to the circulation of the Buddhist imagery on the 2-Afghanis banknote does not appear to be documented, perhaps owing to the diminutive depiction of the Buddha niche set within the panoramic landscape.

In 1951 the state issued another Bamiyan postal stamp. The Second Definitive Monuments Series included seventeen varieties of stamps printed by the internationally recognized firm Waterlow & Sons. Unlike the previous "Bamian" postal stamp, the 1951 beige and black 20-poul stamp depicted a close-up shot of the large Bamiyan statue. It was the only pre-Islamic image in the collection. The other seven stamps depicted Islamic monuments, such as the Ghaznavid minaret and the Qala-e Bost Arch. Given the previous reactions of the ulama to Buddhist iconography, it probably came as no surprise to state officials when they protested against the issuing of the 20-poul stamp, forcing the stamp to be withdrawn three months later (ibid., pp. 51–53).

The following year, the Afghan-Franco cultural agreement was renegotiated, ushering in the "International" stage of the archaeological discipline (1952–79). The arrangement opened the field to foreign teams and centralized archaeological activities, enforcing government ownership of artefacts, export bans on unlicensed antiquities, and guaranteeing excavation permits to international archaeologists (Grissmann 2009). New excavations broadened the temporal scope of archaeological discoveries, with, for instance, American and British teams excavating at prehistoric sites (i.e., Fairservis 1961; Helms 1997) and Italians at the Islamic site of Ghazni at the behest of the Afghan government, then eager to expand exploration of the Islamic tradition (i.e., Scerrato 1959). These advances were a prelude to the so-called "Decade of Democracy", an era of hastened social reform beginning in the early 1960s. During this period, King Zahir Shah oversaw the promulgation of the 1964 constitution, granting greater rights to political parties and minority groups, and barring royalty from holding political positions (Dupree 1973, p. 576).

The second wave of rapid reforms triggered renewed interest in Bamiyan. In the early 1960s the Afghan Tourist Organization (ATO) under the directorship of Wahid Tarzi, the son of Amanullah's foreign minister, launched an advertising campaign touting Afghanistan as the "Switzerland of Asia" (Zhobal 1958, p. 9). As one of the most visible and well-studied archaeological sites in Afghanistan, Bamiyan was promoted as one of the main tourist attractions, particularly to international travellers retracing the routes of the early pilgrims through South Asia along the so-called "Hippie Trail". To aid tourism, the ATO commissioned a series of guidebooks, beginning with Bamiyan.

As Bamiyan blossomed into a major tourist attraction at home, the Buddhist collections also drew large crowds abroad. In 1964 an exhibition of Afghanistan's most prized archaeological collections went on an international tour to prominent museums in Europe and the United States. The patron, King Zahir Shah, praised the "rich and diverse cultural heritage of this ancient nation" on display (Wolfe 1963, p. 8); yet, the exhibition clearly emphasized the pre-Islamic past favoured during the "Concessional" stage. Of the nine collections presented in the exhibition, one originated from Mundigak, an Indus civilization site excavated by DAFA in the 1950s; seven collections from pre-Islamic sites, including Bamiyan; and one from the recent Italian excavations at Ghazni, the former capital of the Islamic world (Rowland 1966, p. 128).

The 1968 guidebook to the National Museum of Afghanistan, more commonly known as the Kabul Museum, showcased a portion of the more than 100,000 finds housed in the museum—all originating from archaeological sites and historical monuments within the country's current borders (Grissmann 2009). The guidebook also plainly reflected the emphasis on the pre-Islamic past during the "Concessional" stage of the archaeological discipline. Most of the guidebook—66 per cent—covered the pre-Islamic period, 13 per cent the Islamic, 13 per cent the modern ethnographic and 8 per cent the prehistoric. Similarly, of the nine exhibition rooms, six dated to the pre-Islamic period, two to the Islamic, and one to the prehistoric. The "Bamiyan Room" occupied a large exhibition room, displaying Buddhist finds from the Bamiyan Cliffs and Kakrak Valley. However, instead of incorporating details of the Bamiyan Valley's two Islamic sites, Shahr-i Gholghola or Shahr-i Zuhak, the exhibition and guidebook included several different pre-Islamic collections (Dupree et al. 1968, pp. 20–21).

After overthrowing King Zahir Shah—now remembered as the last king of Afghanistan—the self-proclaimed president, Daoud Khan (r. 1973–78), expanded archaeological activities as part of his progressive agenda for the new republic. Given the visible deterioration, both natural and as a result of human activity, of the Buddha statues and surrounding niches (Toubekis and Jansen 2013, p. 157), the government sponsored the Archaeological Survey of India from 1969 to 1976 to conserve the site (Sengupta 2002, pp. 48–98). Future directors of the Afghan National Institute of Archaeology, Zemaryalai Tarzi and Abdul Wasay Feroozi, conducted restoration on the niches and paintings in Foladi Valley (Feroozi 2004, p. 10; Tarzi 1977). International scholars from India, Italy and Japan also made significant contributions to the study of Bamiyan (Hichuchi 1983; Klimburg-Salter 1989; Sengupta 2002).

In 1981 these developments helped secure Bamiyan's nomination, along with eight other sites in Afghanistan, to UNESCO's "Tentative List" of World Heritage Sites (Krieken-Pieters 2002, p. 226). It was an inauspicious occasion. A communist coup in 1978 overthrew President Daoud and opened the door to the violent civil war between the Soviet occupying forces and the Mujahideen (1979–92). During this period the archaeological discipline transitioned to the "Independent" stage (1979–2002), when international work essentially ceased, leaving Afghan officials to manage what archaeological activities they could as the countryside was laid waste. Bamiyan plummeted into another state of disrepair after the communist government neglected to send the necessary

World Heritage Site documentation to UNESCO (Manhart 2002, p. 154), and it only re-emerged in international consciousness in the late-1990s when a member of a radicalized Islamic group threatened to destroy the colossal statues.

Afghanistan's Archaeology, Nationalism and Politics: The War Years (1979–Today)

Against this backdrop, fifteen years later the Taliban captured Kabul from the Mujahideen interim-government. Under the leadership of Mullah Omar and the conservative ulama, the Taliban movement embraced a religious nationalism based on a strict interpretation of Sunni Islam and Pashtunwali, the traditional Pashtun tribal code (Pattanaik 2002, pp. 132–33). When the Taliban assumed political control, the major order of business was to restore stability in Afghanistan according to this religious code, and in doing so gain international recognition as a legitimate government (ibid., pp. 123–28; Rashid 2010, p. 4).

The preservation of archaeology played an important role in the campaign. In 1996 the Taliban minister of information and culture (MOIC), Mullah Akbar Khan Mutaqi, undertook the protection of the National Museum after militants had destroyed and looted it during the Mujahideen civil war (1992–25) and had traded the antiquities on the black market via Pakistan (Bailey 1996, p. 50; Rashid 1995). In November that year the Taliban MOIC addressed the rampant looting and smuggling of artefacts in a Radio Shari'at (the former Kabul Radio) broadcast: "All people are called on to give back items from the Kabul Museum in their possession. It is illegal to have such items and Shari'at-i Islamic law will apply to those who violate this rule" (SPACH 1996, p. 1). The announcement was part of a broader effort to restore order by adopting extreme interpretations of sharia law. The Taliban's Department of the Promotion of Virtue and Prevention of Vice enforced strict bans on popular cultural activities, including kite-flying, photography, poetry, singing and sports (Afghanistan Forum 1996).

On 17 April 1997 the Taliban commander, Abdul Wahid, leading the campaign to capture Bamiyan from Mujahideen control, threatened to destroy the Buddha statues (Dupree 1998). The threat was met with a vocal protest by the Society for the Preservation of Afghanistan's Cultural Heritage (SPACH), a non-profit organization founded in Peshawar in 1994 to advocate for the protection of Afghanistan's heritage (Krieken-Pieters 2006, p. 209). In order to appease the international community, the Taliban leadership denounced the commander's actions and reconfirmed their efforts to preserve the country's cultural heritage (ibid.; Dupree 1998).

Bamiyan Valley exchanged hands three times in the following year and a half (Siri 2002, p. 108; SPACH 2000, p. 15), during which time the site was used for artillery positioning and for refugee and militant encampments (Margottini et al. 2015, p. 73). Then, in autumn 1998, Bamiyan Valley fell to Commander Wahid, who, despite earlier reassurances, ordered an attack on the statues. Rocket shells damaged the small Buddha statue's head and midriff before the Taliban's newly appointed governor to Bamiyan had the commander arrested (Siri 2002, pp. 107–8; SPACH 1999, p. 21). Again, the Taliban leadership denied involvement (Krieken-Pieters 2002, p. 211); and, to further assuage international concerns, Mullah Omar issued two decrees in July 1999: "Concerning the Protection of Cultural Heritage" and "Concerning the Preservation of Historic Relics in Afghanistan". The edicts stated: "The famous Buddhist statues in Bamiyan were made before the arrival of Islam in Afghanistan.... The government regards the statues with serious respect and considers the position of their protection today the same as always" (Pattanaik 2002, p. 137). The edicts recommitted the Taliban to safeguarding Afghanistan's cultural and historic relics and to prohibiting illicit excavations of archaeological sites (SPACH 2000, p. 17).

At the time, one of the Taliban's chief goals was to gain recognition from the international community as a legitimate government, though by then only Pakistan, Saudi Arabia and the United Arab Emirates had offered it this. The Taliban also needed international aid to combat the exigencies of severe drought and economic hardships affecting the Afghan people (MacPhail 2002, p. 165). However, their requests for aid and legitimacy were drowned out by the objections of human rights advocates criticizing the Taliban's abuse of women (Coll 2004, pp. 362–63; Rashid 2010, p. 213). On 19 December 2000, the UN Security Council issued Resolution No. 1333 to enforce economic sanctions and seizure of the Taliban's remaining assets (Chakrabarti 2003, p. 201; Rashid 2010, p. 217). The combination of these factors allowed hard-line Taliban leaders to sideline the moderates and enforce even more extreme policies (Dupree 2002a, p. 986). It also provided an opening for al-Qaeda operatives—who were "guests" of the Taliban in Afghanistan after fighting alongside the

Mujahideen during the Soviet occupation (1979–92)—to foster stronger bonds with the Taliban. With al-Qaeda providing urgently needed funding to the Taliban (Bucherer-Dietschi 2002), the National Museum staff noticed the change in the political leadership: In "2000 it was evident that hardliners within the Taliban regime were gaining the upper hand, exerting greater influence under the direction of their foreign Arab 'guests'" (Dupree 2002a, p. 98).

The Taliban's political realignment produced a major shift in their policy approach to heritage (Cassar and Rodríguez García 2006, pp. 25–26). In late 2000 the Taliban Supreme Court clerics began deliberating the suitability of the country's cultural heritage for their Islamic agenda. Then, on 26 February 2001, Mullah Omar dramatically reversed his call for heritage protection after the ulama determined the Buddha statues represented *jahiliyyah*, a "state of ignorance", prior to Islam (Qutb 1980, pp. 173–98). "It has been decided", a new edict declared, "to break down all statues/idols present in different parts of the country. This is because these idols have been gods of the infidels … and all other false gods should be removed" (Coll 2004, p. 555).

Representatives from the UN, including the secretary-general, Kofi Annan, entreated the Taliban leadership to protect the statues. Their pleas fell on deaf ears. From 2 to 9 March 2001, Taliban militiamen armed with guns, rockets and tank shells destroyed the Bamiyan Buddhas (Bahadur 2002, p. 113; Manhart 2002, pp. 150–52; Siri 2002, p. 108). In video replays, the world watched as the Buddha statues crumbled to the cave bottoms after having survived the comings and goings of empires for more than fourteen centuries. A week after the destruction of the Bamiyan Buddhas, Taliban police destroyed a large portion of the museum's pre-Islamic collections, including numerous Buddhist statues (Massoudi 2008, p. 39). The Taliban's radical political repositioning was evident in their change of rhetoric after the destruction. Justifying their actions, Mullah Omar stated: "Allah will ask me, 'Omar, you have brought a superpower called the Soviet Union to its knees. You could not break two statues?'" (Coll 2004, p. 555).

In November 2001 the American-led NATO forces overthrew the Taliban militants. The 2002 Emergency Loya Jirga rapidly established an interim government for the Transitional Islamic State of Afghanistan under the acting president, Hamid Karzai (r. 2002–14) (Barfield 2010, p. 298), whose primary agenda was to steer the failed state back to a period of peace and stability. After two decades of civil war, the Afghan people initially shared a new national unity based on a desire to surmount ethnic and religious divisions in order to end the conflict (ibid., p. 278). Again, archaeology, and Bamiyan in particular, played a pivotal role in the new political agenda. Alongside major state-building initiatives, the government authorized measures to rehabilitate Afghanistan's heritage sites with support from international organizations, including UNESCO and ICOMOS (Ball 2006, p. 44).

These initiatives ushered in the "Negotiated" stage (2002–present) of the archaeological discipline and a third wave of archaeological activities at Bamiyan. In early 2002 a UNESCO mission evaluated the condition of the Bamiyan Cliffs and implemented preliminary preservation efforts, estimating that 80 per cent of the frescoes in the cliffs' niches were missing due to destruction, looting and neglect during the civil wars (Manhart 2006, p. 51). Japan donated $3 million to implement a three-phase preservation project of the niches and frescoes, and efforts were also made to safeguard the fragments of the Buddha statues (Yamauchi 2006, pp. 3–4; ibid., p. 59). In 2003 the Cultural Landscape and Archaeological Remains of Bamiyan was, after a rushed process, confirmed on UNESCO's World Heritage List and Heritage in Danger, more than two decades after its nomination. The government emphasized that "the property ... symbolises the strong hope of the Afghan and Bamiyan people that peace will be constructed in the minds of the citizens of this ravaged country, to enable the Afghan people to restore their lives and cultural heritage" (UNESCO 2003).

After a thirteen-year hiatus, Afghanistan's postal service resumed in 2002. That year, the service issued a 25,000-Afghanis UNESCO Bamiyan postal stamp, depicting the empty niche of the colossal Buddha statue with rubble piled on the spot where the Buddha once stood. This was followed in 2003 by a "Heritage of Afghanistan" series that included four postal stamps printed with Buddhist imagery. Two of the postal stamps illustrated broken fragments from the Bamiyan statues: a 20-Afghanis "Fragment's of a Woman's Face" postal stamp and a 100-Afghanis "Monumental Buddha Hand" postal stamp; the other two depicted a Gandhara Buddha head and Buddha statue. The fragmentation portrayed in each of the images, either as a broken section from the statue and frescoes or the abstract fragmentation bordering the image of the empty niche, captured the country's cultural loss at the hands of the Taliban. The third edition of the guidebook to Bamiyan was also reissued with the same content but with a new introduction (Dupree 2002b). Concurrently, the state issued a new banknote series, but this time the Bamiyan Buddhas were omitted. The only pre-Islamic image depicted was the ancient Bala Hissar fort, a daily scene for Kabulis, with the ancient fortress walls running along the mountainside of Sher Derwaza through the heart of the capital. Of the remaining images, eight depicted Islamic monuments, five modern monuments and one a scenic view of the Salang Pass. So, although the UNESCO stamps highlighted the Buddhist past, the Afghan banknotes clearly preferred the Islamic past.

A joint UNESCO-Italian archaeological team also began conservation at the ancient Islamic remains of Shahr-i Zuhak (Margottini 2014), while DAFA began surveying the ruins of the Islamic-period fort of Shahr-e Ghogholah. Under the auspices of DAFA, Afghan archaeologists Zemaryalai Tarzi and Abdul Wasay Feroozi, who worked at Bamiyan during the second wave of activities in the 1960–70s, also began excavations near the Bamiyan Cliffs. Their work subsequently uncovered a monastery and fragments of an estimated 19-metre paranirvana Buddha statue (Morgan 2012, p. 61; Tarzi 2003), though Tarzi continued to pursue his life's ambition of uncovering a 300-metre paranirvana Buddha described in the 1,400 year-old accounts of the Chinese pilgrim Xuanzang (Tarzi 1987, p. 100; Tarzi 2006, p. 151). Construction of a Bamiyan cultural centre also began in 2015. Situated on a scenic hillside in Bamiyan Valley, the completed centre will boast scenic views of the Bamiyan Cliffs and Buddha niches. The centre will include two exhibition halls to display the finds from the ongoing pre-Islamic- and Islamic-period excavations, a workshop, auditorium and outdoor garden space, amongst other features, for the local community and tourists to engage with the local culture (Bamiyan Cultural Centre 2015).

A central question during the "Negotiated" stage is whether to reconstruct the Bamiyan Buddhas and surrounding cultural landscape. As a "negative heritage" site, storing collective negative memories (Meskell 2002, p. 558), the Bamiyan Buddhas stand at a crossroads: either to be embraced or erased from the national narrative in support of the post-2001 national identity. Though the idea was previously rejected by representatives of both the Afghan government and UNESCO at the International Seminar on the Rehabilitation of Afghanistan's Cultural Heritage in 2002, which recognized the need to channel funds to more urgent state-building initiatives (Manhart 2006, p. 50), during the fortieth session of the World Heritage Committee in 2016 the Afghan government appealed for the reconstruction of one of the Buddhas. The return of antiquities lost or destroyed during the wars would symbolize a resumption of a more peaceful political era.[4] This point was perhaps most eloquently expressed by former president Karzai, who reflected during his opening address at the British Museum's 2011 exhibition, "Afghanistan: Crossroads of the Ancient World", showcasing priceless pre-Islamic antiquities presumed lost in the 1990s: "[they] will remind you of ... a peaceful Afghanistan, of an Afghanistan where societies lived and flourished" (Meharry 2011).

In September 2017 the Afghan and Japanese governments and UNESCO held a conference in Tokyo on "The Future of the Bamiyan Buddha Statues: Technical Considerations and Potential Effects on Authenticity and Outstanding Universal Value".[5] One well-voiced proposal suggested using anastylosis to reconstruct the Buddhist monuments from their original fragments, though a large portion of the reconstruction would require using material that was not original or authentic (i.e., Petzet 2009, p. 46). Critics of the plan highlighted the fragile conditions of the caves because of the harsh climatic conditions in Bamiyan, the difficulty of reconstructing the Buddhas based on the limited remaining materials, and the exorbitant cost of the undertaking, while also questioning whether the project should be undertaken in an ongoing conflict zone. Instead, critics of the reconstruction suggested alternative, less-permanent approaches, such as using lasers to project 3D images at night, which would be easy to disassemble should Bamiyan be consumed by conflict in future (for more on this discussion, see Bevan 2017).

The conference concluded by proposing the formation of a working committee in Afghanistan that would submit a recommendation for further action in Bamiyan to the government of Afghanistan and the World Heritage Committee. While platitudes of peace-making have been provided as justification for rebuilding the Buddhas, it is hoped that the committee will reach out to various stakeholders in Bamiyan province and across Afghanistan to better understand what impact the rehabilitation of the Bamiyan Buddhas would have on the local and national economy, society and identity, as well as to address measures to remove the site from the list of World Heritage Sites in Danger. This issue will continue to be at the forefront of cultural activities in Afghanistan, since, for many in the national and international communities, rebuilding the Buddhas goes part and parcel with efforts to rebuild the Afghan nation-state (Bobin

2015). As the archaeologists F. Raymond Allchin and Norman Hammond highlighted, "For most people Bamiyan is somehow synonymous with Afghanistan, such is the impressiveness of its rock-cut monastic caves and the two huge Buddhas" (1978, p. 271).

Discussion

As this paper has demonstrated, throughout Afghanistan's modern history, successive political leaders have employed archaeology to assert their nationalist agenda. During the formative years of the Afghan state, the monarchy (r. 1919–73) promoted archaeological study and tourism in Bamiyan Valley, displays of the archaeological collections at home and abroad and depictions of the Bamiyan statues in state-sponsored material. Despite archaeology's pivotal role in asserting Afghanistan's independence from imperial powers, it was not until the "Decade of Democracy" that Afghanistan established control over the archaeological discipline from foreign archaeologists; though by this stage a clear focus on the pre-Islamic past had been established, owing to the French monopoly on archaeological enterprises during the "Concessional" stage (1922–52).

An interesting dichotomy emerged from analysis of state-sponsored material during this era. The guidebooks and exhibitions primarily intended for international viewership emphasized the pre-Islamic past, whilst the banknotes and postal stamps primarily intended for national use emphasized the Islamic past. And during the early years of the Afghan state, when pre-Islamic and particularly Buddhist iconography were depicted, the discontented elements of the conservative factions repeatedly resisted it. On the one hand, the recurring attempts to insert Bamiyan into the state's visual lexicon indicated the site's valuable symbolism for the successive nationalist agendas. On the other hand, these events emphasized the diverging value systems between the Islamic conservative and modernist factions of Afghan society, with the foreign emphasis on the pre-Islamic past exacerbating these tensions.

Over the course of the modern history of Afghanistan, archaeology became a political tool for conservative and progressive ideologies. Pre-Islamic archaeological sites and museum displays were symbolic of the progressive political agenda, and one form of protest by dissenters was to attack these sites. The Bamiyan Buddhas were particularly emblematic of modern Western values, given their consistent usage in the progressive nationalist agendas and the foreign involvement at the site. As a result, the iconic Bamiyan Buddhas were susceptible to attack. Combining the assessment of Bamiyan in the nationalist agendas and analysis of state-sponsored material offers a clear trajectory of revolt against the pre-Islamic past: from the 1924 attack at the archaeological site of Hadda, the 1929 destruction of the Hadda collection at the Arg, to the 1932 and 1951 protests following the issue of the 3-Afghanis and 20-Poul Bamiyan postal stamps, respectively.

In 2001 the destruction of the Bamiyan Buddhas by the hardliner branch of the Taliban was a similar protest against Western powers. The international emphasis on the pre-Islamic "idols" exemplified a state of *jahiliyyah*, which served as justification for the destruction of the Buddhas. Like the previous Afghan governments, the Taliban leadership employed Bamiyan to further its own political ambitions, though in a destructive manner. Ultimately, the demolition of the colossal statues underscored the inextricable connection that has emerged between Afghanistan's archaeology, nationalism and politics.

Conclusion

Now, after more than thirty-five years of civil strife, Afghanistan is re-embracing its ancient archaeological heritage to establish its position in the world order. Across the country, extensive preservation work has been conducted at Ghazni, Herat and the Minaret of Jam as archaeological activities have slowly begun to focus on Islamic heritage. Yet, the foreign legacy has left an indelible mark on the country's archaeological discipline. Current large-scale excavations and exhibitions continue to emphasize the pre-Islamic past, including an international travelling exhibition promoting some of the museum's most prized pre-Islamic collections from Aï Khanum, Begram, Tepe Fullol and Tillya Tepe; rescue excavations at the Buddhist monastic complex of Mes Aynak and the accompanying exhibition at the National Museum of Afghanistan; and the third wave of archaeological activities at the Bamiyan Cliffs. The study of Bamiyan ultimately underscores the disputed nature of archaeological heritage in ethno-religious conflicts. It also emphasizes the careful planning that will be required amongst international, national, regional and local stakeholders to utilize the lessons from the history of Bamiyan to preserve and potentially rehabilitate the site in Afghanistan's uncertain future.

TABLE 9.1
Banknote and Postal Stamps Depicting Bamiyan

Issue	Administration	Type	Motif	Image
1932	King Nadir Shah	3-Afghanis First Definitive Monuments Series postal stamp	Large Bamiyan Buddha	
1939	King Zahir Shah	2-Afghanis banknote with portrait of King Zahir Shah on obverse	Bamiyan Valley and Large Bamiyan Buddha Niche	
1951	King Zahir Shah	20-poul Second Definitive Monuments Series postal stamp	Large Bamiyan Buddha	
1965	King Zahir Shah	3.75-Afghanis "Visit Afghanistan" temporary series postal stamp	Bamiyan Valley and Large Bamiyan Buddha Niche	

Year	President	Stamp	Description
2002	President Karzai		20,000-Afghanis temporary series postal stamp — Large Buddha Niche and Buddha Statue fragments
2003	President Karzai		20-Afghanis "Heritage in Afghanistan" temporary series postal stamp — "Fragment of a Woman's Face" from fresco in Bamiyan
2003	President Karzai	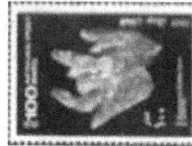	100-Afghanis "Heritage in Afghanistan" temporary series postal stamp — "Monumental Buddha Hand" from Bamiyan Buddha

Source of images: Delcampe 2015, Heindorffhus 2003, Shah M Book 2015, Stamp World History 2015, World Banknotes and Coins 2015.

Acknowledgements

Portions of this work were submitted for an MA dissertation in the Archaeology Department at Durham University. I am grateful to UNESCO Professor Robin Coningham at Durham University for his continued supervision, to the Ancient India and Iran Trust for a generous research grant, and to the photographer Jake Simkin for his stunning photographs of Bamiyan.

Notes

1. For a discussion of this topic, see Flood (2002).
2. This paper agrees with the suggestion by Louis Dupree that the formation of the Afghan state dates to 1880 under the centralization of Emir Abdur Rahman Khan (r. 1880–1901), but it concentrates on the era of nation-building following Afghanistan's independence in 1919 (Dupree 1973, p. xix).
3. The author adapted the stages of Afghanistan's archaeological discipline initially presented by Louis Dupree, accepting that an "Exploratory" stage preceded the advent of modern archaeology (1958, pp. 161–66). The structure of the new categorization utilizes similar divisions presented by Magnus Bernhardsson for the development of archaeology in Iraq (2007, pp. 192–203).
4. As argued by Afghan representatives from Bamiyan at the UNESCO Tokyo Conference in September 2017.
5. The author was an attendee at this conference.

References

Adamec, L.W. 1967. *Afghanistan, 1900–1923: A Diplomatic History*. Berkeley: University of California Press.

———. 1974. *Afghanistan's Foreign Affairs to the Mid-Twentieth Century: Relations with the USSR, Germany and Great Britain*. Tucson: University of Arizona Press.

Afghanistan Forum. 1996. "Afghanistan, Culture is a Casualty of War". *Afghanistan Forum*, pp. 8–9.

Allchin, F.R., and B. Allchin. 2012. *From the Oxus to Mysore in 1951: The Start of a Great Partnership in Indian Scholarship*. Kilkerran: Hardinge Simpole.

Azari, E. 1988. "Afghan Stamps". *Afghanistan Today* 6, no. 18: 38.

Bahadur, K. 2002. "The Bamiyan Buddhas, the Taliban and Islam". In *Bamiyan: Challenge to World Heritage*, edited by K. Warikoo, pp. 112–21. New Delhi: Bhavana Books & Prints.

Bailey, M. 1996. "Taliban Authorities Promise Protection: Ninety Percent of Former Displays Scattered". *The Art Newspaper* 65: 49–50.

Baker, P.H.B., and F.R. Allchin. 1991. *Shahr-i Zohak and the History of the Bamiyan Valley, Afghanistan*. Oxford: Tempvs Reparatvm.

Ball, W. 2006. "The Archaeology of Afghanistan: A Reassessment and Stock-taking". In *Art and Archaeology of Afghanistan: Its Fall and Survival*, edited by J. van Krieken-Pieters, pp. 39–48. Leiden: Brill.

———. 2008. *Monuments of Afghanistan*. London: Tauris.

Bamiyan Cultural Centre. 2015. http://bamiyanculturalcentre.org/summary/ (accessed 25 August 2015).

Barfield, T. 2010. *Afghanistan: A Cultural and Political History*. Princeton: Princeton University Press.

Beal, S. 1885. *Buddhist Records of the Western World*. Boston: J.R. Osgood.

Bernbeck, R. 2010. "Heritage Politics: Learning from Mullah Omar?" In *Controlling the Past, Owning the Future*, edited by R. Boytner, L.S. Dodd, and B.J. Parker, pp. 27–54. Tucson: The University of Arizona Press.

Bernhardsson, M.T. 1999. "Reclaiming a Plundered Past: Archaeology and Nationalism in Modern Iraq, 1808–1941". Diploma dissertation, Yale University.

———. 2007. "The Sense of Belonging: The Politics of Archaeology in Modern Iraq". In *Archaeology in the Construction, Commemoration, and Consecration of National Pasts*, edited by P.L. Kohl, M. Kozelsky, and N. Ben-Yahuda, pp. 189–205. Chicago: University of Chicago Press.

Bevan, R. 2017. "Ruin or Rebuild? Conserving Heritage in an Age of Terrorism". *The Art Newspaper*, 2017. http://old.theartnewspaper.com/features/ruin-or-rebuild-conserving-heritage-in-an-age-of-terrorism/ (accessed 10 October 2017).

Bobin, F. 2015. "Disputes Damages Hopes of Rebuilding Afghanistan's Bamiyan Buddhas". *The Guardian*, 10 January 2015. https://www.theguardian.com/world/2015/jan/10/rebuild-bamiyan-buddhas-taliban-afghanistan (accessed 8 August 2016).

Bryant, M.D. 2002. "The Tragedy of Bamiyan: Necessity and Limits of the Dialogue of Religions and Cultures". In *Bamiyan: Challenge to World Heritage*, edited by K. Warikoo, pp. 184–95. New Delhi: Bhavana Books & Prints.

Bucherer-Dietschi, P. 2002. "How Can Afghanistan's Cultural Heritage be Preserved?" *Asia Society*. http://asiasociety.org/arts/how-can-afghanistans-cultural-heritage-be-preserved (accessed 15 July 2015).

Cambon, P. 2008. "Begram: Alexandria of the Caucasus, Capital of the Kushan Empire". In *Afghanistan: Hidden Treasures from the National Museum, Kabul*, edited by F. Hiebert and P. Cambon, pp. 145–61. Washington, DC: National Geographic.

Cassar, B., and A.R. Rodríguez García. 2006. "SPACH: An Overview of Activities since 1994". In *Art and Archaeology of Afghanistan: Its Fall and Survival*, edited by J. van Krieken-Pieters, pp. 15–37. Leiden: Brill.

Centlivres, P. 2008. "The Controversy over the Buddhas of Bamiyan". *South Asia Multidisciplinary Academic Journal* 2: 1–13.

Chakrabarti, D.K. 2003. *Archaeology in the Third World: A History of Indian Archaeology since 1947*. New Delhi: D.K. Printworld, 2003.

Cohen, L.E. 2012. "America's Foreign Relations through Philately". *American Philatelist*, pp. 836–45.

Coll, S. 2004. *Ghost Wars: The Secret History of the CIA, Afghanistan, and bin Laden, from the Soviet Invasion to September 10, 2001*. New York: Penguin.

Coningham, R., and N. Lewer. 1999. "Paradise Lost: The Bombing of the Temple of the Tooth – a UNESCO World Heritage Site in Sri Lanka". *Antiquity Journal* 73: 857–66.

Daroogheh-Nokhodcheri, R. 2014. "Towards a History of Iranian Archaeology: Nationalism, Politics, and the Practice of Iranian Archaeology". Diploma dissertation, University of Durham.

Delcampe. 2015. "Destruction of Buddha of Bamiyan 6th Century Monumental Statue, 2002 Afghanistan". http://www.delcampe.net/page/item/id,323240871,var,Destruction-of-Buddha-of-Bamiyan-6th-Century-Monumental-Statue-2002-Afghanistan-1v-MNH-PG-10,language,E.html (accessed 17 July 2015).

Dupree, L. 1958. *Shamshir Ghar: Historic Cave Site in Kandahar Province, Afghanistan*, vol. 46. New York: The American Museum of Natural History.

———. 1973. *Afghanistan*. Princeton: Princeton University Press.

Dupree, L., A. Dupree, and A.A. Motamedi. 1968. *A Guide to the Kabul Museum*, 2nd ed. Kabul: Afghan Tourist Organization.

Dupree, N.H. 1974. "Archaeology and the Arts in the Creation of a National Consciousness". In *Afghanistan in the 1970s*, edited by L. Dupree and L. Albert, pp. 203–38. New York: Praeger.

———. 1998. "Museum under Siege: The Plunder Continues". *Archaeology Magazine*. http://archive.archaeology.org/online/features/afghan/update.html (accessed 15 July 2015).

———. 2002a. "Cultural Heritage and National Identity in Afghanistan". *Third World Quarterly* 23: 977–89.

———. 2002b. *The Valley of Bamiyan*, 3rd ed. Peshawar: Abdul Hafiz Ashna.

Eyre, V. 1843. *The Military Operations at Cabul*. London: Murray.

Fairservis, W.A. 1961. "Archaeological Studies in the Seistan Basin of South-Western Afghanistan and Eastern Iran". *Anthropological Papers of the American Museum of Natural History* 48: 2–4.

Fenet, A. 2010. *Documents d'Archeologie Militante: La Mission Foucher en Afghanistan (1922–1925)*. Paris: Memoires de l'Academie.

Feroozi, A.W. 2004. "The Impact of War upon Afghanistan's Cultural Heritage". Archaeological Institute of America. http://www.cemml.colostate.edu/

cultural/09476/pdf/AIA_Afghanistan_address_lowres.pdf (accessed 17 April 2015).

Flood, F.B. 2002. "Between Cult and Culture: Bamiyan, Islamic Iconoclasm, and the Museum". *Art Bulletin* 84, no. 4: 641–59.

Foucher, A. 1923. "Correspondance". *Journal Asiatique* (April–June): 354–68.

———. 1917. *The Beginnings of Buddhist Art and Other Essays in Indian and Central-Asian Archaeology*. Paris: Geuthner.

Fouchet, M. 1931. *Notes sur l'Afghanistan: Œuvre Posthume*. Paris: Maisonneuve Frères.

Giles, H.A. 1923. *The Travels of Fa-hsien (399–414 A.D.), or Record of the Buddhistic Kingdoms*. London: Cambridge University Press.

Godard, Y. n.d. *Interview with Yedda Godard, No. 26*. Cambridge: Harvard University.

Goode, J.F. 2007. *Negotiating for the Past: Archaeology, Nationalism, and Diplomacy in the Middle East, 1919–1941*. Austin: University of Texas Press.

Gregorian, V. 1967. "Mahmud Tarzi and Saraj-ol-Akhbar: Ideology of Nationalism and Modernization in Afghanistan". *Middle East Journal* 21: 345–68.

———. 1969. *The Emergence of Modern Afghanistan: Politics of Reform and Modernization, 1880–1946*. Stanford: Stanford University Press, 1969.

Grissmann, C. 2009. "Kabul Museum". *Encyclopaedia Iranica*. http://www.iranicaonline.org/articles/kabul-museum (accessed 8 August 2015).

———. 2006. "The Kabul Museum: Its Turbulent Years". In *Art and Archaeology of Afghanistan: Its Fall and Survival*, edited by J. van Krieken-Pieters, pp. 61–75. Leiden: Brill.

Hackin, J., and J. Carl. 1933. *Nouvelles Recherches Archeologiques a Bāmiyān*. Paris: Les Éditions G. Van Oest.

Hackin, J., and R. Hackin. 1934. *Le Site Archeologique de Bāmiyān. Guide de Visiteur*. Paris: Délégation Archéologique Française en Afghanistan.

Heindorffhus. 2003. "Cultural Landscape and Archaeological Remains of the Bamiyan Valley". http://heindorffhus.motivsamler.dk/worldheritage/frame-AfghanistanBamiyan.htm (accessed 21 July 2015).

Helms, S.W. 1997. *Excavations at Old Kandahar in Afghanistan 1976–78*. Oxford: Archaeopress.

Hichuchi, T. 1983. *Bamiyan: Art and Archaeological Research in the Buddhist Cave Temple in Afghanistan 1970–1978*. Kyoto: Kyoto University.

Kakar, H.K. 1979. *Government and Society in Afghanistan: The Reign of Amir 'Abd al-Rahman Khan*. Austin: University of Texas Press.

Khan, B. 1969. *My Life and Struggle*. Delhi: Hind Pocket Books.

Klimburg-Salter, D. 1989. *The Kingdom of Bamiyan: Buddhist Art and Culture of the Hindu Kush*. Naples: Istituto Universitario Orientale and Istituto Italiano per il Medio ed Estremo Oriente.

Krieken-Pieters, J. van. 2002. "The Buddhas of Bamiyan and Beyond: The Quest for an Effective Protection of Cultural Property". In *Bamiyan: Challenge to World Heritage*, edited by K. Warikoo, pp. 206–29. New Delhi: Bhavana Books & Prints.

———, ed. 2006. *Art and Archaeology of Afghanistan: Its Fall and Survival: A Multidisciplinary Approach*. Boston: Brill.

The Living Age. 1928. "Afghanistan Visits Europe: An Ancient Land Reborn". 15 March 1928: 507–14.

Maconachie, R.R. 1928. *Précis on Afghan Affairs, 1919–1927*. Simla: Government of India Press.

MacPhail, R. 2002. "Cultural Preservation and the Challenge of Globalisation". In *Bamiyan: Challenge to World Heritage*, edited by K. Warikoo, pp. 164–83. New Delhi: Bhavana Books & Prints.

Manhart, C. 2002. "UNESCO's Response to the Destruction of the Statues in Bamiyan". In *Bamiyan: Challenge to World Heritage*, edited by K. Warikoo, pp. 150–55. New Delhi: Bhavana Books & Prints.

———. 2006. "UNESCO's Rehabilitation of Afghanistan's Cultural Heritage: Mandate and Recent Activities". In *Art and Archaeology of Afghanistan: Its Fall and Survival*, edited by J. van Krieken-Pieters, pp. 41–60. Leiden: Brill.

Margottini, C., ed. 2014. *After the Destruction of Giant Buddha Statues in Bamiyan (Afghanistan) in 2001: A UNESCO's Emergency Activity for the Recovering and Rehabilitation of Cliff and Niches*. Berlin: Springer.

Margottini, C., F. Fidolini, C. Iadanza, A. Trigala, and Y. Ubelma. 2015. "The Conservation of the Shahr-e-Zohak Archaeological Site (Central Afghanistan): Geomorphological Processes and Ecosystem-Based Mitigation". *Geomorphology* 239: 73–90.

Martini, A., and E. Rivetti. 2014. "UNESCO Stops Unauthorized Reconstruction of Bamiyan Buddhas". *The Art Newspaper*, 6 February 2014. http://ukblueshield. org.uk/unesco-stops-unauthorised-reconstruction-of-bamiyan-buddhas/ (accessed 18 August 2016).

Masson, C. 2011. *Narrative of Various Journeys in Balochistan, Afghanistan, and the Punjab: Including a Residence in Those countries from 1826 to 1838*. London: British Library.

Massoudi, O.K. 2008. "The National Museum of Afghanistan". In *Afghanistan: Hidden Treasures from the National Museum, Kabul*, edited by F. Hiebert and P. Cambon. Washington, DC: National Geographic.

McChesney, R.D. 1999. *Kabul under Siege: Fayz Muhammad's Account of the 1929 Uprising*. Princeton: Wiener.

Meharry, J. 2011. "Review of Afghanistan: Crossroads of the Ancient World Exhibition at British Museum". *College Art Association Reviews*.

Meskell, L., ed. 1997. *Archaeology under Fire: Nationalism, Politics and Heritage in the Eastern Mediterranean and Middle East*. London: Routledge.

———. 2002. Negative Heritage and Past Mastering in Archaeology. *Anthropological Quarterly* 75, no. 3: 557–74.

Morgan, L. 2012. *The Buddhas of Bamiyan*. Cambridge: Harvard University Press.

Mousavi, S.A. 1998. *The Hazaras of Afghanistan: An Historical, Cultural, Economic and Political Study*. Surrey: Curzon Press.

Nawid, S.K. 1999. *Religious Response to Social Change in Afghanistan 1919–29: King Aman-Allah and the Afghan Ulama*. Costa Mesa: Mazda.

———. 2009. "Tarzi and the Emergence of Afghan Nationalism: Formation of a Nationalist Ideology". *Boston University*. https://www.bu.edu/aias/nawid_article.pdf (accessed 13 August 2015).

Pattanaik, S.S. 2002. "Religion and Politics in Afghanistan: The Role of Taliban Regime". In *Bamiyan: Challenge to World Heritage*, edited by K. Warikoo, pp. 122–41. New Delhi: Bhavana Books & Prints.

Patterson, F.E. 1964. *Afghanistan: Its Twentieth Century Postal Issues*. New York: The Collectors Club.

Petzet, M. 2009. *The Giant Buddhas of Bamiyan: Safeguarding the Remains*. Berlin: ICOMOS–Hendrik Bäßler Verlag.

Qureshi, M.N. 2014. *Ottoman Turkey, Ataturk and Muslim South Asia: Perspectives, Perceptions, and Responses*. Oxford: Oxford University Press.

Qutb, S. 1980. *Milestones*. Beirut: The Holy Koran Publishing House.

Rashid, A. 1995. "Plundered Afghan Treasures". *Afghanistan Forum*, 1995: 2–3.

———. 2010. *Taliban: The Power of Militant Islam in Afghanistan and Beyond*. London: Tauris.

Ratnagar, S. 2004. "Archaeology at the Heart of a Political Confrontation: The Case of Ayodhya". *Current Anthropology* 45: 239–59.

Rowland, B. 1966. *Ancient Art from Afghanistan: Treasures of the Kabul Museum*. New York: Asia Society.

Sale, F. 1843. *A Journal of the Disasters in Afghanistan, 1841–42*. London: Murray.

Scerrato, U. 1959. "Summary Report on the Italian Archaeological Mission in Afghanistan: The Two First Excavation Campaigns at Ghazni, 1957–58". *East and West* 10: 23–56.

Schinasi, M. 1979. *Afghanistan at the Beginning of the Twentieth Century: Nationalism and Journalism in Afghanistan a Study of Seraj ul-akhbar (1911–1918)*. Naples: Istituto Universitario Orientale.

Sengupta, R. 2002. "Indo-Afghan Co-operation Restoration of Bamiyan". In *Bamiyan: Challenge to World Heritage*, edited by K.G. Menon, pp. 47–112. New Delhi: Archaeological Survey of India.

Shah M Book. 2015. "The Buddha of Bamiyan". http://www.shahmbookco.com/index.php?req=postal-stamp-detail&id=9 (accessed 17 July 2015).

Silberman, N.A. 1989. *Between Past and Present: Archaeology, Ideology, and Nationalism in the Modern Middle East*. New York: Holt.

Simpson, W. 1886. "The Colossal Statues of Bamian". *Illustrated London News*, 6 November 1886: 490–91.

———. 1886. "The Rock-Cut Statues of Bamian". *Illustrated London News*, 13 November 1886: 525–26.

Siri, S. 2002. "Bamiyan Demolition". In *Bamiyan: Challenge to World Heritage*, edited by K. Warikoo, pp. 107–11. New Delhi: Bhavana Books & Prints.

Smith, A.D. 2001. *Nationalism: Theory, Ideology, History*. Cambridge: Polity Press.

SPACH. 1996. "Introduction". *Society for the Preservation of Afghanistan's Cultural Heritage Newsletter*, p. 1.

———. 1999. "Bamiyan Buddha Damaged". *Society for the Preservation of Afghanistan's Cultural Heritage Newsletter*, p. 21.

———. 2000. "Decrees by Mullah Omar". *Society for the Preservation of Afghanistan's Cultural Heritage Newsletter*, p. 17.

———. 2000. "Head of Large Bamiyan Buddha Blackened". *Society for the Preservation of Afghanistan's Cultural Heritage Newsletter*, p. 15.

Stamp World History. 2015. "Afghanistan". http://www.stampworldhistory.com/country-profiles-2/asia/afghanistan (accessed 17 July 2015).

Sykes, P. 2002. *A History of Afghanistan*. New Delhi: Manoharlal.

Tarzi, N. 2006. "Tarzi on Tarzi: Afghanistan's Plight and the Search for the Third Buddha". In *Art and Archaeology of Afghanistan: Its Fall and Survival*, edited by J. van Krieken-Pieters, pp. 150–54. Boston: Brill.

Tarzi, W. 1998. "Translator's Note". In *Reminiscences: A Short History of an Era (1869–1881)*, edited by W. Tarzi, pp. i–ii. East Hampton: Afghanistan Forum.

Tarzi, Z. 1977. *L'Architecture et le Decor Rupestre des Grottes de Bamiyan*. Paris: Imprimerie Nationale.

———. 1987. "Report of Public Lecture at Musee Guimet". *Arts Asiatiques* 42: 100.

———. 2003. "Bamiyan: Professor Tarzi's Survey and Excavation Archaeological Mission, 2003". *Silk Road Foundation Newsletter*. http://www.silkroadfoundation.org/newsletter/december/bamiyan.htm (accessed 9 August 2016).

Thomas, D.C. 2012. "The Metamorphosis of the Minaret of Djām–from Ghūrid 'Victory Tower' to Symbol of the New Afghanistan and Global Cultural Property". Edited by R.O. Riagain and C.N. Popa. *Archaeological Review from Cambridge* 27, no. 2, "Archaeology and the (De)Construction of National and Supra-National Polities", pp. 139–59.

Toubekis, G., and M. Jansen. 2013. "The Giant Buddha Figures in Afghanistan: Virtual Reality for a Physical Reconstruction". In *Archaeologizing' Heritage?: Transcultural Entanglements between Local Social Practices and Global Virtual Realities*, edited by M. Falser and M. Junega, pp. 143–66. Springer.

UNESCO. 2003. http://whc.unesco.org/en/list/208 (accessed 25 April 2015).

Williams, A.R. 2015. *ISIS Smashes Priceless, Ancient Statues in Iraq*. http://news.

nationalgeographic.com/news/2015/02/150227-islamic-militants-destroy-statues-mosul-iraq-video-archaeology/ (accessed 10 August 2015).

Wolfe, N.H. 1963. *The Valley of Bamiyan*. Kabul: Afghan Tourist Organization.

World Banknotes and Coins. 2015. Afghanistan 2 Afghanis banknote 1939 King Mohammed Zahir Shah. http://www.worldbanknotescoins.com/2015/06/afghanistan-2-afghanis-banknote-1939-king-mohammed-zahir-shah.html (accessed 17 July 2015).

Yamauchi, K. 2006. *Preliminary Report on the Environmental Investigation for the Conservation of the Bamiyan Site: 2005 and 2006 Seasons*. Recent Cultural Heritage Issues in Afghanistan, supplement 3. Japan Center for International Cooperation in Conservation.

Zhobal, M.H. 1958. *Afghanistan Past and Present*. Kabul: Government Printing House.

10

Disappearing Voices: The Politics and Practice of Safeguarding *Kunqu* Opera in the People's Republic of China

Min Yen Ong

"Invaluable, Rare, Traditional Aesthetics: A Restoration of the Ming Dynasty Mode of Performance." This was the caption used to market a *kunqu* opera performance in Beijing's Imperial Granary production of Ming dynasty playwright Tang Xianzu's (1550–1616) play *Peony Pavilion*. Such words exude authenticity and seek to attract those curious to experience a rare performance of an antiquarian art form. The exoticism and novelty of experiencing an "ancient" and "authentic" performance appeals to the modern (Ivy 1995, pp. 241–42). It prompts the modern to consider that *kunqu* performances and aesthetics have been irrevocably lost, and thus this performance of *Peony Pavilion* at the Imperial Granary[1] was to be a rare opportunity not to be missed. Captions like these resonate within the individual—that, because of the rapidly evolving sense of time and changes in political history, environmental context and contemporary culture, much has been lost, and this alarming sense of distance[2] appeals to the identity and nostalgia of the Chinese modern, who begins to question their roots and traditions.

Performances like these are also marketed towards the international visitor. Printed in English, the production advertises its performance as the "Ultimate Landscape of Chinese Culture: A Must-see for Tourists in Beijing", with the accompanying words: "Kunqu Opera: A Masterpiece of the Oral and Intangible Heritage of Humanity of UNESCO". The endorsement by UNESCO places *kunqu* on the world stage: a source of pride for the nation. The lead performers are young, good-looking and professionally trained from state-sponsored, government-endorsed *kunqu* opera troupes. The performance has an air of exclusivity. The theatre is small, with intimate seating for an audience of about forty. The setting gives the appearance and allure of the historical home of a member of the literati holding a performance by a private family troupe (*jiaban*). The performance, without microphones, compels audience members to lean in and be entranced. Ticket prices are hefty, ranging from 380 to 1,980 renminbi. The promises of an authentic, professional, spectacular and exclusive performance are all made.

My objective in these introductory paragraphs has been to give the reader a taste of how *kunqu* is often depicted and represented today. *Kunqu* is portrayed as an ancient and complex, elite art form performed glamorously and exquisitely on stage by state-sponsored professional *kunqu* opera troupes to an educated and/or wealthy audience. Little is mentioned about the less-glamorous yet vibrant amateur *kunqu* community that continues to practice this genre today (and scarcely any documentation is publicly available about it). My discussion of *kunqu* in this chapter will highlight the discrepancies between what intangible cultural heritage (ICH) means to different actors and how it is communicated, transmitted and represented in order to manage, safeguard and sustain its practice.

Using Hafstein's (2015), You's (2015) and de Cesari's (2013) arguments that attempts at safeguarding ICH have often in actuality disempowered communities and reinforced the position of the state and its institutions, this chapter illustrates how despite the growing popularity and recognition of *kunqu* as a representational form of Chinese ICH, amateur *kunqu* practitioners who form a vital and significant proportion of the *kunqu* community have been sidelined by the agenda of UNESCO and the state. I argue that despite the long existence of *kunqu*'s amateur and professional traditions, *kunqu* has been decontextualized from its Confucian-based literati amateur practice,[3] and its musical practices and performance traditions have been assimilated and recontextualized through professional theatre-based practices for the political purposes of strengthening national pride and generating a new national image. Relationships have been reformed and a new breed of audiences (such as domestic and international tourists and others from the international sphere) have been sought to generate prestige and sociocultural and economic capital. I feature innovative *kunqu* performer Zhang Jun in my chapter to demonstrate and contrast the different perceptions of managing heritage today.

Kunqu: Its Origins and Practitioners

Kunqu has its origins in Kunshan in Jiangsu Province, China. It grew out of a popular local singing style called *Kunshanqiang* ("Kunshan melody"), which is known to have been practised in the thirteenth century. In the 1500s, *kunqu* was refined by a herbal doctor and singing master called Wei Liangfu (1522–73), who codified a system of tunes, vocal techniques and ornamental elements. Wei devised the "water polishing" style (*shuimoqiang*), which has become synonymous with *kunqu*. This method uses the phonetic principles of Chinese characters and involves clear recitation and a subtle transition from one syllable to another. This singing method gives *kunqu* its unique smooth lyrical singing style, which is a key aesthetic in singing *kunqu*.

The refinement of *kunqu* won the patronage of the literati elite, and it developed into a pastime for them. They were amateurs—a term not to be confused with amateurish (by way of performance standards). In the Chinese historical context, the terms "professional" and "amateur" bore contrasting meanings. The amateur was of high social status and was often closely associated with the educated elite literati interested in painting, poetry and playing music for the purposes of self-cultivation and without financial recompense. The professional, on the other hand, received monetary gain for their services in order to maintain their livelihoods. They were mostly illiterate, and in the Confucian social hierarchy—on account of their service-oriented function—they were classed in the lower strata, together with beggars, prostitutes and soldiers. In *kunqu*, the literati amateurs researched, analysed and cultivated the art of singing and were highly skilled and knowledgeable. They paid meticulous attention to the pronunciation of the syllables of the words, the projection of the voice and the fine embellishments used to release each word and note of the sung text. For the amateur literatus, the process of studying and singing *kunqu* was a form of self-cultivation. They were playwrights, owners of private troupes, anthologists, researchers and practitioners.[4] Joseph Levenson (1967) likens China's (amateur) literati culture in the Ming and early Qing dynasties to the period of Jonathan Swift, the seventeenth-century Irish satirist and writer, describing literati culture as:

> ... an anti-vocational retrospective humanism in learning. Artistic style and a cultivated knowledge of the approved canon of ancient works, the "sweetness and light" of a classical love of letters—these, not specialised, "useful" technical training, were the tools of intellectual expression and the keys to social power. (Levenson 1967, p. 100)

The amateurs and professionals had very distinct boundaries. Neither group overlapped, and it was extremely rare for someone to transition from one to the other.[5]

Kunqu has two performance traditions. It began primarily as a vocal singing form without theatrical elements, known as *qingchang* (pure singing). This tradition is still practised today mainly by amateurs in the context of amateur groups. In this style, meticulous attention is paid to the matching of the text to the music, and this involves the pronunciation of the syllables within a character and the fine embellishments used to transition from one to the next with careful vocal projection. The second performance tradition emerged in the sixteenth century when the playwright Liang Chenyu (1519–91) wrote the libretto for "Washing Silk", which made use of the *kunqu* singing style. This marked the beginning of *kunqu*'s theatre tradition, which is mainly performed by professional performers in the context of professional troupes.

From the 1950s, after the Chinese Communist Party established the People's Republic of China, two pivotal changes occurred that affected professional and amateur *kunqu* practices. Qian Baogang, the leader of one of the oldest existing and respected amateur groups, the Shanghai Kunqu Research Society, describes these changes as a "change in status" and a "change in style".[6] The change in status implied that no longer were professional performers viewed as being of a low status in accordance with the Confucian hierarchical system, but instead they bore an equal status in society and were to play an important role in the new system as part of the propaganda arm of the government by performing plays in line with state policies. In the 1950s, due to theatre reforms, all existing private professional opera troupes were converted to collectively owned troupes controlled by the state (Liu 2009, p. 396), and thus began the formation of state-owned *kunqu* opera troupes. These troupes had training schools akin to the Western music conservatoires. And, because of their specialized training, the performers began to take on a new identity: They were now seen to be respectable and knowledgeable professional specialists. It is worth noting that the initial teachers of these training schools numbered among their ranks both professional performers and learned amateurs. The amateurs and professionals at that time had more similarities in their singing styles than those of today.

With the elevated status of professional *kunqu* performers and the government sponsorship of troupes came added musical pressures to conform. What began in the 1920s as a search for a national music[7] continued after the formation of the PRC and in the 1980s under Deng Xiaoping's leadership. The Westernization of Chinese music, together with the effects of commercialization and an opening up of China to a global economy, led to changes in musical style. State-sponsored professional *kunqu* opera troupes were pressed to meet government demands such as performing specific works with content in line with state ideals and performing works in what was perceived to be a modern Westernized style[8] (tunings of instruments, orchestration techniques, the use of functional harmony, written musical notation) in order to meet this national music style and attract audiences. Local musical traditions without these modifications were viewed as backward and conservative. Traditional *kunqu* methods of singing started to lose their appeal, and professional troupes were pressured to adapt to audience's tastes. According to Qian, as *kunqu* began to change its style the amateur groups became threatened. Today it is very rare, or even unheard of, for a student in a professional school to be learning from an amateur. Students are taught by professional performers, and they are instructed to sing in a style that has been influenced by modernization and Western art music.

There exist today three main kinds of amateurs, grouped according to their levels of commitment and knowledge. There are the *qujia*, which I refer to as "learned amateurs", who possess a wealth of knowledge as they devote themselves to understanding the texts and the fundamentals of singing *kunqu*. They are competent singers and can be defined by their elite lineage and family, with a well-known history of singing or researching theories on the aesthetics of *kunqu*. They often share their knowledge by teaching or via literary means. The second kind of amateur are the *quyou*, who learn from a teacher and diligently research and master methods of singing and pronouncing words. The third group are the *aihaozhe*, who consist mainly of fans who enjoy listening to and watching *kunqu* and who dabble in learning to sing *kunqu*. Their interest can be less analytical or less profound.[9]

During my fieldwork in China (2008–16), I visited *kunqu* amateur groups in Beijing, Tianjin, Shanghai and Suzhou. Many of these groups experienced a revival in the early 2000s, mainly owing to Pai Hsien-yung's production of Tang Xianzu's *Peony Pavilion*, and subsequently in the 2010s when the concept of intangible cultural heritage began to catch on. There were student groups that met on university campuses and studied the aesthetics and complexities of *kunqu* in great depth. Some amateur groups had the privilege of having learned amateurs as their teachers. Most amateur groups meet weekly to practise singing. A session could involve taking turns to perform to one another, singing collectively as a group, or having a teacher teach a piece or scene to the group. The critique would centre around articulation, pronunciation and embellishments. In addition to these weekly meetings, larger gatherings may be held that could include members from other amateur groups or, at times, professional performers. These larger gatherings could involve various individuals performing individually or as a group, or could follow a theme devoted to the remembrance of a prolific playwright or deceased learned amateur. These performances could be sung in the pure singing style or with movement. For the more conservative and tradition-focused groups, a good performance would comprise clear, simple, perfect pronunciation of each word and accompanying embellishments, and a subtle emotive quality to display an understanding of the text and context of the piece. In general, most amateurs adhere to the Confucian aesthetic principles of *zhong zheng ping he* (maintaining equilibrium) and *hanxu* (controlled or restrained), as this implies an internal richness beneath a simple surface. Professional virtuosity is viewed as distasteful by more conservative amateurs. A strong sense of community is felt amongst the amateurs.[10]

Kunqu: A Masterpiece

In 2001, following a successful application[11] by the Chinese Academy of Arts (the state organ entrusted by the Ministry of Culture to make the application), *kunqu* was proclaimed a UNESCO Masterpiece of the Oral and Intangible Heritage of Humanity. This was received with much excitement in *kunqu* circles, who were proud that not only was *kunqu* given national support to rejuvenate the art but also that the international world had recognized its importance. Prior to the successful listing, the practice of *kunqu* had been in sharp decline, having been banned during the Cultural Revolution and only practised outside the PRC in places such as Taiwan.

The selection resulted in financial assistance from UNESCO/ Japan Funds-in-Trust (a fund initiated in 1993 following an agreement between UNESCO and the Japanese government to be used to safeguard awarded submissions from Member States with developing economies).[12] UNESCO's intervention, together with the support and work of the Chinese government, resulted in training courses, prizes awarded to practitioners, collecting and preserving traditional librettos and recordings, sponsored public performances and the creation of policies to enhance the dissemination of *kunqu* opera. The joint efforts focused on training local students and on organizing an annual *kunqu* festival.

More specifically, the action plan (the mandatory procedure following the UNESCO Masterpiece proclamation) for the project implemented in 2002, formulated in close cooperation between UNESCO and the Chinese Ministry of Culture, incorporated the formation of a steering committee, an official launch of the project with regional and national partners, and the funding of the annual National Kunqu Festival in Suzhou. The festival saw twenty-one prizes awarded to *kunqu* practitioners by a jury designated by representatives of the UNESCO Beijing Office and the Ministry of Culture. Master classes were also organized during the event. The project also included the recording and filming of performances, evaluations of potential international *kunqu* opera co-productions, and the organization of more workshops with students from opera schools in Shanghai and Changsha.[13]

The objectives of the project were to "provide thorough training to the *Kunqu* practitioners, to contribute to the strengthening of Chinese professional training and resources in the areas of safeguarding and promotion of *Kunqu*, to work with existing structures of national and local government, specialized institutions and local community organisations and NGOs" at the local, district, regional and national levels in order "to raise awareness within Chinese society at large of the significance of conserving and transmitting the *Kunqu* performing arts heritage". The project hoped to "strengthen the learning and training of the classic plays of *Kunqu* opera, improve the managing level of staff in *Kunqu* opera houses and troupes, improve the artistic performing level of the outstanding performers in *Kunqu* opera houses and troupes in China and continue the support of the seven *Kunqu* companies and the various actor-training schools."[14]

Overall, the goal of the joint project was "to support the transmission of the traditional art of *Kunqu* Opera in order to ensure that this heritage is maintained", "promote the importance of *Kunqu* Opera amongst the Chinese public and seek to mobilise relevant local, regional, and national institutions for the elaboration of appropriate activities and policies on the dissemination of *Kunqu* Opera".[15]

The listing of *kunqu* as a UNESCO Masterpiece vindicated the support given by the government to encourage the continued transmission of *kunqu*, and the listing has also given the Chinese government new incentives and ideas to renew its work in safeguarding intangible cultural heritage, as can be seen in the establishment of a national inventory-making system[16] and administrative and legal measures (the "Law on the Protection of Intangible Cultural Heritage of China" issued in 2006).[17]

Resulting from state involvement in the safeguarding of *kunqu* after the 2001 UNESCO Masterpiece proclamation and the closely formulated project between UNESCO and the Ministry of Culture in 2002, the Ministry of Culture issued a five-year safeguarding plan from 2005 to 2009.[18] The plan included the following: **In relation to performance,**[19] calling for the revival and arrangement of fifteen rarely transmitted traditional plays (three per year) and the creation of ten new plays (two per year), to be carried out and performed by professional state troupes. **Regarding archival preservation**, it proposes the recording of two hundred performances (forty per year) of plays by professional state troupes and the saving and protecting of *kunqu* resources such as notation, photographs and *kunqu* movement manuals. It also seeks to encourage composers, playwrights and performers to publish their works. **With regard to increasing awareness**, it calls for professional state troupe performers to go into schools to teach and perform *kunqu*, for greater coverage in state media (television, newspapers, online), and to send professional state troupes overseas to perform, give talks and support state functions. **For fostering new talent**, it encourages the nurturing of new performance talent through a *kunqu* training school in Shanghai; new directing, composing and choreographing talent in Zhejiang; to strengthen scholarly research on *kunqu* in Suzhou; and to reward potential, existing and retired talent in festivals, competitions and performances in Beijing (in 2005 and 2008), Suzhou (in 2006), Zhejiang (in 2007) and Shanghai (in 2009). **In terms of protective measures and the manner in which the safeguarding was to be implemented**, it established safeguarding measures, which it states must come from the ministry, as it is (according to the policy document) a complicated and difficult process. This comprises the formation of a steering committee (made up of employees from the ministry) and a professional group (invited by members of the steering committee) that will advise and consult with the steering committee. These bodies will review the play applications of professional state troupes, guide the selection and editing of plays, aim to raise standards, and develop research work, amongst other things. A fund will be provided for all these projects. The professional troupes will have the responsibility to lay down measures with the provincial bureaus.

At the local level, detailed safeguarding objectives specific to a locality and its resources have been implemented. For example, Suzhou's *kunqu* safeguarding policies include investing in the annual Tiger Hill Kunqu Festival, its *kunqu* museum, the Chuanxisuo, "The Institute for the Preservation of *Kunqu*", its professional troupe (Jiangsu Suzhou *Kunju* troupe) and its performance venue. Kunshan has also wanted to profit from its importance as *kunqu*'s place of origin, and it has many of its own unique safeguarding objectives and achievements.[20]

The safeguarding work of UNESCO and the PRC government has been beneficial to *kunqu*. In addition to ensuring the continued transmission of staged performances by professional state troupes, releasing DVDs, CDs and publications on *kunqu*, and ensuring more coverage of *kunqu* in state media, the promotion of *kunqu* has signified new meaning for *kunqu* practitioners. It has provided encouragement and brought honour to *kunqu* practitioners, as the genre and its practitioners have garnered national and global recognition through well-received international performances. And for the government, it has brought a sense of national pride in possessing this great cultural asset. For many Chinese people it was an eye-opener for them to see the value in a form of cultural heritage that was once regarded as outmoded and in need of improvement. UNESCO served as a visible endorsement, as can be seen in the numerous publications running the UNESCO proclamation, billboard posters, performance programmes and advertisements in taxis that bear the UNESCO stamp as if to say *kunqu* is "UNESCO Certified". This is reminiscent of what Barbara Kirschenblatt-Gimblett describes as heritage "adding the value of its pastness" (Kirschenblatt-Gimblett 1995, p. 370; also 1998, p. 150). Subsequently, audience numbers for *kunqu* performances increased, as did attendance at amateur groups.

However, despite the success of the nomination and the publicity that came with the UNESCO Masterpiece proclamation, certain issues have aroused debate within *kunqu* circles—concerns that may be gleaned from examining closely the safeguarding recommendations and policies. There is concern about not just what has been written in the safeguarding texts, but also about what is absent from them.

First, from the UNESCO website description of *kunqu* in the proclamation of the UNESCO Masterpieces, it seems evident that *kunqu's* extensive literati amateur tradition—so intrinsically interwoven into its history—has been left out:

> Kunqu is China's oldest and one of its most influential theatrical traditions. It is performed in many areas of the country. A Kunqu play usually consists of more than 24 scenes—accompanied by arias—with a complex plot and subplots involving human or supernatural elements. The performance usually features 12 actors who employ gestures, pantomime, mock combat and acrobatics, as well as stylized dancing and singing... (UNESCO Proclamation of Masterpieces of the Oral and Intangible heritage of Humanity 2001 Kunqu Opera description)[21]

In 2008, after the UNESCO Masterpieces programme was scrapped and entries from the list were moved to the UNESCO Representative List of the Intangible Cultural Heritage of Humanity, an edited version of the description was written. However, once again, *kunqu's* extensive literati amateur tradition was left out:

> Kun Qu [sic] opera developed under the Ming dynasty (fourteenth to seventeenth centuries) in the city of Kunshan, situated in the region of Suzhou in southeast China. With its roots in popular theatre, the repertory of songs evolved into a major theatrical form. Kun Qu is one of the oldest forms of Chinese opera still performed today. It is characterized by its dynamic structure and melody (kunqiang) and classic pieces.... It

> combines song and recital as well as a complex system of choreographic techniques, acrobatics and symbolic gestures. (UNESCO Representative Safeguarding List Kunqu Opera description)[22]

In addition, from this description, *kunqu's* theatre tradition seems to be the focus and the core of what *kunqu* is about. There is no mention of *kunqu's* even longer pure singing tradition, a vital practice mainly transmitted by amateurs in order to preserve and maintain key singing aesthetics in the performance of *kunqu*. *Kunqu* scholar Isabel Wong observes a consistency between the Ministry of Culture's emphasis on the safeguarding of *kunqu* as a theatre practice in its UNESCO Masterpiece nomination and many Chinese and Western writings on *kunqu*, in which *kunqu* as theatre takes the foreground (Wong 2009, p.16).

With a focus on safeguarding *kunqu's* theatre tradition, and in line with rejuvenating performances as a strategy, UNESCO and the state seem to have their sights set on encouraging and nurturing the talents of the professional *kunqu* troupe performers. This is also reflected in the action plan that was implemented after the UNESCO Masterpiece proclamation: "the government plans to support the six existing *kunqu* opera houses [professional state troupes] and the training of new performers".[23] A *kunqu* safeguarding policy derived from the 2005–9 safeguarding plan from the Ministry of Culture also states:

> ... under Central Government leadership, *kunqu* troupes should form the foundation, and currently-active *kunqu* performers should form the backbone, measures on protection should be conscientiously followed, invested funds supported ... and in all aspects promote *kunqu* and build on [the opera] troupes.[24]

This direction can also be gleaned from the UNESCO and state *kunqu* action plans described earlier. The amateur practitioners, who form a substantial proportion of the *kunqu* community, seem not to have been accorded the same level of recognition. *Kunqu* researcher and practitioner Hu Yi reminds us that *kunqu* is a literati practice. He says that the word *wen* (meaning cultured, refined or literary) is used to separate *kunqu* from other forms of Chinese opera, and that the UNESCO descriptions (which were submitted by the Chinese state) fail to acknowledge the crucial role the literati played in *kunqu's* formation, development and transmission over the centuries (Hu 2004, pp. 5–6).

The exclusion of *kunqu* as a non-theatrical pure singing tradition is problematic because this practice lies at the heart of its relevance to communities of amateur *kunqu* practitioners, and it is one of the two performance traditions that make up *kunqu* as a genre. One young amateur observed that the exclusion of amateurs is deep-seated. According to him, it is embroiled in the historical political woes of the country—that the influence and power of the intellectual must be curtailed. Since the founding of the PRC, many intellectuals (or literati) suffered under various campaigns imposed by the state. These included handing their land and properties over to the state through land reforms; the Anti-Rightist movement in 1957, when many were labelled, re-educated through hard labour or purged; and the Cultural Revolution (1966–76), when they suffered persecution, humiliation and torture. I wondered, though, whether there was graver concern of the suppression of amateurs as a whole.

The 2003 UNESCO Convention for the Safeguarding of the Intangible Cultural Heritage draws emphasis on the community[25] as having a central role in safeguarding and transmitting ICH. The convention signalled the final juncture from safeguarding simply the artefact to that of the people, thus emphasizing a sense of identity and belonging and of a role in enriching cultural diversity and creativity. However, as has been demonstrated in this section, managing and representing heritage comes with decisions over which areas to value and sustain and which areas to hide, forget or simply exclude as a representative heritage is sought (Harrison 2013). These processes are strategically thought through and controlled. People, places, traces and practices that are not compatible with contemporary versions of history may be erased in order for them to be created anew. The process of safeguarding heritage is dissonant. It is not just about who possesses the knowledge of the genre with an eye to perpetuating the tradition, but it is also about negotiation and the use of power. The management of heritage is both a political process and an economic enterprise, revealing which values are embodied.

Zhang Jun: "Young, Fresh, Good-looking and Market Savvy"

The promotion of *kunqu* by the state and UNESCO has helped legitimize selected artistic opportunities (Ong 2013), and one example of this may be seen in Zhang Jun, an innovator and transmitter of *kunqu* who has managed to navigate his position in a genre charged with historic and cultural symbolism and performance conventions.

Zhang Jun (b. 1974), dubbed by Chinese media as the "Kunqu Prince", started learning *kunqu* at the age of twelve. He began his training at the Shanghai Drama School, before moving on to Shanghai Jiaotong University and the Shanghai Theatre Academy. He started his professional career with the Shanghai Kunju Opera Troupe, playing the role of *xiaosheng* from the age of twenty. He soon became one of the most promising young actors in the troupe and was taken under the wing of Cai Zhengren (the then head of the Shanghai Kunju Opera Troupe). He eventually took on the position of deputy director. Zhang became one of China's top-ranking *kunqu* performers, and he has won national prizes, including the distinguished Plum Blossom Prize (one of the most prestigious national drama awards). However, in 2009 he left the Shanghai Kunju Opera Troupe to become an independent performer.

Now detached from the opera troupe and with his own private group— Shanghai Zhang Jun Kunqu Art Centre—Zhang is at liberty to promote *kunqu* by revamping its image and reaching out to young audiences. For Zhang, it is about adopting a modern approach and employing the right marketing.[26] With his funky haircut and trendy exterior, Zhang brings a new cool to *kunqu*.

Zhang is keen for cultural exchange and unique collaborations. His first experience of this was with renowned Chinese composer Tan Dun's production of Marco Polo, which premiered in 1996, in which he implemented *kunqu*'s stylized speech into his role as Shadow 1/ Rustichello. The stylized speech, performed in English, was deliberately stretched, accented and reconstructed to resemble *kunqu*. The Marco Polo experience gave Zhang his first taste of experimenting with *kunqu* and of performing this experimental *kunqu* to an international audience. Since then Zhang has used rap as a means of capturing the attention of a young audience. He has collaborated with Taiwanese rap artist Wang Li Hom and Shanghainese music artists Zhang Zhilin and Wang Yuanchao. In 2008, Zhang worked with Belgian pianist-composer Jean Maljean to create a jazz-*kunqu* performance, and in 2010 he collaborated with Emiya Ichikawa II (a Japanese *kabuki* actor who specializes in impersonating females) to perform a *kabuki-kunqu* scene from the play *Peony Pavilion*. This show was performed in Tokyo and used to commemorate the thirtieth anniversary of Sino-Japanese diplomatic ties. In 2016 he created an adaptation of

Shakespeare's *Hamlet*, transformed into a *kunqu* monologue entitled *I Hamlet*.

Zhang is perhaps best known for his version of *Peony Pavilion* known as the "Garden version", set in the Kezhi Garden in Zhujiajiao just outside Shanghai. It was produced in 2010, was co-directed by Zhang and Tan Dun, and saw the usual fifty-five acts condensed to just four. Its first performances coincided with the World Expo in Shanghai in 2010. Zhang's *Peony Pavilion* production was staged with a global audience in mind—its first performance at the World Expo attracted many foreign tourists. The "Garden version" of *Peony Pavilion* was also staged abroad in 2012, at the Metropolitan Museum of Art in New York in its Astor Court (which contains a re-creation of a Chinese garden). There is no doubt that from its initial conception and its first production during the Shanghai Expo, marketing the production to an international sphere was at the forefront of the minds of its creators. Zhang's "Garden version" was well-produced and enchanting, and the quaint ambience of the Ming-style garden combined with the exotic, atmospheric, rhythmic sounds and music made for a unique *kunqu* performance experience. Moreover, the small audience size gave a feeling of intimacy and exclusivity.

With such wide-ranging innovative performances, I was keen to ask Zhang what he valued as the key aesthetics and traditions of *kunqu*. For Zhang, the aesthetic lies within the production of the words. He said, "For *kunqu*, the words come first. We call it *yizixingqiang* (melody-word matching), and then you have the music.... With regards to recordings, if pop or world music methods are used, the singing of words (maintaining the achievements of the predecessors) and melody must be retained, everything else is okay. It doesn't matter ... the most important is the singing of the words."[27] But, according to Zhang, these must not be sung in English. For example, he said that because his speech in the play Marco Polo was sung in English, his performance could not be seen as a *kunqu* performance. "[S]ome people mix *kunqu* and English, but it's a joke. You cannot use English to sing *kunqu*, as there are set rules.... There are limits.... If there are no Chinese characters (*wenzi*), then you will have no music. If you use *kunqu* melodies and slip in English for singing, that is not *kunqu*. With no Chinese characters, there is no meaning.... People think I have a lot of interest in new things/projects, crossover? But no, there are limits!... *Kunqu* must use the rules ...".[28] So, for Zhang, who places the utmost importance on the words sung, the musical arrangement, or genre for that matter, is much more flexible. In 2012, Zhang released his first album, "Kun Plug *shuimo xindiao*" (Water flowing new melodies). The album consists of Zhang singing *kunqu* accompanied by New Age, rock, jazz, rap and electronic rhythms and styles. He says, "why not, you can play with a guitar, you can mix it. I feel for traditional techniques you don't need to be too anxious about it. You can relax a bit."[29] But despite all his daring innovations, Zhang sees himself as traditional, saying, "I am very traditional, I am extremely traditional. I am extremely traditional. You just see an idea that looks like I am not traditional."[30]

He says that not one word sung has been modified. The melody has been kept the same. Zhang feels that collaborations are important in making *kunqu* known outside its usual spheres. "I have a lot of musician friends who originally have no idea what *kunqu* is, but through this process of cooperation they have become *kunqu* enthusiasts. They really respect *kunqu*.... I use my own performance, they add in their own method and emotion, so it creates a new response/expression."[31] For Zhang, he says "tradition and innovation are closely associated with each other, like a shadow following the person. You have innovative ideas which influence traditional research. That's why I find there is meaning. I find that, importantly, at the core, there must lie a free spirit, even when you sing traditional plays. Like with my troupe, I do the things I like, and don't do the things I don't like."[32]

Zhang and the UNESCO Artist of Peace Award

Through his unique innovations and collaborations, Zhang succeeded in capturing the attention of UNESCO. In 2011 he was awarded the UNESCO Artist for Peace Award. According to him, UNESCO representatives present at his 2010 performance during the Shanghai Expo were very impressed that such a traditional genre could be presented in a modern and attractive way. He says, "this [referring to his artistic methods] relates to UNESCO's ICH safeguarding methods, with continued transmission and development as its principle.... When UNESCO director general Madam Bokova came to watch my performance, she felt it was a good model, as it showed how to safeguard China's traditional ICH and move forward with it. This type of innovative method is good. This is why I think UNESCO has made our relationship close.... They see me use this type of method to let such an old genre regain a brand new life, which is inevitably inseparable from its transmission. I feel that this method really suits UNESCO's views on education, cultural development, its basic principles."[33]

The UNESCO Artists for Peace is an award used to promote UNESCO's message and programmes, to heighten public awareness regarding key development issues and as a means of informing the public of its actions in their relevant fields of interest.[34] I asked a senior representative at UNESCO Office Beijing for her views on the decision. She said:

> We do not necessarily support Zhang Jun as an innovator, but as a person who is an artist who can contribute as an artist to the peace through music and the artistic form. We have Artists for Peace in the field of education; it's just that he's a young, dynamic person, who is also active.... For us it is attractive to have someone like him who is actually interested in doing something—not that we see him as one dimensional—we see him as a young dynamic person who is actually moving and shaking something. He is also interested in being this ambassador. We have not subscribed to him as the innovator of *kunqu*. We accept him as this rounded artist that he is. We cannot just take him as one part of the artist. He is, as a whole person, the Artist of Peace.[35]

She added that Zhang was also chosen because he is "young and fresh", "experienced", good-looking, interesting and that he markets himself well. She stated that it is important in today's world to be "market savvy" and to not have someone else do that for you. Zhang was "not leaving and waiting for the government to do something, he's taking his own initiative, which UNESCO also appreciates". She emphasized that ICH is a living tradition, and because of that transmission is the key to safeguarding it. She stated that Zhang Jun's role in transmitting *kunqu* is as important as promoting it.

However, one may be aware that the UNESCO Artist for Peace Award is in reality a political manoeuvre initiated not by UNESCO but by Member States; in this case China's Ministry of Culture and Ministry of Education.

Zhang is a safe and valuable asset for China. As a nation-state, the politics of preservation and the promotion of the hot topic of ICH nationally and internationally can be seen as a form of soft power, which is now viewed as a core resource of a state's power (Glaser and Murphy 2009), as is evident from the sponsorship of state cultural events abroad, which include the touring of national opera troupes and vast cultural spending at the local and international levels. It generates cultural capital and cultural nationalism by promoting national cohesion, strength and image. Zhang's training and background with the Shanghai Kunju Opera Troupe means he is deemed a safe option. And, together with his edgy, well-produced, forward-looking, visitor-friendly performances, he helps to convey to the outside world the sophistication and greatness of Chinese talent and culture. It articulates that an age-old operatic tradition like *kunqu*, brimming in culture and history, has been well preserved and continuously transmitted. This, together with Zhang's innovative elements, demonstrates an affluent modern progressive nation.

One key point to observe is that by no longer being a part of a national professional opera troupe, but a trendy charismatic artist, Zhang has managed to bypass perceptions and associations of being a cultural tool for the state.

Reception of Zhang's Artistic Innovations

Zhang is looked upon with disdain by traditionalist *kunqu* connoisseurs, who vehemently object to his innovative approach. A number of the *kunqu* amateurs I interviewed were dismissive of him. They see him as adulterating the pure and rich tradition of *kunqu*. *Kunqu*, as a genre, bears strong historical and cultural symbols. These amateurs seek to preserve and retain the "original sauce, original flavour" (*yuanzhiyuanwei*). In a personal interview with eminent *kunqu* expert Gu Duhuang, he informed me,

> Nowadays, diction is neglected and not emphasized ... like singing modern songs. When you use *kunqu* diction, the music has a unique character. If you sing a song with *kunqu* diction, any song can become just like *kunqu*. If you de-emphasize the diction, the *kunqu* style is lost ... the de-emphasis on diction has spoilt the music of *kunqu*.[36]

For Gu, it is about *yuanzhiyuanwei*—the aesthetics and singing techniques rooted in the 1930s and earlier must be retained. This echoes the opinion of other elderly traditionalist connoisseurs who see themselves as custodians of the genre and maintainers of the aesthetics of singing *kunqu*. They feel that the singing aesthetics of *kunqu* should be passed on faithfully to future generations (the pure singing tradition plays a vital role in ensuring this), and they feel especially compelled to do so as they perceive that the quality of professional performances is deteriorating. Whilst they acknowledge that modern performances generate an interest in *kunqu*, they resent what is being performed. They criticize such performances for being "a low-grade *kunqu*", void of aesthetics, and they regard the organizers and performers as opportunists looking to make money. They refer to these performances as "genetically modified" *kunqu*. I sense that for many traditionalists their objections lie not only with the music or the technique but also with maintaining the historical tradition and giving it a sacrosanct position. In their eyes, Zhang Jun is now cast as an outsider.

When I probed Zhang on how he felt about keeping *kunqu* authentic, he said "you can in some ways, like the museum's bronzeware is *yuanzhiyuanwei* because it is dead! If you want something alive, then you have to live in that period!"[37] Daphne Lei (2011) articulates that the "original sauce, original flavour" is "imaginary", and that "the concept of modernity in traditional arts is riddled with ambiguities and relativism" and surrounds an "empty core".

A report by critic Chen Yunfa (translated by Qi Chongyu) states:

> Don't create a 'collision' between western and Chinese artificially! I personally feel that if Zhang Jun does not have the ability to present *kunqu* as a wonderful art with traditional instruments, then he should not engage in this career, rather than transforming *kunqu* and making it neither modern nor classic, which has [*sic*] no difference from the counterfeit T-shirt on the market.... I do believe that [instruments such as the] piano, [or] violin can be mixed with Chinese traditional instruments to play *kunqu*, and [I] also have confidence in the outcome that this style of *kunqu* would be attractive to foreign audience[s] and audience[s] who are unfamiliar with *kunqu*. However, just as [this new] *kunqu* sounds good,... what sounds good is not necessarily *Kunqu* opera."[38]

This is a sharp statement, but a poignant one that encourages us to consider and question of where the aesthetical boundaries lie.

A contrasting approach has been taken in statements made by officials charged with developing and implementing policies on intangible cultural heritage. UNESCO Culture official, Beatrice Kaldun, says:

> Special attention needs to be paid to the spirit of Intangible Heritage, referred to by UNESCO as "authenticity" and "creativity".... Repetition is not the point of the expression of intangible cultural heritage. The point is transmission and the preservation within the community and its natural cultural spaces.[39]

Zhang, on account of his formal *kunqu* training, has come from the inside. But because he departed from his troupe and embarked on radical innovations to cater to a wider audience he is now seen as an outsider by *kunqu* traditionalist connoisseurs and professionals.

By creating a cool persona and trendy style that is "audience friendly", and by taking advantage of the contemporary resurgence of cultural traditions, Zhang has created a place for young Chinese audiences to develop a new sense of belonging, where traditions can be seen as progressive and compatible with the modern urban Chinese individual. This has perhaps even also fostered a sense of national pride among some people.

By making his productions progressive, attractive and "foreigner/ visitor friendly", he has been able to reach a transnational audience. Such initiatives have also benefited the state, led to UNESCO's endorsement of Zhang Jun as UNESCO Artist for Peace. For the state, it is about creating and promoting China as a strong cultural power.

Conclusion

This chapter has demonstrated the differences in what the *kunqu* safeguarding process means to different actors. For the amateurs, the significance lies in protecting *kunqu*'s channels of transmission and ensuring that the correct authentic singing aesthetics through the pure singing tradition are passed on and performed. The amateurs are concerned that a standardized homogenized *kunqu* with compromised aesthetics will, in time, become the true representational form. The state, on the other hand, has set its sights on the professional troupes, giving responsibility to them as the true purveyors of the genre. The safeguarding measures of UNESCO and the state have, in their strategies and centralization of heritage management and power, brought in new social actors such as committees and networks, thus institutionalizing social relations and producing more governmentality and bureaucracy. This has resulted in the exclusion of and stifled the expression of the amateur community. Prior to the UNESCO listing, artistic decisions and practices were split between different actors: the state, the professional troupes and the amateurs. Despite UNESCO's 2003 convention, which called for the "widest possible participation of communities"[40] in order to ensure a "democratic" safeguarding process (Blake 2009, p. 46), this has been difficult to implement, as managing heritage is a political task and communities are heterogeneous.

I chose to feature progressive *kunqu* performer Zhang Jun in this chapter as he seems to have received the endorsement of both the state and UNESCO, despite his unique *kunqu* creations—a position which traditionalist amateurs sternly object to, as they disapprove of his creations being classed as *kunqu* for fear of misleading others less in the know. Zhang is an exceptional case as he has succeeded in making *kunqu* "transportable" beyond national borders. By no longer being a part of a national professional opera troupe, Zhang has creative freedom. As an independent international artist and cultural representative, he has managed to circumvent the political and cultural baggage that precedes the professional troupes, which are seen as cultural arms of the government. Moreover, by presenting polished and innovative *kunqu* performances, Zhang has been able to perpetuate a tradition by coming into his own and being seen as a "young, fresh, good-looking and market savvy" *kunqu* performer.

Safeguarding intangible cultural heritage serves a purpose. It is culturally relative, historically specific, politically charged and economically driven. Despite UNESCO calling for communities to play a central role in safeguarding ICH, the safeguarding recommendations made by the organization have, in actuality, disempowered communities and inadvertently reinforced the stronger power, the state.

Notes

1. The Imperial Granary in Beijing was a location formerly used to store crop for the imperial household. It was built in 1409. After being recently restored it has been used as an events venue hosting private functions and performances. The Imperial Granary performance of *Peony Pavilion* is known as *tingtangban* (the "Banquet Hall" edition). It premiered in 2007. I watched the performance in 2009.

2. Drawing from Ning Wang's (2001) application of Georg Simmel's (1950) appeal of distance, three kinds of distance are applied to mobilize the visitor: time (the evolving and linear sense of time), space (the physical and built environment) and culture (the exotic and the unusual) (Wang 2001, p. vii).

3. These include the principles of self-cultivation and virtue ingrained within the *kunqu* performance process, the Confucian ideal of *zhong zheng ping he* for cultivating and educating one's mind and character, which took precedence

over achieving results, and the Confucian emphasis on education and transmission without innovation (Analects of Confucius 7.1). These ideals formed the focus of the *kunqu* musical aesthetic of performing in a balanced, controlled style without virtuosity or extravagance, and an emphasis on the strict maintenance and transmission of singing aesthetics.

4. For more information, refer to Mark (1990).

5. Cases of this were rare because of social stigma. To do so was known as *xiahai* (lit. jumping into the sea). The *kunqu* performer Yu Zhenfei (1902–93) is a well-known case. Not wishing to offend his father whilst he was alive, Yu Zhenfei only turned professional after his father had passed away.

6. Personal interview with Qian Baogang, 26 June 2010, Shanghai.

7. For further discussion of the search for a new national music and for the development of Chinese music, see Lau (1995, 1996, 2008), Kraus (1989), McDougall (1980, 1984), Stock (1996), and Wong (1991).

8. The reader may like to refer to Fang Kun, Keith Pratt, Robert C. Provine, and Alan Thrasher (1981) for a discussion about what is Chinese traditional music.

9. The terms *aihaozhe* and *yeyu* are also used as umbrella words for a non-professional *kunqu* practitioner.

10. For more information on *kunqu* amateur groups, refer to Ong (2013) and Ong (2018).

11. In a personal interview on 11 January 2011 with Wang Ankui, a retired government official who was in charge of the nomination of *kunqu* as a Masterpiece in 2001, Wang informed me that the Chinese Academy of Arts and the Ministry of Culture elected *kunqu* because they felt that Chinese opera had been inextricably linked to the lives of the Chinese people. Wang stated that *kunqu* was the oldest surviving opera and, despite its historical associations with the literati, it was appreciated and accepted by everyone, as opposed to the *guqin*, which was not as widely accepted and only represented the literati. One may speculate in retrospect that the state was keen for China to promote to the international domain genres that were firmly established among the elite; however, Wang's comments about *kunqu*'s relevance to the "masses" suggests that revolutionary era rhetoric had not been entirely forgotten.

12. For more information on the UNESCO/Japan Funds-in Trust, refer to http://www.unesco.emb-japan.go.jp/pdf/brochure-intangible2005.pdf for a list of initiatives and activities (accessed 20 November 2017).

13. Derived from an internal UNESCO document.

14. Derived from an internal UNESCO document.

15. Derived from an internal UNESCO document.

16. For more information on the national intangible cultural heritage list, refer to http://www.ihchina.cn/5/5_1.html (accessed 20 November 2017).
17. http://www.unesco.org/culture/ich/index.php?pg=00311&cp=CN&topic= nat_measure#national- measures (accessed 11 October 2012).
18. http://www.cpll.cn/law7292.html (accessed 1 August 2012).
19. Please note that the categories given here in bold are my own definitions.
20. http://www.kswhg.com/news1.asp?id=368 (accessed 11 October 2012).
21. Extracted from http://www.unesco.org/bpi/intangible_heritage/china.htm (accessed 26 February 2015).
22. Extracted from http://www.unesco.org/culture/ich/en/RL/kun-qu-opera–00004 (accessed 21 December 2016).
23. http://www.unesco.org/bpi/intangible_heritage/china.htm (accessed 26 February 2015).
24. http://www.cpll.cn/law7292.html pg.2 (accessed 11 October 2012).
25. http://www.unesco.org/culture/ich/en/convention (accessed 6 May 2017).
26. Ibid.
27. Personal interview with Zhang Jun, 24 October 2014, Shanghai.
28. Ibid.
29. Ibid.
30. Ibid.
31. Ibid.
32. Ibid.
33. Ibid.
34. http://portal.unesco.org/en/ev.php-URL_ID=8843&URL_DO=DO_ TOPIC&URL_SECTION=201.html (accessed 1 November 2012).
35. Informal interview with UNESCO official, September 2011, Beijing.
36. Personal interview with Gu Duhuang, 3 November 2009, Suzhou.
37. Personal interview with Zhang Jun, 24 October 2014, Shanghai.
38. http://english.eastday.com/e/eastalk/u1a6749013.html (accessed 14 September 2012).
39. Speech by Beatrice Kaldun entitled "UNESCO and its Role in the Safeguarding and Transmission of the Intangible Cultural Heritage" given at the Central Academy of Fine Arts, Beijing, 12–18 June 2006.
40. http://www.unesco.org/culture/ich/en/convention.

References

Blake, Janet. 2009. "UNESCO's 2003 Convention on Intangible Cultural Heritage: The implications of Community Involvement in 'Safeguarding' ". In *Intangible*

Heritage, edited by Laurajane Smith and Natsuko Akagawa. New York: Routledge.

De Cesari, Chiara. 2013. "Thinking through Heritage Regimes". In *Heritage Regimes and the State,* edited by Regina F. Bendix, Aditya Eggert, and Arnika Peselmann. Göttingen: University of Göttingen Press.

Fang Kun, Keith Pratt, Robert C. Provine, and Alan Thrasher. 1981. "A Discussion on Chinese National Musical Traditions". *Asian Music* 12, no. 2: 1–16.

Glaser, Bonnie S., and Melissa E. Murphy. 2009. "Soft Power with Chinese Characteristics: The Ongoing Debate". In *Chinese Soft Power and its Implications for the United States: Competition and Cooperation in the Developing World,* edited by Carola McGiffert. Washington, DC: Center for Strategic and International Studies.

Hafstein, Valdimar Tr. 2015. "Learning to Live with ICH: Diagnosis and Treatment". In *UNESCO on the Ground: Local Perspectives on Intangible Cultural Heritage,* edited by Michael Dylan Foster and Lisa Gilman. Indiana: Indiana University Press.

Harrison, Rodney. 2013. *Heritage: Critical Approaches.* Abingdon: Routledge.

Hu, Yi. 2004. "Daideng shilai fengbian". In *Kunqu reji,* edited by ZhangYunhe and Qiming Ouyang. Beijing: Yuwen Chubanshe.

Ivy, Marilyn. 1995. *Discourses of the Vanishing: Modernity, Phantasm, Japan.* Chicago: University of Chicago Press.

Jones, A.F. 2001. *Yellow Music: Media Culture and Colonial Modernity in the Chinese Jazz Age.* Durham, NC: Duke University Press.

Kirschenblatt-Gimblett, Barbara. 1995. "Theorizing Heritage". *Ethnomusicology* 39 no. 3: 367–80.

Kraus, Richard Curt. 1989. *Pianos and Politics in China: Middle-class Ambitions and the Struggle over Western Music.* New York: Oxford University Press.

Lau, Frederick. 1995. "Individuality and Political Discourse in Solo 'Dizi' Compositions". *Asian Music* 27, no. 1: 133–52.

———. 1996. "Forever Red: The Invention of Solo *Dizi* Music in Post–1949 China". *British Journal of Ethnomusicology* 5: 113–31.

———. 2008. *Music in China: Experiencing Music, Expressing Culture.* New York: Oxford University Press.

Lei, Daphne P. 2011. *Alternative Chinese Opera in the Age of Globalization: Performing Zero.* Houndmills, Basingstoke: Palgrave Macmillan.

Levenson, Joseph Richmond. 1967. *European Expansion and the Counter-example of Asia, 1300–1600.* Englewood Cliffs, NJ: Prentice-Hall.

Li, Xiao. 2005. *Chinese Kunqu Opera.* San Francisco: Long River Press.

Liu, Siyuan. 2009. "Theatre Reform as Censorship: Censoring Traditional Theatre in China in the Early 1950s". *Theatre Journal* 61 no. 3: 387–406.

Mark, Lindy Li. 1990. "The Role of Avocational Performers in the Preservation of Kunqu". *CHINOPERL Papers*, no. 15: 95–114.

McDougall, Bonnie S. 1980. *Mao Zedong's "Talk at the Yan-an Conference on Literature and Art": A Translation of the 1943 Text with Commentary*. Ann Arbor: University of Michigan.

———. 1984. *Popular Chinese Literature and Performing Arts in the People's Republic of China 1949–1979*. Berkeley: University of California Press.

Ong, Min Yen. 2013. "*Kunqu* in 21st Century China: Musical Change and Amateur Practices". PhD Dissertation, Department of Music, School of Oriental and African Studies (SOAS), University of London.

———. 2018. "Safeguarding Kunqu in the People's Republic of China". In *Music as Heritage: Historical and Ethnographic Perspectives*, edited by Barley Norton and Naomi Matsumoto. Routledge.

Stock, Jonathan P.J. 1996. *Musical Creativity in Twentieth-Century China: Abing, His Music and its Changing Meanings*. Rochester: University of Rochester Press.

Wei, Zhou, 2011. "A *Peony* Transplanted: Pai Hsien-yung and the Preservation of Chinese *Kunqu*". PhD Dissertation, University of Edinburgh.

Wong, Isabel. 1991. "From Reaction to Synthesis: Chinese Musicology in the Twentieth Century". In *Comparative Musicology and Anthropology of Music: Essays on the History of Ethnomusicology*, edited by Bruno Nettl. Chicago: University of Chicago Press.

Wong, Isabel K.F. 2009. "The Heritage of Kunqu: Preserving Music and Theater Traditions in China". In *Intangible Heritage Embodied*, edited by D. Fairchild Ruggles and Helaine Silverman. London: Springer.

You, Ziying. 2015. "Shifting Actors and Power Relations: Contentious Local Responses to the Safeguarding of Intangible Cultural Heritage of Contemporary China". In *UNESCO on the Ground: Local Perspectives on Intangible Cultural Heritage*, edited by Michael Dylan Foster and Lisa Gilman. Bloomington: Indiana University Press.

Zhang, Jun. 2008. *Woshi xiaosheng*. Shanghai: Shanghai Cishu Chubanshe.

11

Neoliberalizing Heritage: International Agencies and the Local Dynamics of Heritage Conservation in Bali, Indonesia

Agung Wardana

For Indonesia, culture as a means of economic development has recently become an important policy issue in development discourse and practice. Given the country's richness and diversity of cultural heritage, the deputy to the Indonesian minister of education and culture, Wiendu Nuryanti, claimed that Indonesia is a "cultural superpower state" (*negara adidaya secara budaya*). In order to show its leadership in cultural diplomacy, the government of Indonesia took the initiative of organizing the World Cultural Forum in November 2013, in Bali, as the first multilateral conference to build global partnership around culture-based development. Following the forum, in December 2013 the United Nations adopted Resolution No. 68/233 on Culture and Sustainable Development, which embraces an instrumentalist notion of culture by emphasizing its contribution "to inclusive economic development, since cultural heritage, cultural and creative industries, sustainable cultural tourism and cultural infrastructure are sources of income generation and job creation". In the previous year, the deputy minister also led the Indonesian delegation to the UNESCO World Heritage Committee meeting in St. Petersburg, Russia, where nomination of the Cultural Landscape of Bali Province was finally approved as a World Heritage Site.

For both the World Cultural Forum and the approval of Indonesia's first World Heritage cultural landscape, Bali was the centre of gravity. Not only because Bali's cultural heritage is regarded as a national asset (UNDP, USAID and the World Bank 2003) but also because the island is the international gateway for Indonesia. Since the Dutch colonial era, Balinese culture has been an object of preservation in the service of the development of tourism. More recently, cultural heritage conservation projects for Bali have been promoted and supported by international agencies, including the World Bank and UNESCO. In these projects, the old discourse and practices of the conservation of Bali's cultural heritage, a concept Schulte Nordholt (2008) asserts was "invented" by Dutch Colonial authorities and scholars, has been brought into new structural settings. Not only has the global economic system been restructured, the Indonesian state has been transformed substantially from a colonial state to a developmental state, and more recently to a neoliberal regulatory state where the relations between the state, market and civil society in the heritage conservation sphere are redefined. As the tourism industry is regarded as a major partner in cultural heritage preservation, the role of the Indonesian regulatory state was intended by policymakers to provide a friendly climate where the tourism market could work properly to enhance the management and preservation of cultural heritage (AusHeritage and ASEAN-COCI 2002).

The recent integration of cultural heritage conservation into the global tourism market has become the hallmark of neoliberalizing heritage. In this regard, neoliberalism should be understood not merely as a political and economic phenomena but also as a cultural one aimed at transforming every fabric of society into conformity with neoliberal logic (Aspinall 2013). Academically, neoliberalism has been examined widely in different disciplinary contexts; for example, urban studies (Harvey 2005b; Brenner and Theodore 2002), environmental politics (Duffy and Moore 2010; Fay 2013; Heynen et al. 2007; Igoe and Brockington 2007; Corson 2010), legal studies (Krever 2013; Blalock 2014; Turner 2008), and cultural studies (Rottenberg 2013). However, given the recent interest by and active involvement of the World Bank and other international agencies in cultural heritage conservation and its connection to economic development, neoliberalism in the context of heritage remains under-explored. In this light, this paper aims to examine cultural heritage conservation in the neoliberal era of Indonesia, focusing especially on the role of international agencies in the inscription of the Cultural Landscape of Bali Province to UNESCO's World Heritage List. This paper is not intended to examine heritage in the context of Balinese identity politics, a dominant theme in the debates on Bali studies (Picard 1996; Schulte Nordholt 2008), but it will shift the debates into a political economic sphere to highlight the winners and losers in the project of Bali's heritage conservation.

Neoliberalism and Heritage Conservation

Neoliberalism: From Washington to Post-Washington Consensus

Neoliberalism is understood differently by different people. For many scholars, neoliberalism is defined as an ideological template of economic, legal and institutional reform packages imposed by external forces within a given country to advance market liberalization policies (Saad-Filho and Johnston 2005; Corson 2010; Turner 2008). Others emphasize it as a dialectical process between endogenous forces, in terms of domestic power dynamics, and exogenous forces, in terms of global political economy structures (Springer 2010; Peck 2003; Heynen et al. 2007). In this chapter, neoliberalism refers to "both a political-economic-cultural phenomena and an explanatory concept" (Peck 2013, p. 133) characterized by its directive, utopian projects (Harvey 2005a). It is utopian in the sense that a perfect market order that is seen to be the best way to organize society could never be achieved, but political and economic power-holders and associated intellectuals have continued to push every aspect of life towards market-driven interests. Hence, neoliberalism does not appear to be uniform and monolithic because its outcomes would be influenced by specific political-economic, social and cultural contexts where it is pursued. In this respect, an examination of neoliberalism would need to focus on the specificity of "actually existing neoliberalism" (Brenner and Theodore 2002) so that the consequences of institutional arrangements, policy regimes and practices, and contestations among social forces can be seen (Springer 2010).

Neoliberalism is not a static doctrine. It has been continuously developing and adapting. Conceptually and chronologically, there are two broad paradigm shifts in neoliberalism that each stress different features as the best way to achieve the main objective, a free market society; namely, the Washington Consensus and the Post-Washington Consensus. While the Washington Consensus stresses structural adjustment programmes like privatization, deregulation and fiscal austerity to liberate the market, the Post-Washington Consensus revises this by adding in the important role of institutions (see Carroll 2012). This revision was introduced on account of the failure of the Washington Consensus caused by "problems of governance, issues of reforms sequencing and the influence of coalition of rent seekers" (Carroll 2007, p. 2). The main characteristic of the Post-Washington Consensus is to enhance governance to address such problems. Another is to establish "the relentless specification ... of the state form and function in a market-complementing manner" to indicate the market liberalization progress (Carroll 2012, p. 354). Many models have been introduced to assess qualitatively and quantitatively the position of a state against the standards required for attracting capital investments and fostering economic growth.[1]

The World Bank and Neoliberalization of Heritage

In 1999 the World Bank enacted a framework of action on culture and sustainable development which sets the basic policy for the organization's involvement in development by expanding its concern with cultural heritage, capturing proactively the economic value of heritage patrimony and focusing on the relationship between cultural heritage and development, especially for reducing poverty and creating employment. This framework marked the World Bank's new perspective of seeing cultural heritage not only as patrimony to be safeguarded during development processes but also to be advanced as a tool for development (World Bank 1999). The framework rests upon two cornerstones—the educational value of cultural heritage and its economic value. The former deals with the vital role of cultural heritage in creating self-esteem and national identity. It is observed that "[c]ultural patrimony assets are not just 'commodities.' Their educational capability is unsubstitutable. The patrimony is essential for human capital formation and for inculcating national identity" (World Bank 2001a, p. 33). Regarding the latter, the World Bank (2001a, p. 33) admits that previously it underestimated "the intrinsic economic capacity of the cultural sector for empowering development ...[thus] the economic resources of the cultural patrimony have been seldom mobilised" because of "insufficient information and [an] inadequate pricing mechanism". Consequently, cultural heritage has been threatened because of its low or even unrealized economic value.

The valuation of cultural heritage is therefore seen as an essential step to realize its economic value—to assess whether it is feasible to "capture" an economic value from a patrimony (World Bank 2001a). Following the analogous emergence of environmental economics in payments for environmental services, a model of "cultural economics" has been introduced to calculate, quantify and examine the value of cultural goods and services. Given that both environmental and cultural heritage each share a similar nature as a public good to be used for the benefit of present and future generations, there are at least three propositions that have been claimed by proponents in support of cultural economics: (1) "cultural assets, like environmental goods, have economic value"; (2) "these economic values and potential can increasingly be assessed through improved methodologies"; (3) "their economic value can be captured, and even maximized, through adequate policies and efficient pricing" (World Bank 2001a, p. 43). Cultural economics was one of the key themes discussed officially at the 2013 World Cultural Forum, which recommended in the outcome of the forum—the "Bali Promise"—to find "new modalities for the valuing and measuring of culture in sustainable development".

While waiting for the modalities in cultural economics to be developed sufficiently, the immediate economic value of cultural heritage still relies to a large extent on the tourism industry. In this regard, tourism is seen as the most vital industry to collaborate with in heritage management (World Bank 2001a). In the 1999 framework of action, it is clearly stated that "[w]hen the World Bank supports conservation of monuments and heritage sites it is to achieve economic and social objectives. Most World Bank projects that include site conservation are justified on tourism ground[s]" (World Bank 1999, p. 8). The World Bank (2001b, p. 81) argues that "attracting visitors, whether local or global, vacationers or pilgrims, day trippers or sojourners, is for many countries highly attractive as a development strategy. Tourism offers a way to enhance foreign exchange earnings, stimulate a variety of other economic activities, increase employment, and build national self-esteem for a relatively small public investment." It also observes from its creditor countries that there has been a close correlation between cultural heritage conservation and the tourism industry in the sense that a country which has no aspiration for developing tourism is unlikely to borrow money from the World Bank to undertake cultural heritage conservation projects (World Bank 2001b).

The ways the World Bank has played its role in tourism development has changed over time. Hawkins and Mann (2007) divide this role into four conceptual and chronological periods. The first was the Macro-Development Period (1969–79), where tourism was regarded as an opportunity for pursuing a balance of payments through the maximization of foreign exchange (Hawkins and Mann 2007, p. 354). In this period the bank provided loans for developing the tourism industry in seventeen countries. The second was the Period of Disengagement (1980–90), in which the bank had ceased to provide loans for tourism development to governments (World Bank 2001a). Here the bank embraced the idea that the private sector was the best actor for developing a country's tourism industry, informed by the prevailing ethos of the Washington Consensus (Hawkins and Mann 2007). The third period is known as the Sustainable Development Period (1991–99), when the bank reoriented its development projects, introducing the dimension of "sustainable tourism" (Hawkins and Mann 2007). In this period the bank funded forty-four projects across thirty-four countries dealing with biodiversity conservation, with ten per cent of these focusing on the preservation of cultural heritage (Hawkins and Mann 2007, p. 357). The last era was the Micro-Development Period (2000–2006), where the bank advocated decentralized institutional arrangements, community-based and public-private partnerships in tourism development (Hawkins and Mann 2007, p. 358).

Although these period classifications by Hawkins and Mann (2007) did not tidily apply in the Indonesian context, they do provide a general picture of how the World Bank came to play a significant role in tourism development in the country. The World Bank had already become a major player in Indonesian development after the government of Indonesia had rejoined the organization in 1967. Previously, under the Sukarno presidency, the Indonesian government had given up its membership. Since the early 1970s, the organization had assisted the newly installed President Suharto and his military-backed New Order government, including in the development of the tourism industry in Bali. As a result the influence of the World Bank, conceptually and institutionally, has been very important in shaping the ways in which tourism and cultural heritage conservation on the island are dominantly conceived and practised by policymakers, opinion leaders and academics, and even by NGO activists.

Bali Cultural Heritage in the Tourism Industry

Tourism in Colonial and Post-colonial Bali

The tourism industry in Bali was first introduced during the colonial period. This early development of tourism by the Dutch Colonial government was part of the ethical policy following the shameful wars of conquest ending in *puputan* (mass suicide of the royal courts) in 1906 and 1908, which brought negative press coverage at the international level (Vickers 2012). Tourism development also went hand in hand with a project of *Baliseering* (Balinization), which aimed at enhancing Balinese culture and identity to prevent the spread of nationalism, Islamization and Christianization on the island. In the absence of natural resources for the global market, Balinese culture was seen as an asset for tourism that could be developed by constructing the necessary infrastructure and creating an image of "paradise" to attract international tourists (see Darma Putra and Hitchcock 2007; Vickers 2012). Although it is true that the image of Bali as a "paradise island" was created by the Dutch colonizers to foster the tourism industry on the island, as argued by Vickers (2012), the image was not created out of nothing. As noted by Couch and Ritchie (1999), the economic value of comparative advantage can be realized when factors of competitiveness are developed, very often by external actors who have greater skills and knowledge about the workings of the global market, as product packagers, sellers or travel agents. Accordingly, the creation of a "paradise" image should be seen as the way the colonial administration developed this factor of competitiveness out of Bali's comparative advantages, including its climate, natural environment and, more importantly, cultural heritage. Without these comparative advantages, tourism in Bali would have no material basis to be competitive.

In the 1950s the postcolonial state of Indonesia attempted to rebuild the tourism industry on the material and ideational foundations left over by the Dutch colonial administration (Vickers 2011). Interestingly, many of the actors involved in the industry were former independence fighters who established their own tourism enterprises such as hotels, art shops and travel agencies (see Vickers 2011). During this period, tourism was "largely unplanned and haphazard, with decisions about location, building design, and the provisions of basic infrastructure … generally lagg[ing] behind hotel construction." Consequently, this had led to a concern about negative impacts of tourism on Balinese culture and the island's environmental assets (World Bank 1974, p. 4). Concerned with these impacts and at the same time the need to pursue foreign exchange, a Tourism Master Plan for Bali Province funded by UNDP and with the World Bank as the executing agency came about. The master plan was based on a study conducted by SCETO, a Paris-based tourism consultancy, in the early 1970s, which attempted to resolve these contradictory pressures by redirecting tourism development in Bali into a concentrated site in Nusa Dua. Enclave tourism was promoted to "ensure the most economic utilization of available land without detracting from [the] natural environment, while being sufficiently flexible to accommodate the preferences of potential investors in hotels and other facilities" (World Bank 1974, p. 5). The World Bank's report (1974) argued that enclave tourist facilities that are physically isolated from densely populated residential areas and good agricultural land would ensure that the interaction between tourists and local people would be controllable; hence, local culture and agriculture would not be compromised.

A relatively smooth process to advance the tourism industry on the island during the New Order era was partly ensured by the traumatic experience of the 1965–66 mass killings. During this event it is estimated that around 80,000–100,000 people were killed in Bali alone—up to 8 per cent of the total population—among whom were leftist intellectuals, farmer and labour organizers, women activists, and ordinary people associated with the Indonesian Communist Party and affiliated organizations (Robinson 1995; Vickers 2012). Leftist intellectuals in the past, particularly members of Lembaga Kebudayaan Rakyat (LEKRA/Institute for the People's Culture), had been very suspicious of tourism, which was seen as a form of neo-colonialism (Darma Putra 2003). Hence, the mass killings arguably set the way for Suharto, who came to power in the aftermath, to impose national policies on Bali without significant opposition. In the first Five–Year National Development Plan, Bali was designated as the centre for foreign exchange earning through tourism. This served at least two objectives: the advancement of the tourism industry, taking Indonesia to the global market, and fostering a national cultural identity focused on aesthetics rather than the socialist discourse of the Sukarno era (Picard 2003). The concept of "cultural tourism" was first introduced during this era in order to keep the main commodity of the tourism industry in Bali—that is, the culture itself—in the hands of the local populace as the owner of Bali's cultural heritage. Later, however, as argued by Picard (1996), the concept became conflated with "touristic culture"—touristification of society and the use of tourism for confirming what should be regarded as "Balinese culture".

At the end of the 1980s the Master Plan for Bali Tourism expired and the development of the tourism industry on the island spread rapidly beyond what had been set by the plan. This was also coincidentally advanced by the prevailing ethos of the Washington Consensus, especially its promotion of privatization and deregulation. Indeed, the World Bank during this period had ceased to provide loans to governments for tourism development in order to facilitate market and private sector interests as the engines for such development (Hawkins and Mann 2007). Regionally, the Provincial Government of Bali enacted Governor Decree No. 15/1988 to move away from concentrated enclave tourism by expanding tourism designated areas (*kawasan pariwisata*) to fifteen locations, later expanding the number to twenty-one areas covering 24.7 per cent of the island (UNDP, USAID and the World Bank 2003, p. 61). As a result, tourism investment has increased significantly, benefiting from the national and regional deregulation policies. The key players for this expansion were Jakarta-based conglomerates close to President Suharto working together with their local allies, including Golkar functionaries, regional government officials and local noble families, who were to become future tourism entrepreneurs themselves. Consequently, the integrity of Bali's environment and culture have been compromised by the rapid expansion of tourism, which in turn has triggered island-wide resistance.[2]

After the fall of the authoritarian regime of Suharto in 1998, structural changes in Indonesia brought significant changes in governance through democratization and decentralization policies, with paradoxical effects. This period is characterized by Aspinall (2013) as "a nation in fragments", where organizational fragmentation in contemporary Indonesian politics enables neoliberalism and patronage to work hand in hand. The small island province of Bali has now been structurally divided into eight districts and a municipality, each of which has authority to manage its territory to generate revenues. Here, decentralization should also be seen as a neoliberal spatial strategy through downward rescaling in order to constrain centralistic state structures, facilitate market expansion and foster competition among national territories (see Reed and Bruyneel 2010). In the decentralized era, every district in Bali has been involved in competition to attract investment to its territory, especially for tourism development. The tourism industry is seen as the most feasible way to gain local revenues for district governments, while also extracting "easy money" from rent-seeking practices in the process, developing both tourism projects and patronage politics (Wardana 2015). Consequently, the impacts on the natural and social environments have been intensified across an ever-wider landscape.

The Conservation of Bali's Cultural Heritage

With regard to the effects of rapid tourism development since the 1980s, the World Bank approved funding for the Bali Urban Infrastructure Project (BUIP) during 1997–2004. The objectives of BUIP itself were to improve Bali's urban infrastructure services in accordance with sustainable development principles in order to meet: "(i) basic needs in all important urban centres and (ii) the needs of growing urbanization in South Bali, as a result of tourism and other economic activities" by investments in urban infrastructure, the participation of the private sector, conservation of cultural heritage, and institutional enhancement (World Bank 2005, p. 2). Although the project was not specifically about heritage conservation, it had a component dealing with Cultural Heritage Conservation (CHC), with a budget of around US$15.1 million. This component consisted of five elements: (1) improvements to the Besakih Temple complex; (2) pilot conservation activities; (3) establishing an inventory of historic places; (4) strengthening conservation capacities; and (5) implementing signage at heritage sites (in Indonesian and other languages).

Under this component of the project, an international symposium on cultural heritage conservation entitled "Conserving Cultural Heritage for Sustainable Social, Economic and Tourism Development" was held in July 2000. It resulted in a declaration affirming the relationship of culture to development, stating that "living cultures have the potential to generate wealth, create social harmony and resolve conflict". An important achievement of the project was the establishment of the Bali Heritage Trust (BHT), a semi-private organization that undertakes inventories, runs pilot conservation projects and engages in capacity building and policy advocacy for cultural heritage management and conservation in Bali, such as by drafting a provincial regulation for Bali's cultural heritage (Licciardi and R. Amirtahmasebi 2012). A respected noble from the Ubud Royal Palace, Tjokorda Raka Kerthyasa, who is also a politician and tourism entrepreneur, was appointed as the chair of the BHT by the governor of Bali in 2003. This shows how the cultural conservation project in Bali since the colonial period has very often been intertwined with the revival of traditional ruling elites and their claims as the most legitimate heirs of Bali's cultural heritage. Several pilot conservation projects have also targeted the reconstruction or rehabilitation of the properties of local royal families, including the Royal Water Park of Taman Ujung in Karangasem.

In addition to the BUIP project, the World Bank has also worked closely with other international organizations, specifically UNESCO, to enhance the value of Bali's cultural heritage. In 2000, through a joint mission, the World Bank and UNESCO encouraged the government of Indonesia to take further steps in cultural heritage conservation by nominating a cultural heritage site to UNESCO's World Heritage List (Dharmiasih and Lansing 2014; Darma Putra and Hitchcock 2005). The government of Indonesia had twice attempted to nominate the Besakih Temple complex since the 1990s, but those attempts were rejected by Balinese concerned with the impacts of inscription on the management and ownership of the temple (Darma Putra and Hitchcock 2005). Some Balinese intellectuals even condemned the involvement of UNESCO and the World Bank in the nomination of Besakih Temple by the national government as "an instance of neo-colonialism" because as "the 'Mother Temple' of Bali", they claimed, "Besakih does not belong to the Indonesian government but the Balinese Hindus" (Picard 2003, p. 117). The national government eventually cancelled the nomination of Besakih and redirected its attention to other cultural heritage sites in Bali, such as the Royal Temple of Taman Ayun and the Jatiluwih rice terraces.

After the public rejection of the Besakih Temple nomination, the role of the World Bank has become less prominent, although its conceptual framework on the relationship between cultural heritage and development has persisted. UNESCO, however, as it is part of its mandate, has continued to play an essential role in supporting the Indonesian government in nominating as many sites as possible to the World Heritage Committee. In 2002–3, UNESCO deployed three experts to Bali to assist the government in creating a nomination dossier. Four site clusters were included in a singe nomination entitled the Cultural Landscape of Bali Province: the Royal Temple of Taman Ayun; archaeological sites along the Pakerisan River; the rice terraces of Jatiluwih; and the West Bali National Park. The nomination, however, was deferred on account of a lack of coherence among the clusters—there were no clear cultural or ecological connections among the clusters beyond the fact they were geographically situated in Bali. After being revised and omitting the West Bali National Park from the proposal—considered natural heritage rather than cultural—the dossier was submitted for consideration in 2006. The application was rejected for having missed the submission deadline. The International Council on Monuments and Sites (ICOMOS), the technical advisory body of the World Heritage Committee, also suggested further revisions (Dharmiasih and Lansing 2014).

Once the technical assistance in preparing the dossier had been exhausted, the role of mobilizing support for Indonesia's proposal shifted from UNESCO to the Indonesian government. In this regard, in 2008 the government of Indonesia used diplomatic channels as well as lobbying strategies to approach the World Heritage Committee member countries (Bhaskara 2015). A cultural mission of Balinese artists and dancers was sent by the national and regional governments to perform at the UNESCO offices in Paris. The district government of Badung had contributed financially to the mission in the expectation that the listing of the Royal Temple of Taman Ayun as a World Heritage Site would significantly boost tourism in the district (Bhaskara 2015). Significantly, the district head of Badung at that time was A.A. Gede Agung, who is also the "king" of Mengwi Royal Palace, the owner of the Royal Temple of Taman Ayun. A regular coffee morning was also organized by the Ministry of Culture and Tourism in Jakarta, with ambassadors and other diplomatic officials from World Heritage Committee member countries invited to attend (Bhaskara 2015). Yunus Arbi, a high official at the Ministry of Education and Culture, admits that the World Heritage "nomination process is related to politics; last time we supported South Korea by giving them our vote and they helped us too. Our vote is important because this nomination process is all about voting" (quoted by Bhaskara 2015, p. 248).

Despite such lobbying, the 2008 dossier also failed because it lacked coherency and comparative analyses with similar sites in other countries. For such matters, the role of international experts had been vital. UNESCO's guide for preparing for nomination stresses the need for international experts who understand the place of the proposed site in the international context, who have the ability to undertake comparative and scientific studies on the authenticity and value of the property compared with similar properties at the global level, and who have "useful networks for obtaining wider advice" (UNESCO 2011, p. 53). In fact, the 2008 dossier involved just a single international expert, Professor Stephen Lansing from the University of Arizona, who was asked at the last minute to give a presentation before UNESCO delegates in Paris alongside Indonesia's cultural mission (Bhaskara 2015).

This reflects how the UNESCO heritage regime privileges so-called "international experts" and perpetuates the asymmetrical power relationships between "international experts" and "local experts" in defining what heritage is and is not. As Professor Lansing's field of expertise is on issues surrounding *subak* (Bali's traditional irrigation system) and Balinese agricultural practices, ICOMOS recommended that the nomination should focus exclusively on the *subak* as a traditional irrigation association whose existence has been under threat (Dharmiasih and Lansing 2014). Based on this recommendation the World Heritage Committee (2008) deferred examination of the dossier and suggested that the scope of properties covered be expanded to include other *subak* and the surrounding environment that the *subak* depend upon ecologically and culturally (see the Ministry of Culture and Tourism 2011). Hence, a new team was established to redraft the dossier with Professor Lansing appointed formally as the international expert. He invited his colleagues, local academics, *subak* researchers and non-governmental organization (NGO) activists to join the team to enhance the dossier in accordance with the recommendations of ICOMOS to focus on *subak*. After numerous consultations, visits and evaluations, the Cultural Landscape of Bali Province was finally listed under the World Heritage Convention in June 2012 at the thirty-eighth World Heritage Committee Session in St. Petersburg, Russia.

World Heritage Status and a Contest of Power

The Bali Cultural Landscape and the Management Plan

Learning from the controversies in nominating Balinese Hindu's holiest temple of Besakih, the subsequent nomination to UNESCO's World Heritage List saw better public relations from the government of Indonesia in approaching the Balinese public. The focus on *subak*, the traditional irrigation system, as recommended by ICOMOS in 2008 in line with the international expert's areas of expertise, appeared to be the best way to get the first World Heritage Site in Bali and the first World Cultural Landscape in Indonesia listed. Given that the nomination needed strong justification for a property to be listed, the contemporary threats to *subak*, which have also been a common concern of the Balinese public, became the principal rationale in the dossier (see Ministry of Culture and Tourism 2011). Putting the threatened *subak* system as the focal point in the nomination effectively mobilized wider support from the public without causing public controversy over temple management or issues of commercialization of temples, even though several major temples, such as Batur Temple and Batukaru Temple, were also included in the clusters (Figure 11.1).[3]

To be sure, it was not the entire *subak* system in Bali—which is estimated to include 1,559 *subaks* covering around 81,625 hectares of agricultural land across the island (BPS 2013)—that was included in the dossier; only two particular *subak* landscapes that were considered to have potential for tourism. The World Bank once observed that given the trend in heritage tourism, the use of "cultural heritage as the focal point of tourism" should be directed to improve "underutilized or less known [tourism] sites" (World Bank 2001b, p. 81). This observation seems to fit the inclusion of the rice terraces of Jatiluwih, which had been designated as a tourism destination in the mid 2000s but had not able to attract tourist visits significantly. Thus, the nomination of the rice terraces of Jatiluwih—which later was expanded into the Subak Landscape of Catur Angga Batukaru following the ICOMOS recommendation—as a World Heritage site should be seen as a scaling-up strategy to put the landscape on the global tourism map by gaining recognition of "outstanding universal value" as a factor of competitiveness (Wardana 2019).

It is argued that cultural heritage sites would be better protected if their economic value could be mobilized to generate income through tourist visits (World Bank 2001b). Building economic value based on the symbolic capital of the World Heritage List has been the dominant logic in the government's pursuit of inscription under the World Heritage Convention. In the dossier it explains that there are four major threats to the existence of *subak*: (1) loss of soil fertility due to the overuse of chemical fertilizers and hybrid-rice seeds introduced with the Green Revolution under the New Order; (2) low incomes from rice farming because of the

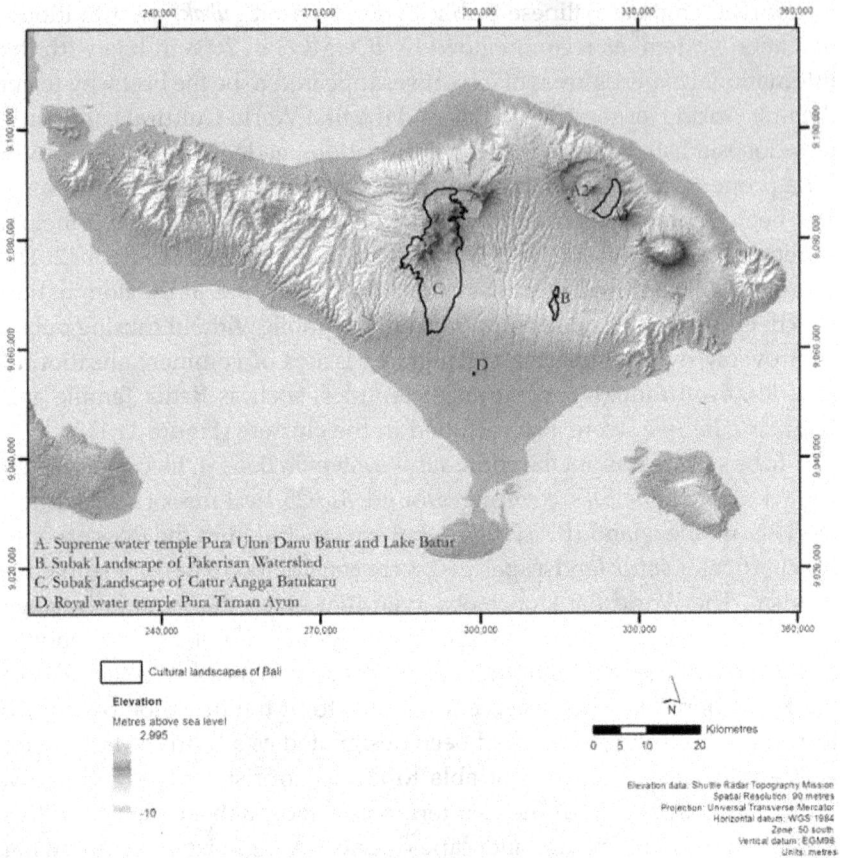

FIGURE 11.1 Map of the Cultural Landscape of Bali Province. Source: Ministry of Culture and Tourism, 2011.

high cost of inputs and the small size of landholdings; (3) forest degradation, which affects the water supply for *subak*; and (4) land conversion due to "unplanned development" (Ministry of Culture and Tourism 2011). Essentially, what is argued in the dossier is that agriculture is no longer economically profitable; and, in turn, many farmers have given up their land for development projects in order to survive, endangering the *subak* system as the backbone of Bali's cultural heritage.

In fact these threats are not a naturally given, but they are interlocked with and to a large extent have been the unintended consequences of state policies.[4] Thus, in order to protect *subak*, what is actually needed is immediate state intervention to change public policy in order to support farmers in coping with these threats in the first place. Putu Sardana, a member of Subak Jatiluwih, insists that "if only the government helped us with subsidies for the cost of fertilizer, land taxes, and supports the market for our harvests, we [the small farmers] would need no tourism".[5] However, as the neoliberal regulatory state has become dominant, the amount of support from the state to this marginalized sector of society has been reducing. Such "support" thus has to be connected to the market process. In the context of this paper, state "support" for the farmers and *subak* has been directed towards market channels. This has been undertaken through the integration of *subak* conservation and farmers' engagement with the tourism industry in order to capture the economic value of the landscape as a heritage site. It was argued that revenues from tourist visits to the *subak* landscape would generate income for local people and make them realize the economic value of their heritage so that it would be worth preserving.

The reality, however, is not so straightforward. The benefits of World Heritage listing have become a source of contestation among different social forces. Institutional arrangements have become a site of power struggles in accessing such benefits and maintaining power in society (Wardana 2020). The management plan, a pledge by the state to the international community on how it would manage the World Heritage Sites, has less impact at the local level, where the district political and economic elites, utilizing the discourse of decentralization, have navigated the plan and institutional framework in pursuing their vested interests. For example, the District Government of Tabanan, where most of the Subak Landscape of Catur Angga Batukaru is located, has established an institution to govern the landscape within its territory known as the Governing Body. Instead of focusing on the management and preservation of the rice terraces and the *subak* system, this body—which consists mainly of district government officials, including the head of district as chairwoman—has been focusing on extracting economic benefit from the listing, particularly revenues from tourist visits (see Figure 11.2). Most of the locals and non-district government officials serving the body were appointed on account of their political and personal connections, either to the Indonesian Democratic Party of Struggle (PDIP), the ruling party in the district or to the high district officials, chiefly Eka Wirsyastuti, the district head.

In fact, the *subak* institution, upon which the preservation of the *subak* depends, is left on the margins and receives little by way of contribution from this revenue (see Figure 11.2). Disappointed with the World Heritage outcome, several members of Subak Jatiluwih have blocked their rice fields with bamboo fences in order to prevent tourists from entering them (Wardana 2020). Nyoman Sutama, the chief of *subak* (*pekaseh*) in Jatiluwih, has many times refused invitations from the Governing Body to explain the *subak* system to visitors, including visiting dignitaries and state officials who would not fit the tourist label.

Professor Windia (2015a), a *subak* expert at a local university, who was also actively involved in the nomination process, admits that the conditions in the *subak* landscape of Jatiluwih are far from what was expected. He proceeded to recommend that UNESCO "boycott" tourism in the landscape. Paradoxically, given the degraded conditions of the rice terraces of Jatiluwih after the World Heritage listing, he recommends that tourists visit Subak Pulagan, another cluster of the Cultural Landscape of Bali Province located in the neighbouring district of Gianyar, as an alternative to experience rice terraces (Windia 2015b). Instead of demanding that the state take the necessary steps to assist *subak* and small farmers in the first place, many academics and opinion leaders share a similar neoliberal logic embracing the concept that the conservation of *subak* and Bali's agricultural heritage should be integrated into the expansion of tourism markets (see Pitana and Adi Putra 2013).

Moreover, the inscription of the Royal Temple of Taman Ayun in Badung District to the World Heritage regime does not appear to contribute to the conservation of the Subak Landscape of Catur Angga Batukaru. In fact, the flocks of tourists visiting the Royal Temple of Taman Ayun, which have doubled due to the World Heritage listing, have provided a greater source of wealth for the Mengwi Royal Family instead of assisting Balinese farmers to cope with the threats to their agriculture. This is because the revenues from tourist visits to the Royal Temple of Taman Ayun are distributed 75 per cent to the Mengwi Royal Palace, as the owner of the property, and 25 per cent to the Badung District Government (Widiarta 2015). This calculation explains why the District Government of Badung—in which A.A. Gede Agung served simultaneously as the district head of Badung and as the king of Mengwi Royal Palace—was very disappointed when Professor Lansing's new team for drafting the dossier had attempted to exclude the Royal Temple of Taman Ayun from

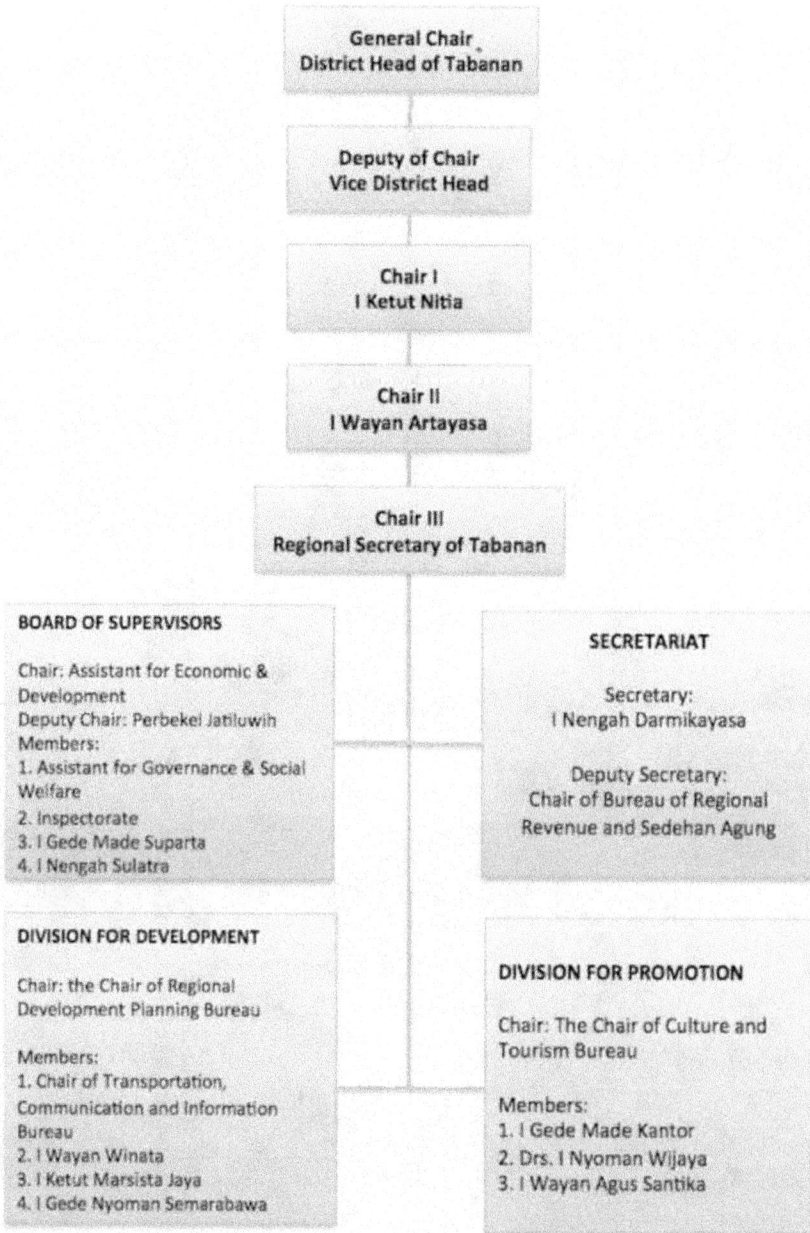

General Chair
District Head of Tabanan

Deputy of Chair
Vice District Head

Chair I
I Ketut Nitia

Chair II
I Wayan Artayasa

Chair III
Regional Secretary of Tabanan

BOARD OF SUPERVISORS

Chair: Assistant for Economic &
Development
Deputy Chair: Perbekel Jatiluwih
Members:
1. Assistant for Governance & Social
Welfare
2. Inspectorate
3. I Gede Made Suparta
4. I Nengah Sulatra

SECRETARIAT

Secretary:
I Nengah Darmikayasa

Deputy Secretary:
Chair of Bureau of Regional
Revenue and Sedehan Agung

DIVISION FOR DEVELOPMENT

Chair: the Chair of Regional
Development Planning Bureau

Members:
1. Chair of Transportation,
Communication and Information
Bureau
2. I Wayan Winata
3. I Ketut Marsista Jaya
4. I Gede Nyoman Semarabawa

DIVISION FOR PROMOTION

Chair: The Chair of Culture and
Tourism Bureau

Members:
1. I Gede Made Kantor
2. Drs. I Nyoman Wijaya
3. I Wayan Agus Santika

FIGURE 11.2 Structure of the Jatiluwih Governing Body. Source: The Decree of Tabanan District Head No. 84/2013 on the Establishment of the Jatiluwih Governing Body.

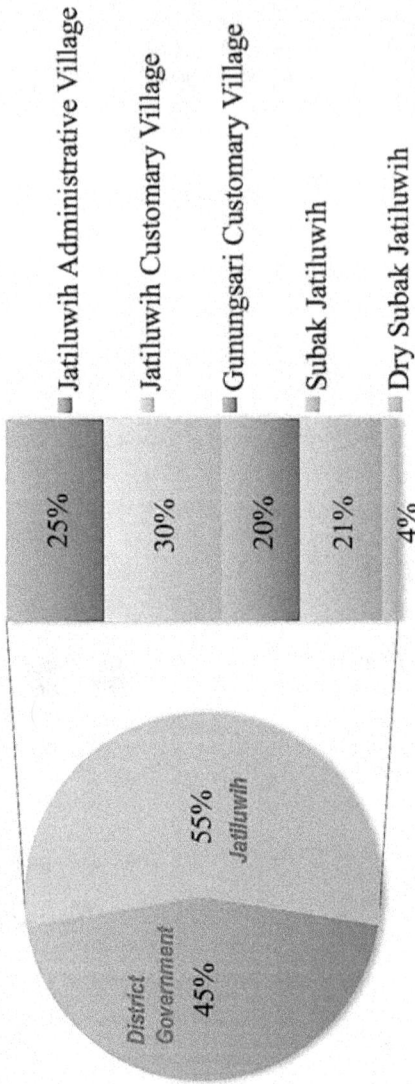

FIGURE 11.3 Allocation of Net Tourism Revenues in the Subak Landscape of Jatiluwih. Source: Joint Agreement between the District Government of Tabanan and Jatiluwih Village.

the nomination.[6] The government demanded the new team re-include the temple in the proposal because Badung had previously contributed a significant amount of financial and political support for the cultural mission to Paris back in 2008 (Bhaskara 2015).[7] In brief, the conservation of Bali's agricultural heritage by integrating it into the global tourism market appears to be navigated by the local elites to advance their interests at the expense of the marginalized *subak* communities.

Conclusion

Bali's cultural heritage has been the object of development policies since the colonial period. This has been an integral part of developing the tourism industry on the island. More recently, the logic behind efforts at heritage conservation in Bali seems to have been no different, although it has been placed in relatively different structural contexts. The recent integration of cultural heritage conservation into the global tourism market has become the hallmark of neoliberalizing heritage. As shown above, the influence of international agencies, particularly the World Bank, both conceptually and institutionally, had been essential in developing the tourism industry in Bali and, later, for the conservation of Bali's cultural heritage, which led to the listing of the Cultural Landscape of Bali Province under the World Heritage regime. However, the role of these agencies has been limited to the initial listing process. Once the inscription was successful, agency for the site fell to local power brokers, and the international agencies were relegated to the role of mere legitimizers.

It had been assumed that by being listed the value of the *subak* system, especially its landscape, would be realized through tourism, and in turn the *subak* as Bali's distinctive cultural heritage would be better preserved. In this regard, the tourism market would change the value of the *subak* qualitatively from its productive capacity to expropriation of its symbolic value as a heritage site. In reality, the conservation of Bali's cultural heritage is more complex than the Post-Washington Consensus neoliberal assumption that sees it simply as an issue of governance that might be addressed by establishing a management plan, putting in place institutional arrangements and providing incentives for the rural economy from the global tourism market.

From the outset, the nomination, and later the management of the heritage landscape, has been a field of competition where differing interests have been articulated, mediated and contested in order to acquire or retain control over the sites and to access the financial benefits arising from the listing. As it is a political act embedded in pre-existing power structures, to date the local elites appear to have been able to navigate the institutional structure governing the landscape to pursue their vested interests at the expense of *subak* communities. This has been made possible under decentralization, through which political power has been distributed to the local political elites. In the case of Bali it appears that the process of neoliberalization has been hijacked by local power holders and it has failed to deliver its promises to the local *subak* communities. Thus, because the local *subak* communities have not benefitted as expected from heritage tourism, to a certain extent they have resisted heritagization of the *subak*.

Although it is true that "UNESCO is watching" (Dharmiasih and Lansing 2014), as are the other international agencies, there is little they can do to affect the power struggles taking place within the sites. What they could do is to recommend moving Bali's sites from the World Heritage List to the endangered list, a decision that would be difficult to take given the recent position of Indonesia as an elected member of the World Heritage Committee. And if such a decision were to be taken it would be followed by financial aid to address the problems of governance without resolving the underlying asymmetric relations of power through which the marginalization of local *subak* communities is perpetuated. In fact, such financial aid itself could potentially become another source of contestation over the use of such funds. Hence, neoliberalization of the heritage in Bali—and this is probably also applicable to other neoliberal projects under the World Heritage regime—has eventually played into the hands of local culture rent-seekers, who are benefiting from the existing power relations and institutional structure by strategically utilizing the neoliberal framework promoted by the international agencies.

Acknowledgments

Research for this paper was funded generously by the Australian Research Council project "Intangible Cultural Heritage across Borders: Laws, Structures and Strategies" (DP130100213 C. Antons, W. Logan, C. Warren, J. Chen) and by Murdoch University. The author would like to thank Dr Carol Warren, his former doctoral supervisor, as well as Melissa Johnston, Rebecca Meckelburg, Lian Sinclair and other colleagues at Asia

Research Centre, Murdoch University, for providing valuable comments on an earlier draft of this paper.

Notes

1. These standards include the World Bank's Worldwide Governance Indicators and Doing Business Indicators. The World Bank's Worldwide Governance Indicators is a report on the state of governance covering more than 200 countries. Six dimensions of governance are measured by the report: voice and accountability; political stability and absence of violence/terrorism; government effectiveness; regulatory quality; rule of law; and control of corruption. The World Bank's Doing Business Indicators is a quantitative report on business regulations and property rights protection that compares and ranks 189 countries around the world. Eleven areas are measured: starting a business, dealing with construction permits, getting electricity, registering properties, otaining credit, protecting minority investors, paying taxes, trading across borders, enforcing contracts, resolving insolvency, and labour market regulation.

2. For example, the cases of Bakrie Nirwana Resort (BNR), Garuda Wisnu Kencana (GWK), and Serangan Island Reclamation, to name a few (see Warren 1998; Suasta and Connor 1999).

3. The Cultural Landscape of Bali Province consists of four clusters: (1) the Subak Landscape of Catur Angga Batukaru in Tabanan and Buleleng Districts, including the Temple of Batukaru; (2) the Royal Water Temple of Pura Taman Ayun in Badung District; (3) the Supreme Water Temple of Pura Ulun Danu and Lake Batur in Bangli District; and (4) the Subak Landscape of Pakerisan Watershed.

4. For example, the Green Revolution was the policy of the New Order imposed upon farmers with little regard for the sophisticated socio-ecological agricultural systems that existed (Lansing 2007). The fact of low-incomes from farming is due to population growth, the unequal distribution of land and the generally poor terms of trade for agricultural products. Furthermore, land conversion in Bali presents a very complex picture. It is frequently argued that farmers choose to sell their land when farming is no longer economical because of the high expenses of paying for fertilizer and seeds, other production costs and land taxes (Ministry of Culture and Tourism 2011; Pitana and Adi Putra 2013). This argument is put within a rational-choice framework and fails to acknowledge the complete political-economic picture behind this "choice". In Jatiluwih the local community is more concerned with preserving their livelihoods as the first priority, since their land is regarded as a *tetamian leluhur* (heritage from the ancestors to be passed to

the next generation). Thus, the land is seen as of symbolic significance rather than solely a factor of economic calculation. Political-economic factors have also been important in the process of land alienation. In many cases, land conversion for tourist development projects in Bali have involved physical or psychological intimidation from brokers, the state apparatus, and vigilantes, sometimes with the collusion of local elites (for further discussion, see Wardana 2014; Warren 1998, 2014).

5.   Interview on 24 January 2014.

6.   It has been difficult to establish the reasons for the new team wanting to exclude the Royal Temple of Taman Ayun. I assume it was partly informed by the long-standing debates of how the *subak* system is conceived among scholars. Stephan Lansing (2007), who was also on the international expert team, argues that the *subak* is a self-governing institution, autonomous from the pre-colonial state. Schulte Nordholt (2011), in examining the role of Mengwi Royal Dynasty, argues that the *subak* system is far from autonomous. The controversy over state control versus *subak* autonomy in pre-colonial Bali is covered thoroughly in Hauser Schåublin's (2003) essay and her response to comments in *Current Anthropology*. In fact, for Professor Lansing, the inclusion of the Royal Temple of Taman Ayun—a representation of the state's power in *subak* affairs—in the nomination dossier would mean contradicting his own thesis and admitting that Schulte Nordholt's argument prevails.

7.   Bhaskara (2015, p. 298) quotes his informant, Alit Arthawiguna, saying that "the problem was that Taman Ayun was excluded from the serial nomination for the new dossier, but the Badung regency insisted they wanted this site to be included because they claimed they spent a lot of money sending the cultural performance groups to Paris back in 2008. I do not know how much they spent on Paris, I have no idea about this…. So, they insisted on it being included. The provincial government told us we should understand the situation that the Badung regency had spent a fortune on the first nomination process. Stephan [Lansing] and I had headaches as it was a hard time … so we had to find a solution to include this site."

References

Aspinall, E. 2013. "A Nation in Fragments: Patronage and Neoliberalism in Contemporary Indonesia". *Critical Asian Studies* 45, no. 1: 27–54.

AusHeritage and ASEAN-COCI. 2002. *ASEAN–Australia Project Development of an ASEAN Regional Policy and Strategy for Cultural Heritage Management: Cultural Heritage Management Profile, Indonesia*. Sydney: AusHeritage.

Bhaskara, G.I. 2015. "The Local Community as a Stakeholder Group and Its Participation in UNESCO's World Heritage Nomination Process: Jatiluwih

Village, Bali, Indonesia". PhD dissertation, Faculty of Management, Bournemouth University.

Blalock, C. 2014. "Neoliberalism and the Crisis of Legal Theory". *Law and Contemporary Problems* 77, no. 4: 71–103.

Brenner, N., and N. Theodore. 2002. *Spaces of Neoliberalism: Urban Restructuring in North America and Western Europe*. Oxford: Blackwell.

Brohman, J. 1996. "New Directions in Tourism for Third World Development". *Annals of Tourism Research* 23, no. 1: 48–70.

Carroll, T. 2007. "The Politics of the World Bank's Socio-Institutional Neoliberalism". PhD dissertation, Murdoch University.

———. 2012. "Introduction: Neo-Liberal Development Policy in Asia beyond the Post-Washington Consensus". *Journal of Contemporary Asia* 42, no. 3: 350–58.

Corson, C. 2010. "Shifting Environmental Governance in a Neoliberal World: US AID for Conservation". *Antipode* 42, no. 3: 576–602.

Crough, G., and B. Ritchie. 1999. "Tourism, Competitiveness and Societal Prosperity". *Journal of Business Research* 44: 137–52.

Darma Putra, N. 2003. "Reflections on Literature and Politics in Bali: The Development of Lekra, 1950–1966". In *Inequality, Crisis and Social Change in Indonesia: The Muted Worlds of Bali*, edited by T. Reuter. London: Routledge Curzon.

Darma Putra, N., and M. Hitchcock. 2005. "Pura Besakih: A World Heritage Site Contested". *Indonesia and the Malay World* 33, no. 96: 225–38.

Dharmiasih, D.A.W., and S. Lansing. 2014. "Can World Heritage Status Save Bali from Destruction?" *Strategic Review – Indonesia* 360 (January–March). http://www.sr-indonesia.com/in_the_journal/view/can-world-heritage-status-save-bali-from-destruction?pg=all (accessed 29 October 2016).

Duffy, R., and L. Moore. 2010. "Neoliberalising Nature? Elephant-Back Tourism in Thailand and Botswana". *Antipode* 42, no. 3: 742–66.

Fay, D. 2013. "Neoliberal Conservation and the Potential for Lawfare: New Legal Entities and the Political Ecology of Litigation at Dwesa-Cwebe, South Africa". *Geoforum* 44: 170–81.

Harvey, D. 2005a. *A Brief History of Neoliberalism*. Oxford: Oxford University Press.

———. 2005b. *Spaces of Neoliberalization: Towards a Theory of Uneven Geographical Development*. Munchen: Franz Steiner Verlag.

Hauser Schäublin, B. 2003. "The Precolonial Balinese State Reconsidered: A Critical Evaluation of Theory Construction on the Relationship between Irrigation, the State, and Ritual". *Current Anthropology* 44, no. 2: 153–82.

Hawkins, D.E., and S. Mann. 2007. "The World Bank's Role in Tourism Development". *Annals of Tourism Research* 34, no. 2: 348–63.

Heynen, N., J. McCarthy, S. Prudham, and P. Robbins. 2007. *Neoliberal Environments: False Promises and Unnatural Consequences*. London: Routledge.

Igoe, J., and D. Brockington. 2007. "Neoliberal Conservation: A Brief Introduction". *Conservation and Society* 5, no. 4: 432–49.

Licciardi, G., and R. Amirtahmasebi, eds. 2012. *The Economics of Uniqueness: Investing in Historic City Cores and Cultural Heritage Assets for Sustainable Development*. Washington, DC: The World Bank.

Ministry of Culture and Tourism of the Republic of Indonesia. 2011. *Nomination for Inscription on the UNESCO World Heritage List: Cultural Landscape of Bali Province*. Dossier submitted to the Secretariat of the World Heritage Committee, UNESCO.

Nijkamp, P. 2012. "Economic Valuation of Cultural Heritage". In *The Economics of Uniqueness: Investing in Historic City Cores and Cultural Heritage Assets for Sustainable Development*, edited by G. Licciardi and R. Amirtahmasebi. Washington, DC: The World Bank.

Picard, M. 1996. *Bali: Cultural Tourism and Touristic Culture*. Translated by Diana Darling. Singapore: Archipelago.

———. 2003. "Touristification and Balinization in a Time of Reformasi". *Indonesia and the Malay World* 31, no. 89: 108–18.

Pitana, I.G., and I.G.S. Adi Putra. 2013. "Pariwisata Sebagai Wahana Pelestarian Subak dan Budaya Subak Sebagai Modal Dasar Dalam Pariwisata". *Journal of Bali Studies* 3, no. 2: 159–80.

Reed, M., and G. Bruyneel. 2010. "Rescaling Environmental Governance, Rethinking the State: A Three Dimensional Review". *Progress in Human Geography* 34: 646–53.

Robinson, G. 1995. *The Dark Side of Paradise: Political Violence in Bali*. Ithaca: Cornell University Press.

Rottenberg, C. 2013. "The Rise of Neoliberal Feminism". *Cultural Studies* 28, no. 3: 418–37.

Saad-Filho, A., and D. Johnston. 2005. *Neoliberalism: A Critical Reader*. London: Pluto.

Sage, C., and M. Woolcock. 2005. "Breaking Legal Inequality Traps: New Approaches to Building Justice System for the Poor in Developing Countries". Paper presented at the World Bank Conference, "New Frontiers of Social Policy: Developing in a Globalizing World", Tanzania, 12–14 December 2005.

Schulte Nordholt, H. 2008. *Bali an Open Fortress, 1995–2005: Regional Autonomy, Electoral Democracy and Entrenched Identities*. Singapore: NUS Press.

———. 2011. "Dams and Dynasty, and the Colonial Transformation of Balinese Irrigation Management". *Human Ecology* 39: 21–27.

Springer, S.D. 2010. *Cambodia's Neoliberal Order: Violence, Authoritarianism, and the Contestation of Public Space*. Abingdon: Routledge.

Suasta, P., and L. Connor. 1999. "Democratic Mobilization and Political Authoritarianism: Tourism Development in Bali". In *Staying Local in the Global Village*, edited by L. Connor and R. Rubinstein. Honolulu: University of Hawai'i Press.

Turner, R.S. 2008. "Neo-Liberal Constitutionalism: Ideology, Government and the Rule of Law". *Journal of Politics and Law* 1, no. 2: 47–55.

UNESCO. 2011 *Preparing World Heritage Nominations*, 2nd ed. Paris: UNESCO.

UNDP, USAID, and the World Bank. 2003. *Bali beyond the Tragedy: Impact and Challenges for Tourism-led Development in Indonesia*. Jakarta: UNDP Indonesia.

Vickers, A. 2010. *Bali: A Paradise Created*. Tokyo: Tuttle.

——. 2011. "Bali Rebuild its Tourism Industry". *Bijdragen tot de Taal-, Land- en Volkenkunde* 167, no. 4: 459–81.

Wardana, A. 2015. "Debating Spatial Governance in the Pluralistic Institutional and Legal Setting of Bali". *Asia Pacific Journal of Anthropology* 16, no. 2: 106–22.

——. 2019. *Contemporary Bali: Contested Space and Governance*. Singapore: Palgrave Macmillan.

——. 2020. "Neoliberalizing Cultural Landscapes: Bali's Agrarian Heritage". *Critical Asia Studies*. https://doi.org/10.1080/14672715.2020.1714459.

Warren, C. 1998. "Tanah Lot: The Cultural and Environmental Politics of Resort Development in Bali". In *The Politics of Environment in Southeast Asia: Resources and Resistance*, edited by Philip Hirsch and Carol Warren. London: Routledge.

——. 2014. "World Heritage and Agrarian Identities: Critical Perspectives on 'The Cultural Landscape of Bali'". *Proceedings of the 4th International Conference on Heritage and Sustainable Development*, edited by R. Amoeda, S. Lira, C. Pinheiro, pp. 619–28. Guimaraes, Portugal, 22–25 July 2014.

Widiarta, I.Y. 2015. "Pengelolaan Daya Tarik Wisata Pura Taman Ayun Sebagai Bagian Dari Warisan Budaya Dunia". Master's thesis, Udayana University.

Windia, W. 2015a. "Opinion: Kawasan WBD Jatiluwih Makin Amburadul". *Bali Post*, 9 July 2015.

——. 2015b. "Opinion: Subak Pulagan Sebagai Alternatif Subak Jatiluwih". *Bali Post*, 8 November 2015.

World Bank. 1974. *Appraisal of Bali Tourism Project Indonesia*. Washington, DC: International Bank for Reconstruction and Development.

——. 1997. *Project Appraisal Document on a Proposed Loan in an Amount of US$110 Million to the Republic of Indonesia for a Bali Urban Infrastructure Project*. Washington, DC: Infrastructure Operations Division Country Department III East Asia and Pacific Region.

——. 1999. *Culture and Sustainable Development: A Framework for Action*. Washington, DC: The World Bank.

————. 2001a. *Cultural Heritage and Development: A Framework for Action in the Middle East and North Africa*. Washington, DC: World Bank Middle East and North Africa Region.

————. 2001b. *Cultural Properties in Policy and Practice: A Review of World Bank Experience*. Washington, DC: The World Bank.

————. 2005. *Implementation Completion Report (SCL-41550 TF-29708) on a Loan in the Amount of US$110 Million to the Republic of Indonesia for a Bali Urban Infrastructure Project*. Washington, DC: Urban Development Sector Unit East Asia and Pacific Region.

World Heritage Committee. 2008. *Decision WHC-08/32.COM/8B*. 32nd Session of the World Heritage Committee, Quebec City, Canada, 2–10 July 2008.

12

Heritage Conservation as Trickle-Down Development

Jayde Lin Roberts

Although the Union of Burma[1] once tried to resist the grand vision of modernization and development with its associated machinery of Western lending and universalist discourses of technology transfer and democracy, the post-1988 governments of Myanmar have gradually adopted international standards as prescribed by the World Bank, the Asian Development Bank, ASEAN and others in order to catch up. They fear that if Myanmar does not become competitive in the regional economy, it will be swallowed up by China and India, and left behind by its ASEAN neighbours.

From 1962 to about 1988, the military-led socialist government drove out foreign influence and endeavoured to develop Burma on its own terms, to make it self-sufficient through *The Burmese Way to Socialism*.[2] Although economic reform from about 1990 onward incrementally improved the national economy, Myanmar was still ill-prepared for integration into the ASEAN Economic Community because it could not compete as an equal.[3] National reform initiated in 2011 has dramatically altered the status of the country on the world stage and opened the floodgates for international aid, but the country's long-term prospects remain uncertain. During the initial honeymoon-like phase between 2011 and 2016, sweeping changes seemed to indicate thorough reform in all sectors. However, the current phase under the leadership of Aung San Suu Kyi seems marked by economic stasis and increasing ethno-religious violence. In November 2015, the National League for Democracy (NLD) won the first openly contested general election since 1990, and came to power in March 2016. While the NLD and its leader, Aung San Suu Kyi, are broadly seen as symbols of hope and democracy, their symbolic significance has been tested by the complex reality of a country where ethno-religious violence continues unabated and basic needs in housing, education and health have yet to be met. It is too early to draw any conclusions, but for this discussion the exponential increase in the number of international actors in Myanmar has certainly increased the complexity of heritage-making and urban development and has unearthed entrenched and often contradictory practices that defy the rationale of linear international development.[4]

Amidst this rush to develop, Myanmar's transnational elite has asserted the significance of Yangon's built heritage and claimed the colonial design of its downtown as a key asset for a liveable and cosmopolitan city. To legitimate their claim, leaders such as Thant Myint-U, the founder of the Yangon Heritage Trust (YHT), have sought support from international organizations such as UNESCO, the World Monuments Fund, the Getty Trust, and the United States Embassy, and solicited foreign and local investment from real estate developers.

This chapter analyses two internationally funded heritage conservation projects and argues that the current approach abides by the logic of trickle-down economics. The two projects are (1) the "EU Project: Economics and Livelihoods Study" and (2) the "Pre-feasibility study (PFS) for Heritage Renovation and Integrated Infrastructure Development to Catalyse Urban Regeneration in Yangon". The Economics and Livelihoods Study was the second part of a three-phase €800,000 programme to build capacity for the Urban Planning Unit (UPU) within the municipal government, the Yangon City Development Committee (YCDC). Undertaken in 2014, it sought to determine explicit connections between heritage buildings and urban livelihood. The second project began as a stand-alone four-month programme with US$350,000 provided by the Cities Development Initiative for Asia (CDIA). The objective was to identify specific heritage buildings to showcase the economic potential of conservation.

In trickle-down or supply-side economics, production (the supply of goods and services) is primary in determining economic growth. This economic theory asserts that supply creates its own demand and it calls for lower taxes and a hands-off approach from governments that will not interfere through excessive regulatory or monetary policies. It strives for a free market wherein market forces are supposed to naturally encourage growth (Chang 2010). This neoliberal premise has disenfranchised many people in both developed and developing nations (Chang and Grabel 2004; Escobar 2011; Harvey 2007; Rahnema and Bawtree 1997), and it poses a particular threat to Myanmar, where the newly elected civilian government must simultaneously promote democracy while making the country economically competitive. Global free market imperatives could tip the balance towards privatization, stripping power from the nascent people-based politics and government before they have time to gain strength. It could also exacerbate existing socio-economic inequalities and perpetuate the abuses of crony capitalism that have beset the country for decades.

For Yangon's conservationists, the supply that would promote economic growth is the city's stock of colonial architecture. Thant Myint-U said,

> There's every possibility that Yangon can become one of the most beautiful and most liveable cities in Asia. I strongly believe preserving its architectural heritage will be a big part of making that happen.... What we need to realise is that Yangon has a unique cityscape. It's a priceless asset. (Kean 2012)

In agreement, Chaw Kalyar, a Myanmar architect who completed a special short course on heritage conservation funded by AusAID in 2013 said, "Old colonial blocks are the treasures of Yangon city and can attract tourists from all over the world" (Htar Htar Khin 2012).[5] In these narratives about Yangon's past and future, colonial architecture is an asset that can drum up international demand. This path forward requires soliciting international and private investment because the Myanmar government proved itself untrustworthy between the 1960s and 2010s, and the current government is confronting multiple issues that are straining its administrative and financial capacity.[6]

Both of these internationally funded projects were intended to promote heritage conservation as an integral part of urban development, and they stipulated public consultation as a part of their pro-poor, democracy-building and liveability guidelines. However, both failed to engage everyday residents except as interview subjects. Given the five decades of political oppression in Myanmar, genuine public participation will require time. However, by prioritizing the conservation of Yangon's built heritage over other liveability improvements, the aestheticism and romanticism of Yangon's transnational elite could override the basic needs of everyday residents. International and normative definitions of architectural value will likely raise the profile of Yangon on the global cultural market, but the cost will be the livelihood and wellbeing of the city's diverse residents.

Although it has become a cliché, the dramatic influx of international aid, expertise and investment since 2011 have shaken up Yangon and Myanmar as a whole. Local activists such as Lahpai Seng Raw, founder of Metta Development Foundation, Myanmar's largest civil society organization, have criticized the distribution and management of international aid money and called for more context-appropriate and locally determined projects and evaluation systems.[7] Indeed, many scholars have questioned the neoliberal premise of international development and its uneven outcomes (Appadurai 2001; Brenner, Marcuse and Mayer 2009; Escobar 1999, 2011; Rankin 2009; Roy 2005, 2012). This chapter investigates heritage-making in Yangon as an elite-led project that has questionable benefits for its less-privileged residents.

Economics and Livelihoods Study

In 2013 the European Union supported a two-year €800,000 project to build capacity for Yangon's Urban Planning Unit (UPU), which had been newly established at the end of 2011. Cognizant of the multiple challenges on the city's horizon, YCDC cobbled together a planning unit of about sixty staff members by culling members from existing departments such as civil engineering and public administration. The EU grant proposal titled, "Capacity Building of the YCDC Urban Planning Unit for a Better Yangon", was initially drafted by Myanmar Egress, a local civil society organization, and later included the YHT as an associate. Myanmar Egress was founded by Nay Win Maung in 2006 to foster critical thinking among Yangon's youth and to establish a Western-style political and economic think tank. By 2012, their more conciliatory approach towards the military had enabled them to participate directly in national reform and sometimes serve as an interlocutor between foreign aid agencies and the different levels in Myanmar's government. Similarly, the YHT, founded in 2013, endeavoured to work with the government as an ally to save the colonial era downtown. With this more accommodating and pragmatic stance, Myanmar Egress and YHT were able to become key players during the earliest phase of reform at the municipal level.

This EU-funded two-year project identified three primary areas to increase urban planning capacity: improve managerial and technical urban planning skills; include community outreach and consultation into urban planning policymaking and implementation; and include heritage protection in urban planning.[8] As a part of the third focus, the YHT managed a three-phase heritage conservation study that included (1) an inventory of built form, (2) an economic study of urban livelihoods, and (3) a comparative legal study that would recommend regulatory approaches for protecting built heritage. All three phases were undertaken by international consultants with the assistance of local research assistants. This chapter focuses on the second sub-project, the study of urban livelihoods, because it deals directly with the everyday lives of Yangon's residents and can serve as a critique of top-down, elite-driven conservation.

This three-phase study focusing on heritage encountered several problems. The Yangon Heritage Trust had a difficult time recruiting specialists with the required local knowledge, and local residents were suspicious of and evasive towards the research. As a spatial ethnographer who had already undertaken two years of fieldwork in Yangon and who speaks Burmese, the author was aware of the various sensitivities in the city and was therefore selected as the lead researcher for the second study. The terms of reference (TOR) specified that the livelihood study would be based on the first phase, the built-form report, and continue the analysis of three downtown blocks selected by the YHT: lower block of Latha Street, lower block of 26th Street, and upper block of Bogalayzay Street. These streets sit within YHT's proposed downtown conservation zone and "were chosen for their heritage character, because they each represent different ethnic groups within Yangon and because they also contain modern infill" (Yangon Heritage Trust 2014). The TOR also stated that the study had to be completed in thirty days and its purpose was to better understand (1) the existing nature, mechanisms and systems by which local residents engage in economic activity; (2) the relationship between urban heritage and existing local economies; and (3) the needs and aspirations of local residents in relation to economic activity. This work was undertaken by the author and two assistants, one from UPU and a local researcher who had worked on rural projects funded by international aid organizations. Although building local capacity was explicitly stated in the TOR, no one from YHT participated in the research. The total cost of the sub-project was approximately €20,000, which covered an honorarium and per diem for each of the three researchers.

While the fact that the study required street-based interviewing of local residents was encouraging, several assumptions raised concerns: the presumed connection between built heritage and livelihood; the unproblematic approach towards those who might be categorized as non-residents such as street vendors; and the barely veiled priority given to architectural aesthetics. Urban heritage as a concept still lacks definition. It is more than the architecture in a city, but the aspects that exceed the physical boundaries of the built form are vaguely lumped together as intangible heritage, which also lacks clarity because the intangible can be all inclusive. In the urban livelihood study, there was clear recognition of the importance of everyday practices, particularly as they relate to generating income, but the project specified the built form as the foundation of all three studies. Therefore, architecture, not people, was given primacy.

The details of the research are not pertinent for this analysis, but a brief description of the cultural context is necessary before discussing key findings. Although national reform was initiated in 2011 with significant improvements in political freedom and freedom of association, Burmese people still evade questions or answer in generalities unless they are talking with family and close friends. Decades of political oppression have engendered a culture of self-policing, and any hint of officialdom raises alarms, rendering survey tools and short research periods problematic. In addition, unemployment has been pervasive and many rely on the informal economy and other undocumented means to earn an income. A researcher must build trust before endeavouring to understand the reality on the ground. Furthermore, except for the few educated elite who have had access to private schools and overseas education, or those who have worked abroad, the bare life in Myanmar has discouraged aspirations beyond making enough money to keep one's family in good health, and if possible to send one's children to university as a pathway towards upward mobility. There is also a pervasive sense that social connections and luck are necessary to find good, high paying jobs. This reduces the sense of individual agency. Given these circumstances, the outcomes of a single, month-long research project into the livelihood of Yangon's residents that requires reliable data about their income is inherently limited. Any information about Yangon is valuable given the absence of reliable statistics and other basic research, but it is critical to recognize the limitations of the data and avoid setting policies without further research.[9]

Urban Livelihoods in Specific Yangon Neighbourhoods and the Economics of Heritage Protection Study

About halfway through the Economics and Livelihoods Study, the YHT recognized the limitations of the research and changed the title of the project to "Urban Livelihoods in Specific Yangon Neighbourhoods and the Economics of Heritage Protection Study". However, this change was likely motivated by the rules and expected outcomes stipulated by EU aid policies rather than an earnest reappraisal of research goals. Otherwise, the second half of the title, "economics of heritage protection", would have been reconsidered as well because interviews from the first two weeks indicated that Yangon's residents saw little or no connection between colonial architecture and their ability to generate income. Indeed, those who lived in or operated businesses within such buildings said that the architecture was a financial liability because the cost of maintenance was so high. Street vendors and others in the informal economy said that beautiful architecture is a hindrance because they are not allowed to sell in front of renovated or new buildings. Their businesses are commonly seen as unsightly. Vendors have managed to survive because government officials and property owners do not bother to police dilapidated and leftover spaces.

Furthermore, the three blocks chosen for the study are known as high-class streets within Yangon. The colonial government imposed an explicit spatial hierarchy in their design of Yangon.[10] The major streets, designated as hubs of colonial trade and representing the face of the Empire, were set at 100 and 150 feet in width. Secondary streets, marking the boundaries of neighbourhoods, were set at 50 feet. Tertiary streets, where townhouses and small businesses were built, were set at 30 feet. Latha, a 100-foot street, has been the most prestigious address for the Sino-Burmese since the colonial era. Similarly, Bogalazay, a 50-foot street, contains colonial townhouses built with steel rather than wood structures, which was a costly material beyond the reach of most residents. From the perspective of heritage conservation, this selection is logical. The wealthy owners of these residences have been able to maintain their properties, making these buildings more viable as conservation projects. However, for an investigation into current urban livelihoods, these buildings contribute little to the economic vitality of Yangon and skew the results towards the financial reality of the moneyed elite.

During the colonial era, the richest ethnic Chinese established their homes and businesses on Latha Street, then known as Latter. They were the rare few who succeeded under the colonial system and became rice traders and middlemen who traded in luxury goods, beans and pulses. During the first decade and a half following independence, Chinese merchants still made handsome profits, but after the enactment of the Enterprise Nationalization Law in 1963 they had to hand their businesses to the government. However, these merchants did not lose all of their assets. In fact, many still had enough money to move overseas, and most held on to their real estate on Latha Street. Residents in Tayout Tan (Chinatown) say that the most desirable properties are on Latha Street, but even if you have money you cannot buy them because the owners do not want to sell.[11] The owners do not need the money. Indeed, the lower block of Latha is lifeless because many of the residential units are empty and few businesses operate on the ground floor. Many of the property owners still live overseas and few people walk along the street because the block offers few services or amenities. Furthermore, the aura of exclusion is still palpable, discouraging informal gatherings and street-side vending. Although Latha Street intersects Mahabandoola Road, an avenue where waves of vendors sell on the sidewalks from six in the morning to eleven o'clock at night, little of that street life filters down to the lower block of Latha. It remains quiet except during Burmese holidays, when local ward officials hire *zat pwe* (traditional Burmese theatre) troupes to perform.

Similarly, Bogalazay Street was the home of colonial clerks and Muslim traders who constituted the most successful Asian professional and business class in Yangon. Compared to most other 50- and 30-foot streets in Yangon, the buildings on this street occupy larger lots, are of higher construction quality, and remain in better shape. However, the quality of architecture has not resulted in economic growth because the larger spaces and better construction demand higher rents, making it difficult for new and small businesses to succeed. Of those who agreed to be interviewed on Bogalazay, almost all said that the rent is extremely high and that many businesses have come and gone in three to six month cycles because they cannot make enough money to pay the rent. The ballooning real estate market post-2011 certainly contributes to the problem, but even before the initiation of national reform upper Bogalazay was known as a high-end tailor street where rich ladies had their *eingyi* and *tamein* (Burmese blouses and *longyis*) made. Just like lower Latha Street, upper Bogalazay sees little economic activity except at the corners that intersect with Anawrahta and Mahabandoola Roads. The corner of Anawrahta Road and Bogalazay Street is a sprawling bus stop for the many routes that cut through the city. Therefore, many betel nut and refreshment vendors sell at the corner. At the southwest corner of Bogalazay Street and Mahabandoola Road is Bogalay Market, a historic wet and dry market, and at the northwest corner is Sein Gay Har, one of the most successful department store chains in Yangon. However, even with the busy street life that caps the north and south ends of upper Bogalazay Street, there is little traffic or street vending within the block itself. The residents in this block said that they liked their street because it was quiet.

By selecting Latha and Bogalazay Streets as the models to study and promote for heritage conservation, the YHT reveals its preference for top-down investment. From the perspective of European and North American urbanism, Latha and Bogalazay are ideal sites for cafe streets that would evoke the feeling of Paris or the pleasantness of Spanish al fresco dining. However, the spaciousness of the streets alone cannot engender a Western-inspired cafe culture. Cafes, unlike traditional Burmese tea stalls, are usually in air-conditioned spaces because cafes are supposed to be higher class. These two blocks could be transformed to resemble the well-designed and pleasant spaces advocated by urban designers such as Jan Gehl and Project for Public Spaces, but they would not become accessible public space for two important reasons: (1) private capital will be necessary to renovate the buildings and improve the streetscape, thus increasing the likelihood of creating exclusive spaces inaccessible to most Yangonites, and (2) public space and public culture has yet to be defined for Myanmar.[12]

In contrast to Latha and Bogalazay Streets, the third site, lower 26th Street, is a lower-middle-class block.[13] The 30-foot street is denser, with smaller lot sizes and taller buildings, housing at least three times the number of residences and businesses as Latha and Bogalazay. Popularly known as "Paint Street", lower 26th is the home of numerous paint, hardware and pipe distribution shops as well as stores that repair and sell fishing nets. This street was most likely chosen because the only synagogue in

Yangon is located at its northwest corner, and this largely unused religious monument has garnered international attention. Near the southwest corner is another religious structure, the Mamsa Sunni Jamai Mosque. This mosque is very active and serves as the community centre for the many Muslims who live on and near 26th Street. However, this mosque is located within a post-1988, four-storey apartment block and has received little attention from YHT. Its architecture does not warrant attention.

Also in contrast to Latha and Bogalazay, lower 26th is busy in the morning and late afternoon. Many shoppers visit this block to purchase paint and other supplies, delivery trucks drive through the block to drop off and pick up goods, residents walk in and out of their homes, itinerant vendors amble through calling out the types of items they are selling, and Muslims go to the mosque for prayers. All of these activities not only contribute to the economic vitality of 26th Street but they also support the trade in Theingyi Zay, a historic market at the northwest corner of 26th Street and Mahabandoola Road. Many small business owners said that they started out in the small stalls within Theingyi Zay, and when their business outgrew the stalls they rented larger spaces on 26th Street. The proximity of lower 26th Street to Theingyi Zay is important because the vendors' customers can easily find the relocated business after the move, and being close to a historic market enables the business to capture the market's customer traffic.

Based on the above research, the author recommended that YHT focus on Theingyi Zay as a top choice for heritage conservation. This market, built during the colonial era, not only has the potential to showcase colonial architecture but can also catalyse economic growth because it has served as a low-risk entry point for entrepreneurial Burmese who want to start a business. It is also a worthy conservation target because it is one of the most frequented markets for Yangon residents. Burmese people say that they can buy everything they need at Theingyi Zay: cookware, clothes, vegetables, fruit, meat, fish, spices and more. If heritage conservation in Yangon is supposed to improve urban livelihoods for the many, not the few, then a historically significant market that remains intimately tied to the daily practices of everyday Burmese people would be ideal.

The research also showed that the economic reality of Yangon's residents is much more evident in streets such as 37th Street, where many vendors store their carts overnight and recent migrants have constructed rooftop units in order to live within walking distance of their place of work. Narrower 30-foot streets such as 37th Street have witnessed dramatic change since the early 1990s because their older two- to three-storey townhouses have been demolished to build six- to seven-storey apartment buildings. For architects and conservationists, this type of architecture is seen as a blight on Yangon, but their lower quality construction and lack of design must not disqualify them as significant places that support urban livelihoods. The disregard for unaesthetic places is not new in the fields of architecture and urban design, but many scholars and activists have drawn our attention to nondescript buildings and informal settlements and their vital role in providing manual labour and other services to cities (Chase, Crawford and Kaliski 2008; Jacobs 1961; Kim 2015; Roy 2012; Roy and AlSayyad 2004). However, the unbeautiful requires mentioning in Yangon because heritage conservation has been written into basic urban planning objectives, and protecting the colonial downtown requires very significant capital. The dollars necessary to save the built heritage has compelled conservationists to appeal to private enterprise and thereby take refuge in the logic of trickle-down economics.

Pre-feasibility Study for Heritage Renovation and Integrated Infrastructure Development

The second project, the "Pre-feasibility study (PFS) for Heritage Renovation and Integrated Infrastructure Development to Catalyse Urban Regeneration in Yangon", also relied on market mechanisms to promote conservation. Financed by the Cities Development Initiative for Asia (CDIA), the project objective was:

> To help YCDC and YHT to define an investment programme for an area-based comprehensive heritage-led regenerative initiative in three pilot areas that details the opportunities and constraints for development of and investment in: a) Infrastructure improvements and, b) Upgrading and renovation of individual properties. (Ringhof 2015)

At first glance, CDIA would seem an unlikely donor for an urban heritage project. Established by the Asian Development Bank and the government of Germany in 2007, CDIA's objective is to provide "assistance to medium-sized Asian cities to bridge the gap between their development plans and the implementation of their infrastructure investments" (CDIA 2017). As of 2017, 79 per cent of their funding has been directed towards infrastructural projects such as flood and drainage management and urban transport. Of the categories funded by CDIA, this heritage project could fit within urban renewal, but the pervasive practice of urban renewal has included significant instances of the demolition of old buildings. The awkward fit between the goals of heritage preservation and infrastructural development is evident in the title of the project: Pre-feasibility study (PFS) for Heritage Renovation and Integrated Infrastructure Development to Catalyse Urban Regeneration in Yangon. It appears that "integrated infrastructure development" was added to make the project fit within the remit of CDIA.

However, Ester Van Steekelenburg, who spearheaded the project, was successful in obtaining CDIA funding and was eventually selected as the team leader. Van Steekelenburg is the founder and director of Urban Discovery, a self-proclaimed social enterprise that "specializes in heritage economics" (Urban Discovery 2017). Without an in-depth study of their process and projects it would be unfair to draw any conclusions. However, based on their work in Yangon and their self-representation through their website, Urban Discovery's key strategy is to sell heritage: to help city governments "capitalize on heritage assets" and "work with developers to make preservation financially feasible" (Urban Discovery 2017). This pragmatic stance is common and even understandable in the context of Yangon, where the municipal government has yet to establish a viable taxation system to build up revenue. However, selling heritage as an asset is prioritizing the exchange value of a built environment without adequate consideration of its use value for the many people who live and work in and around the colonial architecture.

To help YCDC and YHT define an investment programme, a team of ten international and five national experts was recruited.[14] As is common in international development and aid consulting, the experts were to be deployed on an intermittent basis over an extended period and were not expected to remain on site. In the specified four months of the project, no one except for the team leader was expected to spend a significant amount of time in Yangon. In the eight months of the project, each expert was only contracted to work between one and three months, and, depending on his or her role, much of that work could be done from outside the country.

As stated above, if the project objective would have been to address the specific needs and characteristics of Yangon, a locally attuned understanding built upon long-term engagement and trust would have been essential. The globalized norm of parachuting experts in to provide universalized solutions is a problematic practice that has been criticized by many (Atkinson and Bridge 2005; Escobar 2011; Marcuse 2009; Scott 1998). In the case of Yangon and the pre-feasibility study, the problem was exacerbated by the scarcity of trained Myanmar professionals, particularly in the fields specified by CDIA. Therefore, the local grassroots voice remained silent, and the authority of international experts was falsely magnified. In this unequal context there is little opportunity for the preconceptions of globetrotting consultants to be challenged and refined by local understanding.

The pre-feasibility study had a very tight timeline. Recruiting began on 29 January 2015, the start date was set for 2 March, and the entire project was supposed to be completed by 30 June 2015.[15] However, the application and selection process was delayed by two months because none of the parties involved were able to locate Myanmar nationals with the required expertise.[16] At the delayed start date of May 2015, the pre-feasibility study only had one full-time Myanmar national expert to serve as the architect and one part-time social safeguard specialist who had eventually agreed to take on the project despite prior commitments. None of them worked with or for YCDC or YHT.[17] A full complement of international experts was hired, but only one professional, Van Steekelenburg, the team leader, had prior experience in Myanmar. However, her knowledge was limited to a few months of short-term consultation projects focused on the architecture of downtown Yangon, without training in the history, culture or language of Myanmar.

In actual operation, the pre-feasibility study took more than eight months. An executive summary was made public on 23 December 2015 and the final report was not completed until 8 April 2016. Within the context of Myanmar, the extended timeframe is more reasonable than the original estimation of four months, and this allowed the team to recruit additional specialists, filling in the missing local expertise in municipal infrastructure, real estate, social safeguard, and financial management. However, the part-time social safeguard specialist indicated that the team members were rarely ever in Yangon at the same time, and there were noticeable gaps in the research.[18] The international cultural resources and community specialist who was supposed to monitor local welfare was seldom in Yangon, and attempts at surveying local residents met with the same level of reticence encountered in the above built-form and urban-livelihoods studies. Indeed, the social safeguard specialist, a native of Yangon, commented that most people were afraid to speak and were worried that the research would result in government officials evicting local residents. This is a well-known phenomenon in Myanmar and specialists with in-depth knowledge of local customs would have designed the project differently.

Furthermore, in the eight months of the pre-feasibility study, only April and May were dedicated to research. The remaining six months from June to December were committed to problem-solving through deciding the scope of the three pilot areas, architectural design solutions, financial modelling, feedback from selected stakeholders, and marketing (van Steekelenburg 2016, pp. 5, 22). With only one international consultant holding prior knowledge of Yangon, and an incomplete team of local experts, the leap to problem solving without a thorough investigation into the multiple, intersecting problems on the ground is troubling.

A thorough analysis of the entire pre-feasibility study process would be informative for guiding future research and development projects in Myanmar, but neither the written reports nor the team members have offered much detail. Instead, a polished final report with eye-catching graphics presents a seemingly unproblematic set of solutions for the complex and often contradictory development in urban Yangon.[19] The pressure to present credible research and solutions is inherent in international consulting, particularly in projects that demand obvious, and almost immediate, return on investment. However, this widespread practice should not be tolerated as the norm or as best practice. Rather, this semblance of rational problem solving and completeness should be critiqued as a play of globally standardized expertise that can dangerously bury the paradoxes and stresses inherent in any social or urban issue.

This bias towards confident, clear-cut solutions is obvious in the wording in the project brief, executive summary and final report. The pre-feasibility study was to deliver investment programmes for a "comprehensive heritage-led regeneration" and articulate a future for Yangon based on "the shared vision for the downtown conservation zone by the YCDC and YHT through a participatory exercise that includes residents, business operators, religious caretakers, traditional representatives and other stakeholders" (Ringhof 2015). This work was to identify the development potential in the heritage protection zone and estimate the capital investment required for upgrading three types of properties:

A) Properties where owners and/or tenants can initiate and undertake repairs and make improvements to their buildings

B) Properties that are potentially bankable heritage renovation projects, i.e. suitable for commercial exploitation (retail, office, residential)

C) Properties that have redevelopment potential as public/cultural facilities, with specific heritage value or cultural identity (community centre, library, museum, etc.). (Ringhof 2015)

Furthermore, for category A properties, the team, "in collaboration with residents, must propose tools and incentives alongside a communication strategy to help unlock current investment potential" (Ringhof 2015). For categories B and C, the team must "formulate and design a strategy to bring these properties to the market, targeted at local and foreign developers, companies and (institutional) investors seeking a healthy long term financial return" (Ringhof 2015).

In the executive summary and final report, the language is more circumspect. Rather than "comprehensive" and a "shared vision" among all potential stakeholders, the report states, "[T]he PFS demonstrates how heritage can create value and drive economic growth by increasing the competitiveness of the City of Yangon and enhancing the living conditions, economic and tourism potential of the city" (van Steekelenburg 2016, p. 4). However, the premise is still based on a globalized business and marketing model in which words such as *bankable, commercial exploitation, tools* and *incentives* are stated without qualification.

A locally attuned research proposal could hardly specify these outcomes with such surety. Burma specialists and Myanmar people would immediately recognize the herculean effort and countless hours required to articulate a "shared vision" among the various stakeholders, and they would set a more realistic timeline or alternative objectives. They would also remove the words "commercial exploitation" because doing business in Burma is still intimately tied to personal relations and moral rectitude. The *cedana* (intention) behind every action is considered to be more powerful than the action itself, and the greed required to exploit something would be seen as *akutho* (an unmeritorious deed) that would result in negative *kamma* (consequences).[20] Furthermore, Burmese people see life as highly unpredictable and would not presume to be able to create anything comprehensively.

The tremendous challenge in undertaking this type of project in Myanmar was evident in the recruitment process wherein CDIA had to begin the pre-feasibility study with an incomplete team. The extent of the difficulty is more apparent in the executive summary made public on

23 December 2015. In the introduction, the authors stated, "[W]ithin the current political and institutional context, the conditions are not yet in place for firm legislation and planning control for the downtown conservation zone, let alone master planning different heritage precincts within the zone" (van Steekelenburg 2015, p. 2). Furthermore, they remarked,

> While the Heritage Works Team advocates a comprehensive precinct based master planning approach to improve local living and working conditions while safeguarding the historic streetscape, it is recognized that the current legal, political and institutional context and absence of a solid and respected planning framework currently limits the possibilities for implementation of area based regeneration activities. (van Steekelenburg 2015, pp. 3–4)

Despite these challenges and the limited research data, the Heritage Works Team proceeded as originally programmed. The standard practice in international consulting demands that the consultant delivers on the terms of reference (TOR). Therefore, the team divided the properties in the downtown conservation zone into three categories: (1) Typical tenement buildings with apartment units in private ownership dating back to pre-1990; (2) Privately owned (former) commercial or industrial properties that are currently underutilized or vacant; (3) Publicly owned properties that are currently underutilized or vacant. For all three types, the team delivered strategies and investment packages for heritage-led development in the form of financing, regulatory and architectural design solutions. These ready-made templates are meant to attract investors and specify the interventions necessary to protect heritage buildings while simultaneously demonstrating the "positive pro-poor environmental and economic impact" (van Steekelenburg 2016, pp. 7, 37). However, except for a few sentences stating that they undertook a social survey and a series of focus group discussions, there is no mention of how and to what extent common Myanmar people participated in the pre-feasibility study. Indeed, the participants who are listed by name are government officials, Yangon's cosmopolitan elite, and potential investors.

As the executive summary and final report focused on the desired outcomes, not the process, and direct queries about the study have yet to elicit responses, it is difficult to interpret how the team reached its conclusions and recommendations. Additional research is necessary, but the part-time social safeguard specialist indicated that the social side of the equation was likely missing. Without genuine long-term engagement with local residents, the CDIA pre-feasibility study is yet another top-down aid project that presumes large sums of money poured on high levels of government and prestigious organizations will trickle down and benefit the common people.

In December 2015, the Heritage Works Team created a Facebook page called "Heritage Works Yangon" to publicize their project and encourage local residents to appreciate heritage.[21] This was clearly a key tool in the team's communication strategy, with regular posts that included photographs of colonial era monuments, design charrettes, architectural designs by local firms, sketches and paintings of Yangon by local and international artists, and other creative work. It was also their way of encouraging participation through the comfortable distance of social media and a means to announce public events such as "Observation Fridays".

During "Observation Fridays", residents who pass through Mahabandoola Garden and Bogyoke Market were asked to share their views on the city. The Facebook page does not provide details of how many "Observation Fridays" have taken place or of exactly when local residents made their comments, but as of June 2016 thirteen images of people with their written statements had been posted. Of those, eight support heritage conservation, three ask for new buildings, and two recognize the historical value of old buildings but see them as unsafe. This effort is commendable and could gradually raise awareness about Yangon's built heritage without dictating how residents should feel about colonial era architecture. However, even in these gestures towards inclusion, the Heritage Works Team is mainly marketing their work to gain popular support, not to invite public opinion in order to form a people-based vision of Yangon. Furthermore, the Heritage Works Yangon Facebook page has been quiet for most of 2016 and 2017, with no new posts based on activities by the Heritage Works Team. Like-minded organizations such as Doh Eain, a Yangon-based business that renovates colonial era buildings for market housing, and Turquois Mountain, an international organization that promotes heritage preservation in Afghanistan, Saudi Arabia and Myanmar have posted their events on the Heritage Works Yangon page.

Conclusion

In contemporary Myanmar, placing one's hope in neoliberalism appears reasonable. After all, from 1962 to 2011, the governments of Burma failed to serve the people, and any sign of improvement or modernization appeared to be the result of private initiative. Private capital built the first two high-rises in Yangon, the Sakura Tower and Traders (now Shangri-La) Hotel, which stood as emblems of modernity from about the 1990s to 2009.[22] Whenever basic services such as water, electricity and telephone lines were lacking, neighbours and community members pooled together their money to procure and share those resources. Among Myanmar people, there has been little to no expectation that the government would serve the public, and what constitutes the public has yet to be defined.[23] Therefore, organizations such as the Yangon Heritage Trust are focusing their attention on international organizations and private investors as the most viable way of saving Yangon's colonial landscape. YHT has also appealed to the government, but only to the highest national levels, to prevent catastrophic damage, not to gain financial or other tangible support. In this context, where the urban environment has yet to be defined as a public good under the care of the government, and the government has yet to take on this responsibility, private capital and privatization seem to be the most realistic, though not the best, option.

However, the money involved is in the billions of dollars, and there might be a wilful blindness towards the unevenness of development and the inescapability of gentrification. It is possible to make Yangon one of the most beautiful cities in Southeast Asia by conserving its colonial era architecture, but to claim that this effort will make it one of the most liveable is to define liveability by global elite standards without considering how everyday Myanmar people actually live. More research is required, but my analysis to date indicates that Yangon residents do not aspire to live in leisurely neighbourhoods dotted with cafes and boutiques. They value convenience and closeness to family and neighbours. The now-globalized image of green liveable cities with spacious parks are not a part of the Myanmar imagination. The heat and humidity of Yangon requires more intimate shaded spaces for leisure. To hope that private investment in heritage buildings will eventually improve the livelihoods of everyday Myanmar people is to subscribe to the logic of trickle-down economics. A prettier city will draw in more tourists and maybe even entice multi-national businesses to set up offices in Yangon, but this path towards economic growth has created increasing inequality and an underclass of labourers in neighbouring cities such as Singapore and Bangkok. The supply of renovated colonial era architecture might increase global demand and generate wealth for established landowners, crony capitalists and Burma's transnational elite who have the money to invest in high-end businesses. However, it is doubtful that an influx of tourists and foreign investment will improve the livelihood of the average Myanmar person, at least not in the near term.

The two international aid projects above were funded by two different organizations, but both prioritized economics over other considerations. The underlying assumption is that heritage has to make money or it will not be saved. This has been true in many cities, and Yangon hardly has the authority or financing to fight back against the neoliberal world order. However, there is still room for critique and for the search for alternative solutions. At present, dire problems such as flooding, clogged drainage, inadequate water supply and other issues demand the attention of everyday residents and government officials, so little effort has been directed towards less urgent issues such as architectural heritage. Indeed, the unrelenting challenges of living in a poorly maintained and serviced city seems to have encouraged an atomistic society wherein an individual feels incapable of dealing with any problem other than the one that is immediately impinging on her and upon her close circle of family and friends. Problems that are one step removed are believed to be beyond a person's control.

Yangon's educated and cosmopolitan elite have a greater sense of their individual agency and have begun to advocate for a better Yangon. However, their advocacy efforts have yet to solicit public opinion or build mutual, like-minded communities. They remain individuals focused on communicating the importance of their own agendas, and the absence of broader based participation will impede progress towards the formation of a shared urban heritage. Like the wealthy who argue that increased profits for the rich will trickle down to the poor, heritage conservationists in Yangon believe that saving the colonial downtown will benefit Yangon, even if those benefits are not shared equally.

Notes

1. Although the name Myanmar is now widely accepted and recognized as the official name of the nation-state, the two names, Burma and Myanmar, were once used to declare allegiance to different political actors within and outside

of the country. In 1989, the military junta that suppressed the 8 August 1988 popular protests demanded that the world call the country by the name of Myanmar. As the political debates concerning the name are no longer a central issue, I use Burma for all discussions prior to 1989 and Myanmar for the period thereafter.

2. Much more research is necessary to understand what happened during this period, but the apparent reality is that international technical assistance was denied and the country experienced precipitous declines in the national economy, standards of living and education. I briefly discuss this period and its relevance for heritage making in "Heritage-Making and Post-Coloniality in Yangon, Myanmar" (Roberts 2017).

3. For a more thorough discussion regarding the implications of ASEAN integration for Myanmar, see my chapter "The Urban" in *The Routledge Handbook of Contemporary Myanmar* (Roberts 2018).

4. Given the fast pace of change in Myanmar, even the most knowledgeable Burma experts are hesitant to make any predictions. However, for a cogent analysis of Myanmar in transition, see "Drivers of Political Change in Post-Junta, Constitutional Burma" (Callahan 2012).

5. After Australia's Foreign Minister Bob Carr visited Yangon in 2012 and was convinced of the value of the city's colonial architecture, the government of Australia funded heritage conservation projects including the AusAID project that took twelve Myanmar architects to Queensland for a special short course on heritage conservation and reuse (see Invest in Australia 2012; Kean 2013).

6. Under the newly elected civilian government led by Aung San Suu Kyi, there might be more trust in the government. However, the NLD-led government has innumerable hurdles to overcome, the most urgent of which is continued armed conflict in the border regions, particularly Rakhine State. The new government will likely fall short of the unrealistic expectations of the Burmese people. Heritage conservation will be one of the trickier projects to navigate because saving colonial era buildings will require huge amounts of capital and likely result in gentrification. There are too many problems that have to be solved at the same time, all from a basis of unclear regulations and an absence of a shared sense of the "public".

7. See, for example, Laphai Seng Raw (2016), but others such as Vicky Bowman, former ambassador of the UK to Myanmar, have also provided critiques.

8. Conversation with U Toe Aung, director of the YCDC Urban Planning Unit, 1 November 2014.

9. There is already evidence of this type of premature writing of policy and its consequences. The Japan International Cooperation Agency (JICA) produced a master plan called "Yangon 2040: City of Green and Gold" based on a huge set of data that was presumed to be reliable. Since its publication, the JICA

plan has garnered significant authority and was cited as the justification for reducing the widths of all sidewalks by half in order to produce parking spaces.

10. For a more thorough discussion about the design of Rangoon as a colonial imposition, see chapters 1 and 4 in *Mapping Chinese Rangoon* (Roberts 2016). I also discuss heritage-making as a condition of post-coloniality in "Heritage-making and Post-coloniality in Yangon, Myanmar" (Roberts 2017).

11. Interviews with residents and business owners on Latha Street, 13, 14 and 18 November 2014. For more in-depth analysis about Chinatown in Yangon, see Roberts (2016).

12. The terms "public", "public space" and "public realm" have been used in many reports and heritage conservation campaigns in Yangon, but I have yet to see any clear definitions. Indeed, in my current research, those who deploy these terms say them in English without translating or defining them in Burmese.

13. The question of socio-economic class requires serious investigation in Myanmar. I am using the word "class" because Burmese informants have repeatedly used the English word in their conversations with me and because my fieldwork to date indicates that this is an important phenomenon. However, more research is necessary to define "class" in Myanmar society.

14. The international experts were made up of an urban heritage economist/team leader, heritage conservation architect, cultural resources and community specialist, project finance/PPP specialist, and a real estate development specialist. The national experts were a municipal infrastructure specialist, legal/real estate specialist, social safeguard specialist, financial management specialist, and an architect.

15. Email communication with Eva Ringhoff of CDIA, 29 January 2015.

16. As a Burma Studies scholar who places great value on the intelligence of the local and everyday, I wanted to ensure the inclusion of local perspectives. Although I could not participate directly in the study, I assisted in the recruitment process and contacted bilingual colleagues and friends to encourage them to apply.

17. Although this was probably not the case for this CDIA project, the quantified and computerized system for selecting consultants within ADB means that expertise is conceived of as universal, regardless of the specificities of particular places or cultures, and those with more hours of consulting are deemed to be more qualified. In the case of Myanmar, where there are very few national experts, this standardized bias did not affect the selection process. Indeed, anyone who was remotely qualified was recruited. However, the so-called objective selection process might have made it more difficult for members of YCDC or YHT to join the team as paid researchers because that would have been deemed a conflict of interest. Whatever the intentions, staff members in

YCDC and YHT gained little knowledge or know-how through the process of the project.

18. Telephone interview with Yu Yu Khaing, 31 March 2016. Yu Yu Khaing was employed part-time and was replaced by Min Min Han.

19. This is a widespread phenomenon and in the fields of architecture and urban design it is a particularly glaring problem because designers are specifically trained in graphic presentation.

20. Of course, the actions of the top generals in Myanmar contradict this way of being. Many scholars have commented on this contradiction and have noted that Senior Generals Ne Win and Than Shwe and former president U Thein Sein have all undertaken long periods of meditation in order to cleanse themselves of their unmeritorious deeds.

21. https://www.facebook.com/HeritageWorksygn-1644805409093889/.

22. During my doctoral fieldwork from 2006 to 2009, many Burmese people pointed to the Sakura Tower and Traders Hotel as special buildings because they were the first two high-rise towers with elevators. They described these towers as modern buildings and said that there is little that is modern in Yangon.

23. See, for example, Saw and Arnold (2014).

References

Appadurai, Arjun. 2001. "Deep Democracy: Urban Governmentality and the Horizon of Politics". *Environment & Urbanization* 13, no. 2.

Atkinson, Rowland, and Gary Bridge, eds. 2005. *Gentrification in a Global Context: The New Urban Colonialism*. London: Routledge.

Brenner, Neil, Peter Marcuse, and Margit Mayer. 2009. "Cities for People, Not for Profit". *City* 13, nos. 2–3: 176–84.

Callahan, Mary P. 2012. *Drivers of Political Change in Post-junta, Constitutional Burma*. Washington, DC: USAID.

CDIA. 2017. "Cities Development Initiative for Asia: Investing in Asia's Urban Future". http://cdia.asia/who-we-are/what-is-cdia/ (accessed 18 September 2017).

Chang, Ha-Joon. 2010. *23 Things They Don't Tell You about Capitalism*. London: Lane.

Chang, Ha-Joon, and Ilene Grabel. 2004. *Reclaiming Development: An Alternative Economic Policy Manual*. London: Zed Books.

Chase, John Leighton, Margaret Crawford, and John Kaliski, eds. 2008. *Everyday Urbanism*, 2nd ed. New York: Monacelli.

Escobar, Arturo. 1999. "The Invention of Development". *Current History: A Journal of Contemporary World Affairs* 98, no. 631: 382–86.

———. 2011. *Encountering Development: The Making and Unmaking of the Third World*. Princeton, NJ: Princeton University Press.

Harvey, David. 2007. *A Brief History of Neoliberalism*. Oxford: Oxford University Press.

Htar Htar Khin. 2012. "Experts Back Introduction of Downtown Heritage Zones". *Myanmar Times*, 19–25 March 2012. http://www.mmtimes.com/2012/news/619/news61919.html.

Invest in Australia. 2012. "Australia Supports Preservation of Yangon's Urban Heritage". http://www.investinaustralia.com/news/australia-supports-preservation-yangons-urban-heritage-12c3 (accessed 18 September 2017).

Jacobs, Jane. 1961. *The Death and Life of Great American Cities*: Vintage Books.

Kean, Thomas. 2012. "Historic Yangon Cityscape Thrown a Lifeline". *Myanmar Times*, 19–25 March 2012. http://www.mmtimes.com/2012/news/619/news61901.html.

———. 2013. "From Yangon to Sydney. Heritage Tour". *Myanmar Times*, 29 August 2013. https://www.mmtimes.com/national-news/7992-from-yangon-to-sydney-heritage-tour.html.

Kim, Annette Miae. 2015. *Sidewalk City: Remapping Public Space in Ho Chi Min City*. Chicago: University of Chicago Press.

Laphai Seng Raw. 2016. "Work with Us, Not around Us". *Myanmar Times*, 19 August 2016. https://www.mmtimes.com/opinion/22044-work-with-us-not-around-us.html.

Marcuse, Peter. 2009. "From Critical Urban Theory to the Right to the City". *City* 13, no. 2–3: 185–97.

Rahnema, Majid, and Victoria Bawtree, eds. 1997. *The Post-Development Reader*. London: Zed Books.

Rankin, Katharine N. 2009. "Critical Development Studies and the Praxis of Planning". *City* 13, nos. 2–3: 219–29.

Ringhof, Eva. 2015. "Pre-Feasibility Study (PSF) for Heritage Renovation and Integrated Infrastructure Development to Catalyse Urban Regeneration in Yangon".

Roberts, Jayde Lin. 2016. *Mapping Chinese Rangoon: Place and Nation among the Sino-Burmese, Critical Southeast Asian Studies*. Seattle: University of Washington Press.

———. 2017. "Heritage-Making and Post-Coloniality in Yangon, Myanmar". In *Citizens, Civil Society and Heritage-Making in Asia*, edited by Hsin-Huang Michael Hsiao, Yew-Foong Hui, and Philippe Peycam, pp. 40–60. Singapore: ISEAS – Yusof Ishak Institute.

———. 2018. "The Urban". In *Routledge Handbook of Contemporary Myanmar*, edited by Adam Simpson, Nicholas Farrelly, and Ian Holliday. London: Routledge.

Roy, Ananya. 2005. "Urban Informality: Toward an Epistemology of Planning". *Journal of American Planning Association* 71, no. 2: 147–58.

———. 2012. "Entrepreneurs of Millennial Capitalism". *Antipode* 44, no. 2: 545–53.

Roy, Ananya, and Nezar AlSayyad, eds. 2004. *Urban Informality: Transnational Perspectives from the Middle East, Latin America, and South Asia*. Lanham, MD: Lexington Books.

Saw, Kyi Pyar Chit, and Matthew Arnold. 2014. *Administering the State in Myanmar: An Overview of the General Administration Department*. Myanmar: The Asia Foundation and MDRI-CESD.

Scott, James C. 1998. *Seeing Like a State: How Certain Schemes to Improve the Human Condition Have Failed*. New Haven, CN: Yale University Press.

Urban Discovery. 2017. "Urban Discovery". http://urbandiscovery.asia/ (accessed 18 September 2017).

van Steekelenburg, Ester et al. 2015. "New Ideas for Old Buildings – Heritage-led Urban Regeneration in Yangon: Pre-feasibility Study in Three Pilot Areas, Executive Summary". Yangon: Cities Development Initiative Asia (CDIA).

———. 2016. "Heritage-led Urban Regeneration in Yangon: Pre-feasibility Study in Three Pilot Areas". Cities Development Initiative Asia (CDIA).

Yangon Heritage Trust. 2014. "EU Project: Economics and Livelihoods Study".

Index

Note: Page numbers followed by "n" refer to endnotes.

JICA (Japan International
Cooperation Agency), 93–95, 97,
106n35
Jilin People's Press, 208
Jin Yufu, 193
Jordan, Lothar, 191
J. Paul Getty Trust, 130

K

Kabul Museum, 234
Kaldun, Beatrice, 271
Kalyar, Chaw, 307
Kampung Melayu (the Malay
quarter), 144
Kang Sheng, 195, 214n2
Karzai, Hamid, 238, 241
Kauman, 144
kawasan gelap (dark district or no-go
zone), 144
Keiko Miura, 82
Khmer architecture, 26
Khmer Rouge, 59
Kim Dae-Jung, 199
Kim Il-Sung, 192, 195, 196
Kim Jong-Il, 197, 198
Kirshenblatt-Gimblett, Barbara, 263
Koguryo Research Center, 199
*Koreans Who Left Their Names in
Ancient Chinese History* (Fang),
200
Kota Lama
Chinese-descendent Indonesians,
150
"colonial heritage", 162
"Dutch" district, 160
Dutch East India Company, 144
Dutch involvement, 151
kawasan gelap (dark district or no-
go zone), 144
"Little Netherlands", 148
local authorities, 148
perception and management of, 157

preservation and marketing of, 149
UNESCO World Heritage Site, 145
Kota Merah (The Red City), 143–44
Kun Plug *shuimo xindiao* (Water
flowing new melodies), 267
kunqu Opera
amateur groups, 259
in Beijing's Imperial Granary
production, 254
origins and practitioners, 256–59
refinement of, 256
state-sponsored professional
troupes, 255
on world stage, 255
Kunshanqiang (Kunshan melody), 256,
262, 263
Kusno, A., 159

L

Lansing, Stephen, 290, 294, 300n6
Lee Hyun-Kyung, 10
Lei, Daphne, 271
Lembaga Kebudayaan Rakyat
(LEKRA), 285
Levenson, Joseph, 257
Liao River, 195, 214n3
Limthongkul, Sondhi, 28
"Little Netherlands", 148, 159, 162n5
Lopes, Henri, 84
Lowenthal, David, 3, 173
Lowry, W. McNeil, 122
Lunet de Lajonquière, Etienne, 58
Lü Zhou, 203

M

Maceda, José, 127
Ma, Dazheng, 201, 214n5
Malay quarter, 144
Maljean, Jean, 266
Mamsa Sunni Jamai Mosque, 314
Manchuria, 190, 193, 199, 207
Manichi Shimbun, 182